SLAVISH SHORE
The Odyssey of Richard Henry Dana Jr.
By Jeffrey L. Amestoy
Publication Date: August 2015
$35.00 | 383 pages | 25 halftones
ISBN: 978-0-674-08819-1
Harvard University Press

For more information, please contact:
Phoebe Kosman
Publicity Manager
Phone 617.495.0303
Fax 617.495.4051
phoebe_kosman@harvard.edu

Visit our Web site
www.hup.harvard.edu

SLAVISH SHORE

Slavish Shore

THE ODYSSEY OF RICHARD HENRY DANA JR.

Jeffrey L. Amestoy

Harvard University Press Cambridge, Massachusetts · London, England 2015

First printing

Library of Congress Cataloging-in-Publication Data

Amestoy, Jeffrey L. (Jeffrey Lee), 1946–

Slavish shore : the odyssey of Richard Henry Dana Jr. /
Jeffrey L. Amestoy.

  pages cm

Includes bibliographical references and index.

ISBN 978-0-674-08819-1 (alk. paper)

1. Dana, Richard Henry, Jr., 1815–1882. 2. Lawyers—United
States—Biography. 3. Politicians—Massachusetts—Biography.
4. Authors—United States—Biography. 5. Sailors—United States—
Biography.   6. Antislavery movements—United States.   7. United
States—Politics and government—1845–1861.   8. Upper class—
Massachusetts—Boston—Biography.   9. Massachusetts—Biography.
I. Title.   II. Title: Odyssey of Richard Henry Dana Jr.

E415.9.D15A44 2015

324.2092—dc23

[B]   2015002113

For my daughters

CONTENTS

Know ye now, Bulkington? Glimpses do ye seem to see of that
mortally intolerable truth; that all deep, earnest thinking is but the
intrepid effort of the soul to keep the open independence of her sea;
while the wildest winds of heaven and earth conspire to cast her
on the treacherous, slavish shore?

—Herman Melville, *Moby-Dick*

INTRODUCTION

On an August day in 1834 a slight, nearsighted boy boarded a ship he had never seen before, joined a crew to whom his aristocratic family would have never spoken, and sailed where few Americans had ever been. The ship might have vanished with the forgotten lives of its sailors. Richard Henry Dana Jr.'s classic, *Two Years Before the Mast,* immortalized the harrowing voyage from Boston around Cape Horn to the remote coast of California. But when Dana witnessed the sadistic flogging of his shipmates, it prompted more than one of the most compelling scenes in American literature. It was the genesis of his vow to stand for justice. This is the story of how Dana kept his promise in the face of the most exclusive and powerful establishment in America—the Boston society in which he had been born and bred.

The drama of Dana's remarkable life arises from the unresolved tension between the man he became at sea and the Brahmin he was expected to be on shore. The qualities—courage, integrity, and a sense of justice—that led to his acceptance as a common sailor before the mast were the traits least valued by his peers. "He was counsel of the sailor and the slave," wrote Charles Francis Adams Jr., "courageous, skillful but still the advocate of the poor and unpopular. . . . In the mind of wealthy and respectable Boston almost anyone was to be preferred to him."

Dana first broke with convention when he left Harvard to ship as a common seaman. He represented sailors, angering Boston's ship owners. He defended fugitive slaves and their rescuers when the "best people" believed opposition to the Fugitive Slave Act was treasonous. His brilliant argument before the U.S. Supreme Court preserved Lincoln's authority to carry on the Civil War. He was the special prosecutor who indicted Jefferson Davis for treason—and prompted the president to end the prosecution.

No lawyer of equivalent standing did as much on behalf of fugitive slaves and those who aided them, nor paid a higher price for doing so. Dana was socially ostracized, boycotted, and nearly murdered. Charles Sumner refused to join Dana in defending the first of the fugitive slave "rescuers" because he thought it political suicide. George Ticknor, social arbiter of Brahmin Boston, wrote to Dana that they were never to speak again. Rufus Choate, Boston's leading lawyer, publicly insulted Dana before the most prestigious gathering of the Boston bar.

When a prominent lawyer and spokesman for the most influential members of Brahmin society told Dana to either keep silent or leave the city, Dana replied that such a demand "would do in a club, but not in a community of equal rights." He added pointedly, the sentiment "came from persons who thought Boston was a club—their club."

Dana knew the club well. Understood as a social order from which he could not resign, his "membership" was a source of inner turmoil and outward tension throughout Dana's life. Aristocrat? Author? Abolitionist? Advocate? Dana's peers could not define him. "Richard Henry Dana," said the most perceptive speaker at a 1915 Cambridge ceremony celebrating the centennial of his birth, "was an essentially romantic temperament, forced by external circumstances to compete with persons whom he described perfectly in his first book as the people who never walked but in one line from their cradle to their graves."[1]

A buoyant spirit when freed from the slavish shore, Dana was, in the words of his first biographer, Charles Francis Adams Jr., "like so many other men of rare power . . . doomed to waste his life making a living." It was a judgment only an Adams could make ("The Adamses," said James Russell Lowell when asked his opinion of the biography, "have a knack for saying gracious things in an ungracious way.") It would not have surprised Dana that he was evaluated by an Adams. The families were so closely associated that George Washington once used "Adams-Dana" as a password in the Revolutionary War. Virtually all that remains of history's dim memory of Dana is the depiction of a fastidious aristocrat in *The Education of Henry Adams.*

But it was Henry Adams, traveling first-class in Cunard's largest and fastest steamship, who believed he learned more in a single night's ocean gale than he did at Harvard. Dana's education before the mast was infinitely more rigorous, and he never forgot its lessons. "A whale ship was my Yale College and my Harvard," wrote Herman Melville. When Dana completed the intricate task of lowering a sail aboard the brig *Pilgrim,* the first mate's "well done" gave him as "much satisfaction as I ever felt in Cambridge on seeing a 'bene' at the foot of a Latin exercise." "If you want to know the Cape," said Melville, "get my friend Dana's *Two Years Before the Mast*—it must have been written with an icicle."

First published in 1840 when twenty-five-year-old Dana opened his Boston law office, *Two Years Before the Mast* has never been out of print. "Dana's small book is a very great book," concluded D. H. Lawrence, a judgment seconded by scholars of American literature who have lamented the diversion of Dana's literary talent to the "ordeal in the courtrooms of Massachusetts."[2] But that ordeal included nothing less than the challenge of deciding what ought to change—and what ought not to change—in himself and in his country.

The nineteenth century posed a question that Americans could not escape: What price human dignity? The response of America's most powerful and exclusive social establishment—the Brahmin society to which Dana was irrevocably wedded—mattered. The odyssey of Richard Henry Dana Jr. illuminates a society that did not wish to be judged in Dana's light when he was alive and has succeeded in dimming any contrast ever since.

In the selective historical memory of most Americans, Bostonians stood as one against Southern slave owners. The popular tale celebrates the unbroken line of antislavery action from the prophetic abolitionist William Lloyd Garrison, to the courageous Charles Sumner literally fending off a Southerner's blows on the floor of the U.S. Senate, to the heroic Robert Gould Shaw Jr., son of Brahmin Boston and fallen leader of the Fifty-Fourth Regiment of Massachusetts, Infantry, colored. When the monument to her son was unveiled on Beacon Hill, Shaw's mother said to the sculptor Augustus Saint-Gaudens that he had immortalized himself, her son, and "my native city."

It would have been more accurate to observe that Saint-Gaudens's magnificent work paid tribute to a man worthier than many who lived on the Hill the monument now faced. If, in the words of one historian of Boston, "Garrison was the voice, and Shaw the arm," there were in the crucible of history between voice and arm, tests of conscience, character, and courage which many failed.[3] By the time of the statue's unveiling on Memorial Day 1897, the social, economic, and political pressures that Dana confronted were "almost forgotten, and in a few more years, he who speaks the truth about them will be denounced as a maligner."[4]

It was true that the politically correct sentiment of established Boston had been antislavery from the early days of the United States. But it was a "thin, colorless anti-slavery sentiment ... current and fashionable ... having no hold either in conviction or in material interest." When the financial interests of Boston's aristocracy began to align more closely with Southern slaveholders because slave-produced cotton was needed for Northern mills, even the sentiment gave way. Social and business Boston "became in its heart, and almost avowedly, a pro-slavery community; and it so remained until 1861."[5]

Dana began a journal in 1841 at age twenty-six, and kept it for nearly twenty years. Every significant figure in nineteenth-century America seemed to have made an appearance: John Quincy Adams and Daniel Webster; Abraham Lincoln and Andrew Johnson; Robert E. Lee and Jefferson Davis; Charles Dickens and Herman Melville; Francis Parkman and Harriet Beecher Stowe. But Dana's journal is more than a compendium of notables. It is the record of Dana's search for himself beneath the layers of Brahmin society on a shore he could not leave.

On trips away from Boston, Dana would sometimes don sailor's garb to cruise the brothels of a city. He wrote in his journal (his wife had access to it) that he wore a suit under his seaman's clothes and would at the appropriate moment reveal himself to be a proper Bostonian. But it was always the sailor's clothing that was closest to his skin.

The temptations of a "sailor's life" were the least of Dana's challenges as he sought to integrate his experience before the mast with the conventions of his class. It became increasingly difficult for him to reconcile "success" as his culture defined it with a lesson he learned at sea: a ship's captain was "equally answerable for what he does himself and what he permits to be done."

Dana believed that the Civil War had taught Americans what failing to be "equally answerable" cost. His optimism—a mix of idealism and naiveté—was ill-founded. That did not deter Dana from seeking to address the immediate challenges of Reconstruction, including the right to vote for newly freed slaves and the treason prosecution of Jefferson Davis, in terms that had only a single flaw. As always, he forgot the politics. "My life has been a failure," a momentarily despondent Dana wrote at age fifty-seven.

That verdict could be sustained only in the context provided by an Adams. When news of Dana's death in Rome reached Boston in January 1882, Charles Francis Adams Jr. spoke to a somber gathering of the Massachusetts Historical Society, whose members included Emerson, Longfellow, and Holmes, among other luminaries. "We are all bookish men here," said Adams, "with possibly one single exception, he alone of us all, has added a recognized classic to the world's literature.... If you do not admit that it is genius, you will admit that it is something not easy to distinguish from it."

Adams recounted Dana's confrontation with America's most powerful establishment over the moral issue of the century. "Even as a young man ... to browbeat him or break him down was hopeless. They tried in the fugitive slave cases, where with a courage which was simply superb, he faced the law officers of the government and denounced in measured terms none could misunderstand." Yet, Adams added, Dana was "still a man of promise to the end ... no matter what he did—and he did a great deal—it amounted to nothing in comparison with what he himself, and his friends too, knew that he could do."

Adams and Oliver Wendell Holmes Sr. each reached back to Odysseus to pay tribute to Dana. The reference was apt at least in its recognition that when Dana left Boston as a nineteen-year-old Harvard dropout to sail to the western edge of the North American continent, the speed of communication had changed little in 2,500 years. One evening less than a decade after the voyage, Dana's friend "Finley" Morse stopped by to give "a most interesting account of his magnetic telegraph. He says he can cross a river without wires." The invention modernized the world.

But the impetus for Dana's leap into history was timeless. A few years before Dana left the suffocating atmosphere of his family, a young French aristocrat described his own departure from home in words nearly identical to those Dana was to use: "I was nineteen years old but it seemed I was not fit for anything. . . . Time pressed, and it was humiliating to remain a burden on my family . . . any change could but be a change for the better, as far as I was concerned."[6]

The restless youth of the Old World became a staff officer for Napoleon. The New World offered no such path for nineteen-year-old Dana, no matter how prominent his family. Adventure was no distinguisher of persons in the new America. Dana would have to make his way among men who cared nothing for his culture, connections, or college. His real odyssey began when he returned. After two years before the mast, he was about to embark on a life's passage through the most tumultuous controversies of nineteenth-century America. But Dana was prepared for the storms. He had taken another voyage first.

1

TRUE SPIRIT

In the cold early morning of a Massachusetts winter, a boy enters a Cambridge schoolhouse. The stove in the middle of the single room is not yet warm, though by mid-day it will glow fiercely. The boy knows well the stove's punishing heat. The day before, he was made to stand next to it until he fainted.

This day, the boy has a note from his father. But the headmaster does not believe the boy is ill. The boy is ordered to put his left hand on the desk. Six times, the master strikes the slender youth with the full weight of an iron-capped rod. The boy does not flinch. The master calls for the right hand. Six more blows are delivered with all the strength the master possesses. No sound from the boy.

The master is determined to break the boy with repeated blows to the boy's bloodied hands. Now the schoolhouse is in an uproar—students hissing, groaning, scraping their desks on the floor. The master turns to confront the disorder. Lessons *are resumed. The heat rises from the stove. The master speaks not another word to the boy.*

The boy, too, keeps his silence. The pain is intense. His outrage at the indignity of the assault overwhelms him. An hour after school is dismissed, he still cannot speak. Then the boy rises. He goes to the school's trustees. He states his case. His hands are examined. The next day only four boys attend school. The following day, the master is gone.

In 1841, twenty-six-year-old Richard Henry Dana Jr. began a journal. He was the eldest son of one of America's oldest and most distinguished families. He had opened a Boston law practice and married. Dana's *Two Years Before the Mast,* an account of his voyage around Cape Horn to the western coast of North America, had been published to international acclaim. But what he most remembered of his first twenty-six years was that winter's day when the master had taught the fourteen-year-old Dana a lesson he would never forget.

"My whole soul was in my throat," wrote Dana. "I could have gone to the stake for what I considered my honor." Dana confided to his journal that for several years after the incident the thought of revenge "was frequently in my mind." Once, mistaking a passing stranger for the despised headmaster, Dana closed upon him rapidly, intent on forcing "a full and unequivocal apology . . . Had I been in a dueling country, I should have challenged him instantly."

Dana never got the chance to confront his tormentor. By the time he began his journal, the master had died. In self-reproach, Dana wrote that the denial of the chance to avenge the insult was God's rebuke to Dana for his pride. Yet he could not resist summarizing what the assault had taught him: "There are some insults to which natural man cannot quietly submit. *Something must be done.*"[1] The emphasis was Dana's.

He was always a plucky boy. On the first day of August 1825—his son's tenth birthday—Richard Henry Dana Sr. wrote to a friend: "If I understand Richard, he is a boy of excellent principles even now I am afraid he is too sensitive for his own happiness; yet he . . . is a boy of true spirit."[2]

The Cambridge Danas, like the Braintree Adamses, settled in Massachusetts before the middle of the seventeenth century. John Adams believed Dana's great-grandfather, Richard Dana, would have been "one of the immortal names of the Revolution" had he not died before 1775. It was Richard Dana, a Tory judge, who in 1765 drafted "the first treasonable document of the American Revolution," compelling Andrew Oliver, the crown's "Distributor of Stamps," to swear, "I will never directly or indirectly . . . take any measures for enforcing the Stamp Act in America, which is so grievous to the People."[3]

Dana's grandfather, Francis Dana Sr., traveled with John Adams to Paris in 1779 when Adams was chosen by Congress as minister plenipotentiary to France. The following year, when Congress instructed Francis Dana to proceed to the St. Petersburg Court of Catherine the Great to seek Russian recognition of the United States, Dana took with him the fourteen-year-old son of John Adams. John Quincy Adams was to name his third son, Charles Francis, in honor of his former mentor.

Francis Dana did not procure Catherine the Great's recognition— or even an audience with her, for that matter—but he did return with a great sable coat. When he became chief justice of the Supreme Judicial Court of Massachusetts, Dana was often seen in sable, embroidered waistcoat, and white muff. He traveled to court in a magnificent horse-drawn coach attended by servants.

But by the time of Richard Henry Dana Jr.'s birth in 1815, the Danas were more to be pitied than envied—especially by the Adamses. The unremarked passing of Dana's grandfather in 1811 was evidence of the dwindling fortunes of the distinguished family. The death of Francis Dana Sr., member of the Continental Congress, friend of George Washington, American envoy to Russia, and chief justice, went unnoticed. Abigail Adams was prompted to write, "If my absent son had been in America, the grave would not have thus silently closed over him."[4]

Chief Justice Dana's eldest son, Francis Dana Jr., brother to Dana's father, invested the bulk of the family fortune in a spectacularly unsuccessful venture to make Cambridgeport a hub of Boston shipping. The Dana mansion, carriages, and horses were sold to satisfy debts. The forced sale of the Dana estate dispersed the sons and daughters as well.

Francis Dana Jr. escaped creditors by surreptitiously taking passage to Archangel. His brothers Edmund Dana and Richard Henry Dana Sr. found themselves no longer in a mansion atop glorious Dana Hill, but beside a marsh in lower Cambridgeport. The simple frame house on Green Street would have seemed bleak under any circumstances, but their three unmarried sisters moved in as well.

It was in this house that Richard Henry Dana Jr. was born on August 1, 1815. Richard Henry Dana Sr. had brought his wife and one-year-old daughter there the previous year. Generations of Dana men had chosen their brides with a keen eye for improving their fortunes. Francis Dana Sr. inherited two fortunes and married a third when he wed Elizabeth Ellery, daughter of William Ellery of Newport, Rhode Island, a signer of the Declaration of Independence.

Richard Henry Dana Sr.—ever the romantic, as his son was to be—broke with family tradition and married for love. Dana's mother was Ruth Charlotte Smith, daughter of a penniless Taunton, Rhode Island, laborer. The Taunton Smiths were not the Newport Ellerys. Chief Justice Dana adamantly opposed the match and the couple did not marry until after his death.

True spirit was better protection than distinguished ancestry in the schools of early nineteenth-century New England. Dana possessed both qualities in abundance, but it was his mettle that enabled him to survive an educational system that seemed designed to crush all but the hardiest. Dana was always small for his age (the crew manifest for the brig *Pilgrim* listed the nineteen-year-old's height as 5 feet 5 inches; weight 125), but the boy could not be cowed.

The brutal and degrading application of corporal punishment was especially prevalent in the schools favored by the "best families." In 1822, at seven, Dana was enrolled in Reverend Samuel Barrett's school in Cambridgeport. His first response was to abandon his habit of prayers, "which would make me ridiculous among the boys." Dana made an exception "in times of alarm," and alarmed he must have been upon seeing his first teacher: "The master was a thin, dark-complexioned, dark-haired and dark-eyed man . . . and by the side of the door stood a chest in which I knew was kept the long pine ferrule with which all punishment was inflicted."

"How often did our hearts sicken at the sight of that chest and that ferrule!" recalled Dana. Punishment was inflicted "for every misdemeanor"—leaving seats, laughing, and poor recitation. Each boy who was "noted" was punished at the end of the day. If a boy had a note early, there were several dreaded hours before the blows to the hands were delivered. "A few of the older boys never cried but only changed color violently," Dana remembered, "but the other boys always cried . . . and with good reason."[5]

Reverend Barrett had another mode of punishment "rather peculiar to himself," Dana noted dryly. It was the master's habit to sometimes drag recalcitrant students by their ears "a good part of the way across the school room and over the benches." But, Dana stated proudly, "this mode of punishment however came to a stop with me."

In a celebrated incident, still spoken of many years later, the irrepressible Dana nearly sacrificed his ear to his "natural propensity to laugh." He had been reciting a lesson when a fellow student made him giggle. The master "pulled my ears pretty severely." This quieted Dana for a time but "the necessity of preserving my sobriety only made the temptation to laugh stronger." The master pulled Dana to his seat by the ear. Dana laughed a third time, motivated he conceded "to a little desire not to seem intimidated."

The enraged master dragged Dana by one ear back and forth across the classroom. Dana's ear was partly torn from his head. He was escorted home by a procession of classmates eager to attest to the drama. Dana's father petitioned the school to end ear-pulling. It did so, but Dana ruefully observed, "the ferrule resumed its full sway."[6]

The smallest boys "who were slow to learn and needed encouragement" suffered the most. Dana remembered one—broken in spirit—who was "weeks and weeks upon a few pages of his Latin grammar, which he had blotted with tears and blackened with his fingers, until they were hardly legible."[7] "A boy's will is his life, and he dies when it is broken" was one of the earliest lessons in the education of Henry Adams.[8]

Dana's own spirit was all the more remarkable given his father's lethargy. Although Richard Henry Dana Sr. was for a brief period considered America's greatest poet, he was most noted for his inertia. A lapsed lawyer, literary dilettante, and armchair sailor, the senior Dana was satirized in a James Russell Lowell poem:

> That he once was the Idle Man none will deplore,
> But I fear he will never be anything more;
> The ocean of song heaves and glitters before him,
> The depth and the vastness and longing sweep o'er him,
> He knows every breaker and shoal on the chart,
> He has the Coast Pilot and so on by heart,
> Yet he spends his whole life, like the man in the fable,
> In learning to swim on the library-table.[9]

Dana's mother died in February 1822, leaving Dana's father with four children: seven-year-old Ruth Charlotte, six-year-old Richard Henry, four-year-old Ned, and two-year-old Susan. The apparent cause was tuberculosis, and Dana records his mother constantly suffering ill health in the last year of her life. The death of Dana's mother had a far greater impact on his father's spirit than on his own.

His father's grief, "which no description . . . short of madness has equaled," manifested itself in ways that might have irreparably damaged a different boy. The deep and solemn impression the death made upon Dana was reinforced by his father's elevating the mother's memory to a sacredness Dana described as "peculiar and lasting." Reference to his mother was not permitted except at private moments orchestrated by his father. Twenty years after her death Dana wrote, "Her name has never been mentioned among us or anything connected with her alluded to."[10]

To his father's inherent predisposition to morbidity, came a tragedy entirely unremarked upon by either father or son. In April 1822, two months after his mother's death, Dana's two-year-old sister Susan died of injuries sustained in a fall. Beyond a passing reference in a later Dana family history, there is no mention of the child's death except that it occurred "at home."[11]

Home was Wigglesworth House in Harvard Yard where Dana Sr. had moved his young family when he became an occasional lecturer at the college. Wigglesworth House was two centuries old but it is unlikely that any resident ever had more misfortune there than Dana's father. Not only did his wife and youngest daughter die there, but it was there that he ceased publication of his literary periodical, *The Idle Man,* because of lack of subscribers. Even someone with a temperament better equipped to sustain those losses would have had difficulty. For Richard Henry Dana Sr., the events of 1822 were to deepen the melancholia that was the most characteristic aspect of his personality.

It may well have been the death of little Susan that compelled Dana's aunts to bring Dana's father and the surviving children into their home. Elizabeth and Sarah Dana were no strangers to sudden death in early nineteenth-century New England. In the autumn of 1817, just days before a planned double wedding in which the sisters were to marry the brothers George and James Foster, there swept through Cambridge an epidemic to which both brothers succumbed.

Six years later a surviving elder brother, Dr. William Foster, fulfilled a pledge he had made to his dying bothers to build a house for the bereaved Dana sisters. The house, which today stands next to the Harvard

Faculty Club, held a commanding position on a small hill in the southeast corner of Harvard Yard. A Greek portico extended the length of the south side of the home. From the porch one could look over the salt marshes and Winthrop Duck Pond, to the shimmering Charles River below.

In February 1823, Richard Henry Dana Sr. moved his family from the rickety Wigglesworth House to his sisters' new home. They were joined by a third sister, Martha Remington Dana, making a household of Dana's three aunts, his father, and his sister and brother. The Dana house was relatively spacious, and Harvard thought it "sufficiently firm to support a telescope of some power" when the college purchased the property a few years later and put an observatory atop it.[12] But the interior was made somber by the veil of tragedy that Dana's elders seemed unwilling to relinquish.

Aunts Elizabeth and Sara, who were to die spinster maids, still wore black to mourn the death of the Foster brothers. Dana's father remained morose despite his relocation to a home that provided him a private library and "a very beautiful prospect from it." "Must the kindred stillness and gloom of our dwelling be changed for . . . the talk of the passersby, and the broad and piercing light of the common sun?" he wrote in an essay about a boy and the death of his mother.[13] The studied melancholy with which the elder Dana greeted visitors—"smiling sadly with his soft blue eyes while extending a pale white hand"—was often remarked upon.[14]

Eighteenth-century tradition suited Dana's father. There were still Cambridge residents who regretted the "late unhappy separation" from England. The village was devoid of foreigners, except, one observer noted, "two Scotch gardeners."[15] A contemporary description declared that Cambridge "eminently combines the tranquility of philosophic solitude, with the choicest pleasures and advantages of refined society."[16]

It is not surprising that Dana thought adventure lay beyond his Cambridge home. An attempt to bring excitement indoors when Dana and his boyhood friend, James Russell Lowell, tried to ride a pony up the Dana staircase was not well received. Outdoors and free of his family, there was little that Dana did not explore. At age seven he once walked fourteen miles and was none the worse for it, an early demonstration of a prodigious physical stamina that was to amaze future shipmates. "I was a noted wanderer," Dana wrote, with more accuracy than he realized.

Cambridgeport was much closer to Cambridge than Quincy was to Boston, but in Dana's boyhood it meant "country," and that meant—as Quincy had to Henry Adams—"liberty, diversity, outlawry."[17] The greater part of Cambridgeport was still huckleberry pasture in the 1830s, but there were several inns with huge barns and courtyards. Wagons drawn by double teams of six to eight horses brought country wares for market and seaport. The local brewer's white-roofed cart was adorned with two large cardboard bottles. It attracted boys to whom the brewer provided a discount "and wisely for they were his chieftest patrons."[18]

"I went where I was told not to go, played with boys whom I was warned against as vulgar, was always found out and wondered how . . . went whortle-berrying and ate all before I got home; followed soldiers, droves of cattle, showmen and anything else that was attractive and noisy, was imposed upon by larger boys, had my hat run away with, which I thought was a grievous loss to the whole family as well as myself," remembered Dana.[19] The wagon drivers filled the inns and they could be heard late into the night carousing behind barrooms' red curtains. There were some houses next to the taverns but "by whom or why inhabited" was a puzzle to Dana and his friends.

Dana welcomed the freedom afforded him by his timid father. "My father always adopted the course with me of allowing me to knock about for myself and get into such dangers as I dared to," he noted in his journal.[20] Dana ascribed the surprising permissiveness to a well-considered parental belief in encouraging habits of self-reliance, but his father's letters suggest a different motivation of which Dana was unaware.

The elder Dana wrote a friend that he thought of his son "with an impression that if he lives he will not be happy; and so constant is this feeling . . . that should he die early, tho it would be a sad thing to part with him, my first and last thought of him would be, he has escaped the evil to come." Dana Sr. acknowledged it was a weakness to think this way, but added, "When have I been other than a creature of weakness and folly?"[21] One suspects that the letter's recipient silently answered "Never."

The father's strange sensibility did, however, make him an astute observer of his son. "I have great hopes for Richard," he wrote to his sister-in-law shortly after his wife's death. "With all his fondness for laughter and fun, he has great thoughtfulness and tenderness." The elder Dana may have had in mind an incident recounted in Dana's journal. One holiday, Dana heard a small black boy crying because a large white boy had taken his money. Dana was so upset "that my father was obliged to . . . walk a long distance, hunt the boy up and give him some money before I could be comforted."[22]

For all Dana's escapades and what his future would hold, there is almost no mention of ships and sailors despite his proximity to Boston Harbor, then one of the busiest seaports in the world. First memories are often of color (for Henry Adams it was "a yellow kitchen-floor in strong sunlight") and Dana's earliest recollection was of "a pitcher of remarkably rich blue" which brought to his mind "something . . . which the simple water it contained did not answer to."[23]

The extent of his preparation for one of the most celebrated voyages in history was sailing a homemade raft on the pond that was visible from his house. Dana's inspiration to try his hand on simple water may have been the sloop *Harvard,* owned by the college and often seen on the Charles River. So thought James Russell Lowell, who recalled "those first essays at navigation on the Winthrop duck-pond of the plucky boy who was afterwards to serve two famous years before the mast."[24] It was Harvard—not its sloop—that was to be instrumental in Dana's decision to go to sea, but inspiration was not part of the curriculum.

On a warm July morning in 1831, fifteen-year-old Richard Henry Dana Jr. made the short walk from his home to Harvard's University Hall. There, the formidable Harvard president, Josiah Quincy, was already examining prospective students. The Dana path to Harvard was well-trod. His great-grandfather, grandfather, and father had preceded him. Indeed, the Danas were soon to literally be a part of Harvard, for in 1835 the college purchased the former Dana house and extended Harvard Yard to include the property.

"Was it possible . . . to conceive a greater potentate than the President of the University?" wrote Lowell.[25] But if Dana had any trepidation about conjugating Latin verbs, reciting Cicero, or otherwise satisfying President Quincy as to his fitness to enter Harvard, it is not reflected in his journal. Harvard College no longer ranked members of the freshmen class according to the social standing of their families, but the Danas had sufficient pedigree to withstand their current reversal of fortune. Dana's great-grandfather Richard, class of 1718, was ranked fifteenth of nineteen, but grandfather Francis, class of 1762, had ascended to sixth of forty-seven, trailing only a Danforth, an Oliver, a Winslow, and two Hutchinsons.[26]

President Quincy assumed the Harvard presidency in 1829, determined "to make the College a nursery of high-minded, high-principled, well-taught, well-conducted, well-bred gentlemen."[27] Among the many impediments to this lofty goal one may start with two: the average age of Harvard freshmen was sixteen, and the academic year began in August and continued to the following July. To these formidable obstacles, Josiah Quincy added one of his own—the abominable "Scale of Merit." The marking system was to be castigated by Harvard graduates for the next quarter century. It was this Harvard that Dana, class of 1835, entered in August 1831.

He began well enough, finding himself "unexpectedly second . . . in mathematics," twelfth out of sixty in Latin, and "in Greek not quite so high."[28] But a system of instruction premised upon rote learning and recitation that discouraged teachers from answering questions or explaining texts could not hope to engage students. President Quincy's marking system required instructors to grade each student daily on a scale of eight for each recitation. A student's marks could be reduced for a variety of reasons. There was a sixteen-point penalty for absence from chapel. Every week the president personally totaled the marks of each student. It was this "stupid method of teaching" to which a historian of Harvard has ascribed the revolt against the classics—and, he could have added, to much else.[29]

Student "rebellions" were so prevalent at Harvard College in the first half of the nineteenth century that it became necessary to distinguish them by name. The "Bread and Butter Rebellion" of 1805, a protest against bad food in the dining commons, was not to be confused with the "Butter Rebellion" of 1766, though the cause ("Behold our Butter Stinketh") was identical.

But rebellions had consequences. The college authorities always suspended—and often expelled—students who took part in the protests. Dana's father, class of 1808, was dismissed for his role in the "cabbage rebellion," another riot provoked by unhappiness with poor food in the dining commons. Harvard would not confer a degree on Richard Henry Dana Sr. until 1866, and then only because of the prominence of his son. The forty-three students—out of a class of seventy—expelled for the

"Great Rebellion" of 1823 fared even worse. Only twenty-five were eventually acknowledged A.B. "as of" 1823. Though a son of John Quincy Adams was among them, the degree was not conferred until after both father and son had died. Harvard has a long memory.[30]

The "Great Rebellion" did prompt the college to institute some reforms relating to administration and student discipline. The vacation schedule was changed in recognition of perhaps the only educational theory of the nineteenth century that remains uncontroverted: warm weather contributes to student riots. President Quincy, however, had little doubt that he could handle recalcitrant Harvard students irrespective of the weather. A former Boston mayor, Quincy once single-handedly faced down an unruly mob of Bostonians.

Given the institution, the president, and the student, it was only a matter of time before Dana himself was in rebellion. It did not take long. The cause was so common that the rebellion has not been deemed nameworthy. In the spring of 1832, Dana's freshman year, an infraction of college rules had been committed and the faculty was determined to identify the culprit. Another student was thought to know the offender's name but refused to disclose it.

The unfortunate Rugg—as unlucky in circumstance as in name—was a "charity-student," an easier target than the sons of wealthy families. President Quincy threatened to bring him before a grand jury. Whatever benefit grand juries may have to mayors, they are a singularly unhelpful tool for college presidents. Josiah Quincy was to learn this lesson two years later when, in 1834, his attempt to compel students to testify against each other in grand jury proceedings led to an undergraduate revolt explosive even by Harvard standards.[31] The lesson could have been grasped earlier had Quincy the wit to recognize the motivation that spurs all similar protests—"an aversion," in Dana's words, "to tale-bearing." The determination to sustain Rugg, "a very worthy, unpretending man," in his refusal to be an informer prompted a meeting of Dana's classmates attended by "all but two or three very timid and mean spirited lads."[32]

At Friday evening prayers, as the eminent Professor of Divinity, Dr. Ware, began to read from the Bible, Dana's class "set up a hissing, groaning, and scraping which completely drowned his voice." This immediately brought President Quincy down from his seat and tutors down from the galleries. Despite their presence the noise continued. At Saturday morning prayers the demonstration was repeated.

"Here," wrote Dana, "was an open rebellion . . . suspension or expulsion was the certain consequence." Dana was to later learn that President Quincy had gone to Dana's father and advised him that if he could persuade his son to stay away from Harvard Yard for a day or two, he would not be among those disciplined. Richard Henry Dana Sr. asked his son for an explanation of his reasons for the protest.

"I . . . told him that I had joined the rebellion because I thought the class was contending for a principle of honor and good faith between young men." His father asked if he would consider staying away from Harvard for a few days. Dana replied that he had given his word to go forward with the protest and "if I stayed away, it would not be because I had changed my view of the right & wrong of the thing . . . but it would be a desertion of those who kept their word at great risk, merely for my own preservation."

Dana's father, to his great credit, left the decision to his son by telling him "if I could not stay away without feeling that I had done a dishonorable thing, I must go, though punishment would be a certain consequence."[33] The Harvard faculty minutes of March 5, 1832, reflect the result: "Voted: That Dana being concerned in making noise in chapel be suspended and directed to pursue his studies in some place out of the limits of the Town of Cambridge."[34]

Dana's suspension was for six months. "My banishment at Andover passed in a most delightful and improving manner," Dana wrote in his journal. He studied with the Reverend Leonard Woods Jr. of Andover Theological Seminary. Woods, then twenty-four, was to become president of Bowdoin College at thirty-two. Dana credited him with doing more to interest him in learning and "worthy" ambition than anyone he ever met. "What a man is, and not merely what he has done became the standard of emulation and effort," Dana said of his tutor.[35]

Dana was to internalize that standard with consequences he could not have foreseen. But in the spring of 1832, sixteen-year-old Dana was delighted to have found a kindred spirit. He could barely conceal his joy at being able to study to learn, "not for the sixes, sevens, and eights, which [Harvard] put against every word that came out of a student's mouth." Dana was particularly struck by two aspects of his tutor's approach, also rare at Harvard. Reverend Woods, observed Dana, was remarkably free of the prejudices and strong opinions that were typical of persons of faith, and he was so welcoming of questions from students that he was "much sought after by the unlearned, a thing not usual with the learned."[36]

Dana was often in the company of Woods' large family. His tutor had six sisters, one of whom, Sarah, was two years younger than Dana. She apparently became enamored with the suspended Harvard student, for there is a suggestion that Woods admonished Dana for trifling with his sister's affections. Dana was more amused than concerned by the girl's attention, but there came a time when the episode was to have a profound effect upon him.

Dana's suspension ended in August 1832. "I would have given a great deal to have my sentence extended six months more," wrote Dana. If it were not for family, he complained in a letter to his father, he would not return to Cambridge as there was "nothing to benefit one at all." But the choice was not his to make, and Dana returned to Harvard "as a slave whipped to his dungeon."[37]

Dana worked hard his sophomore year, rising early to study by candlelight. At the end of the academic year he ranked seventh in his class. Dana rewarded himself with a visit to family friends in Plymouth, where he spent several weeks in "fishing, boating, shooting, and idling of all kinds." The pleasant and otherwise unremarkable vacation was to have consequences that "changed suddenly and to an extreme my whole course of life for years after and perhaps for all my days."[38]

Dana contracted measles. Although sick for only a few days, his eyesight was severely weakened. When he found he could not read without extreme pain, he decided not to begin his junior year at Harvard. Nine months of treatment failed to yield any sign of improvement. His confinement in the suffocating atmosphere of the Dana house was exacerbated by a father "embarrassed in his pecuniary condition." Dana's younger brother Ned, never ambitious to begin with, claimed to have eye problems too, and was kept home from school.

"I lingered about at home," wrote Dana, "a useless, pitied and dissatisfied creature." Then there arose "a strong love of adventure which I had always with difficulty repressed." Dana hit upon a plan "to relieve myself from ennui, to see new places and modes of life, and to effect if possible a cure of my eyes which no medicine has helped."[39] He would take a long voyage. Before the mast.

Dana's family and friends were aghast at the idea. Though a voyage to cure ills, imagined or otherwise, was an acceptable and conventional response among the best families even in the early nineteenth century, no one meant sailing "before the mast" in the unimaginably squalid conditions of a merchant ship's forecastle. Dana's determination to become a common seaman provoked nearly as much horror as if he had volunteered to become a slave. Indeed, the comparison was not far-fetched, for the authority of a ship's captain was absolute, and depending upon the master's inclination, the discipline inflicted upon a sailor thousands of miles from the safe harbor of Boston could be as brutal and degrading as that on a Southern plantation.

Dana's father attempted to persuade his son to choose a more sensible course. Although he did not have the means to send Richard on a tour of Europe—the preferred option of his social class in dealing with restless sons—the elder Dana did have sufficient connections to secure a reasonable alternative. J. Ingersoll Bowditch was preparing to embark for India and, as an owner of the ship, offered Dana passage to Calcutta. He added that Dana would, of course, be provided a room in his house when on shore.

Dana's eyesight was still poor and, as a passenger on a lengthy voyage, he would have little to do but read. He remained determined to go to sea as a member of the crew. Bowditch would hear none of it and he enlisted his father, the mathematician and celebrated author of *The Practical Navigator*, Dr. Nathanial Bowditch, to talk sense to young Dana.

Dr. Bowditch told Dana he liked his spirit. That, said Dana, only added fuel to the fire, for "the . . . old gentleman had been . . . before the mast himself when a boy and he knew that it had done him good." Dana declined the offer to sail as a passenger. "When I recall the motives which governed me in this choice," wrote Dana, "I can hardly tell which predominated, a desire to cure my eyes, my love of adventure & the attraction of the novelty of a life before the mast, or anxiety to escape from the depressing situation of inactivity & dependence at home."[40]

Dana was able to procure a berth as a common seaman on the brig *Pilgrim*. He knew little of the ship and nothing of the sea. He was the eldest son of the fifth generation of a family that had spent two centuries in one town in a country with one coast. But he was nineteen years old. And the *Pilgrim* was bound for a land called "California."

2

PILGRIM

On August 14, 1834, Richard Henry Dana Jr. stood on a Boston wharf waiting to board the brig *Pilgrim*. Outfitted in white duck trousers, checked shirt, and tarpaulin hat, Dana thought he looked "as salt as Neptune himself." In fact, the slightly built, nearsighted Dana looked like a ship's "boy" of twelve rather than the "jack tar" of nineteen he supposed himself to be when he changed from the dress coat and kid gloves of a Harvard undergraduate. Once aboard, Dana realized that his appearance was the least of his problems. Completely bewildered by the "unintelligible orders . . . strange cries and stranger actions," Dana made his first observation of the voyage: "There is not so helpless and pitiable object in the world as a landsman beginning a sailor's life."[1]

The two-masted, two-decked *Pilgrim* was an intimidating ship of sail, rope, and rigging to one whose "sailing" had been on Winthrop duck pond. But an eighty-six-foot brig with a crew of fifteen was a modest vessel for a voyage around perilous Cape Horn to the edge of the North American continent. The *Pilgrim*'s thirty-year-old master, Captain Frank Thompson, was to prove even more dangerous than the ocean, but floggings, death, and desertion were far from Dana's mind as he made his way to the "inexpressible sickening smell" of steerage after having been sick several times on deck. "I could not but remember that this was the first night of a two years' voyage."[2]

Captain Thompson addressed the crew from the quarterdeck. With cigar in mouth, "dropping the words out between the puffs," the master advised obedience or "we shall have hell afloat." Dana did his best to remain unnoticed, but five days out he made the mistake of sitting down after swabbing the deck. He was immediately ordered to climb the main mast. Dana was still seasick but realized "that if I showed any sign of want of spirit . . . I should be ruined at once." Ordered to "slush" the masthead, "the rocking of the vessel which increases the higher you go . . . and the smell of grease which offended my fastidious senses" sickened Dana again.[3]

The call to breakfast held little appeal, but the cook gave the green hand advice: "You are well-cleaned out . . . pitch all your sweetmeats overboard, and turn—to . . . good hearty salt beef and sea bread." After gnawing on salt beef and biscuits, Dana could not believe the change: "I was a new being . . . and could begin to learn my sea duty with considerable spirit."[4]

Duty began with acknowledgment that the captain was "lord paramount" and "must be obeyed in everything without a question." Dana had already learned that there was no idleness on deck. "In no state prison are the convicts more regularly set to work and more closely watched." Conversation among the crew was prohibited when on duty, though sailors talked when aloft or if the officers were not near. Sundays were to be the crew's day unless the ship was entering or departing a harbor—a "coincidence" that Captain Thompson always seemed to manage. There were no religious services aboard, for the *Pilgrim* "had a crew of swearers from the captain to the smallest boy."[5]

There must have been oaths aplenty on the morning of September 22. A black-hulled ship—sailing without colors and full of armed men—

began pursuit of the *Pilgrim*. Dana and the crew remained on deck all day with "arms in order," though there was little they could have done had the stranger been what they feared. The tiny brig was slightly faster in light wind than its menacing pursuer and by nightfall increased its lead. In the moonless night, the *Pilgrim* doused its lights and by daybreak there was no sign of the mystery ship.

On October 1, Dana crossed the equator and felt himself "for the first time . . . at liberty, according to the old usage, to call myself a son of Neptune." By the end of October the *Pilgrim* was in "the latitude of the river La Plata" off the coast of Argentina, when Dana experienced the first storm "which could be really called a gale." Dana was ordered aloft to reef the sails. A hopeless landlubber two months before, Dana proudly reported "I had now become used to the vessel and to my duty, was of some service on a yard and could knot my reef-point as well as anybody." It was well he could, for a few days later came the cry "All hands ahoy!"[6]

Coming on deck, Dana saw "a large black cloud rolling on toward us from the south-west, and blackening the whole heavens." "Here comes Cape Horn!" exclaimed the chief mate. Dana had never seen such heavy seas. The little *Pilgrim,* "no better than a bathing machine," plunged into the waves and "the forward part of her was under water . . . the sea pouring in . . . threatening to wash everything overboard." The storm's fury continued through the night—"rain, hail, snow, and sleet beating upon the vessel"—and at daybreak "the deck was covered with snow." By morning it began to clear, and "a glass of grog was sent to each of the watch."[7] It was benign weather for Cape Horn.

The seas had calmed enough to afford Dana "my turn to steer" and "inexperienced as I was, I made out to steer to the satisfaction of the officer." Dana never had to surrender the helm because of ineptness, and "this was something to boast of, for it requires a good deal of skill . . . to steer a vessel close hauled, in a gale of wind, against a heavy head sea." There were other rewarding moments as well. Off the Falkland Islands, Dana heard the "near breathing of whales." Unable to see them because of heavy fog, Dana leaned over the bulwarks "listening to the slow breathings of the mighty creatures."[8]

On November 9, as the *Pilgrim* continued to beat against the wind, a "true specimen of Cape Horn" struck. Again, "the little brig was plunging madly into a tremendous head sea." The chief mate called "lay out there and furl the jib!" It was dangerous work, and "John the Swede," the best sailor on board, sprang to the bowsprit. But another hand was needed and Dana jumped forward, as he "was the near the mate." With the brig diving into the seas, Dana "hardly knew whether we were on or off." The two men finally managed to furl the jib, and "were not a little pleased to find that all was snug." Dana noted "we had now got hardened to Cape weather."[9] But there were harder things ahead.

George Ballmer, a young English sailor, was "prized by the officers as an active and willing seaman." A good shipmate, at 5 feet 4 inches he was the only member of the crew shorter (by an inch) than Dana, except for the ship's boy. On the morning of November 19 Dana was awakened by a cry of "All hands ahoy! A man overboard!" Ballmer had gone aloft to fit a strap around the main topmast. Burdened by a strap and block, a coil of rope, and a marlinespike around his neck, he slipped and fell into the sea.

Dana got on deck in time to jump into a lowered boat, "but it was not until out upon the wide Pacific, in our little boat, that I knew whom we had lost." Balmer could not swim "and with all those things around his neck, he probably sank immediately." Though the crew knew there was no hope, "yet no one wished to speak of returning, and we rowed about for nearly an hour." At last the crew bowed to the inevitable and returned to the ship.

"Death is at all times solemn, but never so much as at sea," mused Dana. "When a man falls overboard at sea and is lost, there is suddenness in the event, and a difficulty in realizing it, which give to it an air of awful mystery. . . . Then, too, at sea . . . you *miss* a man so much. A dozen men are shut up together in a little bark, aboard the wide, wide sea and for months and months see no forms and hear no voices but their own, and one is taken suddenly from among them, and they miss him at every turn. It is like losing a limb."[10] Yet the voyage must continue.

The young sailor's effects were auctioned off according to the custom of the sea. Though the seaman's clothes were sold, "sailors have an unwillingness to wear a dead man's clothes during the same voyage . . . unless they are in absolute want." Dana thought a sailor's life linked "the beautiful . . . with the revolting, the sublime with the common-place, and the solemn with the ludicrous." Seamen had a more blunt expression: *"To work hard, live hard, die hard, and go to hell after all, would be hard indeed!"*[11]

A week after death at sea, the *Pilgrim*—now round Cape Horn and sailing north—raised the island of Juan Fernandez, made famous by

Daniel Defoe's *Robinson Crusoe.* The ship entered the small harbor "and our anchor struck bottom for the first time since we left Boston—one hundred and three days." The island was used by the Chilean government to imprison convicts, some of whom Dana found "locked up . . . in caves dug into the side of the mountain." But Dana was under Crusoe's spell, and thought the beauty of the island "and its solitary position in the midst of the wide expanse of the South Pacific" made it "the most romantic spot of earth that my eyes had ever seen."[12]

On November 27 the *Pilgrim* left the island "and saw no more land until we arrived upon the western coast of the great continent of America." Though the sailing was benign ("We caught the south-east trades, and ran before them for nearly three weeks, without so much as altering a sail, or bracing a yard"), the mood aboard was malignant. The crew was without fresh provisions, and when bread rations were cut, the sailors "went aft in a body with [John the] Swede for spokesman" to petition the master. True to form, Captain Thompson snarled, "Well what the devil do you want now?" When the crew began to state grievances "as respectfully as we could," Thompson interrupted, calling them fat and lazy. "This provoked us and we began to give word for word," Dana added. "This would never answer."[13]

Nor did it, for Thompson was as fearless as he was malicious. "You've mistaken your man! I'm Frank Thompson, all the way from 'downeast.' . . . I'll *haze* you! . . . I'll make a hell of this ship!" "Haze" was a word frequently used aboard ship, though Dana had never heard it elsewhere. "It is very expressive to a sailor, and means punish by hard work. Let an officer say, 'I'll *haze* you' and your fate is fixed."[14]

When Thompson cooled off, the chief mate was able to restore rations, though the captain insisted on berating the men again. But Dana took it all in stride, because he and shipmate Ben Stimson, another green hand from Boston, were at last given permission to move from steerage to the forecastle. Though the berths were as dark and dank, Dana could now bunk and eat with the crew. "No man can be a sailor or know what sailors are, unless he has lived in the forecastle with them—turned in and out with them, eaten of their dish, and drank of their cup."[15]

It was a new year. Dana was a sailor. On January 14, 1835, after a voyage of 150 days, the *Pilgrim* anchored in a lonely bay off a remote coast of the continent. From the deck, Dana "looked about us to see what sort of country we had got into, and were to spend a year or two of our lives in." Dana was immediately struck by an aspect of the country that millions who came later noticed too. "In the first place it was a beautiful day, and so warm that we had on straw hats, duck trousers, and all the summer gear; and as this was mid-winter, it spoke well for the climate."[16] They were in Santa Barbara, California.

Just before sundown the mate ordered a boat lowered, and Dana was among the crew who rowed the three miles to shore. "I shall never forget the impression which our first landing on the beach of California made upon me. The sun had just gone down; it was getting dusky; the damp night wind was beginning to blow, and the heavy swell of the Pacific was setting in, and breaking in loud and high 'combers' upon the beach."[17]

The *Pilgrim*'s master had not disembarked in Santa Barbara to sightsee. The ship was there to pick up an agent of the Boston firm of Bryant, Sturgis and Co., owners of the vessel. For the past half-dozen years, the firm of Yankee traders had been the principal importers of cattle hides from Mexico's California. "California hides" were in demand by New England shoe manufacturers, and never more so than in 1835–1836, the sixteen months Dana spent on the California coast.[18]

Dana had little idea of the drudgery and almost literally back-breaking work that the "hide trade" had in store for him, but he got an inkling on the Santa Barbara beach. "Sandwich Islanders" from the ship *Ayacucho* were already at work carrying hides. The stiff cattle hides had to be carried through the surf as there was no wharf. They were so large that the Islanders carried them, one or two at a time, on their heads to keep them out of the water. "Well, Dana," said the second mate, "that does not look much like Cambridge college does it? This is what I call '*head work*.'" Dana added his own thought: "To tell the truth, it did not look very encouraging."[19]

At Santa Barbara, Captain Thompson took aboard Alfred Robinson, the company agent, as well as the captain's brother, a trader on the coast. The brother's Mexican wife accompanied him, and Dana—who had not seen a woman in five months—was one of two crew members who "took the senora in our arms, and waded with her through the water."[20]

Two weeks later the *Pilgrim* entered Monterey Bay in "the rainy season, everything was as green as nature could make it." Red tiled roofs on houses ("about a hundred in number") dotted the "extreme greenness of the lawn." The brig came to anchor on a fine Saturday afternoon: "The

Mexican flag was flying from the little square Presidio, and the drums and trumpets of the soldiers who were out on parade sounded over the water, and gave great life to the scene."[21]

Ships intending to trade on the California coast were required to be inspected by Mexican customs officials. The cargo the *Pilgrim* carried from Boston to trade for cattle hides "consisted of everything under the sun." Dana's list included "spirits of all kinds (sold by the cask), teas, coffee, sugars, spices, raisins, molasses, hard-ware crockery-ware, tin-ware, cutlery, clothing of all kinds, boots and shoes from Lynn, calicoes and cottons from Lowell, crapes, silks; also, shawls, scarfs, necklaces, jew-elry, and combs for the ladies, furniture; and in fact, everything that can be imagined, from Chinese fire-works to English cart-wheels." Dana was astonished at how little Californians made for themselves. "The country abounds in grapes, yet they bad buy wine made in Boston." The boots and shoes from Lynn were "as like as not, made of their own hides which have been carried twice round Cape Horn."[22]

Yet the excitement may be imagined when a ship brimming with goods opened its emporium. An account by a twelve-year-old Mexican girl nearly contemporaneous with the arrival of the *Pilgrim* described her rancho learning that a ship "with two sticks in the center" had arrived to trade for hides. Among the goods secured by her father in exchange for "California bank-notes" (the sailors' term for hides) were brass but-tons which the little girl proudly sewed on her dress. A friend "offered me a beautiful black colt for six of the buttons, but I continued for a long time to think more of the buttons than anything I possessed."[23]

The trade between the *Pilgrim* and Monterey residents lasted more than a week. The crew ferried customers between ship and shore, a wel-come break for seamen. It was even better for Dana because he parlayed his limited Spanish into a reputation as a "great linguist." The captain began using Dana to carry messages to different parts of town and to buy provisions. "I was often sent to get something which I could not tell the name of to save my life; but I . . . never pleaded ignorance."[24]

The only other vessel at Monterey was the tiny *Loriotte* with a crew of Sandwich Islanders and two English sailors, one of whom Dana de-scribed so vividly that he confessed "it is strange that one should be so minute in the description of an unknown, outcast sailor, whom one may never see again, and whom no one may care to hear about." Bill Jackson—"a fine specimen of manly beauty"—had "cheeks of a handsome brown . . . teeth brilliantly white . . . hair of a raven black, waved in loose curls . . . and his eyes he might have sold to a duchess at the price of diamonds for their brilliancy." Dana knew him well enough to know he "was very fond of reading" and that "on one of his broad arms he had the crucifixion, and on the other the sign of the 'foul anchor.' "[25]

Dana's keen eye and "fluency" in Spanish enabled him to capture other scenes as well. He was fascinated by California. Its geography presented "two different faces." North from Monterey "the country becomes more wooded, has a richer appearance, and is better supplied with water." South to San Diego "there is very little wood, and the country has a naked level appearance, though it is still very fertile." Dana was enchanted by California attire: "The fondness for dress among women is excessive. . . . Nothing is more common than to see a woman living in a house of only two rooms, and the ground for a floor, dressed in spangled satin shoes, silk gown, high comb, and gilt, if not gold, ear-rings and necklace." Men wore broad-brimmed dark hats with "a gilt or figured band around the crown, and lined inside with silk; a short jacket of silk or figured calico, . . . the shirt open in the neck; rich waistcoat, if any; pantaloons wide, straight, and long, usually of velvet . . . and always wear a sash round the waist, which is generally red, and varying in quality with the means of the wearer. Add to this the never failing cloak, and you have the dress of the Californian."[26]

Dana was mesmerized by the language. "It was a pleasure simply to listen to the sound . . . before I could attach any meaning to it." The "fineness of the voices and beauty of the intonations" made every speaker eloquent; "a common bullock-driver on horseback, delivering a message, seemed to speak like an ambassador at an audience."[27]

The impact of the "Ingles"—mostly "Yankees by birth"—was already apparent. No Protestant could hold property, so Americans who intended to live in California "became Catholics, to a man; the current phrase among them being—'A man must leave his conscience at Cape Horn.' " The new converts "married Californians . . . and acquired considerable property. Having more industry, frugality, and enterprise than the natives, they soon got nearly all the trade into their hands." Though Dana exclaimed, "In the hands of an enterprising people, what a country this might be!" he saw no virtue in Yankee "values."[28]

There was more than a hint of Dana the Brahmin in his account of Don Juan Bandini, who had "the bearing of a man of high birth and figure." Bandini "polite to everyone . . . gave four reals—I dare say the last he had in his pocket—to the steward who waited upon him." Dana contrasted the refined Spanish Californian to "a fat, course, vulgar, pretending fellow of a Yankee trader, who had made money in San Diego, and was eating out the very vitals of the Bandinis . . . grinding them in their poverty; having mortgages on their lands." The impact of his fellow countrymen on "Californians" appeared to Dana to be "a curse" that "stripped them of everything but their pride, their manners, and their voices."[29]

Dana's ruminations about the fate of Californians soon became secondary to thought of his own fate. The brief hiatus in Monterey ended with the *Pilgrim*'s return to San Diego and the "hide-houses." The crew's disdain for the Sandwich Islanders' method of carrying hides quickly gave way to acknowledgment that "head-work was the only system for California." Lined caps were a must for heavy hides as stiff as boards and as wide as arms could stretch. A little gust of wind could overturn hide and sailor. It was "always wet work," the stony beach cut bare feet, and when the boats were loaded, there was "a long pull of three miles" to the *Pilgrim* anchored offshore.[30]

But for Dana the "labors would have been nothing . . . were it not for the uncertainty, or worse than uncertainty, which hung over the nature and length of our voyage." Dana left Boston believing he and his ship would return within two years. Now word began to circulate among the crew that Captain Thompson intended to collect hides for another ship and "we were to collect all the hides we could, and deposit them at San Diego, when the new ship, which would carry forty thousand, was to be filled and sent home, and then we were to begin anew, and collect our own cargo." Rumor was reduced to certainty when the name of the other ship, the *Alert,* became known. The *Pilgrim* seemed certain to spend three to four years in hide gathering. "The older sailors said they never should see Boston again, but should lay their bones in California."[31]

For Dana, it was "bad enough for them, but still worse was it for me." Dana did not plan to spend his life as a seaman, but he knew that three or four years "would make me a sailor in every respect mind and habits as well as body." There seemed no choice except to resolve: "A sailor I must be, and to be master of a vessel, must be the height of my ambition." Yet, even to remain a sailor, Dana had to first survive the master of the *Pilgrim,* and "there was trouble brewing on board."[32]

Captain Thompson's remedy for a disgruntled crew was to work them hard in port, and at sea to call all hands "to come up and see it rain." The men were kept "on deck hour after hour in a drenching rain, standing round the deck so far apart as to prevent talking with one another." The master's displeasure was often directed at Sam, a sailor "rather slow in his motions" who "hesitated in his speech," a defect that provoked Thompson.[33]

On a Saturday morning following several days in which "the captain seemed very much out of humor," Dana stood at the main hatchway awaiting Thompson, who was below deck. Suddenly the master's voice was raised in violent dispute, followed by sounds of a fight. Dana ran for "John the Swede" and the two men peered down the hatchway where the captain's voice arose "loud and clear."

"You see your condition! You see your condition! Will you ever give me any more of your *jaw!*"

"I never gave you any, sir." It was Sam, his voice "low and half choked."

"That's not what I ask you. Will you ever be impudent to me again?"

"I never have been sir," said Sam.

"Answer my question or I'll make a spread eagle of you! I'll flog you, by God."

"I'm no negro slave," said Sam.

"Then I'll make you one," said the captain.

Thompson ordered the first mate to seize the hapless sailor: "Make a spread eagle of him! I'll teach you all who is master aboard!" Sam did not resist and was carried to the gangway, the crew following.

"What are you going to flog that man for, sir?" asked John the Swede.

Thompson quickly ordered the questioner put in irons. Sam was tied to the mast's rigging, wrists made fast against the ropes, "jacket off and back exposed." The captain stood a few feet from him "and a little raised, so as to have a good swing at him."

Dana could not believe what he was seeing: "A man—a human being, made in God's likeness—fastened up and flogged like a beast!" Dana's first impulse was to resist, but the captain and officers had seized the crew's two strongest men. Thompson flogged Sam until the sailor could stand no more. The captain ordered him cut down, and John the Swede brought forward.

The captain stood on the quarter deck "his eyes flashing with rage, and his face as red as blood." When John the Swede was made fast, he turned to Thompson and asked why he was being flogged. "I flog you . . . for asking questions." The master delivered blow after blow: "As he went on, his passion increased, calling out as he swung the rope—'If you want to know what I flog you for, I'll tell you. It's because I like to do it—because I like to do it!—It suits me! That's what I do it for!'"

The sadistic flogging escalated until John the Swede, writhing in pain, called out, "Oh Jesus Christ! Oh Jesus Christ!" The captain shouted. "Don't call on Jesus Christ, *he can't help you. Call on Captain Thompson.* He's the man! He can help you! Jesus Christ can't help you now!" The bloodied sailor was at last cut down. The crew remained on deck where the captain "swelling with rage and . . . importance" cried, "You've been mistaken in me—you didn't know what I was! Now you know what I am! . . . You've got a driver over you! Yes, *a slave-driver—a negro-driver!* I'll see who'll tell me he isn't a negro slave!"[34]

Dana, sickened, leaned over the ship's rail. John the Swede came aft, "his bare back covered with stripes and wales in every direction, and dreadfully swollen." The captain heard the sailor ask the steward for salve. "No," said the captain, "tell him to put his shirt on . . . and pull me ashore in the boat. Nobody is going to lay-up on board this vessel."[35]

Dana now pondered his own fate, "living under the tyranny . . . the length of the voyage, and . . . the uncertainty attending our return to America." But he thought most of how little prospect there was of "obtaining justice and satisfaction for these poor men." Thousands of miles from home, at the mercy of a master and an uncertain fate, twenty-year-old Dana made a promise that was to alter his life: "I vowed that if God should ever give me the means, I would do something to redress the grievance and relieve the suffering of that poor class of beings, of whom I then was one."[36]

No seaman aboard the *Pilgrim* believed a return to Boston was probable. "The flogging was seldom if ever alluded to by us, in the forecastle." Dana thought the sailors' "delicacy and . . . sense of honor . . . worthy of admiration in the highest walks of life." The crew had its own method of retaliation. The captain could not "notice officially" the slowdown, but Dana believed Thompson "must have seen the change."[37]

Returning to Santa Barbara Bay, the *Pilgrim* nearly ran afoul of three vessels. Thompson's seamanship was as bad as his temper—and the crew was in no mood to respond to his urgency when the vessel began to drift toward two small brigs, the *Loriotte* and the *Lagoda.* When Thompson's maneuvers threatened a third ship, the *Ayacucho,* its captain came aboard the *Pilgrim* to assist the flustered Thompson. The even-tempered Captain Wilson soon put matters right. Thompson resumed his command but the last laugh belonged to the *Pilgrim*'s crew.

Dana and another sailor rowed their captain to the *Lagoda,* where the mate announced "Captain Thompson has come aboard, sir!" The *Lagoda*'s master responded in a voice heard fore and aft: "Has he brought his brig with him?" The response became "a standing joke among us for the rest of the voyage." It put the *Pilgrim*'s forecastle in the mood for off-color stories "one must always hear" but, said Dana, "are perhaps, after all no worse, nor, indeed, more gross, than that of many well-dressed gentlemen at their clubs."[38]

The crew's morale increased when lots were drawn for a day ashore in San Diego. The "larboard watch"—of which Dana and Ben Stinson were a part—won. Dana thought he now understood for the first time the meaning of "liberty." The two friends planned to get horses and explore the countryside, but Dana was savvy enough to realize that "you must be a shipmate on shore, or [seamen] will not be . . . shipmate[s] to you on board."[39]

A one-eyed Yankee whaleman from Fall River had a one-room mud "pulperia." Sailors from the *Pilgrim* and other vessels crowded the grog shop. Dana and Stinson "followed in our shipmates' wake, knowing that to refuse to drink with them would be the highest affront." They hoped to buy the first round and leave, but "old sailors did not choose to be preceded by a couple of youngsters." There was nothing to do but drink round after round until their turn, though they ran the risk of being late for the horses and "of getting *corned.*"[40]

Sailors' etiquette satisfied at last, Dana and Stinson secured horses, though their shipmates thought that "a sailor has no more business with a horse than a fish has with a balloon."[41] Nothing was more plentiful in California than horses. A traveler to San Joaquin Valley a decade later wrote, "I think I may say without exaggeration that I have seen in the course of two days travel, forty thousand wild horses."[42] Dana and Stinson paid only for the use of saddles, "they care but little what becomes of the horse."[43]

Dana quickly realized that "California horses have no medium gait . . . between walking and running." That posed no problem for Californians—"there are probably no better riders in the world"—but the two sailors adjusted well enough. "The fine air of the afternoon; the rapid rate of the animals, who seemed almost to fly over the ground; and the excitement and novelty of the motion to us, who had been so long confided on shipboard, were exhilarating beyond expression."[44]

They rode to the mission where an inquiry brought forth "baked meats, frijoles stewed with peppers and onions, boiled eggs, and California flour baked into a kind of macaroni." With wine, the repast "made the most sumptuous meal we had eaten since we left Boston." A visit to a house brought forth those curious to see "los Ingles marineros." A young woman admired Dana's silk handkerchief—"of course, I gave it to her, which brought us into high favor."[45]

But midnight and the end of liberty were fast approaching. Dana and Stimson rode "at full speed, and were on the beach in fifteen minutes." Stragglers soon followed in assorted states of inebriation, including some who "were rather indifferent horsemen." A quarrel between two shipmates as to which one had caused a fall from horseback awoke the crew, but the next sound Dana heard was "All hands ahoy!" It was daylight and "our liberty had now truly taken flight."[46]

It had been seven months since Dana procured a berth on the *Pilgrim* "because California was represented to be a very healthy coast, with a fine climate, and plenty of hard work for the sailors."[47] But neither Dana nor the crew had bargained for the work of "hide-droughers"—the dressing, brining, and hauling of thousands upon thousands of cattle hides. "What the oxen would not do, we were obliged to do."[48]

The harbor of Santa Barbara was chosen as a depot for the hide ships because there was no surf and vessels could anchor near the beach. Hide houses built to hold 40,000 hides were to be filled before the hides were carried to ship. The *Pilgrim*'s crew had gathered only 3,500 hides, and "there was not a man on board who did not go a dozen times into the house, and look around, and make some calculation of the time it would require." George Foster, the former second mate whom Captain Thompson had broken in rank, deserted. The master was enraged, but though the crew thought Foster "shiftless and good for nothing," they "rejoiced" to hear of his escape.[49]

The consequences of the flogging were still being felt, especially by the two victims. Dana's observation of the different effect on each man provided an insight that was to later inform his understanding of slavery. John the Swede talked of revenge. But Sam "was an American . . . and this thing coming upon him, seemed completely to break him down. He had a feeling of the degradation that had been inflicted upon him."[50]

For the next three months the *Pilgrim* coasted California, where whales were "so common that we took little notice of them." The "hide-agent" needed to go ashore at San Juan Capistrano. The brig anchored "in twenty fathoms' water, almost out at sea . . . and directly abreast of a steep hill, which overhung the water and was twice as high as our royal-mast head." Dana had been told by the crew of the *Lagoda* that "it was the worst place in California."[51]

Dana was part of the crew that rowed the agent to shore. They were told to wait but Dana wandered off. He found "grandeur in everything around . . . no sound heard but the pulsations of the great Pacific! and the great steep hill rising like a wall, and cutting us off from all the world but the 'world of waters!'" Alone for the first time since he left home, Dana found "my better nature returned strong upon me." He was delighted that what "poetry and romance I ever had in me had not been entirely deadened." His reverie was broken by shouts from his shipmates preparing to row the agent back to the ship. Dana thought he was leaving "the only romantic spot in California."[52] His name remains at "Dana Point."

In early May 1835, the *Pilgrim* returned to San Diego. All the hide houses were shut except the one to be filled by the crew. A dozen Sandwich Islanders were living on the beach in "complete idleness—drinking, playing cards, and carousing in every way." Captain Thompson was anxious to recruit some of the men to bolster his crew. He had no luck until their money ran out, but just before the *Pilgrim* was to resume cruising the coast to gather hides, four islanders agreed to come aboard. To make room, Thompson summoned Dana and the ship's boy and told them they were to join the gang at the hide house. "In the twinkling of an eye," Dana found himself "transformed from sailor to 'beach-comber.'"[53]

3

ALERT

The change was welcomed by Dana for "the novelty and . . . comparative independence." Dana, the ship's boy, and "a giant of a Frenchman named Nicholas" were quartered in the hide house. An officer from the *Pilgrim* much despised by the crew, Mr. Russell, was left in charge of them and the Sandwich Islanders to "cure the hides." The brining, beating, stretching, and scraping of the hides was disagreeable work that could be done only in the mornings because the hides became too dry in the afternoon sun. Once the morning's work was complete, the men's time was their own with "nobody to *haze* us and find fault."[1]

Characteristically, Dana used his four months as a hide curer to learn all he could about the Sandwich Islanders with whom he worked.

They called themselves "Kanakas" but "by whatever names they might be called, they were the most interesting, intelligent, and kind-hearted people that I ever fell in with." Dana was struck by the Kanaka belief that "whatever one has, they all have." He delighted in the refusal of a Kanaka to keep money from a Yankee trader for himself. Dana asserted, "I would have gone to them all, in turn, [for a favor] . . . and seen it done, before my own countryman had got half through counting the cost."

Dana became particular friends with a Kanaka called "Hope," whom he never saw angry though he was often "imposed upon by white people." Hope and the other Kanakas "were all astonishingly quick . . . things which I had thought it utterly impossible to make them understand they often seized in an instant." No caste nor society—Brahmin or otherwise— ever meant as much to Dana: "I would have trusted my life and my fortune in the hands in any one of these people." Dana never lost his attachment to the Kanakas, "a feeling . . . which would lead me to go a great way for the mere pleasure of seeing them."[2]

The monotony of hide curing was occasionally broken by the need to gather wood, though this proved rather too exciting when Dana encountered a rattlesnake, "very abundant here." Dana kept cutting wood—"I knew that so long as I could hear the rattle, I was safe, for these snakes never make a noise when they are in motion." After an ominous silence, "the big Frenchman . . . was as little inclined to approach the snake as I had been." The dogs, too, seemed afraid, "barking at a safe distance." The Kanakas, however, "showed no fear" and soon disposed of the snake.[3]

A more welcome interruption came a few weeks later. Dana had paid no special attention to the cry of "Sail ho!" as it "did not always signify a vessel but was raised whenever a woman was seen coming down from the town." This time it signified the arrival of guests far more infrequent—two ships: the Italian *Rosa* and *Catalina* from Valparaiso. Soon both crews were ashore. Dana recounted the remarkable amalgamation of sailors: "We had now, out of forty or fifty, representatives from every nation under the sun: two Englishmen, three Yankees, two Scotchmen, two Welshmen, one Irishman, three Frenchmen, one Dutchman, one Austrian, two or three Spaniards (from old Spain) half a dozen Spanish-Americans and half-breeds, two native Indians from Chili . . . one Negro, one Mulatto, about twenty Italians, as many more Sandwich Islanders." At the *Rosa*'s hide house, the nationalities vied with each other in song ("We three Yankees made an attempt at the Star-spangled Banner") but it was the Italian crew's "operas and sentimental songs . . . which produced a fine effect."[4]

The cry "Sail ho!" was heard most often to signal that a woman had come to the beach. Dana's shipmate Ben Stimson later chided him for neglecting to mention *"the beautiful Indian lasses,* who so often frequented your humble abode in the *hide house.*"[5] Dana did recount the common practice of Indian men—a man would "bring his wife . . . down to the beach, and carry her back again, dividing with her the money which she had got from the sailors." Dana thought California women had a "good deal of beauty" though "their morality, of course, is none the best." This, however, afforded no real opportunity for an enterprising sailor, because "the jealousy of their husbands is extreme . . . [t]he difficulties of the attempt are numerous, and the consequences of discovery fatal."[6]

Though Dana was never one to exclude attractive women from his mind, his thoughts were centered on the whereabouts of the *Alert.* It was this ship that was to take hides gathered by the *Pilgrim* back to Boston. Dana "was anxious for her arrival, for I had been told by letter that the owners in Boston . . . had written to Captain Thompson to take me on board the *Alert* in case she returned to the United States before the *Pilgrim.*" On August 25, 1835, "Sail ho!" meant "ship," not "woman," and Dana was delighted to see "a fine, tall ship, with royal and skysails set, bending over before the strong afternoon breeze, and coming rapidly round the point." She was the *Alert.*[7]

The ship had been under the command of Captain E. H. Faucon, but now that it was on the coast, Faucon took charge of the *Pilgrim,* and Frank Thompson became master of the *Alert.* Dana did not relish returning to sea under Thompson's command, but though the *Alert* was to spend several months gathering hides of its own, the *Pilgrim*'s crew faced two years of hide work. Thompson agreed to take Dana aboard the *Alert* while it was on the California coast, as long as Dana could find a crew member to exchange places. That was easily arranged, for sailors were glad to spend a few months on shore.

Dana went aboard the *Alert* in early September. The three-masted ship was more than twice the tonnage of the *Pilgrim.* Its forecastle "was large, tolerably well-lighted by bulls-eyes . . . and far better than the little, black dirty hole in which I lived so many months on board the *Pilgrim.*" Dana was delighted with the change: "Give me a big ship. There is more room, more hands . . . more life, more company." The *Alert*'s chief mate was so proficient that Captain Thompson was seldom on deck. But Dana's former shipmates "seemed to think I had got a little windward of them; especially in the matter of going home first."[8]

His new shipmates included "the most remarkable man I have ever seen." Forty-year-old sailor Tom Harris astonished Dana with "the power of his mind." Dana knew no Harvard man who exhibited such remarkable reasoning powers. On one evening's watch Dana found himself at a disadvantage in an argument over the "Corn Laws," a subject about which Dana was certain Harris had less knowledge, "if, indeed, he had any at all." But Harris had picked up a pamphlet on the topic at a boarding house years before and made arguments to which Dana "was entirely unable to reply." Years at sea had provided Harris with other knowledge, too. "Twenty years of vice! Every sin that a sailor knows, he had gone to the bottom of." Dana asserted: "Taking together all that I learned from him . . . I would not part with the hours I spent in the watch with that man for any given hours of my life past in study and social intercourse."[9]

The *Alert*'s hide gathering sent the ship north from San Diego in October. Anchoring off the point at San Juan Capistrano, the captain sent Dana—the only member of the crew who had been there before—ashore to pitch hides off the cliff. Some of the hides became lodged on the side of the cliff, and "as hides are worth in Boston twelve and a half cents a pound and the captain's commission was two percent," Dana found himself dangling precipitously secured only by a rope fastened to a stake. He managed to free the hides and was lowered to the rocky shore below. If he had hoped to impress his new shipmates, he failed: "I got down in safety, pretty well-covered with dirt; and for my pains was told, 'What a d—d fool you were to risk your life for a half a dozen hides!'"[10]

Becalmed halfway between Santa Barbara and Point Conception— "the Cape Horn of California"—a wind "seemed to come from nowhere. No person could have told . . . that it was not a still summer's night." Instead of stiff oil-cloth suits, southwester caps, and thick boots needed for the snow and sleet of Cape Horn, the crew wore duck trousers and light shoes. "It was sport to have a gale in such weather as this." In early December, after twenty days sailing, "we arrived at the mouth of the bay in San Francisco."[11]

The only other vessel in the "magnificent bay" was a Russian brig. Dana's enthusiasm for his new surroundings soon dampened as "the rainy season set in, and, for three weeks it rained almost every hour, without cessation." The crew gathered wood on Angel Island, where there was "a white frost on the ground, a thing we had never seen before in California." Rowing from the island in the middle of the bay, "we found a strong tide setting out to seaward [and] a thick fog which prevented our seeing the ship." Only "the utmost exertions . . . saved ourselves from being carried out to sea."[12]

By December's end the *Alert* prepared to sail. The commandant of the presidio at San Francisco, "Don Guadeloupe Villego [Vallejo], a young man and the most popular among the Americans and English of any man in California," came aboard. On a fine day, "the first of entire sunshine . . . for more than a month," the *Alert* sailed under the high cliff on which the presidio was built. From the middle of the great bay, Dana surveyed the scene: "small bays, making up into the interior on every side; large and beautifully-wooded islands; and the mouths of several small rivers." He saw even more than that, for he added: "If California ever becomes a prosperous country, this bay will be the center of its prosperity."[13]

The *Alert* stopped briefly in Monterey, where a passenger on the Russian brig offered to take letters and deliver them to Vera Cruz when they could be forwarded to the United States. Those who could dashed off letters dating them January 1, 1836. Dana wrote to his father, describing California and its people—and included a self-appraisal: "As for myself, I have grown somewhat in stature and I am confident that I have gained a great deal in robustness. . . . My eyes are certainly much better than they were. . . . At all events, if I should be compelled to follow the sea, I shall have gained some hardihood and experience; and if not . . . the knowledge that I shall have acquired, of all kinds, is not to be despised, and may be of great use to me and others."[14] The letter reached Boston in mid-March 1836, "the shortest communication ever yet made across the country."[15]

The *Alert*'s voyage from Monterey to Santa Barbara was unusually brisk because Alfred Robinson, the hide agent, was engaged in an endeavor more lucrative than hide gathering. He was to be married to Doña Annetta De Guerra de Noriega Carrillo, youngest daughter of Don Antonio Noriega, "head of the first family in California." Robinson was no favorite of the crew, but the festivities promised to put all ashore. Aboard the *Alert* the crew awaited the captain's private signal, and when the bride stepped from the great doors of the mission church, the ship fired its guns in salute "and instantly . . . was dressed in flags and pennants from stern to stern."[16]

After supper the crew went ashore and joined "nearly all the people of the town" in a huge tent erected in the courtyard of the house of the bride's father. Dana was particularly interested in seeing the bride's sister—the beautiful Doña Augustia—who had sometimes been aboard the *Alert*. His initial disappointment at her slow movement in the "California fandango" was soon replaced by the fascination of watching her waltz with Don Juan Bandini, who "moved about with the grace and daintiness of a young fawn."

The "great amusement of the evening" was the women's breaking eggs over the heads of unsuspecting men. Dana was standing next to "a tall stately Don, with immense grey whiskers, and a look of great importance." Dana felt a light touch on his shoulder and looking back saw Doña Augustia "with her finger upon her lip, motioning me gently aside." With one motion, she knocked off the Don's sombrero, broke the egg upon his head "and springing behind me, was out of sight in a moment." The guests roared with laughter so "old Don Domingo had to join in the laugh."

The festivities continued for three days, the *Alert*'s crew returning each evening. "We found ourselves . . . great objects of attention." They resisted calls to do a "sailor's dance" because after seeing the Spanish Californians dance "we thought it best to leave it to their imaginations." When newly married agent Robinson took the floor, "with a tight, black swallow-tailed coat, just imported from Boston, a high stiff cravat, looking as if he had been pinned and skewered . . . we thought they had had enough of Yankee grace."[17]

They remained in Santa Barbara three weeks before sailing south to San Pedro. It was the port for Pueblo de los Angeles, thirty miles inland. The "desolate-looking place" was "the best place on the whole coast for hides" as it was "filled with herds of cattle."[18] The *Pilgrim*, not seen in five months, had gathered 3,000 hides. Dana reported that his old shipmates were glad to see him, but they could not have been pleased when their hides were put aboard the *Alert*. Nor could his former shipmates have felt warmer toward Dana when they learned the *Pilgrim* was to sail north to San Francisco to obtain more hides while the *Alert* sailed south to San Diego.

In San Diego, Dana did the math. Over 30,000 hides had already been secured; with what the *Alert* could procure in a short voyage back to Santa Barbara "and the *Pilgrim* would bring down from San Francisco, we would make out our cargo." Dana's high spirits were tempered by a visit to the Sandwich Islanders. "The curse of a people calling themselves Christian seems to follow them everywhere." The friend whom Dana "preferred . . . to any of my own countrymen" was dying of venereal disease.[19]

"Hope, was the most dreadful object I had even seen in my life: his eyes sunken and dead, his cheeks fallen in against his teeth; his hands looking like claws; a dreadful cough, which seemed to rack his whole shattered system." He lay on a mat unable to move. When Hope saw Dana, he whispered "Aloha Aikane!" Dana promised Hope to do what he could, telling the Kanaka that he would bring help from the ship.

Dana told Captain Thompson of Hope's condition, requesting that he go and see him.

"What? A d—d Kanaka?"

"Yes sir," said I, "but he has worked four years for our vessels."

"Oh! He be d—d!" the captain said and walked off.[20]

Dana was able to procure medicine from the chief mate. With no time to do more than instruct Hope to take the medicine regularly and in strong doses, Dana left his friend.

In late February word came that the ship *California* had arrived in Santa Barbara. "Our hearts were all up in our mouths" because the Boston-based vessel was sure to be carrying letters and newspapers. When the mail was distributed, each man took his letters below and returned immediately, for "not a letter was [to be] read until we had cleaned up the decks for the night." When Dana was at last able to read his mail, he was relieved that all appeared well at home. Yet the letters were dated August 1835 and "it was already six months [later], and what another year would bring to pass, who could tell?"[21]

A Boston newspaper of the same date carried a full account of Harvard commencement exercises, class of 1835, Dana's own class. "I could see them receiving their A.B.s from the dignified feudal looking President . . . and walking off the stage with their diplomas in their hands; while upon, the very same day, their classmate was walking up and down California beach with a hide upon his head."[22]

The last of Dana's California "head-work" was now in sight. Forty thousand hides, dried and cured, were in the San Diego hide house. The transfer of the hides to the *Alert* would take six weeks of work from "the grey of the morning til starlight." But the crew was in the best of spirits, for a filled ship meant "homeward bound." The principal food was fresh beef ("fried beefsteaks, three times a day") "and every man had perfect health." The sailors' songs "seemed almost to raise the decks of the ship." When hides got heavy, "a lively song like 'Heave, to the girls!' or 'Nancy oh!' . . . put life and strength into every arm."[23]

With the *Alert* filled "within four feet of her beams," the ship awaited the *Pilgrim* for a final stowage of hides. "It was a sad sight for her crew to see us getting ready to go . . . while they, who had been longer on the coast . . . were condemned to another year's hard service." Dana went aboard the *Pilgrim* and "found them making the best of the matter." Ben Stimson had even persuaded the *Alert*'s Tom Harris to trade places for thirty dollars, some clothes, and the chance to be an officer on the *Pilgrim* under their new captain. The *Pilgrim*'s crew said Captain Faucon was "a good seaman . . . a thing [sailors] are not always ready to say." Faucon assured Dana that he would visit Hope and get him what medicine he could.[24]

The *Alert*'s cargo was all aboard and the *Pilgrim* was set to renew its dreary coastal duty. Wrote Dana, "I was just thinking of her hard lot, and congratulating myself upon my escape from her when I received a summons into the cabin." Captain Thompson, Captain Faucon, and the agent Robinson were there. Thompson turned abruptly to Dana:

> "Dana, do you want to go home in the ship?"
> "Certainly sir," said I. "I expect to go home in the ship."
> "Then," said he, "you must get someone to go in your place on board the *Pilgrim*."[25]

Dana could not believe what he was hearing. He knew that Thompson was under orders to bring Dana home on the *Alert*, but he knew as well "that it would be hopeless to prevail upon any of the ship's crew to take twelve months more upon California in the [*Pilgrim*]." Dana decided "to put on a bold front." He told Thompson that he had a copy of the owners' letter telling the captain to bring him home. Thompson "turned fiercely upon me, and tried to look me down." Unable to intimidate the young sailor, the master "changed his ground and pointed to the shipping papers of the *Pilgrim,* from which my name had never been erased." Here was real trouble, because the captain had "absolute discretionary power" over a seaman listed on a ship's manifest. Thompson told Dana "he would not hear another word."[26]

Dana, facing "a fate which would alter the whole current of my future life," continued to insist on his right to sail on the *Alert.* Thompson then "changed his tone entirely." Dana recognized that it was only because "I had friends and interest at home to make them suffer for any injustice they might do me." Thompson asked Dana if he was willing to pay someone to exchange places—as Ben Stimson had done. Dana willingly agreed and "went forward with a light heart."[27]

But Tom Harris, who exchanged places with Stimson, had voluntarily agreed to go to the *Pilgrim.* The sailor with whom Dana was to change places, "English Ben," was given no choice. When the *Alert*'s crew learned that their popular shipmate was being made to take Dana's place, they challenged Dana: "The captain has let you [on] because you are a gentleman's son . . . and know the owners; and taken Ben [off] because he is poor, and has got nobody to say a word for him!" Dana knew "this was too true to be answered."[28]

Dana's dilemma was now greater because he knew that to embark with a crew who thought he was not "one of them" would be nearly as miserable as hauling hides. Dana began a search to find a true "volunteer" among the *Alert*'s crew. He posted a notice that he would pay "six months' wages . . . clothes, books, and other matters." The crew wished to keep English Ben, "a good sailor," on board and prevailed upon "a harum-scarum lad we called Harry Bluff." Dana finalized the exchange quickly "lest his purpose cool," and the next morning Harry Bluff went aboard the *Pilgrim* "apparently in good spirits." Dana had a "regret at taking the last look at the old craft in which I had spent . . . the first year, of my sailor's life." But "the feeling I had for my old shipmates condemned to another term of California" soon passed with the thought that in one week the *Alert* would be Boston bound.[29]

On May 8, 1836, to the tune of "Time for Us to Go," the *Alert*'s crew weighed anchor and the ship was homeward bound. She was so fully laden with hides that Dana thought she was waterlogged. But the older sailors said the *Alert* would work herself loose "and then she'll walk up to Cape Horn like a race-horse." A greater concern was the prospect of being off Cape Horn in July, the very dead of winter. The crew was undermanned, no larger than the fifteen who had sailed the smaller *Pilgrim* round Cape Horn in "summer weather." But "never mind—we're homeward bound" was "the answer to everything."[30]

There would be warm weather until the Pacific Ocean showed "its other face." The crew took advantage of the time to make suits of oil cloth, grease and tar boots, mend mittens, and line southwesters. The *Alert* crossed the equator on May 28, and there was "glorious sailing" into June. "The next time we see the North Star," said a shipmate to Dana, "we shall be standing to the northward, the other side of the Horn." On June 27 the morning was warm enough for the crew "to work in our common clothes."[31]

In the afternoon Dana was asleep below, having finished his watch. "All hands, ahoy!" roused him from his berth. He was still in thin clothes but there was a "bank of mist" coming directly at the ship. "I had seen the same before, in my passage round in the *Pilgrim,* and knew what it meant." Within minutes, rain, sleet, snow, and wind made "the toughest turn his back to windward." The decks were standing at an angle of nearly forty-five degrees "and the ship was going like a mad steed through the water." The sleet- and snow-covered decks meant "Cape Horn had set in with good earnest."[32]

Dana hoped to get below and put on his oilskin jacket and southwester, but a break came only after hours on deck "wet through . . . every moment growing colder . . . hands stiffened and numbed." To make matters worse, "I had been troubled for several days with a slight tooth-ache." It soon swelled "so that my face was nearly as large as two." Dana was unable to chew the salt beef, so the steward asked Captain Thompson if rice could be boiled for Dana. "No! D___ you! Tell him to eat . . . like the rest of them." But the first mate smuggled a pan of rice from the galley and Dana made the best of it, though the pain allowed no sleep.[33]

On the Fourth of July, while Boston "dandies in their white pantaloons and silk stockings" were eating ice cream, the *Alert* was surrounded by ice. Forty-eight hours before, the crew had been called on deck at the sight of an immense iceberg. Dana estimated its size between two and three miles in circumference and several hundred feet in height. "But no description can give any idea of the strangeness, splendor, and really the sublimity, of the sight." The "field-ice" the *Alert* found itself in on the Fourth was more dangerous. Chunks of ice large enough to puncture the ship spread for miles. A constant lookout was necessary, "for any of the pieces, coming with the heave of the sea . . . would have been the end for us."[34]

The sleet and snow were constant. "Our ship was now all cased with ice—hall, spars, and . . . rigging . . . the sails nearly as stiff as sheet iron." The crew was on deck continuously: wet, cold, and worse—without grog. The *Alert* was "a temperance ship" (though the *Pilgrim* had not been). That made little difference to the captain, who could have brandy in his cabin. "Sailors will never be convinced that rum is a dangerous thing, by taking it away from them, and giving it to the officers," observed Dana. Moreover, he believed ship owners who piously embraced the "temperance movement" did so only to save the expense of the grog.[35]

Dana's abscess had not diminished, and when the mate saw Dana's swollen face, he ordered him below. For three days Dana—"as weak as an infant"—lay in the forecastle "cooped up alone in a black hole, in equal danger, but without the power to do."[36] Above, his shipmates began to murmur that the captain was not equal to the dangers before them.

After days adrift the weather began to clear and the crew looked for orders to "make sail." It did not come, and the ship's carpenter, an experienced seaman respected by his shipmates, urged the crew to take the ship from Thompson and give command to the mate. The proposition was "open mutiny." Dana and others argued against it. Then came word that the captain wanted all hands on the quarterdeck—he knew of the crew's murmurings.

Dana anticipated "violent measures, or, at least, an out-break of quarter-deck bravado" from Captain Thompson, but "a sense of common danger and common suffering seemed to have tamed his spirit." In a manner "almost kind," he said the crew had always been "good men," explained why he delayed making sail, and promised the matter would be forgotten if men did their duty. The captain's language "had a very good effect upon the crew, and they returned quietly to their duty."[37]

The *Alert*'s first attempt to "double the Cape" had begun when the ship was nearly 1,700 miles to the west of the Horn. Now the captain determined to run for the Straits of Magellan. No one on board had been through the straits, but Dana had a book that recounted a previous passage. This was shared with crew, and as the account was favorable, it raised spirits. Moreover, because the ship was now only 400 to 500 miles west of Cape Horn, they expected to be clear of ice.

But once again the cry "All hands!" brought the crew to deck; the *Alert* narrowly avoided "a large ice island, peering out of the mist, and reaching high above our tops." The ship finally ran clear of the ice fields. With a good wind, the vessel passed the latitude of Cape Horn, having sailed "southward to give it a wide berth." The *Alert* now sailed east "with a good prospect of being round, and steering to the northward on the other side in a few days." But "ill luck" struck again.[38]

The fiercest storm yet encountered roiled the ship for days. It was as if, said Dana, the Cape "roused at finding we had nearly slipped through ... said ... 'No, you don't!'—No, you don't!" The fear that the ship would drift back into ice eliminated bright talk about the future. "From saying—'*when* we get home'—we began ... to [say] '*if* we get home'—and at last the subject was dropped by tacit consent."[39]

After days of easterly gales, the wind began to shift. It seemed like progress and there was "hope of soon being up with the Cape." But the weather had not cleared enough for observation, "and we had drifted too much to allow our dead reckoning being anywhere near the mark." But on July 22 there was a beam of sunshine, followed by the cry "Land, ho!" It was Staten Island just east of Cape Horn. "It told us we had passed the Cape—were in the Atlantic ... the captain now knew where we were, as well as if we were off the end of Long Wharf."[40]

Up from below came the ship's only passenger "who we almost forgotten was on board." He "came out like a butterfly, and was hopping about bright as a bird." It was Professor Nuttall, who months before had appeared on the San Diego beach to Dana's astonishment. "I should have not have been more surprised to have seen the Old South steeple shoot up from the hide house." Dana had last seen the professor "quietly seated in the chair of Botany and Ornithology of Harvard University." Nuttall had crossed the continent and come down the California coast examining birds and fauna. Finding the *Alert* about to sail to Boston, the professor asked to be taken as passenger.[41]

"In the general joy" of seeing Staten Island, the professor told the captain he should like to be put ashore to collect fauna and fossils. Thompson's response, that he would see Nuttall and his specimens in hell first, drew no protest from the crew. The *Alert* was on the Atlantic Ocean—where "the Boston girls have ... hold of the tow rope." The ice began to melt from the rigging and spars, and the *Alert* added sail after sail as the weather improved. By the end of July, the ship had sailed 2,000 miles in nine days—"allowing for changes of course." It was warm enough for the crew to scrub each other down and to dry clothes. "The whole ship looked like a back yard on washing day."[42]

The contrast in a sailor's life between the commonplace and sublime was never more striking than a night when the *Alert* reached the tropics. Dana observed that despite "all that has been said about the beauty of a ship under full sail, there are very few who have ever seen a ship, literally, under all her sail."[43]

One evening Dana was "out to the end of the flying-jib-boom, upon some duty." When he finished, he lay upon the boom, where "being so far out from the deck, I could look at the ship, as at a separate vessel . . . and, there, rose up from the water, supported only by the small black hull, a pyramid of canvas, spreading out far beyond the hull, and towering up almost . . . to the clouds. The sea was as still as an island lake; the light trade-wind was gently and steadily breathing from astern; the dark blue sky was studded with the tropical stars; there was no sound but the rippling of the water under the stern; and the sails were spread out, wide and high. . . . So quiet too, was the sea, and so steady the breeze, that if these sails had been sculptured marble, they could not have been more motionless. . . . I was so lost in the sight, that I forgot the presence of the man who came out with me, until he said, (for he, too, rough old man-of-war's man as he was, had been gazing at the show,) half to himself, still looking at the marble sails—'How quietly they do their work!'"[44]

The ship prompted a different emotion a few days later when Dana almost fell from a towering mast. At a height of ninety feet, "the tie parted, and down the yard fell. I was safe, by my hold upon the rigging, but it made my heart beat quick." A fall to the deck would have been fatal, but Dana was now a sailor and "an escape is always a joke on board ship." Sailors knew too well "that life hangs upon a thread, to wish to be always reminded of it."[45]

On August 19 the *Alert* crossed the equator. The North Star was visible: "Next to seeing land, there is no sight which makes one realize more that he is drawing near home, than to see the same heavens, under which he was born." Near Bermuda the crew's unvarying diet of salt beef caused an outbreak of scurvy. English Ben was the most stricken; his legs and gums swollen, and "his breath, too, became very offensive." The ship had neither medicine nor fresh provisions, but a brig bound to the West Indies from New York was hailed. To the inquiry "have you fresh provisions to spare?" came the jovial response that girls had strung onions just for them. The fresh onions did the trick.[46]

Dana was untouched by the scurvy. Indeed, once his toothache was gone, he noted that he "was never in better health." By September 15 the *Alert* was in the Gulf Stream. The irregular pitching of the vessel caused queasy stomachs among even the most experienced sailors. Two of Dana's shipmates sent to work on the masts became sick. Dana was ordered aloft, where he worked for two hours. "I was not positively sick, and came down with a look of indifference."[47]

On September 20, 1836, Dana awoke to "the low sand-hills of Cape Cod . . . and before us, the wide waters of Massachusetts Bay." The bay was filled with sails in every direction, "a stirring sight for us who had been . . . over two years without seeing more than three or four traders on an almost desolate coast." The *Alert* was now close enough to run up its signals, "and in half an hour, the owner . . . in his counting-room knew that his ship was [in]; and the landlords, runners, and sharks . . . learned that there was a rich prize for them in the bay: a ship from round the Horn, with a crew to be paid off with two years' wages." The ship needed only to be made pretty, and Dana "was sent up with a bucket of white paint and brush, and touched her [up]."[48]

Dana had one last turn at the helm, where he calculated he had spent between "nine hundred and a thousand hours . . . at the helms of our two vessels." There was little wind, and with the tide running against her the *Alert* was unable to reach the wharf by nightfall. The order was given to anchor, "and for the first time since leaving San Diego—one hundred and thirty five days—our anchor was upon the bottom."[49]

With the ship snug in Boston Harbor, the crew looked upon "the well-known scene . . . the dome of the State House fading in the western sky; the lights of the city starting into sight." With only one more night aboard ship before going ashore, Dana's shipmates, unable to sleep, stayed on deck. But "as for myself . . . I found that I was in a state of indifference, for which I could by no means account. A year before, while carrying hides on the coast, the assurance . . . we should see Boston, made me half wild; but now that I was actually there, and in sight of home, the emotions which I had so long anticipated feeling, I did not find."[50]

Even then, the twenty-one-year-old Dana knew himself well enough to recognize that the remedy was "some new excitement." The next morning all hands were called and Dana—"busily at work"—found that his "mind and body seemed to wake together." With "a fair wind and tide, a bright sunny morning, royal and sky-sails set, ensign, streamer, signals, and pennant, flying, and with our guns firing, we came swiftly and handsomely up to the city." With a rousing chorus "which waked up half the North End," the crew hauled the ship to the wharf.[51]

"The city bells were just ringing one when the last turn was made fast, and the crew dismissed, and in five minutes more, not a soul was left on the good ship *Alert*."[52] But Dana would again fill her sails with wind, her decks with life, and his voyage with lessons he would never forget.

4

THE VOW

When Dana stepped upon Boston soil for the first time in two years, he was shocked. The pallid faces of his relatives, the emaciated frames of his friends, and the women who "looked like mere shades" convinced him that he had arrived in the city during an epidemic.[1] Dana realized it was merely the contrast between the visages of Boston Brahmins and the sunburned, hardy faces of his shipmates.

There was a greater shock ahead. Cousin Frank, son of the uncle who had dissipated the Dana fortune, was entrusted with Dana's sea chest. In the confusion of disembarkation the cousin lost the trunk. It contained a lengthy journal Dana had kept of his two-year voyage. Neither the trunk nor the manuscript was ever found.

If Dana had any thought of immediately publishing an account of his years before the mast, it vanished with the sea chest. His remaining mementos were a few notes and letters, and the sailor's clothes he stored away when he put on gentlemen's attire. One did not return to Harvard looking like a common seaman.

No Harvard student directed to pursue his studies out of the limits of the Town of Cambridge ever did so to greater advantage than Dana. Nonetheless, Dana was required to pass an examination before readmission. He did and entered as a member of the senior class of 1837. Mature and flourishing in his freedom from the forecastle, Dana excelled in his studies, finishing first in his class. He was chosen by both Porcellian and Hasty Pudding, Harvard's most exclusive social clubs, "an honor at that time very unusual," he noted with pride.[2] The Brahmin was back.

But there was a difference between Dana and his Brahmin peers beyond his adventure at sea—he had to work for a living. His idle father and irresponsible brother spent as though they did not. They, and the extended Dana family, became a financial burden Dana never escaped. Only two professions were considered appropriate to the social standing of a Dana: divinity and the law. Religion was to be a significant aspect of Dana's life, but he felt unfit for the divinity. "I stood more in dread [of it] than the law," wrote Dana, though he did not reveal his reasons.[3] It was clear enough, however, that Dana could not reconcile his continuing attraction to a "sailor's life"—by which he meant more than the sea—and the moral obligations of a minister's life.

Dana believed the legal profession "hard, dry, uninteresting, uncertain, & slavish." His perception was shaped by his father, who despite (or because of) being the son of a chief justice, said he had practiced law "only long enough to keep the chain whole, for the legal profession had run in our family lines, unbroken, quite as long as any family in the country."[4] Richard Henry Dana Sr. had given up the legal profession at age twenty-five. In August 1837 his son entered Harvard Law School, "having always considered it a settled thing I must be a lawyer."[5] It was the legal profession by default—the chain unbroken.

Dana did have the distinction of becoming the first of his family to enter law school. Law "schools" were as new to the legal profession as Dana himself. The apprenticeship system, whereby entry to the legal profession could be gained only by clerking for an attorney, was centuries old (and was to last a century more) when, in 1815, Harvard University took the first tentative step toward a school of law. Isaac Parker, who had succeeded Dana's grandfather as chief justice of the Massachusetts Supreme Court, was appointed Royall Professor of Law. Memorably described as "a good-natured, lazy lawyer, and a good natured, lazy judge," Parker was an equally dedicated professor.[6] By 1828 Harvard had one student studying law.

Less than a decade later, an infusion of money—and, of far greater significance, the appointment to the two-professor faculty of one of the remarkable figures in the history of American law, revolutionized legal education in America. Joseph Story had been appointed to the U.S. Supreme Court by James Madison in 1811, at age thirty-two. There, Story had proved the intellectual equal of his colleague, Chief Justice John Marshall, with whom he shared a vision of nationalism. Law's "true glory," wrote Story, "is that it is flexible and constantly expanding with the exigencies of society."[7]

It was similar vision—from much the same impetus—that prompted Harvard to invest in a law school. A system of legal apprenticeship suitable to the localized economic structure of eighteenth-century colonial America could not supply the law and lawyers needed to meet the increasing demands of national and international markets. It was not mere luck that Harvard's concept of a national law school coincided with the advent of the railroad, steamboat, and corporation.

Nor was it coincidental that Harvard President Josiah Quincy used a fortunate collaboration between the wealthy Nathan Dane and Joseph Story to entice the celebrated justice to accept an endowed professorship at the revitalized law school. In recognition of its benefactor, the professorship, the school's first building, and initially the law school itself, were all named for Dane.

By the time of Dana's admission in 1837, there were students from fifteen of the country's twenty-six states. Story's reputation, as well as the growing recognition of the law school, attracted not just those acquainted with the justice (three of his Supreme Court colleagues sent their sons) but also the progeny of Boston's establishment—Otis, Bowditch, Appleton, Lowell, and Holmes among them.[8]

Story and colleague Professor Simon Greenleaf, familiar with the havoc caused among Harvard's undergraduates by President Quincy's detested "scale of merit," wisely avoided "the unwholesome stimulus of college marks." The absence of grades did not make the course of study any less rigorous. A description of Greenleaf as a professor "whose scrutiny was dreaded . . . by indolent students who had skimmed over the lesson" has an unsettling familiarity.[9]

Greenleaf was also a stimulating lecturer, and after eighteen months of law school Dana told his professor "I had not come across any dry places yet." Greenleaf replied, "No sir, and you never will," adding the caveat so long as one practiced law "upon the principles of Christianity and professional honor and conscientiously as . . . a member of the body politic."[10] Dana was to live this truth as a lawyer, for he was never as fulfilled as when he advocated for the rights of the oppressed against authoritarian power—and never as empty as when mired in "the time-wasting of ordinary lawsuits."

If Dana was indebted to Professor Greenleaf for a newfound interest in jurisprudence, he owed his enthusiasm for advocacy to Justice Story. The student affection for Story was nearly universal. He was, said Dana, like "an elder brother, the patriarch of a common family." Charles Sumner, who began his legal studies in 1831 and was to later to characterize his years at the law school as "the happiest of my life," wrote that students "love [Story] more than any instructor they ever had before." Dana was never fond of Harvard's college but its law school "I love, as far as a man can love a mere institution which has no soul."[11]

In later years Story apparently exhibited a weakness inherent in all retired justices, for one student thought Story "might omit, with great profit to his audience, many of the stories about himself and his brethren on the Supreme Court."[12] But Joseph Story was not yet sixty when Dana entered law school, and he was at the peak of his capacity, reputation, and authority.

Story's return from the Supreme Court's winter session in Washington was eagerly anticipated. Students filled the library to ask about lawyers and cases from their states. Justice Story enthralled his listeners with anecdotes of the great advocates Webster, Clay, and Choate "as one would have described to a company of squires and pages, a tournament of monarchs and nobles on fields of cloths of gold."[13]

Story did more than talk. He implemented a vigorous "moot court" where law students were required to argue cases before him. Students compelled to practice advocacy before a professor who was still on the U.S. Supreme Court expected "a fearful amount of stiffness, starch, and dignity," but were greeted by "a sunny smiling face which bespoke a heart full of kindness." With his ringing declaration, "Gentlemen, this is the High Court of Errors and Appeals from All Other Courts in the World" signaling its beginning, a Story "moot" became an event to celebrate.[14]

Dana made his first moot court argument before Justice Story in 1838. Dana kept extensive notes of the cases he and his classmates argued. It was a practice that was to serve him well as an appellate lawyer. He was particularly proud when after one moot court, Story asked Dana to write out his argument so the justice could show it to his colleagues on the Supreme Court "as a specimen of what could be done upon a two years education at a law school."[15]

It was scarcely possible to imagine a better situation than Dana's for a student entering his final year at Harvard Law School. True, the Danas were no longer wealthy, but to be the eldest son of the fifth generation of one of America's most distinguished families, related by marriage to the estimable old names of New England, Ellery and Trowbridge, and grandson of a chief justice of the Massachusetts Supreme Court counted for more than money. Of even greater value was Dana's immense talent and singular energy. Add the high opinion of a distinguished Supreme Court justice who was also one's professor, and there was not a visible obstacle in a privileged path to every reward that could be bestowed upon Dana by the legal profession and the establishment it represented. It was at this moment Dana decided to keep the vow he made before the mast— even if meant challenging Justice Joseph Story.

In May 1839, Boston newspapers were filled with coverage of a prosecution of a captain and first mate for maltreatment of a seaman. The ship *Caravan* had departed Liverpool for Boston in March. Captain Nichols and First Mate Couch were charged with the cruel and unusual punishment of crew member Henry Burr. Angered because Burr had misrepresented himself as a cook, Nichols and Couch subjected the hapless sailor to continuous beatings.

At trial, members of the *Caravan*'s crew testified that the captain and first mate fashioned a "pricker," described as a bamboo stick to which was attached a sail-needle that "stuck-out about three-fourths of an inch." The first mate was heard to say, "This will put life into Burr." On April 2 the beatings of Burr were particularly severe. A fellow seaman testified, "After the mate beat Burr very bad until he fell . . . and then stomped on him...I heard mournful cries...and saw the captain beating Burr with a rope...I thought he was dead."[16]

Burr was carried below, bloody and senseless. The next day, unable to move, he complained of great pain in his chest. On April 4, as Burr was struggling to get his trousers on, the first mate told him the captain wanted to see him on deck. A crew member testified that Burr neither resisted nor said a word when he was pricked and beaten. The *Caravan's* log for April 5 recorded the burial at sea of a crew member "who died very sudden during the night."

A sailor who examined Burr's body before it was thrown overboard testified that it had over one hundred needle holes. When the captain's dog was seen "with its head all swelled up from use of the pricker," the second mate said that Burr "died of the same disease as the dog had." The jury returned guilty verdicts in less than thirty minutes.

The case was tried before Joseph Story sitting as a trial judge in federal court. Story's charge to the jury indicated he found the story of the "pricker" incredible: "It would be inhuman to use it even upon a dog as it has been said," Story conceded, but he prefaced his remark with the observation "What master of a vessel ever heard of such a weapon of punishment?"

At sentencing, defense witnesses testified to the captain's and first mate's good conduct while on shore. Story noted the relative youth of the defendants (Nichols was twenty-five, Couch was twenty-two) and his awareness "of the trials and dangers which they must pass through." Judge Story sentenced Nichols to a $100 fine and ninety days in jail; Couch to a $10 fine and thirty days in jail. Story gave the defendants the option of serving their sentences in Newburyport, where they lived.

The *Boston Morning Post* reported, "The lightness of these sentences excited universal astonishment in the courtroom which was crowded and there was some hissing behind the Bar....It was whispered that [others]...had frequently been sent to State Prison for life for much inferior offenses than had been proved against the prisoners."[17]

Here was the first great test of the vow Dana had made to himself when he watched, horrified and helpless, the brutal flogging of his shipmates. Dana decided to submit an essay to the *American Jurist,* the most prominent legal periodical in the country, castigating Story for his leniency. A student's decision to write an article critical of a justice of the U.S.

Supreme Court who was his law professor was extraordinary enough. But Story was also the presiding judge in the federal courts where Dana hoped to practice law.

To risk the ill will of the judge before whom he would appear seemed to Dana "little short of suicide."[18] Charles Sumner and George Hillard, editors of the *American Jurist* who practiced law before Story, certainly thought so. Hillard refused to publish Dana's essay unless Dana made it clear to Story that the editors bore no responsibility for its content.

In September 1839, Dana wrote to Justice Story: "While at sea it was my lot to witness many instances of cruelty and oppression. . . . One in particular, which I saw, was of so shocking a character . . . that, being unable to interfere at the time, I made a vow that if God should put it in my power in the course of my future life to do anything on behalf of seamen, I would do it." Dana said he had taken "the recent case of Nichols and Couch" to illustrate matters "not known to most of the public and our profession." He added, "If there is anything relating to yourself in the article which you may object to, I wish the blame to rest entirely on myself, and none upon the editor."[19]

Story replied the very next day. The letter's opening was entirely consistent with Story's character: "Your article for the *Jurist* requires no apology to me, because, in the first place, free and full comments on the proceedings of the Courts of Justice are essential to its due administration; and because I know full well that your own just feelings and right principles on all subjects must have my sympathy." And the letter closed, "Affectionately, your friend, Joseph Story."[20] Still, Story's response must have given his student pause. Justice Story offered several explanations for his sentence, any one of which, if accepted by Dana, was sufficient to rebut Dana's pointed criticism.

Story cautioned Dana that the accounts upon which criticisms of the sentence were based "were misrepresented and misunderstood by the newspapers." He wrote that he had not placed "the slightest confidence in the exaggerated statements of cruelty given by some witnesses." Story added cryptically, "I have since learned from very unexceptional sources on further inquiry, that the real facts were not misunderstood by the Court." Justice Story provided an experienced judge's perspective to an inexperienced law student: "If you had been so long in the courts of justice as myself you would be astonished and humbled by the vast extent of exaggeration and even of perjury which characterizes . . . causes where seamen and officers are concerned." "I lament," Justice Story concluded, "the painful necessity of saying so."[21]

Story may have reasonably expected that a letter sent to his pupil within twenty-four hours, graciously but firmly emphasizing that Dana had neither accurate knowledge of the facts nor the judicial experience to evaluate sailors' testimony, would mute his student's criticism. In that expectation, Joseph Story became the first of many prominent nineteenth-century Americans to misjudge Dana's commitment to those who suffered at the hands of authority.

Dana's essay "Cruelty to Seamen" appeared in the October 1839 issue of the *American Jurist*.[22] It is little wonder the editors sought to distant themselves from the source. It was a devastating critique of Story's sentencing of Nichols and Couch. Dana did not pull any punches, least of all in his statement of the case: "Except intentional murder, a worse case than that of captain Nichols, attended by fewer mitigating circumstances, and supported by stronger evidence will not be likely to occur. What slighter punishment there is left for a case less aggravated, we do not know."

Dana may have lacked the experience to evaluate courtroom testimony, but Story could not doubt Dana's familiarity with the seamen's world. "This sentence upon Nichols and Couch," wrote the ex-sailor, "is already known far and wide among the masters, mates, seamen, landlords and shipping masters of our city, and it is the common topic in cabins and forecastles." Dana knew what the effect of the sentence would be on that world: "By it masters and officers are continued in their notion that seamen are not to be believed in courts of justice, and sailors made to feel, that however aggravated may be the cruelty practiced upon them, if there are none to testify to it but themselves, a conviction will be hardly worth procuring."

Dana implicitly questioned Story's invocation of judicial experience as a basis for "want of confidence in the testimony." Dana acknowledged, "There is false swearing among all classes; and interested men are apt to exaggerate." But, asked the law student of one of America's greatest judges, what was the purpose of cross-examination? If sailors could withstand the most rigorous and searching cross-examination by the ablest of lawyers to the satisfaction of a jury, upon what basis could a judge disbelieve the witnesses—except upon "a rule of court that seamen, as a class, are not to be believed?"

Dana aimed his sharpest barbs at his elder's reliance on the "youthfulness" of the defendants as a reason for leniency. Story must have been astonished at his student's tone, but the impassioned voice of one who knew what it was like to be at the mercy of a youthful sadist had force: "That his honor should have held that a man of twenty-five years of age, the father of a family and old enough to have command of a ship, was too young to be fully answerable in law for an act of cruelty, it is impossible for us to believe." Dana added an example of the powerful combination of logic and rhetoric that was to make him a great advocate: "If a man of five and twenty is too young to suffer the full penalty upon a conviction for deliberate and aggravated cruelty, how much of the penalty is a man of thirty to suffer, and how old must a man be before he is to be fully answerable?"

But it was a broader point Dana most wished to make—one that he would soon amplify far beyond the limited readership of a legal journal. A law intended to deter the abuse of sailors by officers was meaningless if judges were so gullible as to accept, at sentencing, testimony of a captain's "good character" while on shore. The "very same man," wrote Dana, "when far from all the restraints of friends and superiors and public opinion, possessed of despotic power, and with none to see or hear him but those who stand to him in the relation of slaves, may show himself a very fiend."

The tactic of calling friends, family, and employers to certify the convicted master's good character while on shore was particularly effective with Justice Story. Dana noted that Rufus Choate, the lawyer of choice for ship owners, did not even bother to put on a defense for a captain charged with cruelty. Choate saved his advocacy for the sentencing, where he successfully argued that the captain's good character on shore mitigated any serious punishment. Dana thought "it would be the strangest thing in the world" if a master, whose next command of a vessel depended upon preserving a respectable appearance before ship owners and insurers, publicly exhibited cruelty while on shore.

Dana equally disdained the "invariably made argument" that imprisonment of a master for abuse would work a hardship on the master's family. "There is not one master or mate in a thousand of a merchant vessel who could not make the same argument," asserted Dana. When a ship captain's sentence was suspended because of his family's dependence on him, "the question is never asked whether the sailor, who has been killed, or maimed . . . , was not also poor and had not also a mother or sister . . . to whom his small and hard earnings might have been a relief."

Story's lenient sentencing excited public comment, but the justice was editorially praised for his practice of reminding the defendants of their obligation to the law. Dana did not believe the abuse of sailors would be diminished "by an address, however moving, from the judge on the bench." Dana was not advancing a law student's theory of the purpose of criminal law. He was urgently asserting what his voyage had taught him about what desperate men could do if not protected by the law: "It is not in human nature to bear the treatment which crews are often subject to . . . with a knowledge that any redress is slight and uncertain."

Despite the withering critique, Story must have found much to admire in the power of his student's essay. Dana's remarkable article was a demonstration of his instinct for the essential. It never for a moment colored Justice Story's treatment of Dana in a courtroom. Indeed, Dana would later write to Story's son, "I honestly believe the truth to be, that he entirely forgot it."[23] It was a rare quality in a judge—rarer still in Brahmin Boston, as Dana was soon to learn.

5

THE BOOK

In January 1839, midway through law school, Dana accepted a position as an instructor of elocution at Harvard College. It provided him with a small stipend that he badly needed, and reunited him with Edward Tyrrel Channing, Harvard's professor of rhetoric and oratory, whom Dana had as an undergraduate. There was a family connection as well. Dana's father was cousin to Channing, and together they helped establish the *North American Review,* the country's most respected literary periodical.

Channing had held the prestigious Boylston Professorship of Rhetoric since 1819. His predecessors included John Quincy Adams, whose Harvard lectures on rhetoric and oratory emphasized the importance of eloquence to every significant calling a Harvard graduate might undertake, from pulpit to politics. Adams was impressed by the flourishes in the sermons of young Edward Everett, who—after a stint as professor of Greek—entered politics. Everett's oratory was considered to embody the eloquence of the Age; it was Everett who spoke for over two hours at Gettysburg, before Abraham Lincoln rose to say a few words.

Channing and Everett were the models for the measured, modulated, and distinct diction that typified Boston's social elite. But if Channing shared Everett's passion for enunciation, he detested any writing in the pompous, self-indulgent style so characteristic of Everett's oratory. Once while assisting Channing in an elocution class, Dana had a student declaim an excerpt from a sermon by William Ellery Channing, Boston's most celebrated minister. The piece aroused the displeasure of Professor Channing, who kept muttering, "poor stuff, very poor stuff." Finally he whispered, "What is this Richard? It is wretched." Dana, without turning to face Channing, answered, "A selection from your brother, sir."[1]

Channing's antipathy to purple prose was not lost on his students. The professor's manner was as severe as his standard:

> Channing, with his bland, superior look,
> Cold as moonbeam on a frozen brook,
> While the pale student, shivering in his shoes,
> Sees from his theme the turgid rhetoric ooze.[2]

Measured by the accomplishments of his students, Channing was the greatest teacher of English in nineteenth-century America. Holmes captured Channing's austerity, and others, including Emerson, Prescott, and Thoreau (who credited Channing with teaching him to write) were a testament to his insistence on simplicity when it was not thought a virtue.

Professor Channing required his students to write essays on a variety of themes: "the cultivation of the imagination," "the superior and the common man," and "the duty and dangers of conformity." Thoreau kept the college themes he wrote for Channing, and if Dana did not, he put to good use one of Channing's topics, "the anxieties and delights of a discoverer."[3]

Dana's extensive journal of his sea voyage having vanished with his sea chest from the Boston wharf in 1836, all that remained of his record of the voyage and his time in California were eight sheets of paper folded to form sixteen pages. But one winter's evening in early 1838, Dana retrieved the sheaf of notes from the remaining mementos of his voyage. Then, amid the burdens of a first-year law student, with the barest of outlines, he began to write.

By Christmas 1838, Dana had completed his narrative. He showed the manuscript to his father and to Washington Allston, a celebrated artist related to Dana's family by marriage. Allston's contemporaries considered him to be the greatest artist America had produced (the Allston section of Boston was named for him). But by 1839 Allston found it increasingly difficult to work in the claustrophobic atmosphere of Cambridge. It was, he said, "like a bee trying to make honey in a coal-hole." Henry James wrote of "the beautiful colorist . . . withering in a cruel air."[4]

The bracing freshness of Dana's voice was particularly striking to Allston, who was at work on a novel that was as stale as his painting. Here was irrefutable evidence—from a twenty-four-year-old law student, no less—that something new could come out of old Cambridge. Dana's father recognized what his son had learned from Professor Channing: "The distinctness of description, the absence of vanity, and uncommon degree of simplicity make up the interest."[5] Dana Sr. and Allston were astute judges of the manuscript's merit, but they had the disadvantage of being related to the author.

A distinguished and disinterested reader was at hand. William Cullen Bryant, poet and essayist, had by 1839 secured the fame and critical acclaim that once seemed in reach for Dana's father. Dana Sr. helped bring Bryant to public notice through publication of Bryant's poetry in early issues of the *North American Review*. Bryant's most recent work was published by Harper and Brothers, a relatively new but growing New York publishing house.

In May 1839, Leonard Woods, Dana's former tutor and now president-elect of Bowdoin College, was on his way to New York City. Dana asked Woods if he would take the untitled manuscript to Harper, with a request that Harper seek Bryant's opinion of the merit of the work. Woods agreed to do so, and Bryant quickly let Dana's father know what he thought of his son's effort: "I like the book immensely . . . I like its picturesque simplicity—the power which the writer has of producing effect without aiming at it, and I am very sure the public will like it too. It is something novel also, the life of sailors before the mast, unaffectedly and intelligently described: the work will succeed I have no doubt."[6]

Bryant conveyed his opinion to Harper as well. Leonard Woods returned to Boston with an oral offer from the publisher; a royalty of 10 percent on each copy after 1,000 copies had been sold. Dana relied on his father as his literary agent. But—as he so often did—Richard Henry Dana Sr. proved to be a "Jonah," the sailors' name for someone believed to bring bad luck to a voyage.

Dana's father thought an offer contingent upon the sale of 1,000 copies was "next door to nothing."[7] In a lifetime of timid literary excursions his sales had never approached that number, so he believed the threshold a bar to any payment at all. He asked Bryant to seek a better deal from Harper. Dana Sr. did correctly assess the negotiations in one respect. "From all appearance," he wrote his son, the brothers Harper were "sharp & vulgar men."[8]

In late June, Bryant reported to Dana Sr., "I have seen the Harpers, and do not find them disposed to publish the book at all at present."[9] Harper's bluff—if bluff it was—unnerved Dana's father. He immediately wrote to Bryant with a new directive: "I do not know but what you already understand that it is Richard's wish to publish, even though he would not get a cent for it—as acceptable as cash would be to him & that if he must choose between the two, a wide circulation, & higher offer,—he would elect the wide circulation. With this understanding, I wish you to consider the [manuscript] as put into your hands to dispose of just as you may think best."[10] Bryant tried Lea and Blanchard, a prominent Philadelphia publisher. It rejected the manuscript, citing the struggling economy, as did two smaller publishing houses. In October 1839 Bryant returned the manuscript to Dana.

The New Year appeared to promise better times to a recovering economy. In early 1840 Dana's father was in New York City to deliver a series of lectures on Shakespeare. Bryant was with him and they approached Harper once more. On February 4, 1840, Dana Sr. wrote his son: "I have seen the Harpers again. Should they like the [manuscript] I think I could get a couple of hundred from them. They wish to have it sent to them. . . . They did not seem to like the proposition to have you interested in the copyright. I think the book will continue to sell; yet I do not know that you had better take what you can get."[11]

Harper's interest in securing the copyright had more to do with its business plan than an expectation that Dana's book would be a best-seller. In 1839 the brothers Harper had secured an exclusive agreement to furnish the New York State superintendent of schools with a multi-volume library that could be placed in school districts throughout the state. The New York State legislature appropriated five years of funding to be matched by the local districts. Harper was soon busy signing authors for little money and printing the books in a small uniform size of "unprecedented cheapness."[12]

Dana's father alerted his son that a book for the "Harper's School District Library" would first have to be reviewed for suitability by the New York school superintendent. He advised Dana to review the manuscript for anything that might be objectionable in a "school book," but added, "Don't sacrifice *anything* going to the merit of the work in any way:—better take the smallest sum than do that."[13]

With the prospect of publication apparently at hand, Dana quickly began a final review of his manuscript. He checked with knowledgeable sources for help with his Spanish and Hawaiian vocabulary. At his father's request, Dana added a preface and concluding chapter. On February 20, 1840, Dana wrote his father: "I shall send by Hamden's Express tomorrow my manuscript, complete, I believe & in order for the press. . . . I propose as a title 'Two Years Before the Mast: A Personal Narrative of Sea Life.' For the latter I am indebted to Ned [Dana's brother] who thinks . . . the design of the work is to give rather my experience of a sailor's life, than a description of places visited. I think he is right."[14]

As to Harper's insistence on retaining the copyright, Dana added, "I wish, of course, to do the best I can, but if the Harpers make it a point, we had better give it up . . . as I consider that if they have the general copyright, they will be anxious to promote the sale & getting out of a new edition which would all be an advantage to me in various ways."[15]

Dana's father provided Harper with the revised manuscript on March 2, 1840. Two weeks later he reported to his son that one of the Harper readers objected to the oaths in the book but if these could be deleted, "they will give you Two Hundred & Fifty dollars for the entire copyright & allow you Twenty-five copies to distribute. They will also send you the proofs for correction. These were the best terms I could make with them."[16]

Dana eagerly awaited the proofs, but then began a process familiar to authors. Weeks elapsed without a word from the publisher. On May 20, 1840, in response to an inquiry from an anxious Dana, Harper evasively replied that the manuscript "shall be carefully preserved," adding, "We shall probably have occasion to be in Boston shortly, when we will see you on the subject."[17]

Unbeknowst to Dana, the manuscript was actually in the hands of Professor Alonzo Potter of Union College in Schenectady, New York. Potter was a reader for Harper, and the publisher sent Dana's work to him for an opinion of its merit and appropriateness for the school district library series. Years later Dana learned from Potter that he had predicted great success for the book and urged Harper to "purchase it at any price."[18]

Potter's endorsement was the likely prompt for Harper's decision to add the book to its own "Family Library Series." On August 20, 1840, Wesley Harper wrote to Dana that after consultation with "judicious friends," Harper would publish *Two Years Before the Mast* at "five times" the normal print run of 1,000 copies.[19] The Harper brothers did not undertake risks unless they were very sure of benefits.

Bryant, now aware that Harper foresaw a commercial success, tried in vain to turn its new interest to Dana's advantage. He proposed a $500 payment for the copyright. It was rejected. He then proposed $300. Dana's journal depicted the final negotiation: "Mr. Bryant told them . . . that they ought not to stand for $50 with a young author, but should give me the round $300. This they refused & the bargain was at last made at $250. We were fairly beaten down to this, & I consented to it against the advice of several friends, from ignorance of the value of the book, & because I was anxious to have it published before I opened my office."[20]

Dana's impatience to see the publication of *Two Years Before the Mast* coincide with the opening of his law practice was based on his calculation that his book "would be of some use to me in Boston in securing . . . a share of maritime business."[21] Thirty years of writing had brought his father less than $400. Dana had already exceeded half of that, but if there was a lesson to be drawn from his father's literary life, it was that a writer was "all gentleman and no pay."[22]

Harper copyrighted *Two Years Before the Mast: A Personal Narrative of Life at Sea* on September 1, 1840. The book went on sale in mid-September as Volume CVI (106) of the Harpers' Family Library series. It was an instant success. Less than a month after publication, Bryant wrote to Dana's father: "The book takes wonderfully, everybody likes it, the newspapers all praise it . . . it is read by all orders, ages and conditions of men . . . I have rarely known a book so generally spoken well of."[23]

With more prescience than he realized, Dana Sr. said, "I expect to be hence forth spoken of as the Father of the writer of *Two Years Before the Mast*." He was constantly stopped by those who wished to praise his son's book, but the encounters were not welcomed: "I . . . can hardly go out on the street without being attacked for disposing of the entire copyright . . . & especially for such a mere song."[24]

Public demand for *Two Years Before the Mast* continued unabated throughout the fall. Harper also published the volume as part of the New York School District Library series, and the book's success compelled the publisher to do a second printing of the Harper's Family Library volume before year's end. The new edition contained the author's name for the first time; the first Family Library edition had only the initials R.H.D.

There was no mystery, however, about either the author or the book's popular and critical reception. Ralph Waldo Emerson was among those who wrote favorable reviews. Emerson, whom Dana briefly had as a teacher, wrote to his brother: "[Dana] was my scholar once, but he never learned this of me: more's the pity."[25] Charles Sumner and Fanny Appleton (Longfellow's future wife) each sent copies of *Two Years Before the Mast* to friends in England who forwarded the book to the London "publisher of poets," Edward Moxon. The publisher of works by Tennyson, Wordsworth, and Browning immediately recognized the book's merit.

Moxon's edition of *Two Years Before the Mast* was published in England in February 1841. Two other British publishers also brought out editions. None were under any legal obligation to Dana (nor Harper) because the American copyright did not extend to international reprints. Nevertheless, Moxon sent Dana a check for $500—twice what Harper had paid. Dana was showered with letters of praise from English authors, including Charles Dickens—already internationally renowned and preparing for a much anticipated first visit to America, where he hoped to meet the young Dana.

Perceptive literary critics hailed the author of *Two Years Before the Mast* as a new voice in American literature. But sailors who spent years in ships' forecastles—the "small, black, and wet holes which few landsmen would believe"—heard a new voice as well.[26] It was from one who sailed with them and returned to speak truth to the authority of the class to which he belonged. In Liverpool, it was said that 2,000 British sailors bought

Two Years Before the Mast in a single day.[27] In Boston, sailors looked for the author as well as the book.

Dana's expectation that his personal narrative of life at sea would generate clients in maritime cases underestimated his book's impact on "that body of men, of whose common life it is intended to picture." Dana's concluding chapter, "in behalf of men who I believe are every day wronged by it," reasserted his unprecedented criticism of judicial leniency for abusive masters, typified by Story's sentence of Captain Nichols.[28]

The twenty-five-year-old Dana opened his law practice in early September 1840. After "3 or 4 weeks with almost nothing to do," his small office next to the courthouse, three blocks from Boston's Long Wharf, was besieged by seamen.[29] A visitor to the law office of Brahmin Richard Henry Dana Jr. in the autumn of 1840, "and indeed long afterward," noted it "was apt to be crowded with unkempt, roughly dressed seamen, and it smelled on such occasions much like a forecastle."[30] The common seaman had found an uncommon advocate.

6

BOSTON, BRAHMINS, AND THE BUSINESS OF LAW

"I am told on excellent authority that now the book is worth $10,000 to them," Dana wrote in August 1842. His estimate of Harper's profit was undoubtedly low. Harper never revealed its sales figures for *Two Years Before the Mast*. A laudatory history of the publisher, unable to favorably portray the negotiation tactics of the Harper brothers, simply omitted any reference to the book—one of the most celebrated works ever published by Harper or any other house.[1]

Dana was resigned to his bargain: "Perhaps it is better for me that the money should be in their hands than in mine." Taking refuge in the biblical injunction "It is good for a man to bear the yoke in his youth," Dana added, "I would not take the money if I had to take one tithe of their spirit with it. I should wish it only for S's sake."[2]

"S" was Miss Sarah Watson of Hartford, Connecticut. Dana met Sarah in the summer of 1838 when his aunts entertained a family friend who brought her two nieces to Boston. Dana had heard an aunt speak of one of them "in a manner which interested me exceedingly." The young women were not expected to arrive in Boston until Monday, and on Sunday July 15 Dana decided to go to Cambridge to hear Ralph Waldo Emerson lecture. It was the occasion of Emerson's controversial "Divinity School Address," in which he questioned the divinity of Jesus. But to Dana it was notable because, at the lecture, "without my knowledge I was for an hour or more [for the] first time in the same room with the woman who [was] afterward to be my wife."[3]

Sarah thought Emerson "preach[ed] the doctrine of human depravity." Dana was attracted by Sarah's rigorous piety—in part because he believed himself in need of a corrective for the temptations of a "sailor's life." Sarah's journal recorded a more enthusiastic response to meeting Dana than to hearing Emerson: "I must to go to bed & for a wonder I don't feel tired & sleepy & I believe I know the reason I do not."[4]

Dana courted Sarah for the next three years, waiting, in strictest adherence to custom, for the chance to express his intentions. The opportunity finally came when Dana, traveling to his brother Ned's commencement from the University of Vermont, orchestrated a trip up the Hudson River accompanied by Sarah and her sister, who were to visit their brother in Albany. Dana had a year of law school remaining but the couple committed to each other. His brief journal entries ("blind man's bluff," "the last evening," "the locket") are shorthand for the episodes that stirred the ever romantic and sentimental Dana.

There was, though, something more at work within Dana than a young man's romance. Sarah was pretty enough to evoke admiring comment, a fact not lost on Dana, who had an eye for physical beauty. But Dana's relationship to Sarah was to play itself out in increasing complexity, never fully recognized by either husband or wife. Dana's aunts thought Sarah looked like Dana's mother, and it may well have been a remark commenting on the resemblance that made Dana "exceedingly" interested in meeting her. Beyond whatever physical likeness there may have been, Dana's description of Sarah's spiritual qualities idealized virtues he believed his mother had possessed: "nobleness & elevation of soul, sincerity of feeling, purity of intention."[5]

It was Sarah who could weigh Dana's own portion of these virtues. Dana believed himself to be in particular need of someone fit to read the scale. His periodic bouts of guilt over his sailor's life, as well as his suppressed desire to revisit the sexual freedom it afforded, engendered a need to look for a wife who could "direct & inspire to all that is noble, holy & good."[6] It was a role Sarah Watson Dana was to master, at least as measured by her capacity to induce in her husband a sense of guilt.

But the life of their marriage was yet to be lived, when on the evening of August 25, 1841, the couple was married in a modest ceremony in Hartford. Sarah at twenty-seven, a year older than Dana, was living with her widowed mother. Her father, a merchant remembered for having led opposition to billiard parlors, died bankrupt. Sarah could offer only to bring a small dowry of $300, which Dana declined. Charles Francis Adams Jr., for one, admired their start: "So far as worldly possessions went Miss Watson was no better off than Dana himself, nor did she have any family connections in Massachusetts. It was a healthy, natural case of young people of slender means marrying simply because they were attached to each other, and had perfect confidence in their ability to face the world and take care of themselves."[7]

The couple honeymooned for a week in Rockport, then returned to Boston, where Dana leased rooms in the United States Hotel. It was to be ten years before the Danas had a house of their own. Sarah resented the necessity of renting, but Dana could not have been happier at where they started married life: "Our parlor . . . has a beautiful view of the harbor. . . . At night we see both the lighthouses."[8]

Dana had good reason for perfect confidence in his future. Despite slender means, his pedigree, profession, and talent provided entree to the most exclusive and powerful social establishment in America. New England society in the 1840s and even later, said Henry Adams, "was still directed by the professions. Lawyers, physicians, professors, merchants were classes, and acted not as individuals but as though they were clergymen and each profession were a church."[9] When the church leaders gathered, they could anoint as well as excommunicate.

A dinner invitation from wealthy Abbott Lawrence may not have been anointment, but Dana was eager for his elders' blessing. Dana quickly replied by note, "It will give me great pleasure to dine with you on Friday & meet Lord Morpeth."[10] And well it might, for the twenty-six-year-old Dana was to be the youngest guest at the most exclusive dinner of Boston's most influential leaders. It was more than coincidence that Dana chose December 17, 1841, to write: "With this day I begin my journal, writing down the events of each day, as they occur. All before this has been from memory." There was more than a touch of pride in his first entry: "Am to dine at 5 at Abbott Lawrence's with Lord Morpeth."[11]

The Boston visit of George William Frederick Howard, eldest son of the Earl of Carlisle, prompted a frenzy of competing invitations from Boston society. Morpeth, said Longfellow, was "a very pleasant, jolly, sociable, ruddy-faced man . . . a laughing bachelor of forty."[12] He was not much more—but he was an English lord. For anglophile Brahmin society, the title elevated the man. Dana's journal described Lord Morpeth as "an honorable, amiable, thorough bred & talented man." Upon reflection, Dana struck "& talented."[13]

But reflection was to come later. Each of the twelve guests who joined Lord Morpeth at the mansion of textile manufacturer Abbott Lawrence were there to pay homage to a representative of an aristocracy they admired. "There was plenty of high conservatism talked," Dana noted, "& by no one more than by Judge Story, who began his life as a radical."[14] Joseph Story's presence was a given for he was the high priest of the legal profession.

But the dinner was at the Beacon Hill residence of a merchant, not a lawyer. Tocqueville's view that American aristocracy is "not among the rich, who are united by no common tie, but [among] the judicial bar and bench" was less applicable to Boston, where the masters of State Street had united commercial success with political power and social status.[15] If the point needed further emphasis, Lawrence made it by ensuring that lawyer John Davis was there only at the sufferance of the Whig elites who controlled the legislature that elected Davis governor and senator.

Yet a Beacon Hill dinner given for an English lord could never be mistaken for a crass display of commercial political power. Tocqueville thought the Boston society to which he was introduced "resembles almost completely the upper classes of Europe."[16] Abbott Lawrence knew how to make a table that was as good an imitation of aristocracy as Boston could produce. True, a third of his guests were fellow merchants, but each moved effortlessly between business and society.

Lawrence included among his guests Samuel Lothrop, pastor of the Brattle Square Church, and Francis Gray, a minor literary figure—though Lord Morpeth was unknown to have demonstrated an abiding interest in either religion or literature. But no Beacon Hill dinner intended to exhibit to the British aristocracy the cultivated manners and refined taste of Boston society was complete without the presence of the two gentlemen who epitomized that society: Harrison Gray Otis and George Ticknor.

Otis, the elder of the two, had long taken "the first place in Boston when there was decidedly a first place to take."[17] Nephew of James Otis, famed orator of revolutionary Boston, Harrison Gray Otis was still, at age seventy-six, the handsome and elegant figurehead of Boston society. A devout Federalist who stood by the principles of the defunct party of George Washington when others (Joseph Story, for one) had found it politically expedient to join the Democrats, Otis could still hold a table. "Mr. Otis was in his best vein, & we young men could easily believe he had been, in his prime, the best conversationist in the land," Dana wrote in his journal. "Indeed, as soon as a word comes from him, all stop speaking."[18]

George Ticknor, at fifty, had succeeded Otis as leader of Boston society. His affinity for the rich was coupled with a literary sophistication and cosmopolitan aura that conveyed good breeding. Ticknor, "having the distinction of having seen Europe [when] this was a distinction," exuded a self-assurance nurtured in his early years as Harvard's professor of French and Spanish Languages and Literatures, and professor of Belles Lettres; he was succeeded in the latter position by Longfellow.[19]

By the time of the Lord Morpeth dinner in 1841, Ticknor had become "a gentleman of letters"—a calling to which there were many aspirants. Ticknor owed much of his success to marrying culture to commerce. His wife, Anna, was a daughter of Samuel Eliot, whose rise from apprenticeship to wealthy merchant left a sizable estate. Ticknor's path to a leisurely life of letters was not unique; when, in Francis Gund's satire of Boston's aristocracy, a merchant is asked why so many literary men seem so well off, he replies: "They marry rich women. . . . They show their common sense in that. It's quite the fashion for our rich girls to buy themselves a professor."[20]

In the social circles that counted, it was said Boston was more aptly named "Ticknorville."[21] The Ticknor house at the corner of Beacon and Park Streets overlooked the Boston Common, and its elegant library was the most exclusive drawing room on Beacon Hill. Nine Park Street was quite a setting for the son of a grocer, who unlike Otis (or Dana) had no hereditary claim to his patrician air. James Russell Lowell (who did) delighted in recounting Thackeray's retort to Ticknor's declaration that a gentleman of eminent standing could be determined by his looks: "A pretty speech," cries Thackeray, "for one broken nosed man to make to another." "All Boston," wrote Lowell "has been secretly tickled with it."[22]

Thackeray may have been the only person on either side of the Atlantic with the standing to mock Ticknor's vanity. Certainly, no Bostonian who wished to enter the charmed circle would dare a remark that could be misconstrued as questioning Ticknor's authority to define a proper gentleman—or worse, to do so as a jest. Otis was "Harry" to his friends, and "his old-fashioned stories were full of rollicking fun."[23] Ticknor preferred sober conversation that paid homage—if not directly to him—to the persons and places that a gentleman should know. It was why Ticknor was particularly pleased that Abbott Lawrence had invited to the dinner a serious (many said humorless) young man with whom Ticknor was very pleased: Charles Sumner.

Sumner was considered a promising representative of the respectable conservatism treasured by Boston's elite. On a trip through Maryland in 1834, Sumner wrote to his family after his first exposure to Negro slaves: "My worst preconception of their appearance and ignorance did not fall as low as their actual stupidity. They appear to be nothing more than moving masses of flesh, unendowed with anything of intelligence above the brutes. I now have an idea of the blight upon that part of our country in which they live."[24]

But Sumner's views about slavery were of little interest to a Beacon Hill dinner in 1841. Sumner's presence was entirely because of the triumphant tour of Europe he had taken four years earlier. Through sheer dint of intellect, perseverance, and ambition, Sumner's campaign to establish his social credentials with aristocracy abroad was "more brilliant . . . than was ever achieved by his countrymen before."[25] It did not hurt that Ticknor was in Paris during his visit. Sumner was given letters of introduction to everyone who counted, including Lord Morpeth, who as Lord Lieutenant of Ireland entertained him in Dublin.

Now it was Sumner who made himself indispensable. "Sumner has introduced me far and near," Morpeth wrote in his diary.[26] At Abbott Lawrence's, Dana noted Sumner's proximity to the lord: "The company all arrived punctually between 1/4 before 5 & 5 minutes after. While in the room, observed that Sumner now & then whispers to Ld. M. the names of persons as they come in & tells him whether he has met them before. I was talking with Ld. M. when Sumner said in a low tone—'That is Mr. Quincy (the tall gentleman) whom you have met. The other gentleman not, a Unitarian clergyman, etc.' Accordingly Ld. M meets Mr. Quincy half way, with 'How do you do Mr. Quincy' etc. This is very convenient."[27]

The zeal and ingratiating opportunism with which Sumner pursued his social ambition to be at the lord's side were to be more evident in a future unimaginable to the guests. "Poor Sumner can't take a joke of any kind," wrote Dana, "He's as literal as a Scotch guideboard."[28] It was the only lament of a privileged gathering that reflected traditions and relations Henry Adams thought "solid and sure to continue."[29]

The aristocratic edifice of 1840s Boston appeared solid because so much had gone into laying the foundation. It was Oliver Wendell Holmes Sr. who famously labeled Boston's aristocracy, "if you choose to call it so," the "Brahmin caste." Holmes conceded that it was wealth, not ancestral lineage, that initially counted, but "money kept for two or three generations transforms a race . . . I don't mean merely in manners and hereditary culture, but in blood and bones."[30]

It was politic of Holmes to limit the generational pedigree to "two or three" since so many families he considered "Brahmin" owed their status to ancestors whose distinction was to have gone from rags to riches. But it was heredity, not domesticity, Holmes had in mind when he declared that "other things being equal, in most relations in life, I prefer a man of family."[31]

Dana agreed—or at least thought he should. But the refinement and class consciousness that typified Abbott Lawrence's dinner for Lord Morpeth were at war with Dana's experience before the mast. If he could find "the most remarkable man I ever met" in Tom Harris, a common sailor, or unsurpassed honor and loyalty in his friendship with the Sandwich Islanders, how much credence ought he to give to his caste's dictate on whom to prefer?

When Charles Dickens made his first visit to America in early 1842, much of Boston was agog. The response of Brahmin Boston was considerably more reserved. Dickens was not Lord Morpeth. Thomas Appleton spoke for the caste after seeing Dickens: "Take the genius out of his face and there are a thousand young London shop-keepers, about the theaters & eating houses who look exactly like him." Dana's journal entry of January 18, 1842, expressed a view appropriate to his class:

"Nothing talked of but Dickens' arrival. The town is mad. All calling on him. I shan't go unless sent for. I can't submit to sink the equality of a gentleman by crowding after a man of note."[32]

When Dickens sent a note expressing surprise that Dana had not called upon him, caste convention was satisfied, and on January 26 Dana (and Longfellow) were shown into Dickens's rooms at Boston's Tremont House. Dana was pleased by Dickens's offer to call upon Dana's father "if he is unwell." Dana believed he could tell much from Dickens's appearance: "You admire him & there is a fascination about him which keeps your eyes on him, yet you cannot get over the impression he is a low bred man."[33]

The next evening it was Dana's peers who deigned to host a dinner for the celebrity. George Ticknor's presence conveyed the necessary social approval. William Prescott, whose monumental history *Ferdinand and Isabella* had been recently published, attended with others whose literary (and social) standing were meant to impress—if not intimidate—a guest who was "by no means patrician."[34]

"The gentlemen are talking their best," wrote Dana, "but Dickens is perfectly natural & unpretending. He could not have behaved better. He did not say a single thing for display. I should think he had resolved to talk as he would at home & let his reputation take care of itself." At one point during the dinner Dana noticed an amused Dickens exchanging a smile with the servants. "As soon as he saw that I observed him, he changed his expression instantly."[35]

After their guest departed, the gentlemen were in agreement that Dickens was a "natural & unassuming man," though Prescott—perhaps to impress Ticknor, who was his benefactor—disparaged Dickens's long hair. This was too much for Dana, who said, "My hair is long." "Prescott," Dana noted, then "blew up [at] all persons who wear long hair."[36]

"Like Dickens very much," Dana wrote of the dinner. The feeling was mutual. Dickens wrote to a friend: "Dana the author of *Two Years Before the Mast* is a very nice fellow indeed."[37] Dana would have been found it instructive to learn that Dickens added, "and in appearance not at all like the man you would expect."

It had been more than five years since Dana disembarked from the *Alert,* but contemporaries noted (not always with approval, as Prescott's remark suggests) that Dana "still wore his hair long, sailor-fashion . . . [and] rolled a little in his gait by no means unconscious of exuding the same air of outdoor hardiness which he has brought back from Cape Horn."[38] Dana's established elders might have been forgiving if his appearance was merely affected, but the young lawyer demonstrated an unsettling pattern of representing those who wore their hair as he did.

If it were true—as Henry Adams contended—that the legal profession of 1840s Boston was being directed as if it were a church, the "clergymen" who led it did not share Dana's belief that its lawyers should represent clients irrespective of their social standing or ability to pay. The Boston bar was said to have the best lawyers in America, and if Justice Story and Harvard Law School unduly amplified the assertion, none could dispute that the city contained some exceptional legal talent. Story's duties as a Supreme Court justice included "circuit riding," which required him to sit as the presiding judge in the federal courts of New England (excluding Vermont and Connecticut). In three decades of holding term in Boston, Story presided over cases argued by the most celebrated lawyers in the country, from Harrison Gray Otis to Daniel Webster to Rufus Choate.[39]

Boston's establishment had a nose for extraordinary lawyers and the purse to pay for them. When thirty-five-year-old Daniel Webster arrived in Boston in 1816, State Street and Beacon Hill were fully familiar with Webster's reputation as New Hampshire's best lawyer. The Cabots, the Lowells, and Harrison Gray Otis himself were Webster's clients within two months of the opening of his Court Street office. Ship owners, manufacturers, and prominent merchants sought the services of the best lawyer money could buy. Two years after coming to Boston, Webster's annual income of $15,000 was more than that of any other lawyer in the city.[40] Daniel Webster's value to Boston's elite, like the money he extracted from them, was to become much greater in the political arena, but he first made his mark where it mattered most to his clients: in the courtroom.

Webster was succeeded in court mastery by Rufus Choate, a trial lawyer of almost legendary status. It was Choate, almost twenty years older than Dana, who represented the interests the younger lawyer most often opposed. Dana's description of Choate, whom he fought fiercely yet admired, captured the almost mystical effect "this strange product of New England" seemed to have on juries and fellow lawyers. It was as if, wrote Dana, "by the side of our time-enduring granite, there had risen, like an exhalation, some Oriental structure, with the domes and glittering minarets of the Eastern world."[41]

Choate's exalted reputation extended far beyond New England. In fact, it was his notoriety that prompted a rare misstep. Choate was cross-examining a witness who claimed that he joined in larceny only because of a promise made by Choate's client. When Choate asked what the promise was, the witness replied: "He said there was a man in Boston named Choate, and he'd get us off [even] *if the money was found in our boots.*"[42]

Rufus Choate was retained by clients who had far more money than they could put in their boots. He combined his extraordinary courtroom skill with an equal capacity to rationalize its exercise on behalf of only those who could afford his fees. Choate's occasional representation of the notorious, together with his steady retention by the wealthy, provided him the platform to retain his status as Boston's most celebrated lawyer.

If there was to be a successor to Choate—as Choate had succeeded Webster in reputation for courtroom advocacy—Boston Brahmins believed they had ample stock upon which to draw. Charles Sumner, who Judge Story said was the best student he ever had at Harvard Law School, appeared to be a fitting candidate to ordain, but lacked the skills essential for courtroom success. Sumner possessed a rare talent for invective, but he was not nimble enough for cross-examination. His ponderous closings, weighted with the scholarship in which he excelled, were ineffective with juries.[43]

George Hillard, Sumner's law partner and classmate at Harvard Law School, was a particular favorite of George Ticknor. Ticknor's blessing was enough to ensure Hillard's standing as a preferred attorney for Boston's mercantile interests. Hillard provided one clue to his fitness when he refused to publish Dana's "Cruelty to Seamen" essay unless Dana cleared it with Judge Story. He would provide much more evidence of his eagerness to do the bidding of State Street and Beacon Hill, but Hillard was more useful to them outside a courtroom than in it.

But Dana, still three years shy of thirty, was establishing a reputation in the arena that intimidated Sumner and Hillard. Story, of course, recognized his former student's rhetorical force, having been stung by it, but other judges began to see it as well. Dana's journal recorded a judge's "rare & valuable compliment" after a jury trial in which Dana had defended a boy charged with larceny: "I met Judge Thatcher in the lobby & he told me that the mother of the lad had been to him to ask him, in case her son was convicted, to send him to the house of reformation instead of jail & that he asked her who was to defend him. She said, 'Mr. Dana.' 'Then,' said the judge, 'I told her he would not be convicted.' "[44]

The young lawyer's reputation as a remarkably talented advocate grew, but so too did his reputation for being on the "wrong side." Dana's first clients were almost all seamen who eagerly sought the services of one who had lived their grievances. The merchant-princes of Boston's State Street predicated the economic efficiency of ships that spent years voyaging to the far side of the world upon brutality and slave wages.

In the decade before Dana became a lawyer, a movement to protect sailors from the most flagrant abuses resulted in a law prohibiting cruel and unusual punishment. In 1840, Congress passed a statute that authorized American consuls in foreign ports to discharge a seaman from further duties with three months' advance pay if the consul determined that he had been mistreated. But the likelihood of a consulate taking the side of a common seaman in a dispute with a ship owned by Boston merchants was as remote as persuading a judge that a captain had brutalized a crew member. It was not that Brahmin Boston was unconcerned with the sailors' plight. But it preferred the benevolence of old-age homes for sailors to legislation protecting seamen from abuse. Dana had a different idea of how to fulfill his vow to help seamen. He wanted justice.[45]

The unkempt, roughly dressed, and decidedly odorous sailors who crowded Dana's small law office wanted their wages. On voyages of two to three years, a sailor rated "ordinary" might be paid ten dollars a month, twelve dollars if rated "able." The handful of dollars was a fraction of the wealth derived by ship owners from a successful voyage, but it was the whole of a sailor's living. Even that small sum was seldom at risk in a claim for unpaid wages. It was not just that the playing field was uneven; sailors seldom got on it at all. Unscrupulous lawyers, little regarded by judges or ship owners' attorneys, often took a fee from seamen who got nothing more than an unfulfilled promise of a day in court.[46]

Dana represented sailors for ten or fifteen dollars—or nothing if they could not pay—and he went to court. "In connection with the law . . . the word 'business' . . . had in Dana's ears a vulgar and most unprofessional sound," wrote a lawyer who clerked with Dana. "The mere use of it always brought from him a correction and a rebuke."[47] In the fall of 1842 Dana recorded an unusual event: "The last week argued *Wentworth v. Nickerson* and the schooner *Harriet*—both cases of seaman's wages. . . .

Lost them both."[48] They were the first cases of seamen's wages Dana had lost in eighteen months of nearly constant litigation. His string of victories over ship merchants and their lawyers was unprecedented.

In a suit against the captain of a New Bedford whaler, the jury awarded $200 to the seaman, a verdict that may have surprised Dana's client, but stunned owners of merchant ships. Dana received "compliments" more valuable than a judge's—ship owners began settling claims for unpaid wages when they learned Dana represented the seaman.

Even a "mutiny" was—to the disbelief of the U.S. attorney and the ship's owners who procured the prosecution—transformed by Dana's legal acumen into a successful claim for wages. The crew of the whaler *Hibernia,* lying at Port Louis in the Isle of France, refused to man the ship for a return voyage to New Bedford unless the master agreed to a survey of the ship's masts, which the crew believed to be dangerously rotted. The master refused to order the survey, as did the American consul whom the crew also petitioned.

The master attempted, with sword's point, to compel the crew to sea. They resisted, police were called, and the sailors were imprisoned at the direction of the American consul. The *Hibernia* safely returned home with another crew. When the *Hibernia*'s original crew reached the United States (after forty-seven days in jail) via another vessel, they were indicted for the revolt. Dana represented all fourteen crew members.

Not the least of Dana's difficulties was that the *Hibernia*'s masts had proved safe enough to bring the ship home. But Dana argued to the jury that it was the reasonableness of the crew's apprehension of the unseaworthiness of the masts at the time the ship was in Port Louis that ought to be determinative. If their belief was reasonable, contended Dana, sailors had a right to ask for the survey and were justified in refusing to go to sea without it. Dana asserted that the master had no right under such circumstances to use force to compel the crew, and force used by the crew in resisting the master was lawful self-defense.

The jury acquitted all fourteen defendants. Dana immediately asked the court for the wages that had been withheld from the crew. The official report of the case of the *Hibernia* concludes: "The court decided that the refusal of the men to obey the master's orders was justifiable, and that the men were entitled to their full lays."[49] It was not only seamen who believed Dana could not lose. Ship owners were beginning to believe it too.

Dana's success did not go unremarked. "I often have a good deal to contend with in the slurs & open opposition of masters & owners of vessels whose seamen I undertake to defend or look after. It is more unpleasant when this is retailed by counsel." He was quick to note that the hostility was limited to the "petty traders." He added, "I never have trouble with the upper class of merchants."[50] Nor was there any reason for Dana to anticipate difficulty from his own caste. Dana's success in obtaining wages due seamen was little more than an irritant to those secure in their fortunes.

Though he would have to make his own way, the twenty-seven-year-old Dana looked to a future that seemed as free from obstacles as the view from Beacon Hill. He closed his journal for 1842 by noting that Longfellow gave Dana's father and Dana each a copy of his new book. It was entitled *Poems on Slavery*.

7

THE MASQUERADE

Dana's debut as a lawyer was nearly as extraordinary as his debut as an author. Within two years of opening his office, Dana's reputation as a litigator was unmatched by any attorney his age and was exceeded only by the acknowledged lion of the Boston bar, Rufus Choate, who had practiced for two decades. On the first day of October 1842, Dana tallied his accounts for one year.[1] He had made over $2,500, a sum that would have been the envy of most Boston lawyers. It was all the more remarkable because it largely represented an accumulation of the small fees charged to his sailor clients.

Dana's early success did not go unnoticed by grasping members of his extended family. A day after closing his accounts, Dana felt compelled to answer an inquiry from his wife's brother-in-law: "When I was in

Hartford, you asked about my income, etc. I have since heard that there is a report there that I am making a fortune. It is very bad to have such reports, as they lead persons to expect things of one which he cannot do. . . . I tell you that you may set one right who has such a notion."[2]

The notions were not limited to distant relatives. Dana's brother Ned sought to join a law practice he perceived as lucrative and, he hoped, undemanding. Dana agreed to allow Ned to go into partnership "for 6 months—as an experiment."[3] No such limitation could be put on Dana's partnership with Sarah, whose notion of her husband's wealth was difficult to dispel. "Our expenses have been much larger than they ought to have been," Dana wrote to Sarah in 1843. "You do not understand the positive value of certain sums."[4]

Sarah's leverage in the couple's frequent disputes over money was considerable. It was, after all, Dana who was born to a family and social class that put great stock in appearances. It was important that what must be done "be done handsomely." That was a maxim by which Dana's father lived, though he never had the least idea of cost, nor the least inclination to know. "Think what an example you have been and are," Dana Sr. wrote to his son—sole supporter of father, brother, and aunts—"yet it has not once roused me out of my elbow chair! Am I not ashamed? I don't know about that. I only know I ought to be."[5]

Sarah's resistance to Dana's fitful warnings to economize was all the greater in the face of what she saw as her husband's ample income and father-in-law's sloth. Dana's response to the increasing financial demands of an unsatisfied wife and insatiable relatives was simple: he worked harder.

There were alternatives. Others in his social class, when confronted with insufficient resources to fund an appropriate lifestyle, had not hesitated to draw upon the largesse of Brahmin Boston. Sumner funded the European tour that launched his career in part with contributions from wealthy Bostonians. More notoriously, Daniel Webster explicitly demanded and received cash from those Bostonians who understood the linkage between favors asked and favors demanded.[6] The Adamses were above reproach, but unlike the Danas their sagacity in land purchases and marriages freed them from having to confront the issue.

But to an exuberant, brilliant young lawyer filled with energy equal to his obligations, "the calling of a man is to labor among men for the support and honor of his family."[7] Dana believed that two years before the mast had taught him the value of labor. An ordinary seaman was expected to have competent knowledge of his tasks, but it was "the day's work" aboard ship that was the "chief test of seamanship." Dana, at twenty-eight, could not conceive of work that would test him beyond the limit of his strength.

The value of a dollar, however, was easily recognized. Dana must have often thought of the thousands of dollars the brothers Harper were receiving for the sale of *Two Years Before the Mast*. The substantial sums being made by others from his writing could not have been far from Dana's mind when he toiled over the lectures he prepared to supplement the income from his law practice.

In New England in the first half of the nineteenth century, the spoken word was the public's chief entertainment. Political speeches could last hours and orators like Edward Everett and the incomparable Webster attracted audiences in the thousands. But smaller venues like courtrooms also drew listeners who could then retell stories used by lawyers in closing arguments (which often lasted hours as well). Every town, it seemed, had its own "lyceum"—a rather grandiose label for the town hall or similar building that played host to lecturers of all stripes.

Dana began his own travel on the lecture circuit in 1842, often traveling to Boston's neighboring towns on a winter's evening after a long day in court. He prepared meticulously crafted lectures on "The Sources of Influence" and "American Loyalty," topics of his own choosing. They were not always the first choice of his audience.

Appearing in Brighton on a January evening in 1843, Dana was introduced as "Squire Daney from Boston." The audience was told that the speaker after Dana would be "a reformed drunkard, a New York woodsawyer named Hadduck & an odd fish with one eye & lame," lecturing on the subject of total abstinence. "There was more curiosity to hear him than to hear my lecture," Dana conceded. Like lecturers before and since, Dana gauged his success by interaction with his listeners: "Not one word was said to me when I got through. Either they did not like me, or did not know what to think." To make matters worse, "they had no one to take my horse."[8]

A week later Dana rode to Milton on a "clear cold night & I in an open sleigh." The "lyceum" had a desk between two small coal stoves. Dana stood there "with a pipe running over my head, & a malignant heat coming from it, beating upon my brain, which to a person just from a cold was particularly stupefying." Nonetheless, after his "American Loyalty" lecture, "a great many persons came up to me."[9] Riding back, Dana's host pointed out a house built by a young man who won $10,000 in a lottery. The sum was exactly what Harper's was rumored to have made in the first year of publication of *Two Years Before the Mast*. If that did not emphasize the gap between effort and reward, Dana's lecture fee of fifteen dollars did.

The distance between effort and income began to be reflected in Dana's relationship with his wife. It was easy enough to see why Sarah, to say nothing of her brother-in-law, equated Dana's growing reputation as lawyer, author, and lecturer with an anticipated increase in wealth. As Sarah reminded her husband after the couple moved into a rented home on Beacon Hill's West Cedar Street in November 1842, there were many women whose husbands were far less busy, far less well-known, and far richer.

The tension between Dana and Sarah had the familiar characteristics of marriage-related stress over money, but Dana's frenetic pace was not simply a manifestation of his ambition to maintain his family's standing among Boston's Brahmins. There was a part of Dana that could not be reconciled with the life to which he was born. His inner turmoil over his inability to fully embrace what convention said should satisfy him—social standing, profession, and family—could not be contained despite Dana's belief that a "day's work" could impose the same discipline on his desires as on a ship's crew.

Dana's journal entries for the summer of 1842 reveal the extent to which he grappled with the parts that made him who he was, but which he could not see whole. In June he exulted over the birth of the couple's first child. By July he was cruising the red light district of Halifax.

Dana was a far more sympathetic and involved father-to-be than was typical for his time. On June 12, when "the great event was drawing near," Dana described "poor S. in the pangs of labor. I stood beside her and held her hand all the time, whispered in her ear, & in her moments of ease she whispered to me and pressed my hand. . . . There is surely no pain like it in the world. At ¼ before 5 P.M. the end comes & a living daughter is born. In an instant S. is awake to all the feeling of a mother. . . . and the beautiful expression peculiar to the new made mother take their place."[10]

Dana's joy at the couple's first daughter (they were to have four more and a son) was unbounded: "God be praised. If ever man had reason to bless God with his whole heart, it is I." The new baby was named Sarah Watson Dana after "the best, the most tender, affectionate & faithful, as well as superior & charming wife that man ever had." Dana was back at work the next day. Two weeks later he noted that he had left home at 7:00 A.M., traveled nearly 120 miles, taken three depositions, and made four calls on clients. Rushing to get home before 7:00 P.M., Dana saw "Mr. Ticknor & his daughters & servants, bound to their residence on the seashore."[11]

On a Saturday in mid-July, Dana impulsively decided to go to Halifax "solely to change the scene." Sarah's mother had come to help with the new baby and Dana's brother Ned could, for a brief period at least, be entrusted with cases. At 5:00 P.M. Dana boarded the steamship *Caledonia*, observing that one no longer "set sail" but instead "made steam."

Dana was fatigued by hard work but "no sooner had we got outside of the lighthouse & the cool salt wind of ocean come over us than I felt myself a new creature." He stayed on the ship's damp and foggy deck until 1:00 A.M. and returned to walk it again before sunrise. His frequent indigestion, a symptom of his stressful schedule and gulped meals, was gone: "At breakfast I had a terrific appetite & ate more than I have at any meal for months." Dana described the object of his weeklong visit to "clear my mind completely from business & cares." He refused invitations to dinners and parties for he "could not go fishing all day & then sun burnt & blackened, dress for a party in the evening." Dana "walked about the street."[12]

Dana was as cognizant as any sailor before the mast of the diversions available in a seaport. His account of his night wanderings among the brothels of Halifax Hill and his later journal entries about cruising the far more dangerous "Five Points" section of New York City are a mixture of revelation and denial. Sarah had access to Dana's journals, and he occasionally read her excerpts including those of his "excursions."[13] It is unlikely that the readings amused Sarah since she had great distaste for his sailor past. That Dana wrote of his visits to prostitutes— much less read of them to his wife—suggests a deep-seated need for confession to—and remonstration from—the woman he had chosen to remind him of what was "pure and noble."

Dana began his journal with the disclaimer that he would not pretend his account would be a faithful transcript: "A private journal . . . [is] a sort of masquerading; a quiet hatching of an egg in secret, which the layer knows will at some future time break & come out a living & speaking thing." When Dana "presumed" the brothels on Halifax Hill were "fair specimens . . . of most other places on the globe," it was a presumption for Sarah's benefit.[14]

"I felt a sudden interest in the younger girl," Dana wrote of his first evening in a Halifax brothel. It was an interest—at least in the telling—that was not sexual: "I told her at once I did not want her in the way of her calling but wished to say a word to her. I then in a careless manner opened my coat to show her I had the dress of a gentleman." Dana related a story of his effort to persuade "poor Kitty Morricay! (for that is her name)" to abandon her way of life. It took more than one visit. Dana often began his conversation with a prostitute by insisting that his visit was of "no object but curiosity." He observed that this seldom seemed to surprise the women. "Perhaps they are used to having visits of persons like myself," Dana wrote with unconscious irony.[15]

It is conceivable, of course, that Dana went to Halifax Hill for the sole purpose of a good deed. Visits to whorehouses by gentlemen interested only in reformation of fallen women were not unheard of. But such tales were more often told when a gentleman was confronted with the unfortunate need to explain one's presence at a brothel. When, a year later, Dana found himself in a precarious spot in the notorious Five Points, he realized "I could ill account for my being found in such a place."[16]

Dana said of "Kitty" that "had she been seduced by a man of wealth or gentility she would have been passed about as a kept mistress, for she was very good looking." It is doubtful that a visitor truly dedicated to improving the plight of prostitutes begins by searching for the prettiest woman. Dana was at least candid in describing the world of which he was a part: "How unjust . . . the world! . . . any . . . admired & successful strumpet . . . will be applauded & followed after & the world sees nothing but her grace & the 'poetry of motion'; but if to vice is added poverty & misfortune, the virtue of the world is stern & has no eye for pity."[17]

Dana continued his cruise of Halifax Hill, going to "a third & a fourth house, in which the "scenes varied between the two first I had seen, neither quite so bad as the second & neither superior to the first."[18] Dana later compared the ladies of Halifax unfavorably with those of Five Points. He found the girls of the Hill unappealing, "with one exception."

On the return to Boston there were rough seas that delighted Dana: "the worse the weather the better I felt." He arrived in Boston Harbor at daybreak in late July, and raced home unannounced. "It is 6½ A.M. as I pass the church." Dana ran up the stairs to meet a surprised Sarah. He was for the moment in the safe harbor of his marriage: "This is the true happiness of married life, when the fervor, the deferential address, & the sentiment & romance of courtship are not worn away. They never need be. If they are, it is the fault of one or both of the parties. There are married persons who are always lovers."[19]

But guilt, if not fault, plagued Dana. A week after his return from Halifax, Dana stood in an Andover cemetery where a plain marble marker read: "Sarah Woods, died September 3, 1836, aged 19 years." At fourteen, Sarah Woods had been infatuated with sixteen-year-old Dana when the suspended Harvard student was tutored by her brother Leonard. Sarah died two weeks before Dana returned from his voyage before the mast. Upon learning of the girl's death, Dana wrote a "formal letter of condolence" he believed appropriate for the death "of a young lady whom I had known for a year or two before I went to sea . . . yet whom I had no reason to suppose particularly attached to me." Dana received a reply from her family that profoundly altered him.

He was told that Sarah Woods had been interested in his voyage, but had never mentioned his name. In the delirium of her sickness she talked only of Dana. Upon recovering from the delirium, she asked her mother privately if she had spoken of Dana. Told that she had, Sarah "opened her whole heart to her mother." Dana learned that Sarah "prayed for me—for my safety . . . she said if the spirits of those in the other world . . . watched over those in this & God would permit it for her, her prayer would be that she might watch over me, keeping me from sin, influencing me toward God & holy things."

There could have been no event more designed to shake Dana to his core. Characteristically, Dana contrasted idealized female virtue with his own conduct. The deceased girl represented "delicacy . . . & purity" while Dana "fell into [sailors'] ways. When I did, I was as bad as any of them. Not a man in my ship was more guilty in God's sight than myself." For several days after receipt of the letter, Dana could find no relief "but in solitude and tears." Dana believed "that God had nicely attuned this last call to all my feelings." "In time, I bowed to God. I gave myself up to him & sought pardon through Christ as the appointed way & by uniting myself with the visible Church." Dana never abandoned the path he believed religion set for him, but he well knew when he deviated. At the girl's grave "a sickness was over me the whole afternoon . . . What a poor creature of vanity, pride & degrading sinfulness am I."[20]

Less than a month after his invigorating trip to Halifax, Dana felt as weak in body as in spirit: "Find my strength & activity decreasing which will never do." Dana joined "Sheridan's gymnasium and boxing school." He reported spending an hour "sparring & exercising" on the last day of August, but never records another appearance at the gym.[21]

It was not exercise Dana needed as much as a break from the grueling law practice that kept him in court or at his office from early morning to late evening. His stamina was prodigious, as his shipmates had learned, but even Dana could falter under the pace he set for himself. The summer of 1842 was the template for a pattern Dana was to repeat throughout his life. He would work to the point of exhaustion and then abruptly seek the sanctuary of a voyage or wilderness trek that removed him from work, family—and Boston's Brahmins.

But Dana sought no such isolation from the best society in his conventional life. A November evening in 1842 found him dining at Ticknor's Beacon Hill mansion with, among others, the Spanish ambassador, Josiah Quincy Jr., William Prescott, and "Longfellow, the poet." Dana's presence was evidence that Boston's aristocracy did not hold Dana's representation of sailors against him. For host George Ticknor, it was enough that Dana was wellborn and presumably faithful to Brahmin political orthodoxy. Ticknor made sure Dana understood what that meant: "Mr. Ticknor said . . . he had always thought [Daniel] Webster the greatest man he ever saw."[22]

New Year's Day 1843 brought Dana a gift of a gold pencil case from Sarah with a note: "For my dearest, to use always for the sake of his wife."[23] Dana's lecture circuit now included New York City, where in January he spoke to an audience he estimated at 2,000. The next night he paid a series of calls upon the city's social elite, starting with the elderly daughters of "the great John Jay," first chief justice of the U.S. Supreme Court. "They are intelligent, religious, & well bred ladies of the old school & spend a large fortune charitably." Dana called on Daniel Lord, "the most prosperous lawyer in N.Y." Lord was to be one of the appellate attorneys Dana would oppose in the most momentous case heard by the Supreme Court during the Civil War. But Dana's first impression was that Lord "appears to be only a little, dapper, talking, smart man of an ordinary range of mind."[24]

Dana's visit to New York City's most successful lawyer was the fourth social call he made that evening, but as he walked down Broadway "the name of Anthony St. struck me, & I had a sudden desire to seek that sink of iniquity & filth, the Five Points."[25] The notorious area was rivaled only by London's East End for crime, disease, and prostitution. Charles Dickens, who saw it within months of Dana's visit, wrote, "Debauchery has made the very houses prematurely old."[26]

The risk for Dana could scarcely have been greater. Unlike when he visited Halifax Hill, Dana had not changed into his sailor's garb of peacoat, old trousers, and watch cap. He was still dressed in the attire of a gentleman making social calls in New York's most exclusive neighborhood. Dana had more than fifty dollars in his pocket (the going rate for a Five Points prostitute was fifty cents). He carried a gold watch, a gold double eyeglass, and the gold pencil case from Sarah.

Dana had no weapon, "not even a cane." "I might be looked upon as an object of plunder," Dana correctly calculated. Dana's explanation for risking life, limb, and reputation demonstrated that he knew the limits of his calculation: "When adventure is . . . uppermost, we seldom weigh chances." Dana ducked into a small house, "it being comparatively early & people passing in the street." Judging from a voice and face that one of the two women in the house was "rather young," Dana noted, he "stopped in almost before I knew what I was doing." Dana's account again portrays his visit as solely to satisfy curiosity. His response—"What do you ask?"—to the girl's question of what he would pay, elicited the observation that she appeared ready to lower her price below a half-dollar.[27]

Whether the bargain was consummated or not, Dana soon realized "it was getting late, I had no more time to waste, & I felt a little uneasy in my situation." Dana began retracing his steps back to Broadway past "close, obscure, & suspicious looking places of every description." He observed "a great many girls of from 8 to 10 to 12 or 14 years of age in the street & going in & out of the houses."

It was but a few blocks from "these dark, filthy, violent & degraded regions" to Ninth Street where "the servant opened for me the parlor door." There, "seated round a pleasant fire, sat a family solely of women, one the beautiful mother of five daughters, all of whom were yet to try the world or be tried by it." Dana, overwhelmed, "felt as though I was wandering in a dream, made up of strange extremes & unnatural contrast." His conscience was troubled by more than the contrasts within society. Dana believed to a moral certainty that an all-seeing God knew "I have done things worse in me."[28]

In his more despondent moods, Dana ascribed his perceived moral failings to his life at sea. But nothing made him more alive than word of his old ship and shipmates. In early May 1843, "on coming to my office, I found [in the shipping news] 'the *Alert* from California, San Diego 125 days.' I hastened down to the wharf." Dana immediately went aboard. The rigging, spars, blocks, and paint were all as he remembered, though the *Alert*'s voyage had been more than three years long. The crew had all returned "except one who was drowned at Santa Barbara."

In the forecastle, Dana found his old berth. The sailor who occupied it "insisted upon my accepting from him two shells which he got at Monterey." Dana was even more grateful for information about the West Coast. Two crew members returned with Dana to his office "& we spent several hours talking over California." Monterey had "increased very considerably and was an important town." A former shipmate married into a Spanish family and quit the sea, finding "he could earn a living in California much more easily." The greatest change was in "St. Francisco" where "there [had been] but one house between the Mission and the Presidio. Now there were more than one hundred." Dana's exploit of dangling from a cliff to salvage hides was well remembered. A sailor told Dana he had gone to San Juan Capistrano "& saw the bank wh. I went down for the hides & told me that the stake was standing in its place still to which we fastened the rope."[29]

Sarah did not welcome a Dana stirred by news of California. On the first day of August in 1843, Dana took a long walk with his wife. "S. talked upon serious matters & we agreed that we had been too negligent of them lately. Spoke of more attentive reading of the scriptures & of self-examination daily. Determined that we would aid one another in aiming at a better life." It was Dana's twenty-eighth birthday "but I mentioned to no one, except S. for birthdays are not pleasant occasions for hilarity with me."[30]

In fact, the month of August was difficult for Dana. He had embarked upon the voyage that was to change his life in August 1834, and a repressed longing seemed to arise when the anniversary of his odyssey approached. His decision to go to sea had been motivated, in part, by his need to escape the suffocating atmosphere of family. When the emotion resurfaced, Dana's relationship with Sarah was complicated by a mixture of duty, devotion, and guilt.

In August 1843 Dana returned to Boston from Hartford, leaving behind "my wife & child, the dearest things I have." Sarah often extended her Hartford visits, where the company of her mother, sisters, and aunts led her to prefer it to Boston. Her absence distressed Dana, who recognized that his behavior contributed to their separation. "Read & meditated at night & made efforts to live a more religious life. My loneliness always helps me in this."[31]

But meditation did little to lift Dana's spirits, and once again in August he found himself "so much worn out that I determined on the spur of the moment to go at once to the Isle of Shoals." Unlike his trip to Halifax the previous August, Dana knew he would not be tempted by evening diversions. On the island on which he was to stay, only one of its twenty houses took in guests. "You will not stay here more than a day or two," said his fisherman host.

Dana was there a week. Once again the sea air gave Dana "a glorious appetite . . . I ate large meals . . . apple pie, fried fish, cake, hot bread." In the evenings he "stayed out until between 8 & 9 listening to the roar of breakers upon the rocks, watching the beautiful revolving lights of the light house on the neighboring island, & thinking not a little how much I could enjoy it with S. by my side."[32]

Dana returned home at the end of August "much burned, roughened & improved in healthiness of appearance." He entered his house "glad . . . [to] see the places made dear to me by so many months of happiness & sanctified by the relations of a husband & a father." Yet, said Dana, "it was solitary and somewhat sad." Alone in his rented house, Dana "met with an affliction of spirit." Sarah and little Sally were still in Hartford. He acknowledged his depression ("I know it will die away") but could do nothing to alleviate it. His journal revealed the depth of his anguish: "Come to me S., my comforter, for I am alone & none can help me."[33]

Dana's August sickness extended into September. Sarah delayed her return to Boston, excusing herself, as she frequently did, on account of unspecified illness. When she did agree to come home, a misdirected letter delayed her arrival. Dana waited eagerly at the train depot but there was "no wife or child for me." Dana's melancholia deepened as he internalized his conflicting values of independence and duty. "Could it be possible that if independent, I could lead a more satisfactory life . . . & have my soul . . . more alive?" Dana's work offered no relief. He "loathed the business & petty things of the world." But duty allowed no escape. "I worked with tears in my eyes. At noon could not endure the dullness of another half day & went out to Cambridge."[34]

That evening Dana "felt suddenly relieved & happy." The change was "as sudden as the relief from bodily sickness." He wrote to Sarah "in a delightful state of mind." A Saturday in early autumn found Dana writing in his journal while "S. was trimming & watering her garden & little Sally playing about her." At Sarah's insistence, the couple's day started in religious reading. He noted "S. does the same but separately."[35]

There appeared to be separation in their social engagements as well. Dana was pleased when he learned that the eminently respectable ladies Mrs. Sedgwick and Mrs. Channing each praised Sarah for "her manners, the grace she showed in little things, her taste in dress, her motion." Mrs. Channing added that Sarah looked "high born." It was, said Dana, "music to my ear & my soul."[36] But the ladies had seen Sarah in Hartford.

At a reception for Dickens, Sarah noted that Mr. and Mrs. Ticknor "talked to me somewhat."[37] But when Dana dined at "Mr. Ticknor's" on Beacon Hill, there was no mention of Sarah, nor was there when, a few days later, he had tea at the mansion of the wealthy R. B. Forbes. She was not present at "a superb party at David Sears' . . . house, the most tasteful and sumptuous in Boston." There, twenty-eight-year-old Dana was quite taken with Jane Norton, one of the daughters in his "ideal" family: "I was very near [to] calling [her] my dear Miss Norton . . . we talked pleasantly together . . . she refusing to dance, as she said, for me."[38]

Husband and wife were together when visiting Dana relatives, but after one such call on a Dana aunt in Cambridgeport, Sarah could not be coaxed to go with Dana to a scene "exciting in the extreme." Boston Harbor had frozen over. Dana joined "people of every description, some of whom had not been on skates for 20 years." Dana skated "as far as the ice would allow," from Long Wharf to within a mile of Long Island Light, a distance of five miles. The next morning "being so much pleased with my excursion on the ice, I went again . . . & skated down as far as before."[39] If he did his religious reading first, there was no mention of it.

The Boston winter held no such charms for Sarah. With Dana preparing to leave for Washington by way of New York to lecture, she determined to go to Hartford even if it meant leaving eighteen-month-old Sally with the housekeeper in Boston. Dana reluctantly yielded to "Sarah's health & her strong desire to see [Hartford] & make a change after her long winter." When the couple departed, "poor little [Sally waved] her hand for 'bye bye.'" The Danas traveled first to Hartford and then to the nearby village of Wethersfield. There to greet Sarah were her mother, sisters, aunts, and brother-in-law. "I stayed but a few hours," Dana noted.[40]

Dana was soon in New York City, where he took a room at the Astor House, then "shaved, dressed, & bought a new hat." His hosts were the socially elite Sedgwicks to whom the Dana family was distantly related. Dana was struck by the beauty of one of the daughters, who "will be a woman to die for, a woman of sentiment & passion."[41] It was late when Dana returned to the Astor after dinner with the Sedgwicks, but Dana put on his "rough coat & cap & walked about the city."

It was not a random stroll: "Turned down Anthony St. to 'Five Points.'" This time—free of gentlemen's attire—Dana could more openly engage the girls: "Here & there are the signs of great previous beauty." One girl who "must have been under 18" gave Dana "an inquiring glance that said 'Do you want me?'" In Dana's account, he curbed his desire, "knowing it was but a vain curiosity & tending to no good." When some sailors arrived and called for drinks, he slipped out. Dana saw something in the gutter of Anthony Street, "which I found to be a man." The man lay amid "the filth the pigs wallow in," and Dana pulled him onto the sidewalk. "I stopped a young lad with a cigar in his mouth to inquire the nearest way to the Astor. He was well dressed . . . but too drunk to understand me."[42]

Dana reached his hotel "late but safely." Sunday morning, Dana's thoughts were still of Five Points. "I had great curiosity to see how [the prostitutes] appeared & what they did in the day time especially on the Sabbath." But Dana checked himself: "I had already allowed my curiosity, *my passion for seeing human life in its extreme developments* to lead me too far."[43] The emphasis was Dana's. It was passion that Dana sought to masquerade. He knew that "if a man wishes to deal faithfully with his heart by pen & ink, let him first (or he will lie in secret) make sure no eye can see it but his own."[44]

But Dana lifted his mask enough to tell us who he might be. Describing a young man from Virginia, whom he found "striking and interesting," Dana could see he lacked "New England prudence" and that his "want of self-control [made] him unsafe." Dana "conceived a sort of wild attachment for him." The young man had recently wed. "People wonder that . . . a young, tender retiring girl should have married such a hair brain. I do not, at all. He might be loved with romantic devotion."[45]

8

THE GREAT MAN OF THE AGE

For a young man of romantic temperament, Dana had an extraordinary capacity to channel his energies to the business at hand. Within a year of publication of *Two Years Before the Mast,* Dana wrote *The Seaman's Friend,* a compendium of practical seamanship, nautical custom, and maritime law.[1] Complete with a "Dictionary of Sea Terms," the book became the standard treatise on seamanship in America and England, where it was published as the *Seaman's Manual.* Dana went from "hapless and pitiable" landsman to indispensable guide for sailors in little more than a half dozen years.

Dana's manual included a cautionary note on mutiny: "In all these cases . . . of mutiny . . . it is to be remembered that the acts are excusable if done from a sufficient justifying cause. . . . But an excuse of this kind is received with great caution and the crew should be well assured of the necessity of such a step, before taking it, since they run a great risk in so interfering."[2] That risk was made real in 1842 when Captain Alexander Slidell Mackenzie hanged three sailors aboard the U.S.S. *Somers*.

"All the world is talking about the *Somers* mutiny and the execution of Spencer," Dana noted.[3] If not all the world, Americans certainly were, because one of the hanged sailors was midshipman Phillip Spencer, son of President Tyler's secretary of war, John Spencer. The 266-ton brig *Somers* was returning to New York from Africa when Captain Mackenzie heard rumors of mutiny among the hundred-man crew. After consultation with his seven officers (one of whom was Herman Melville's cousin), the captain was persuaded that Spencer and two accomplices were determined to lead an armed revolt. On December 1, 1842, the three men were hanged from the yardarm. The public outcry over the hangings stemmed from the landsman's view that the captain could have confined the suspected mutineers until the ship reached port.

Upon the return of the *Somers* to New York, the secretary of the navy ordered Captain Mackenzie to be tried by court-martial for willful murder. Dana attended the court-martial, where he was impressed with the demeanor of Captain Mackenzie, "a modest man . . . entirely without any swagger." A visit to the U.S.S. *Somers* made an even stronger impression: "One needs to see this vessel to appreciate the defenseless situation of the officers."[4] Dana transformed his impressions into a widely published letter providing a vivid picture of a vessel where "half a dozen resolute conspirators could have swept the decks and thrown overboard all that opposed them before aid could come from below." His opinion had weight because seamen and readers of *Two Years Before the Mast* knew Dana opposed "despotic use of power at sea."[5] The court-martial exonerated Captain Mackenzie, and Dana's piece was instrumental in diminishing adverse response to the verdict.

Dana was at an age where he readily ascribed nobility to men and their deeds. (Captain Mackenzie was given an elaborate testimonial in Boston after his acquittal.) Experience would soon enough impart its lesson that greatness is a complicated concept, but on June 17, 1843, the idealistic Dana sprang to the window eager for "the great man." Thousands were pouring into Boston to witness the dedication of the Bunker Hill Monument. Dana was delighted by the procession from Boston Common, "a glorious pageantry which rarely in one man's life can be furnished."[6] But what he most looked forward to was the chance to hear his political idol, Daniel Webster.

Although President John Tyler was also to speak at the ceremony, it was the incomparable oratory of Webster that drew citizens from all over New England. Indeed, Webster's oratorical reputation and political path had been forged at Bunker Hill, when, in 1825 on the fiftieth anniversary of the battle, the young congressman declared, "That these twenty-four states are one country. . . . Let our object be *Our Country, Our Whole Country, and Nothing but Our Country.*"[7]

In 1827 the Whig-controlled Massachusetts legislature sent Webster to the Senate (senators were not chosen by popular vote until passage of the Seventeenth Amendment in 1913). They did so at the behest of the "Boston Associates," a group of elite Bostonians who supplemented Webster's income over the next quarter century. It was "a mutually beneficial arrangement."[8] The gifted Webster was a powerful advocate for the Whig Party and the economic interests of Boston's Brahmins. In 1841 Webster resigned his Senate seat to take a position even more valuable to the establishment—secretary of state for President William Henry Harrison.

The Whig Party had swept to victory in 1840 when voters, reeling from the economic panics of 1837 and 1839, rejected Democrat Martin van Buren's bid for a second term. (A Whig campaign slogan called the president "Martin van Ruin.") It was an even more memorable slogan—"Tippecanoe and Tyler too"—that enabled General Harrison to capitalize on his exploits as an "Indian-fighter." Webster had turned down the offer to be Harrison's running mate, but he and the Boston Associates welcomed his appointment to the cabinet's most powerful position.

Webster volunteered to write the president's inaugural address but Harrison demurred, saying he had written his own. Webster asked to see a draft and was appalled at both its length and its text (Webster told a friend that the draft had no more to do with the United States "than a chapter in the Koran").[9] Undaunted, on a damp and chilly March 4, 1841, William Henry Harrison gave the longest inaugural address in the history of the American presidency. One month later, the sixty-eight-year-old Harrison, the oldest president up to that time, was dead of pneumonia. John Tyler became the first vice president to succeed to the presidency upon the death of the incumbent and, at fifty-one, then the youngest president ever to hold the office.

Tyler's single-minded devotion to his own election prospects was the only constant of his presidency. When every Whig in Tyler's cabinet (save Webster) resigned in protest of his vetoes of bank bills, Tyler replaced many of them with states' rights Democrats. By the time of President Tyler's visit to Boston in June 1843, a caucus of congressional Whigs had expelled Tyler from the Whig Party and the Whigs had lost their House majority in the midterm elections. Webster was beset with criticism from Whigs, who believed he should have resigned the office of secretary of state in protest of Tyler's fiscal policies and courtship of Democrats. Webster finally did so in the spring of 1843, shortly before the president was to come to Boston to dedicate the Bunker Hill Monument.[10]

The impending visit of the slave-owning Tyler prompted meetings of abolitionists. In early June 1843, Dana went to hear William Lloyd Garrison speak at an abolitionist meeting in Boston. The establishment's opinion of abolitionists, and most particularly William Lloyd Garrison, had been made abundantly clear nearly a decade before when the "Garrison mob" had come close to lynching Garrison. The abolitionist's antislavery newspaper, the *Liberator,* began publication in Boston in 1831 with his famous declaration of editorial policy: "I will be as harsh as truth, and as uncompromising as justice. On this subject, I do not wish to think, or speak or write with moderation . . . I will not retreat a single inch. *And I Will Be Heard.*"[11]

By the summer of 1835, Boston's aristocracy was sufficiently alarmed to organize a meeting at Faneuil Hall to denounce abolitionist agitators. The meeting was presided over by the mayor. Abbott Lawrence and Harrison Gray Otis, with whom Dana and Sumner were to dine at the Lord Morpeth dinner a few years later, were among the principal organizers and speakers. The incendiary rhetoric alarmed Garrison, who foresaw trouble ahead.

On October 21, 1835, an unruly gathering of "gentlemen of property and standing" stood outside the Boston office of the *Liberator.* They were ostensibly there to protest the rumored appearance of English abolitionist George Thompson, but upon learning that Garrison was in the building, the mob called for Garrison. He was seized when he attempted to escape through a back door. Garrison was roughed up, but before worse could be done he managed to get to nearby City Hall. The mayor had no intention of sheltering Garrison and spirited him to a safer venue—the Leverett Street Jail. Garrison was released the next day.[12]

Two of the abolitionist's earliest supporters were young lawyers with impeccable Brahmin credentials. Samuel Sewall—whose namesake ancestor had apologized for taking part in the Salem Witch trials and had authored an antislavery tract in 1700—was at Garrison's side during the fracas and remained a staunch ally. Ellis Gray Loring, descendant of another distinguished family, joined Sewall at the 1831 founding of the New England Anti-Slavery Society.[13] But their early embrace of abolitionism and Garrison was odious to proper Boston.

Dana concurred with the far more prevalent Brahmin opinion that Garrison was "a fanatic by constitution and hater of everything established and traditional." He conceded the infamous agitator had "logic and force," but Dana thought "dreadful" the "heated, narrow minded, self-willed ,excited, un-christian, radical energies set to work upon a cause which is good, if rightly managed, but which [abolitionists] have made a hot bed."[14]

Dana was especially dismayed by "two conceited shallow-pated negro youths . . . among the chief speakers . . . spoiled by the notice taken of them & evidently had but little strength of mind by nature."[15] One was Frederick Douglass. In less than a decade Dana and Douglass would be sharing a speaker's platform at Faneuil Hall.

Dana at least went to hear abolitionists. Other up-and-coming Brahmin lawyers did not. Garrison was later to say of Charles Sumner and the many abolitionist meetings held in Boston in the early days of the antislavery movement: "Mr. Sumner's presence was never recognized at any one of them. Why he never came—at least among the curious to hear—I know not."[16] Despite Sumner's instructive absence from meetings where attendance might be misconstrued as support for abolitionists, Dana went to another antislavery meeting two days after hearing Garrison for the first time. Dana described abolitionist Wendell Phillips—a Brahmin peer—as "a gentleman & scholar" although "exciting the blacks to insurrection and war."[17] Phillips was designated by the New England Anti-Slavery Society to meet with President Tyler and call upon him to free his slaves. Tyler refused to meet Phillips.

Brahmin Boston's distaste for Tyler owed more to his failure to adopt the Whig economic agenda than his ownership of slaves, but Dana observed a wider public antipathy. The president's horse-drawn coach in the procession to Bunker Hill prompted "not a sound, nor a cheer from the great multitude. . . . When the carriage appeared, he was seen to be standing up & bowing on one side & the other, but not an answering sound."[18] President Tyler, said John Quincy Adams, had "all the interests and passions and vices of slavery . . . with talents not above mediocrity."[19]

The thousands gathered for the Bunker Hill celebration were not there to hear the mediocre Tyler. Dana stood on top of a shed to get a glimpse of "the great man of the age, with a voice, action & presence almost god-like." Webster's second Bunker Hill address was no match for his first, but that mattered little. Dana could not make out Webster's words, but "it was enough . . . to see Webster's face, the style & grandeur of his action & to hear the tones of his voice without attending to the meaning of his words."[20]

Dana's idolization of the sixty-one-year-old Webster was not exceptional. The phrase "godlike Daniel" was already in vogue. Even if one did not go that far, something of his impact was captured by one who upon hearing Webster exclaimed, "He is a small cathedral by himself!"[21] For Dana, who devoutly believed in the greatness of Daniel Webster, the celebration was a glorious day. Dana saw no need for Webster to reprise his famous reply to Hayne made in the 1830 Senate debate when he declared, "I regard slavery as one of the greatest of evils, both moral and political."[22] In 1843 Dana was as comfortable as any other Brahmin whose antislavery principles were yet to be tested.

But there was no telling how an individual would respond when antislavery sentiment and self-interest collided. Even the pure-hearted Longfellow dropped his antislavery poems from an anthology of his poetry when his Philadelphia publisher advised him that including the poems would diminish sales in the South.[23] The response depended on character. Seventy-five-year-old John Quincy Adams had a much less exalted view of the "great man of the age" than did twenty-eight-year-old Dana: "What a burlesque upon [Bunker Hill] is an oration of Daniel Webster and a pilgrimage of John Tyler and his cabinet of slave-drivers, to desecrate the solemnity by their presence . . . Daniel Webster is a heartless traitor to the cause of human freedom."[24]

In early spring 1844, twenty-eight-year-old Dana made his first visit to Washington, D.C. Dana's lecture circuit was widening, and an invitation to speak in Baltimore enabled him to plan a trip that included admission to practice before the U.S. Supreme Court.

The train to Baltimore provided startling contrasts with Boston. Tobacco spitting was not a new sight, but Dana was amazed at its prevalence as he traveled south. Even late at night "the constant spitting could be heard, now at one end of the cars then at the other, like the irregular firing of Militia." On the train, "waiters were black & white indiscriminately." In Baltimore there were more blacks than in Boston, but "whites were engaged with them in the performance of menial duties." Blacks and whites worked together digging cellars, working on the wharves, and waiting tables. Dana noted "a white man . . . blacked my boots at the hotel."[25]

In Washington, Dana paid a courtesy call on John Quincy Adams. The former president, now a member of Congress, "had told me he wished to see me and talk with me, yet he had nothing to say." After thirty minutes of near silence, Dana rose to leave. Adams clasped Dana's hand and said, "Your grandfather was my friend and patron when I was setting out on my life and a friend of my father." Dana thought the "awkward" Adams "seemed to feel something when he said this."[26]

Dana was equally disappointed by the location of the U.S. Supreme Court in the basement of the Capitol: "I felt indignant, at first, that the highest court of the nation should have so inferior a place, but I found the judges liked it, as they preferred to have no crowd in the galleries for the lawyers to talk to."[27] Dana's admission to practice before the court was moved by prominent New York City lawyer Daniel Lord.

Dana watched Rufus Choate and John J. Crittenden, a Kentucky lawyer well known for his appellate advocacy, argue a case before the court. Dana was amused when Justice Story and Choate sparred over the meaning of a classical reference in the poetry of Alexander Pope. He doubted Crittenden knew the allusion, but was impressed with his "natural, frank, and Western manner." Dana's exposure to "the southern & western men" prompted him to muse on their differences from "those of the New England race." Unlike many in Brahmin Boston, "they are not aiming after a precocious & half attainable gentility." It was refreshing to meet men who "think for themselves . . . speak for themselves . . . dress to suit themselves & not because such & such is the way of such & such people in this & that circle."[28]

His idealized conception of such a man lived in his devotion to the memory of George Washington. Dana's grandfather, Frances Dana, had been sent to Valley Forge by the Continental Congress as a member of a "Committee of Inquiry." Washington correctly suspected that some members sought to remove him from command, but Francis Dana became a fervent admirer. According to a story long repeated in the Dana family, when President Washington visited Harvard, he said to Frances Dana—alluding to Valley Forge—"Mr. Dana, we have seen worse times."[29]

Dana was determined to make a pilgrimage to the home of his hero. It was to be another fifteen years before Mount Vernon was bought to preserve its historical significance, but a distant relative, Reverend Charles Dana, knew the house well. On a spring day in 1844 the two men set out on horseback through "ancient forest, primeval, untouched with its dead silence, except when broken by the loud & wild cawing of the crow."

The wooden mansion had "turned to a venerable gray color for want of paint." Reverend Dana "opened the door without ceremony" and went in search of the family. Dana stood in a vestibule filled with "the simple relics of a mixed military, agricultural, and sporting taste." He stepped out on a piazza where "the noble Potomac, wide & deep, with waves like a small sea, was rolling almost at my feet. . . . While I was wrapped in the spirit of the place, a small voice reached my ear & a little black boy with a pleasant intelligent face told me to please sit."

The proprietor of the once great estate soon appeared. John Augustin Washington, the great-grandnephew of George Washington, was twenty-two. Dana liked him immediately. Their bond further strengthened when he learned that Washington's first child, a daughter, had just been born. Dana thought his host was "probably . . . a good specimen of the Virginia gentlemen, who lived quietly on their estates." John Augustin spoke "with some feeling" about Virginians whom he thought reflected "degeneracy in the tone & character of the Virginia gentleman."

Dana was stuck by "the custom of calling female members of the family by the first name & usually by nicknames, as Nelly, Polly, Nannie & the like [and] in the presence of strangers went no further than to say 'Miss Nelly', 'Miss Nannie', etc." Dana took leave of his host with "real regret. I could not forebear expressing . . . my hope that his child would . . . be . . . a dear companion to him."[30] John Augustin Washington was to die on Valley Mountain, Virginia, an officer in the Confederate Army killed in a skirmish with Union troops.

Dana made another stop at an Alexandria home where the guests "were of all the old federal stock." He was particularly impressed with an Army captain who graduated first in his class from West Point and was the new son-in-law of Major Custis of Arlington: "Mr. Robt. Lee has a very high reputation for intelligence & superiority of character." Dana rode through Alexandria, where he saw the Armfield slave market and slave jail. It sobered him: "After seeing the fair side of the 'patriarchal system' at such places as Mt. Vernon . . . we need to see the other consequence of the system in the slave jail & slave market, the shipping of negroes to the southern market & the like, to restore the proper balance to our feelings & opinions."[31]

Dana's admiration of the Virginia that produced George Washington did not extend to the Virginia that produced John Tyler. He wrote enthusiastically to Sarah of his visit to Mount Vernon, "You can see I am quite insane about Virginia." But, added Dana, "it has a dark side . . . and the issues of its life are uncertain."[32] Neither Dana nor the country at large knew that President Tyler had secretly engaged in negotiations that would expand the dark side and ultimately confront Americans with the uncertain issue of the life of the Union itself.

Unable to cobble together a coalition of Whigs and Democrats for his domestic initiatives, Tyler devised a new political strategy he hoped would pave the way for election to the presidency in his own right in 1844. He decided to annex Texas. Slaveholding Texas had been an independent republic since 1836. Mexico—which itself had gained independence from Spain only in 1821—was compelled to grant Texas sovereignty after Sam Houston and his troops defeated Santa Anna and the Mexican Army at the battle of San Jacinto.

Tyler correctly calculated that Northern objection to the extension of slavery would be overwhelmed by public support for western expansion. His political strategy aligned with fellow slave owners who believed annexation would enhance the slave market while eliminating British antislavery interests in Texas. By early 1844, Daniel Webster's successor, Secretary of State Abel Upshur, had nearly completed negotiation of a secret treaty with the Republic of Texas. The secretary of state pledged to Texas negotiators that President Tyler would use military force to repel a Mexican invasion, even if the event should happen before congressional ratification of annexation. With that commitment, the representatives of the Republic of Texas agreed to execute an annexation agreement.[33]

In the early evening of February 28, 1844, Dana and his Washington host, Rufus Griswold, were admiring the view of the Potomac River from south of "The President's House." Griswold expressed his regret that Dana had not arrived in Washington in time to join a large party that included President Tyler and members of his cabinet aboard the U.S.S. *Princeton,* now sailing on the Potomac River. Dana very much wished to see the Navy's newest warship and especially the heavy gun "Peacemaker" designed by the ship's captain, Robert F. Stockton. Griswold promised to get Dana an invitation to visit the ship the next day.

"Just at this moment," wrote Dana, "we saw a cloud of smoke on the river . . . & supposed it to be from the *Princeton.*"[34] It was. Captain Stockton had brought guests on deck to demonstrate the new weapon. The president remained below to toast those still at the table, but others, including the secretary of state and the secretary of the navy, went to see the gun in action. The "Peacemaker" exploded, killing both. Six others were also killed and many were injured, including Stockton.

The tragedy shook Washington, not least because it was seen as further evidence of "the ill luck that has attended this John Tyler from the first."[35] Tyler was already known as "His Accidency" because of his accession to the presidency upon the death of Harrison. Tyler's wife died shortly after he became president, and one of those killed in the *Princeton* explosion was David Gardiner, father of Julia Gardiner, whom Tyler was engaged to marry.

Dana thought Tyler's tact to be as bad as his luck. He was appalled when the president's message to Congress about the tragedy "had the bad taste of ending with an expression of undiminished confidence in the boat [and] her armament."[36] The message may have been evidence of Tyler's vulgarity, but it was also proof of his single-mindedness. The display of the *Princeton*'s new weaponry was intended to demonstrate Tyler's willingness to use force in any confrontation with Mexico over Texas.

More evidence of Tyler's relentless focus came days later when he appointed John C. Calhoun to succeed the deceased secretary of state, Upsham. Less than two weeks after the deaths aboard the *Princeton,* Secretary of State Calhoun and Texas negotiators signed a secret treaty of annexation. Word of the negotiations had begun to circulate in various press accounts, but the provisions of the treaty were closely guarded and Tyler intended to keep it that way until the Senate ratified it.

To Tyler's surprise—if not to South Carolinian Calhoun's—the provisions of the treaty were leaked to newspapers before the Senate began debate. The most substantive terms of the annexation agreement (that Texas would become a U.S. territory eligible for future admission to the Union as one or more states, and that the federal government would assume $10 million of Texas indebtedness in exchange for Texas public lands) were far less controversial than Calhoun's letter to the British minister to the United States, declaring that Texas was being acquired to prevent Britain from interfering with slavery.

Tyler was later to reflect that Calhoun's letter explicitly describing the Texas annexation as a pro-slavery initiative undermined Tyler's bid to be elected president in his own right. Calhoun was too sophisticated a politician not to have foreseen that result, but his principal objective was to compel Whig Henry Clay and Democrat Martin Van Buren to take positions on the proposed treaty. Each announced their opposition. The proposed treaty was, in fact, soundly rejected by the Senate in June 1844, but Calhoun's letter achieved his aim of making Texas annexation the most significant issue of the 1844 presidential campaign.[37]

The first casualty of Calhoun's strategy was Van Buren. The former president's opposition to annexation was essential to retain his support among Northern Democrats. But his stance made him unacceptable to Southern slaveholders and—of greater consequence—cost him the support of his patron Andrew Jackson, who embraced annexation of Texas as critical to America's westward expansion. At a deadlocked Democratic Convention, James Knox Polk, who had recently lost an election to be governor of Tennessee and was angling for the vice presidential nomination, emerged as the party's unlikely nominee.

Conventional political wisdom held that the obscure Polk had no chance of defeating the far better known Whig candidate, Senator Henry Clay of Kentucky. But Clay's campaign was bedeviled by the Texas issue. A Clay statement that he might favor annexation of Texas in the future did not have the political benefit Clay intended. It made little difference to Southerners but some Northern Whigs—alienated by the statement—supported the Liberty Party candidacy of abolitionist James G. Birney. Although Birney received just over 2 percent of the presidential vote nationally, his candidacy cost Clay the state of New York. When New York declared for Polk, Clay had lost his last best chance to win the presidency and voters had elected the first "dark horse" candidate ever to be president of the United States.[38]

Democrat Polk's stunning victory did not extend to Massachusetts, where the Whigs remained dominant. Daniel Webster campaigned for Henry Clay, though much to Clay's consternation, he seldom mentioned his old rival by name. The unanticipated victory of James Polk dismayed

Boston Whigs, but they were most troubled by the loss of Whig majorities in Congress. Without Webster in either Congress or the administration, the Boston establishment lacked a figure powerful enough to look after their interests.

Rufus Choate, selected by Boston Whigs to succeed to Webster's seat in the Senate when Webster was appointed secretary of state by William Henry Harrison in 1841, wished to return to his law practice. Webster, deeply in debt, was less enamored with earning a living as a lawyer. He informed David Sears, who inquired of his interest in returning to the Senate, "I should prefer suitable public employment, to returning to the bar at my age."[39] But, added Webster, it would require a financial sacrifice that he was reluctant to make.

Wealthy Brahmins rose to the occasion. A "subscription" of $100,000 was raised by the "Boston Associates"—a group that included, almost without exception, every leading Boston banker, manufacturer, and merchant. The Appletons, Lowells, Quincys, and Cabots all subscribed. David Sears wrote Webster a letter—as self-serving as untrue—advising him that the fund was created "without your sanction or knowledge." But there could be no doubt that Sears spoke for Boston's aristocracy when he stated the money was "evidence of their grateful sense of the valuable services you have rendered."[40]

It was unclear to Brahmin Boston what services Dana might be prepared to render on behalf of Boston's Whigs. In the 1844 presidential campaign, Dana made brief remarks on behalf of Henry Clay at a Whig meeting in Cambridge, the "first political speech of any kind I ever made."[41] Dana did not conceive of his speeches as testing the political waters, but if he was not thinking of himself as a potential politician, others were. Webster returned to the Senate. Choate—never enamored of political life—returned to full-time practice of law. In October 1845 Dana received a visit from P. W. Chandler, a Whig political emissary, with an inquiry that was bound to come to a rising young lawyer with impeccable Brahmin credentials: Would Dana be interested in running for office?

Of all the lessons Dana drew from the life of Washington, none had a greater impact on his future than his hero's disdain for political parties. Though Dana blamed Democrats Jefferson, Jackson, and Van Buren for the rise of the spoils system that rewarded party loyalty, he acknowledged that "the Whigs of 1840 were afraid to . . . disavow[it] & . . . when in power they carried out as far as any before . . . now . . . [it has] become the standing rule of practice in this country."[42]

Dana had witnessed the unhappy effect of patronage over proficiency when he met the lighthouse keeper at the Isle of Shoals. Dana hoped to talk of the sea, but the keeper "always went back to his one subject." He owed his job to the Portsmouth collector of customs who had just been replaced by a Tyler appointee. It was unclear to the lighthouse keeper (and not only to him) whether the president was a Whig or a Democrat. Could Dana advise him "where to put his foot? What were the chances of Clay, Calhoun, & Van Buren?"[43] The keeper could not support his family if he lost his position.

Several months later the lighthouse keeper came to Dana's office: "Poor fellow! He has been turned out of office, but worse than all he seems to have lost his integrity & self-respect." The former keeper asked Dana to vouch for him as a Democrat but "this he said in a low tone & no part of this did he look me in the face, for he knew very well that I knew he was a Whig." Dana promised a letter testifying to the man's capable discharge of his duties, but added he would "say nothing about the political part of the matter, for I detested this ruinous system which was corrupting the political morals of our republic."[44]

The Whig emissary, Chandler, began by explaining that if Dana were interested in running for office, a nomination for an open seat in the Massachusetts legislature could be arranged. He hastened to add that it was not a safe seat, and would understand if Dana preferred to wait for a Whig nomination to a seat that provided more certainty of success.

Dana's response was enough to cool the ardor of any party official sent to recruit a "suitable" candidate. Dana declared he was not an "adventurer in politics" and would never stoop to "manage & select my times & seasons." If the Whig Party wished to nominate him, he would be honored, but he "should never allow myself to be considered as one of those who aim to secure a nomination." Dana added: "I would rather never hold an office than to leave it in the power of any man to say that I had avoided the risk of defeat from fear of personal consequences." The startled Whig Party emissary "said, at last, that he thought I was right to say nothing, but let it take its course."[45]

When Dana paid his visit to John Quincy Adams in Washington a year earlier, it was only by reminding himself of Adams's "independence

[and] fearlessness" that he could avoid his sense of Adams as a "wrong-headed man." Dana wrote, "How such a man could ever have been elected . . . I cannot imagine."[46] Imagining Dana's own electability was even more difficult. He heard nothing more from the Whig Party about running for political office.

9

THE INHERITANCE

"All his correction must come through bitter experience—because he always or most always thinks he is right," a Dana aunt wrote of her thirty-three-year-old nephew in the summer of 1848. She was reacting to the news of July 7, laconically noted by Dana in his journal: "Make my debut in political life as Chairman of the Free Soil meeting at the Tremont Temple."[1] Dana's aunt explained the decision to her sister: "You ought to know by this time that he is very ambitious, that he is determined to make the family name felt and he will sacrifice everything but principle to do it."[2]

To Brahmin Boston, "Free Soilers" (so named because they sought to keep newly acquired territories free of slavery) were a species of abolitionist. Whigs saw Dana's political debut as further evidence of his unfitness to represent Boston's establishment. In Dana's social circle "feeling ran high...and it ran all one way." The drawing rooms of Park and Beacon Streets, the bankers, the lawyers, the ship owners, the marine insurance companies, and the respectable merchants, "were Whigs almost to a man."[3] Dana was a Whig, too. But he was the wrong kind. "You may well imagine what a storm of protest was raised about my ears by the Cotton Whigs," Dana wrote to his brother.[4]

Dana was a "Conscience Whig." The phrase was used to describe Whigs whose antislavery views were anathema to the "Cotton Whigs" of establishment Boston. The latter preferred to be known as "Conservative Whigs," but "Cotton" rightly suggested their close affiliation with the Southern slave owners whose plantations produced the crop so essential to Northern textile manufacturers. Dana did not use the phrase "Conscience Whig" because he assumed the latter word embraced the former. When he stood to accept the chair of the Free Soil meeting, Dana described himself as "a Whig of the old school; I may say, without affectation, a highly conservative Whig."[5]

Prominent New York lawyer Daniel Lord later wrote Dana expressing astonishment that someone as "conservative" as Dana could be a Free Soiler. Dana responded that conservatism, properly defined, demanded "risking or sacrificing of material advantages." The "false conservatism" Dana saw among his peers was "a compound of selfishness and cowardice" that made "material *prosperity and ease* its pole star, [and] will do nothing and risk nothing for moral principle."

"A technical Abolitionist I am not," asserted Dana. But he knew he risked much by declaring himself a Free Soiler. Dana could not foresee the price he would pay, but he knew why he was prepared to make the sacrifice: "I am a Free Soiler by inheritance.... I am a Free Soiler because I am (who should not say so) of the stock of the old northern gentry, and have a particular dislike to any subserviency or even appearance of subserviency on the part of our people to the slave-holding oligarchy. I was disgusted with it in college, at the Law School, and have been since in society and politics."[6]

The simmering division between Conscience Whigs and Cotton Whigs had come to full boil with astonishing speed. It had been less than three years since Dana was approached by the Whig emissary who represented the respectable Whig conservatism with which Dana had long been comfortable. Dana's rebuff of an invitation to become a Whig candidate had more to do with his lofty and unrealistic aspiration for a political system without parties than any concern with the potential consequences of territorial acquisition by the United States.

Dana continued to move in an exclusive social circle. When proper Boston decided that going to the theater would be socially acceptable if the galleries were eliminated and seats assigned, Dana noted with pride that he sat with "the Ticknors, Nortons, & Eliots . . . on one side . . . the Sedgwicks & Minots on the other." Propriety compelled him to assert, "I have made it a point not to go to the theater, for it [is] but an assignation house & sink of iniquity." Whatever the truth of this assertion, Dana was certain that the English actor George MacCready had "rarely . . . played before an audience more select in America."[7]

Samuel "Finley" Morse, a portrait painter of Dana's society friends, had a more revolutionary idea than respectable theaters. He stopped by to give a "most interesting account of his magnetic telegraph. He says he can cross a river without wires." Morse told Dana that he had given a demonstration to a congressman who refused to believe that Morse had sent a telegraph and received an answer: "Do you mean to say that went to Baltimore? Nonsense!"[8]

The rising tide of history that separated the world before and after Samuel Morse's invention was also to separate Dana from the select company with which he sat. Polk's election in 1844 led to the annexation of Texas by congressional resolution. The decision to admit Texas as a slave-holding state through resolution may have been constitutionally dubious, but it had the advantage of requiring only a simple majority rather than the more burdensome two-thirds required for a formal treaty. Accordingly, a resolution approving admission of Texas easily passed the Democratic-controlled House and survived Northern Whig opposition in the Senate, where a coalition of Southern Whigs and Northern Democrats narrowly approved it.

The difficulties Texas annexation posed for Northerners were, however, only beginning. President Polk's aggressive agenda for an expansive United States presence on the American continent included designs on the Oregon territory and Mexican-owned California. Polk's settlement with the British of American claims in the Northwest came after much saber rattling ("Fifty-Four Forty or Fight!"), but Polk never seriously considered a military challenge to the British Empire. Mexico, on the other hand, was perceived as a much less formidable adversary.[9]

In January 1846 Polk ordered General Zachary Taylor to advance to the Rio Grande to press the American claim that the river represented the Texas boundary. Several deliberately provocative moves by the U.S. Army predictably led to a military response from elements of the Mexican Army, providing Polk with the pretense to ask Congress for a declaration of war. The declaration was attached to a military appropriation for troops fighting in the field. Even those Whigs who believed Polk started the war and then lied about its cause did not wish to be accused of not supporting American soldiers.[10] Polk had his war. He expected it to end quickly, cost little, and be politically advantageous. Like several American presidents to follow, he was wrong on all counts.

The premise that the poorly equipped Mexican Army and weak Mexican government would be unable to fight beyond a few weeks was mistaken. The war began in May 1846. The Treaty of Guadalupe Hidalgo concluding the Mexican War was ratified in March 1848. The United States suffered over 15,000 casualties (including over 11,000 deaths from disease) and incurred almost $100,000,000 in military expenditures. An estimated 25,000 Mexicans were killed. But the greatest costs were the incalculable political consequences. "Mexico will poison us," said Ralph Waldo Emerson.[11]

The symptoms were apparent early. Although moderate Whigs voted for funds to continue to equip troops fighting in Mexico, they were deeply troubled by the potential for expansion of slavery into territory acquired by the war. In the beginning, at least, Boston Whigs were united in their opposition. The economic and political interests of Brahmin Boston coincided with their antislavery sentiment, the strength of which was yet to be tested. Senator Daniel Webster, who continued to represent the view of Boston's establishment, opposed the acquisition of new territory as a fruit of the war (except the port of San Francisco, whose value New England shipping merchants knew as well as Dana did).

By the time the Mexican War ended—notwithstanding a military victory that had secured Texas, California, and New Mexico for the United States—the issue of whether to extend slavery to the "new territories" had divided the country. Instead of reaping political gains for the Democrats, the Mexican War made Whig generals Winfield Scott and Zachary Taylor military heroes and potential presidential candidates. President Polk tried to discredit both generals in hopes of undermining their political appeal. Worse yet for Polk, the war fractured the Democratic Party.

Democratic congressman David Wilmot of Pennsylvania created the fault line with his "proviso." First offered in 1846 as an amendment to an appropriation intended to acquire Mexican territory, the Wilmot Proviso asserted that all future territory acquired by the United States must be kept free of slavery. Although the proviso was never adopted, support for it became a litmus test for Northern Democrats and Whigs of conscience.[12] Neither the Democratic Party nor the Whig Party yearned to take the test. When the Democratic Party met in Baltimore in May 1848 and nominated anti-proviso Senator Lewis Cass of Michigan, New York's antislavery "barnburner" Democrats bolted the party.

Conscience Whigs were equally dismayed when Conservative Whigs nominated General Zachary Taylor, the "rough and ready" hero of the Mexican War. Boston's most prominent Whigs sought to finesse the Free Soil question by avoiding the subject. "The South," said Dana, "triumphs at the nomination of General Taylor, and proclaims it as a defeat for the Wilmot Proviso and the North is silent. . . . Acquiescence in General Taylor's nomination is to abandon the Free Soil question."

Dana privately and publicly challenged Boston's most powerful figures: "I have the honor of personal friendship—they will allow me to say so—of many of the leading Whigs of this city. . . . Private conversations are to be kept private, but I may say they were entirely unsatisfactory. The farther I inquired the worse it became." When he took the chair of the July 7 Free Soil meeting in Boston, Dana called out Boston's establishment Whigs by name: "Mr. Choate has spoken in Boston, and Mr. Lawrence in Burlington. They have talked upon tariffs, currency, war, internal improvements, cotton—everything but the new territories."[13]

A week after the Boston Free Soil meeting, Dana was asked if he would go to the Free Soil Convention in Buffalo as a Whig delegate. The impetus for "a great convention of all anti-slavery men" had been building for well over a year as Conscience Whigs and antislavery Democrats saw their respective parties embracing candidates opposed to the Wilmot Proviso. The request surprised Dana; he thought the more obvious choice was Charles Sumner. Dana agreed to go "on the condition it was explained to Sumner." Waldo Higginson, who approached Dana on behalf of Boston's Conscience Whigs, said Sumner "was as much a Democrat or Liberty man as a Whig." This was true, but it owed more to the ambitious Sumner's political motives than his principles.

Sumner—despite denials even to himself—hungered for elective office. In any event, it was agreed that Dana "was more decidedly a Whig."[14]

Before leaving for Buffalo, Dana found it necessary to justify his involvement to Sarah. He wrote to her after the July 7 Free Soil meeting, "I am in it, in my heart. I think the honor of Massachusetts requires it, and I will hope you sympathize with me."[15] She did not. Sarah had not welcomed Dana's announcement that he was a Free Soiler, knowing that his antislavery views would not endear him to their Beacon Hill acquaintances.

Sarah's reluctance to embrace Dana's political views was a symptom of a rift between the couple that had widened in the past two years. Her resentment of Dana's absences, failure to buy a house even after the birth of their third child, and quarrels over money prompted a brief separation in 1846. The exchanges between them were bitter enough to cause Sarah to later destroy letters to her husband—and to clip from Dana's journal almost every entry for that year.

In the summer of 1847, Dana wrote to Sarah, who had retreated to the sanctuary of her mother's Connecticut home: "I have tried to cure all my fancy. To relive my life, to be a different person from what I was." Dana's familiar struggle with "those temptations & sins of the flesh which easily beset me" led to marital conflicts not readily resolved. The distance between an ambitious young husband determined to make his mark, and an overwhelmed young mother of three children who was neither understood nor understanding, was evident. "You are my only friend," wrote Dana, "What is the condition of a man who thinks that . . . his circumstances are not interesting & dear to his wife & that she would have preferred others."[16]

In 1848 Sarah wrote a story (marked "To Be Burned") of an innocent country girl's marriage to a city lawyer. The young wife of the story saw her husband playing chess with a beautiful neighbor and give "a look as a lover might give a mistress." The woman who attracted the husband of the story was "superior . . . in personal & intellectual attraction . . . how proud he would be to show her to his friends—far prouder than he has ever been of me." When confronted, the husband proved himself innocent of infidelity but asked his wife "if she supposed he would never ride with any person but herself."[17]

Dana left for Buffalo in early August. Though not his typical August sojourn, he was swept up in the excitement of his first political convention. Rallying under the banner "Free Soil, Free Speech, Free Labor, and Free Men," Conscience Whigs, disaffected Democrats, and members of the antislavery Liberty Party nominated former president Martin Van Buren and Charles Francis Adams Sr., son of John Quincy Adams, as the Free Soil presidential and vice presidential candidates. "Never, since my ears first admitted sound, have I heard such an acclamation," wrote Dana, declaring the Free Soil Convention "noble and providentially successful."[18]

Although Dana believed that "if the North can be brought to act with independence and spirit, we may be able to give the Free Soil candidate a very large vote," he conceded to a skeptical Sarah, "it is a rather forlorn hope in Boston, where the moneyed interest is so strong and so utterly indifferent to slavery."[19] Nor was the nomination of Democrat Van Buren as a Free Soiler well received by those who remembered President Van Buren's opposition to the proposed abolition of slavery in the District of Columbia. But Dana was determined "even as a Whig . . . nurtured in a dislike and suspicion of Mr. Van Buren," to campaign for the Free Soil nominee.

In his maiden speech at Faneuil Hall, given shortly after his return from Buffalo, Dana challenged those unhappy with the results of the convention: "If there is a Whig in Faneuil Hall who doubts about the nomination of Mr. Van Buren, let him name to me a single Whig statesman of the first class, fit to be head of our party, we could have put in nomination, or let him forever hold his peace."[20] Dana's energetic political engagement kept his August depression at bay. He made five speeches in the last week of the month, but on the first day of September 1848 Dana was again immersed in the drama of family responsibility.

Sarah, pregnant with the couple's fourth child, went into labor. She hemorrhaged badly and for several hours it was not certain she would survive childbirth. Dana wrote, "I love my children, but I really believe I would rather lose *them all* than to lose their mother." By evening, the crisis passed and the Danas had their fourth daughter. When told the new baby was a girl, Sarah "was pained in the extreme." "As for myself," Dana wrote, "I cared nothing about it. I even forgot to ask." Out of danger, Sarah was under doctor's orders to sleep as much as possible. Dana was grateful for the intervention of the mayor of Cambridge "who kindly ordered the ringing of the bell to cease for three days, it being so near us."[21]

As soon as Sarah began to recover, Dana made plans to return to the campaign trail. Writing to Sarah's sister-in-law to tell her of the birth, Dana added, "You would be surprised how much I am interested, for the first time, in politics . . . I shall speak at . . . perhaps six evenings next week."[22] Dana reprised his speech in appearances in several Massachusetts towns. He was encouraged by the size of the audiences ("very full house," "hall crowded") and his reception ("great enthusiasm & constant applause," "very successful & cause looking well").[23]

Dana's compelling campaign speech may be glimpsed in an excerpt where he used a rhetorical device much fresher in 1848, though even today no political convention is without it. To his own rhetorical question "Where are the Free Soilers?" Dana answered: "They are beside our rock-bound or our sandy coast; along the hills and valleys, and in the cities and towns of New England. They are at the South, by the banks of the Potomac and the Shenandoah; in the cities and villages of the great West, beyond the Falls of St. Anthony and the Sault Ste. Marie. They are beside the domestic hearths and domestic altars of an American people. And with such advocates, such missionaries, such evangelists, sooner or later, we cannot but succeed."[24]

Dana and other Conscience Whigs hoped Daniel Webster—who claimed allegiance to the Wilmot Proviso—would reject the Conservative Whig candidacy of Zachary Taylor and embrace the Free Soil Party. "One speech from Webster at Faneuil Hall," Dana wrote to his father, "would put an end to the Boston Taylor faction forever."[25] On the day of the birth of Dana's fourth daughter, Webster made his long-awaited announcement of his choice for president. Citing economic issues important to Boston's conservatives, Webster endorsed Taylor and ended any Free Soil chance of carrying Massachusetts.

Dana knew that "the spindles and day-books are against us just now, for Free Soilism goes to the wrong side of the ledger."[26] One could not know in 1848 what or who the right side of the ledger might ultimately contain. Dana's appearances in Woburn, Chelsea, Lynn, and Lowell, where he asserted the Free Soil Party's opposition to the extension of slavery, were followed by a thirty-nine-year-old Whig congressman from Illinois advocating the election of Zachary Taylor, choice of the Cotton Whigs.[27] "We have no power to assign parts in the drama of political life," declared Dana in his July 7 speech to Boston's Free Soilers.[28] The parts citizen Dana and Congressman Lincoln were to play were yet to be assigned.

Daniel Webster's endorsement of Zachary Taylor and failure to support the Free Soil Party ended any illusions Dana had about his political hero. "Young as I am," said the thirty-three-year-old Dana in a speech at Faneuil Hall, "I would not have stood on this spot as Mr. Webster stood, and when these great questions vital to the national honor . . . are at stake . . . put the whole issue upon the lowest, the most ignoble objects, mere money questions—no not for all the honor and all the glory that belongs to Daniel Webster—So help me God."[29]

Dana continued to actively advocate the Free Soil cause. Ralph Waldo Emerson was in the audience when Dana spoke in Concord in February 1850. He invited Dana to spend the night at his house, where Dana noted "he . . . complimented me highly—said my Faneuil Hall speech in '48 was the best speech of that campaign."[30] A day later Dana was again at Faneuil Hall, where a Dana-drafted resolution to sustain the Wilmot Proviso was endorsed by a Free Soil convention. At Dana's urging, copies of the resolution were sent to the Massachusetts congressional delegation, including Senator Webster.

The Faneuil Hall meeting of Free Soilers was convened in the midst of the momentous Senate debate over Henry Clay's Compromise of 1850. Webster had yet to disclose his position on the proposal to admit California as a free state, prohibit the sale of slaves in the District of Columbia, allow the slavery issue to be settled by "popular sovereignty" in the New Mexico and Utah territories, and enact a new fugitive slave law.[31]

On March 7, 1850, Webster began his remarks to the U.S. Senate in support of what eventually formed the basis for the Compromise of 1850, dramatically declaring: "I wish to speak today not as a Massachusetts man, nor a Northern man, but as an American. I speak today for the preservation of the Union. . . . Hear me for my cause."[32] Conscience Whigs heard one cause above all—Webster's desire to placate the South in furtherance of his ambition to be president. Webster did more than declare his opposition to the Wilmot Proviso. He characterized support of it as "a taunt, an indignity" to the South. With respect to fugitive slaves, Webster asserted, "The South, in my judgment is right, and the North is wrong." All Northerners "who are not carried away by some fanatical idea," said Webster, ought to recognize a moral and constitutional obligation to return fugitive slaves to their rightful owners.[33]

One paragraph of Webster's speech must have struck Dana with particular force. Webster complimented the favored lawyer of Ticknor's Beacon Hill clique for opposing resolutions like the one Dana had drafted. "I wish these sentiments could become more common," said Webster, noting, "with pleasure," the remarks of "a young man of talent and character of whom the best hopes may be entertained. I mean Mr. [George] Hillard." It was a pointed reminder to Dana that he was on the wrong side of Boston's establishment.

The "Seventh of March" speech was another painful lesson to Dana about the character of New England's most celebrated political figure. "The truth is," Dana wrote to his brother Ned, "with all his gigantic powers there is one thing [Webster] lacketh. He lacks confidence in the moral sentiment of the people. He will run no personal risk for a principle."[34] The establishment quickly coalesced behind Webster when his Senate address set off a firestorm of criticism in Massachusetts. A letter of support published in Boston and Washington newspapers was signed by more than 800 prominent Massachusetts citizens, including George Ticknor, Rufus Choate, Joseph Quincy, and Oliver Wendell Holmes Sr.[35]

There was far more at stake in the great debate over Clay's proposed compromise than Webster's political future. In Washington, deliberations continued into the summer as Congress sought a grand bargain that would end the drift to disunion. Paradoxically, although President Taylor was a slaveholder from a slave state, Free Soilers thought the president more receptive to their arguments than Daniel Webster. But on July 9, 1850, lightning again struck the Whig Party. President Taylor died after a short illness, leaving the presidency in the hands of an unknown Whig vice president for the second time in less than a decade.

President Millard Fillmore quickly nominated Daniel Webster to be secretary of state. Webster's return to the most influential position in the cabinet was welcomed by Boston and New York money interests, who again responded to Webster's lament of the financial sacrifice he was making (he told Boston banker Franklin Haven that a secretary of state would need a house for entertaining). The usual names—Appleton, Lowell, and Curtis—were among those who raised over $20,000. One absent benefactor was Abbott Lawrence, though his brother Amos contributed.[36]

In mid-September, President Fillmore signed a series of laws to implement the Compromise of 1850, including the Fugitive Slave Act (amending the 1793 Fugitive Slave Act). It empowered slave owners to secure the assistance of federal marshals to seize alleged fugitive slaves. The alleged fugitives were to be brought before a federal "commissioner" for a summary proceeding in which a certificate introduced by the slave owner "was full and conclusive evidence of the fact of escape." The alleged fugitive slave could not testify. The writ of habeas corpus was not available. There was no right of appeal. It was a crime to hinder or obstruct the seizure of an alleged fugitive slave. It was a crime to aid, abet, assist, rescue, or conceal an alleged fugitive slave. Commissioners had the authority to command citizens to assist as a *posse comitatus* in the seizure of an alleged runaway slave.[37] It was the most draconian statute ever enacted into American law. Daniel Webster believed that if he could enforce the Fugitive Slave Act in Boston, he would be the next president of the United States.

The difficulty of enforcement soon became apparent. In November 1850 Daniel Webster arrived in Boston "to put this business of the attempt to arrest the Crafts in better shape."[38] He was too late. Ellen and William Craft were on their way to England, beyond the reach of the American secretary of state. The attempted seizure of the most recognizable fugitive slave couple in the United States was a fiasco for the slave owner and Webster.

The Crafts had settled quietly in Boston after a daring escape from Georgia slavery made them prominent on the abolitionist lecture circuit. When agents of slave master Robert Collins appeared in October seeking warrants to arrest the couple under the new authority of the month-old Fugitive Slave Act, Boston's abolitionists, Free Soilers, and the African American community were galvanized into action.

Lawyer members of the Vigilance Committee, including Samuel Sewall, Ellis Gray Loring, and Dana, were remarkably inventive in procuring state criminal complaints (including one for smoking in the street) to harass the master's agents. Dana warned U.S. Marshal Charles Devans that he would be sued if any improper authority was used against the Crafts—a warning that was sufficient to deter the marshal from forcibly entering William Craft's furniture shop, where Craft had barricaded himself. Reverend Theodore Parker was more direct, telling the agents they "were not safe in Boston another night."[39] It was as much a threat as a warning, and the slave owner's agents left the city the next day.

President Fillmore sent a letter to Robert Collins, "owner" of the Crafts, apologizing for the failure of the U.S. government to secure his "property." Webster, upset with the tepid response of federal officers in Boston, prompted a massive rally at Faneuil Hall in late November to demonstrate establishment support for vigorous enforcement of the Fugitive Slave Act. Benjamin R. Curtis, second only to Rufus Choate as a leader of the Boston bar, declared that Massachusetts had "nothing to do" with "whatever rights" fugitive slaves might have: "Our peace and safety they have no right to invade."[40] Black residents of Boston were soon to learn that "peace and safety"—like "law and order"—is a phrase fraught with danger when coupled with political ambition.

On Saturday morning, February 15, 1851, Dana was in his office next to the Boston courthouse when, "at about 1030 A.M. Charles Davis . . . told me that the Marshal had a fugitive in custody in the U.S. courtroom before Mr. Curtis as Commissioner. I went immediately over to the Court House."[41] Dana could scarcely believe his eyes. The U.S. government had seized a Boston resident from his place of work and intended to send him into slavery.

If the stakes were not so high, the scene could have been as a comic opera. George Ticknor Curtis, lawyer and nephew of Beacon Hill's George Ticknor, was "actually occupying the judge's seat." Curtis, a stalwart "Cotton Whig," was a commissioner authorized to preside over fugitive slave proceedings under the new Fugitive Slave Act. Now, "dressed in a little brief authority," Commissioner Curtis "was swelling into the dignity of an arbiter of life and death with a pomposity as ludicrous as that of Riley."[42]

"Riley" was Patrick Riley, deputy U.S. marshal for Massachusetts. His boss, U.S. Marshal Charles Devans, was thought too timid in his enforcement of the new law and had been conveniently called to Washington. Deputy Marshal Riley, with an inflated self-importance equal to that of Curtis, "was making the most absurd exhibition of pomposity in ordering people about and clearing the courtroom."[43]

Dana could see a "good looking black fellow" seated between the guards. There was nothing in the display that Shadrach Minkins found amusing. Surrounded by specially deputized constables, Minkins was still wearing the waiter's apron he had on when he was seized from Boston's Cornhill Coffee House. Robert Morris, Boston's only African American attorney, spoke briefly to Minkins (who used the alias "Frederick Jenkins"). Minkins gave Morris verbal authority for Dana to prepare petitions seeking the prisoner's release from custody. Dana quickly drafted a petition of habeas corpus stating that "one Frederick Jenkins of Boston, laborer was imprisoned in the courthouse by Patrick Riley, that the pretense was that he was a fugitive from service and labor, and that the petitioner did not know whether there was a warrant or not."[44]

The courtroom had been cleared except for Minkins and the constables, but the stairways of the courthouse filled rapidly "chiefly [by] negroes," who for the moment were "perfectly peaceable." Outside the courthouse a crowd was "increasing every minute."[45] With petition in hand, Dana went in search of the one man who possessed the authority to bring order to the deteriorating situation: Chief Justice Lemuel Shaw of the Supreme Judicial Court of Massachusetts.

Lemuel Shaw had been chief justice for more than two decades (Dana was fifteen years old when Shaw was appointed chief justice in 1830). With a demeanor "uncourtly not to say, rough," Shaw did not welcome conversations with lawyers. An otherwise sympathetic biographer found "the almost utter lack of reminiscences of Shaw indicate pretty clearly that he did not have this tendency." Even Rufus Choate dared not trifle with Shaw, though out of his hearing Choate once proposed the toast: "The Chief Justice! We contemplate him as the East Indian does his wooden-headed idol—he knows that his is ugly, but he feels that he is great."[46]

The chief justice's chambers were in the Boston courthouse but Dana got only as far as the lobby of the supreme court. There he confronted Shaw, who had little interest in hearing from Dana. The young lawyer quickly summarized his purpose as "a case of an alleged fugitive slave and that our object was to test the constitutional power of the Commissioner to issue a warrant." Shaw glanced at the petition "and said in a most ungracious manner, 'This won't do. I can't do anything on this.'" The chief justice laid the petition on a table and turned away.[47]

Dana persisted: "I asked him to be so good as to tell me what the defects were, saying that I had taken pains to conform to the statute." But Shaw was "unwilling" and "seemed desirous" of dismissing the petition and Dana. "In short," Dana wrote in his journal that evening, "he attempted to *bluff me off*."[48] There was no surer way to guarantee Dana's presence. The thirty-five-year-old Dana went head-to-head with Shaw, twice his age and capable of making a young lawyer's future very difficult.

Compelled to identify a defect in the petition, Shaw asserted it was not signed by the petitioner. Dana reminded the chief justice that the statute permitted the petition to be made by the party "or by someone in his behalf." Dana observed that Shaw "must also have known that in the worst cases, where the writ is most needed, a prisoner cannot sign the petition himself. Sometimes even the place of his imprisonment is unknown."[49]

Recognizing that Dana had correctly countered that the petition could be presented in behalf of a prisoner without his signature, Shaw retorted: "There is no evidence that it is in his behalf—there is no evidence of authority." This was a direct affront to Dana because it implied he acted without permission of his client in violation of legal ethics. An angry Dana responded: "Do you require proof of authority? What proof do you require, sir?" Challenged, Shaw retreated to the last refuge of a chief justice: "It is enough for me to say that the petition is not sufficient."[50]

Dana and Shaw sparred over the chief justice's bald assertion of authority, with Shaw adding further objections that Dana found "frivolous and invalid." There was, however, no mistaking "the temper which the Chief Justice was in and his evident determination to get rid of the petition." Dana returned to his office and pondered possible legal alternatives to free Minkins from custody, when suddenly he heard "a shout from the court house, continued into a yell of triumph."[51]

In an instant "down the steps came two huge negroes bearing the prisoner between them." Minkins appeared so dazed by the rescue that he almost sat down. Dana thought he had fainted, "but the men seized him and being very powerful fellows, hurried him through the Square into Court Street where he found use of his feet and they went off toward Cambridge, like a black squall."[52] A well-conceived plan of escape provided Minkins a hiding place in an attic in the black neighborhood on the edge of Beacon Hill. From there a series of clandestine wagon rides carried him north. Six days after his rescue from the Boston courthouse, Minkins was in Canada. He was, for the first time in his life, beyond the grasp of slave masters and the U.S. government.[53]

The suddenness of the rescue amazed Dana: "It was all done in an instant, too quick to be believed." Dana admired the rescuers' efficiency, "so successful was it that not only was no negro arrested, but no attempt was made at pursuit." The "sympathy of the masses was with the successful rescue," though it was condemned, said Dana, by an occasional "old hunker" or "young dandy." Dana was with the masses: "How can any right minded man do else than rejoice at the rescue of a man from the hopeless, endless slavery to which a recovered fugitive is always doomed."[54]

But in a matter of days Dana found himself in the center of a white squall precipitated by his former political idol, the "god-like" Daniel Webster. From his exalted position as new secretary of state, Webster thundered against Boston's "insane" abolitionists and Free Soilers. President Fillmore convened an emergency meeting of his cabinet. Word immediately began to circulate that Webster was prepared to resign within twenty-four hours if the president did not use federal authority to respond to the crisis. A New Orleans newspaper reported, "No man in that cabinet stands up for the South in a manner more decidedly prompt and efficient than Mr. Webster."[55]

But Webster needed more than newspaper articles to show the South he could be counted on to enforce the new Fugitive Slave Act. Upon learning of the escape, Webster telegraphed Commissioner George Ticknor Curtis demanding to know the circumstances of the rescue. Curtis responded by blaming the marshal's office and the city of Boston for gross negligence in failing to anticipate the attack. Curtis described the episode in terms that suggested it fell within the legal definition of treason.

It was a characterization the secretary of state quickly embraced. "It is, strictly speaking, an act of treason," wrote Webster a few days later.[56] The commandant of the Boston Navy Yard and the commanding officer of Fort Independence in Boston Harbor were directed by the secretaries of navy and war to ready their forces to support the U.S. marshal's office if further rebellious acts could not be contained by civil authorities.

On February 18, 1851, President Fillmore signed a proclamation drafted by Webster, "Calling on Citizens to Assist in the Recapture of a Fugitive Slave Arrested in Boston, Massachusetts." Millard Fillmore may have believed the proclamation was no more than a call "on all well-disposed citizens to rally in the support of the laws of their country." But the man who wrote it saw the document as nothing less than an edict to suppress those in Boston who dared to challenge enforcement of the new Fugitive Slave Act. Lest there be any doubt of his interest, the proclamation bore Webster's signature as well as the president's.

Webster deliberately used language that implied that the rescue of Minkins from the Boston courthouse was part of a broader plot. The proclamation commanded "all officers, civil and military, and all other persons, civil or military . . . within the vicinity of this outrage" to do all in their power to assist "in quelling this and other such combinations."[57] The secretary of state knew the "combination" he wished to quell and he knew how to do it. "I do especially direct," ordered the president of the United States in his Webster-drafted proclamation, "that prosecutions be commenced against all persons who have made themselves aiders or abettors . . . and I do further command that the District Attorney for the United States cause . . . all such as aided, abetted, or assisted . . . be immediately arrested."[58]

Federal authorities in Boston had already gotten the word to begin arrests. On Monday February 17, two days after the rescue, the U.S. marshal (at the direction of the federal prosecutor) arrested Charles G. Davis, a white attorney who first alerted Dana that Minkins was in custody, and Elizur Wright, the white editor of Boston's *Daily Morning Commonwealth,* a paper critical of Webster and Boston's Cotton Whigs. In the next few days there were eight more Bostonian arrests, of citizens black and white, prominent and obscure.[59]

The federal government was to spend the next two years prosecuting what become known as the "rescue cases." Long after the Civil War, a lawyer who witnessed the defense of the accused wrote of Dana: "With a courage that was simply superb he faced the law officers of the government and denounced them in measured terms which none could misunderstand."[60] A time would come when the United States would commit its blood and treasure to the cause for which Dana stood.

But all he could know when he entered Boston's federal courtroom on the morning of February 20, 1851, was that the U.S. government intended to prosecute "all persons" suspected of preventing the return of a man to slavery, and that Secretary of State Daniel Webster—the voice of the president, the government, and the Boston establishment—had ordered the prosecutions to begin.

10

A MONSTROUS THING

"Mr. Commissioner, we are assembled here this morning, under extraordinary circumstances. I am not aware that . . . since we became an independent people . . . a case similar to this has once arisen."[1] Dana's representation to Commissioner B. F. Hallett, sitting as presiding judge in the prosecution of Boston attorney Charles G. Davis for aiding and abetting "with force and arms" the escape of Shadrach Minkins, was not hyperbole. "How," Dana asked, "is this extraordinary spectacle to be accounted for?" Dana would provide the answer, but before he did so the federal government attempted to use the hearing to chill the exercise of free speech, free assembly, and the right to counsel. The federal prosecutor twice threatened Dana with criminal prosecution.

No one interested in fairness would have chosen the forum in which Dana had to defend Charles G. Davis. It was, Dana said, "a political state trial." The nation's newspapers had been in full cry since Minkins's escape. It was difficult for even Southern papers to exceed the Northern rush to condemn the rescue. "If we are not mistaken this is the greatest outrage that has ever occurred in the United States," proclaimed the *New York Herald.* "Such a disgrace never fell on Boston before," asserted the *Boston Daily Courier.*[2]

The case of the United States against Davis alleged that the lawyer had given a signal to the African Americans who freed Minkins from the Boston courthouse. The hearing was to determine if the prosecution had sufficient evidence to proceed to a criminal trial of the defendant. But it was much more—it was the forum in which Daniel Webster intended to use a federal prosecutor to demonstrate that "certain resolutions . . . in conventions held in Boston are distinctly treasonous."[3]

Dana considered George Lunt, U.S. district attorney for Massachusetts, "the oddest mixture of obstinacy, ignorance of legal principles, vanity and irritability I ever met in such a place."[4] Dana's father thought it remarkable that his son was threatened by "the ill-bred District Attorney." But Lunt had more behind him than the prosecutorial authority of his office. Proper Boston was strongly supportive of the Webster-initiated prosecution and "deeply mortified" by the Minkins rescue. "The feeling of the community here in Boston is just as it should be," Amos Lawrence wrote to fellow Brahmin Samuel A. Eliot.[5]

Dana Sr. wondered why it was that "not a man of weight at the bar" could be found to assist his son—"a young man with a large and growing family working like a slave to support it"—against "the wealth and rank of this overbearing City."[6] Even Charles Sumner refused to get involved. Dana asked Sumner to appear with him as counsel, but Sumner feared that doing so would jeopardize his election to the U.S. Senate, then in the hands of the Massachusetts legislature. Sumner frankly admitted to Dana that "the delicate state of affairs at the State House required him to withhold any public action." Dana ruefully noted that "no one wished to be in the [rescue cases] who had much to lose."[7]

There was more evidence of Webster's heavy hand in the proceeding. The decision to bring the first rescue case against a lawyer who volunteered to assist alleged fugitive slaves was intended to deter legal challenges to the Fugitive Slave Act—particularly by any attorney who had professional and social standing in Boston. "You cannot find a lawyer in the profession whose income reaches [forty dollars] a year" who believes the law is unconstitutional, Webster infamously asserted.[8] If there were any, the federal prosecution of Davis was an unmistakable message to them.

Dana knew exactly what the message was, and he delivered his response in open court: "I think there is pressure brought to bear against the free expression of popular opinion . . . a pressure felt even in the courts of law, intimidating counsel, overawing witnesses, and making defense of liberty a peril. There is pressure of fear of political disfranchisement, of social ostracism which weighs upon this community like a nightmare." Dana asserted that the pressure of political and mercantile interests meant "that if a man stands . . . charged with being a fugitive slave, he will find it difficult to retain counsel in this city of Boston."

That was the result sought by Webster and the interests he represented. They had reason to anticipate success. Dana observed, "Two years ago no man could have stood before this bar, with perpetual servitude impending over him, but almost the entire Bar would have come forward to his defense." Now "except from a small body of men peculiarly situated," none dared step forward.

Dana knew what had changed. "I think it a monstrous thing," Dana said of the government's decision to prosecute an attorney who volunteered to assist persons alleged to be fugitive slaves: "If there be a person against whom no intimidation should be used it is counsel for a poor, unprotected fugitive from captivity. The question is whether a man and his posterity forever, the fruit of his body, shall be slave or free. It is to be decided on legal principles. If there is a case in the world that calls for legal knowledge—that calls for counselors to come in and labor without money or price,—it is a case like this."

It was the "small body of men peculiarly situated" that Lunt, Webster's prosecutorial instrument, aimed to intimidate. Dana's phrase reflected the precarious ground upon which they stood. Dana anticipated the prosecution would allege much more than that the defendant had given a signal. District Attorney Lunt was prepared to demonstrate to the court and the country that Boston could quell the "combinations" of abolitionists, African Americans, Free Soilers, and lawyers who bore responsibility for the flagrant disregard of the fugitive slave law.

In Webster's eyes, no combination was more dangerous than the melding of Boston's black leaders, abolitionists, and attorney sympathizers who met in Faneuil Hall on October 14, 1850, to denounce the Fugitive Slave Act. For Lunt's purpose at trial, of greatest interest was the formation of a "Vigilance Committee" to assist alleged fugitive slaves in the event of arrest in Boston. The defendant was on the committee. So was Dana.

"I understand that there is to be a great deal done on this case of an unusual character," said Dana to Commissioner Hallett. "We cannot know what limit is to be put to this. And so, not knowing what is before me, with no ordinary rules of procedure to guide me, [I hope] the Commissioner will allow me to anticipate the attacks as well as I can." Dana had little faith in Hallett—"the higher you put him the more he shows his tail."[9]

Dana anticipated that Lunt, at Webster's direction, would characterize opposition to the Fugitive Slave Act as criminal. "We have been threatened with the reading of newspapers," asserted Dana, "public meetings and political principles are to be charged as treasonable." Commissioner Hallett responded that the district attorney merely "proposes to read, as part of his argument, an article from the newspapers." Dana retorted: "He proposes to read it as evidence to affect the mind of the court on the facts." Dana added: "I cannot object to it now. When it is offered, I have no doubt it will be properly met by the Commissioner." It was not.

The degree to which Dana was himself "peculiarly situated" with respect to the court, the prosecutor, and Webster's implementation of the Fugitive Slave Act soon became apparent. The prosecution presented evidence that defendant Davis had said to a city constable on the day of the rescue that the constable "was engaged in a dirty business" because he was paid for catching slaves.

Dana defended the remark: "I have said the same. I saw a man I knew in court the other day letting himself by the dollar a day in slave-catching. I begged him if he could find any honest mode of getting a living to abandon it." The prosecutor for the United States was immediately on his feet: "A very improper remark!" Dana replied, "I venture to suggest not." Commissioner Hallett interjected: "I see no distinction between attempting to deter men from executing the law and assisting in violating it." This was nothing less than the court putting Dana on notice that he was a target for prosecution. The commissioner persisted: "It is the equivalent to saying to the officer that execution of the law is a mean business." Dana was not to be cowed: "That I propose to argue. It [slave-catching] is a mean business. . . . That is what I myself have said, and what every high-minded man must feel."

Lunt, with the imprimatur of the commissioner's remarks, prosecutorial authority of the U.S. government, and the political sentiment of Brahmin Boston—without which he would never have dared threaten one of their own—asserted to the court "that Mr. Dana might find himself changing places at the bar, and be a defendant instead of counsel." Dana paused, looked directly at Lunt, and bowed.

Dana then turned and delivered a withering retort to Commissioner Hallett's contention that the Fugitive Slave Act compelled citizens to assist in the return of fugitive slaves: "No citizen is bound to an active execution of this law, unless called upon as one of the *posse comitatus*. Did your honor feel bound to join in the pursuit last Saturday, when the mob passed you at the corner of Court Street? Do you feel bound, of a pleasant evening, to walk about the neighborhood and see what fugitives you can find and dispose of? Would any compensation tempt you to do it?"

Dana's response to Commissioner Hallett was proof that he could not be bullied. But Dana was more than a fearless advocate—he was an extraordinary trial attorney. Years later, reflecting on the economic hardship he suffered when the Boston establishment boycotted his office because of his defense of the rescue cases, Dana observed that among the few Boston attorneys willing to challenge the fugitive slave law, he alone had a court practice.

District Attorney Lunt had a prosecutor's forum, a sympathetic court, and a low threshold of evidence—all factors that Webster was certain would enable Lunt to advance the prosecution to a full trial. Lunt claimed that "the defendant was not arrested until after full personal investigation of the facts." But as the hearing progressed it became obvious that a very weak case was being tested by a very strong lawyer.

The government's allegation that Davis had issued the verbal order for the rescue of Minkins rested almost entirely on the testimony of Deputy Marshal Frederick Byrnes. Byrnes swore he heard the defendant exclaim to the African Americans gathered outside the courtroom door, "Take him out boys—take him out!" Dana's cross-examination shredded the government's primary witness.

Dana elicited an admission from Deputy Marshal Byrnes that he was somewhat hard of hearing. Asked why he could be sure that he heard Davis cry "Take him out boys!," Byrnes lamely replied, "I think Saturday was one of my hearing days." Other officers called by Lunt to corroborate Byrnes's testimony could not do so. Dana summed up the government's evidence: "It is reduced to an exclamation on the staircase, sworn to, not very confidently, by a deaf man, who was too far off to hear well at any rate of hearing, denied by three officers with good hearing . . . while a dozen voices were calling out the same thing at the same moment."

The United States did not expect to be put to its proof in a preliminary hearing. Lunt advised the court that the government had additional evidence that would be presented at a later stage of the prosecution. Dana countered: "This not a game of brag! It is not upon the evidence that is not here, but the evidence that is here, that this case is to be decided." But Webster had not urged the filing of the case because he was interested in the evidence. The purpose of the prosecution—as Lunt well understood—was to brand political opposition to the fugitive slave law as criminal, disloyal, and possibly treasonous. In pursuit of his objective, the district attorney got what looked like a lucky break.

Charles G. Davis, in addition to using Dana as his counsel, represented himself. The lawyer was as committed as Dana in his opposition to the Fugitive Slave Act, but he was not nearly Dana's equal as a litigator. Davis blundered. To Dana's surprise, defendant Davis called Dana to the stand to testify on his behalf. Dana immediately advised the court that he would have declined to act as counsel in the case had he known he would be a witness; not the least of the consequences was that Dana would no longer be able to represent Davis if the case went to a jury trial. But Commissioner Hallett quickly brushed aside any objection to Dana testifying. "There is no impropriety in it in a preliminary inquiry," said Hallett, gratuitously adding, "and in your case, never."

With Dana on the witness stand, the district attorney could do directly what he sought to do indirectly. Lunt asked Dana if he had participated in the October 14, 1850, Faneuil Hall assembly protesting the Fugitive Slave Act. Dana responded: "I object to these questions as a matter of right. I am not obliged to answer them." Lunt pressed: "I think it would be a satisfaction to the community to know from yourself how the matter stands as to these meetings."

The purpose of the political trial was now unmasked. Lunt believed he confronted Dana with an inescapable dilemma. If Dana did not answer the questions, the prosecutor would argue that Dana's reluctance was evidence that the Faneuil Hall meeting was for illicit purposes. Or Dana could choose to attempt to explain to the satisfaction of the community why he was associated with abolitionists, African Americans, and radicals. There was no mistaking that by "the community," Lunt meant Dana's own Brahmin Boston.

"I have no objections to answering," replied Dana. As to the Faneuil Hall meeting of last October 14, Dana said, "I wrote a set of resolutions, which I believe were adopted. These I am ready to stand or fall by." Commissioner Hallett interjected: "I read them, they were unexceptionable." Dana responded: "Unexceptionable in a legal view; but your Honor could not agree to the opinions expressed." The real issue was now joined, for it was opinion that the U.S. government sought to criminalize.

As Dana had foreseen, Lunt attempted to use a newspaper account of the Faneuil Hall meeting as evidence. "Now with whom is [the defendant] associated? I hold in my hand an account of meeting held in Faneuil Hall, on the 14th of October last." Dana's objection was in vain: "For what purpose is this narrative to be read here? It is an account from a hostile paper, of a political meeting." But it was the *Boston Post* account that the U.S. government believed was the best evidence of the unlawful intent of those with whom the defendant associated, Dana most of all.

District Attorney Lunt read the newspaper account emphasizing Dana's role: "Richard Henry Dana Jr. expressing regret that the meeting was not made up . . . of the leading men in all branches of business, and men of property and reputed respectability . . . read a series of resolutions, author unknown, declaring that the moral sense of the individuals composing the meeting revolted against the law." Among the sentiments expressed in Dana's resolutions were that the Fugitive Slave Act was contradictory to the Declaration of Independence and inconsistent with the purposes of the Constitution, and "that all present pledge themselves to endeavor to aid and cooperate with all colored people endangered by the law."

Lunt emphasized the purported unlawfulness of a resolution "for a committee of vigilance to secure the fugitives and colored inhabitants of Boston and vicinity from any invasion of their rights by persons acting under the law." The district attorney conceded that defendant Davis was not in Boston when the committee was formed. Lunt asserted: "But he admits that he volunteered upon his return. Why didn't he publicly disclaim any assent to these proceedings? And if he did not, is he not to be presumed to have assented? I want the public to know whether Mr. Davis and those associated with him, abide by the doctrines avowed in Faneuil Hall."

It was a question Dana was prepared to answer. But he first wanted the court, his city, and his country to know why he must: "Why should the criminal proceedings of this day have taken place at all?" Dana left little doubt of the impetus: "Instructions come from a distant power that knows nothing of the facts." He ridiculed the Webster-inspired response: "Then the Executive shrieks out a proclamation. A standing army is to be ordered to Boston. . . . The chief magistrate of fifteen millions of people must launch against us the thunders from his mighty hand."

Dana's caustic description of Fillmore and Webster did not minimize the consequences of their actions: "Excited men suspect everybody. Every person who ever attended a public meeting is suspected. A political party is to be put under the ban." Dana knew the cause: "Here has been the dread specter of executive power stalking across the scene, appalling the hearts and disabling the judgments of men."

When Dana rose to make his argument on the afternoon of February 25, 1851, the judgments of men were as disabled as at any time in American history. The disability was greatest among those with greatest authority. It was a time, wrote Emerson, "when judges, bank presidents, railroad men, men of fashion, and lawyers universally, all took the side of slavery."[10]

The government's case against Davis for aiding and abetting the rescue of Minkins collapsed under Dana's relentless cross-examination. But it was not only the defendant that was at risk. The U.S. government was prosecuting conscience, not crime. The disabled judgment that procured the rescue case prosecutions sought to compel obedience to the Fugitive Slave Act as a matter of law. To do so it was necessary to deter free assembly, disrupt right to counsel, and demonize opponents. The necessary predicate for success was for good men to remain silent.

"The doings of these last few days are now part of history," said Dana, "if counsel have been intimidated or witnesses threatened; if liberty of speech and action have been periled; if the dignity and duty of office have yielded to political agents . . . the inquest of public opinion is to sit upon the whole transaction and it will be held up to the world." Dana was making a closing argument to the country.

Because District Attorney Lunt had been so unwise to ask whether Dana "abided by the doctrines avowed in Faneuil Hall," Dana began with his opinion of the Fugitive Slave Act: "I do not hesitate to say, here, that if the act of 1850 had been imposed upon us . . . by a monarchy, we should have rebelled as one man." But, Dana acknowledged: "We are a republic. We make our own laws. We choose our own lawgivers." The Fugitive Slave Act "was passed by the vote of the representative of our own city. . . . It was advocated by our own senator." The law "was constitutionally passed, though not constitutional, we think, in its provisions. It is the law until repealed or judicially abrogated."

For repeal, "it is political courage that is wanted." But that was an unlikely remedy, as Dana well knew. The exchange between Commissioner Hallett and Dana over the obligation of a citizen to assist in the execution of the Fugitive Slave Act illustrated the government's prosecutorial objective. It was to compel adherence to the fugitive slave law. Dana had a different view of a citizen's duty. "I understand that the duty to the Constitution is above the duty to the statutes," asserted Dana. Resistance to a law for purpose of raising a constitutional issue "ought to have the approbation of the courts . . . and every person true to the Constitution and the laws."

But there was something more dangerous at the root of the government's argument than the contention that citizens must assist in the execution of the Fugitive Slave Act. It was that the law was not repealable. "Take from us that great argument, and what can the defendant and myself do? What can the defendant say to discourage colored men from the use of force?" Dana was now making an argument that was as urgent for him as for the defendant: "If we are to be told that this is part of the organic law, sunk down deep into national compact, and never to be repealed—then neither you nor I can answer for the consequences."

If a citizen could not speak to his fellow citizens "at Faneuil Hall where I still think we have a right to go," or if a lawyer could not say to a man arrested in Boston as a fugitive slave, "I will aid in your defense!," then the right to be invoked was "a case altogether out of law." It was, said Dana, "the active ultimate right of revolution. It is the right our fathers took to themselves, as an ultimate remedy for unsupportable evils."

There was no mistaking Dana's own statement of principle when he asserted, "If the defendant had made up his mind that here was a case for revolution, that here was a case for civil war and bloodshed . . . he would have exhibited himself in a far different manner." The place for one who invoked the right to forcibly resist was at the head of resistance. "A gentleman of property and education . . . whose ancestors [are] of the ancient Pilgrim stock" would not dishonor himself by instigating others "to an act he dares not commit himself, of putting forward obscure and oppressed men to dare the dangers . . . from which he screens himself."[11]

But if Dana could speak to what a gentleman would not do, he could also speak to what oppressed men will do: "The blacks, feeling themselves oppressed and periled by this law, standing at that door, behind which their friend is held a prisoner, rush in." Dana knew what it was like to witness the shackling of a crewmate and to stand helpless. When he asserted that "every right-minded man rejoices that Shadrach is free," it was more than the political abstraction of an abolitionist. Dana spoke with the voice of one who had lived with desperate men at the mercy of a master.

Lunt's summation for the prosecution revealed the extent to which he took his cue from Webster and the political sentiment of the Boston establishment. Before the district attorney began to address the evidence, he sought to intimidate Dana for alluding "to constitutional doctrines and opinions which a small class of the community entertain." Dana's remarks, said the prosecutor, "come with an ill grace from him . . . the gentleman should take care how he is associated."

The prosecutor for the U.S. government left no doubt why "it is dangerous and mischievous to recommend such doctrines as the gentlemen avows." Lunt threatened Dana: "The relation of counsel in which he appears may be changed. The sentiments he has uttered here place *him* in peril. He will find it so, *to his cost,* unless he changes the tone of his remarks, on this and future occasions."

Compelled to address the evidence in the current prosecution, Lunt conceded that it was insufficient to prove Davis guilty beyond reasonable doubt. Nonetheless, asserted the district attorney, sufficient evidence had been introduced to bind the defendant over for a jury trial. The case was submitted to Commissioner Hallett on February 25. That evening Dana noted, "Finished my argument in the Davis case. From all I can learn it is the best thing I ever did. I managed to keep Hallett good-natured and Lunt ill-natured . . . which was the best state of things."[12]

And so it proved. The very next day, Commissioner Hallett decided there was no evidence to connect Charles G. Davis criminally with a pre-conceived plan of rescue. "I take pleasure in adding," wrote Hallett, "that the conduct of the defense by the learned counsel, and his testimony and disavowals, have greatly aided me in coming to that conclusion."

The pleasure did not extend to Washington. Dana's closing argument identified the reason: "There is nothing so rash as fear. There is nothing so indiscriminating as fear. There is nothing so cruel as fear unless it be mortified pride—and here have they both concurred." Fear and pride would soon concur again. Webster knew that proper Boston would redeem itself by sending into slavery the next black man his agents seized.

11

CHAINS

Daniel Webster's singular devotion to enhancing his presidential prospects by demonstrating to the South that Boston would enforce the Fugitive Slave Act "produced a curious moral spectacle." The question Bostonians confronted was whether to return men to slavery or not. By the spring of 1851 there was no doubt where the great majority of Boston's "best people" stood. A slaveholder or his Harvard son was more welcome in Boston society "than any guest except a foreigner."[1]

The close economic affiliation between Northern manufacturers of cotton goods and Southern producers of cotton—between "the lords of the loom and the lords of the lash" in Sumner's telling formulation—was seldom invoked by Conservative Whigs as justification for support of the Fugitive Slave Act. Instead, social and business Boston cloaked its defense of Webster's arrests and prosecutions in terms of national security that "approached hysteria."[2] "Shrieks out" was Dana's apt description of the tone Webster set in President Fillmore's hastily issued proclamation calling on all persons to quell the "outrage" of resistance to the fugitive slave law.

Dana's measured denunciation of "disabled judgments" gave others pause. A bouquet of flowers and a note "for the noble defense of us all" came from the Benjamin Watsons, wealthy friends of Emerson. "I believe I have never done anything professionally that has gained me so much credit," Dana recorded in his journal.[3] But the best evidence of the impact of Dana's principled stand came from Charles Sumner's new eagerness to assist Dana.

For the better part of three years, forty-year-old Sumner had maneuvered his way toward political office. He was on the verge of election to the U.S. Senate if a deal between Democrats and Free Soilers could be consummated by the Massachusetts legislature. The unlikely coalition of the two parties owed much to Sumner's earlier machinations; he was "a far better politician than even his friends believed."[4]

In the summer of 1850 Sumner met with Free Soil leaders to discuss the expediency of a political coalition with Democrats in the upcoming fall election. The idea of becoming political bedfellows with Democrats, who opposed Free Soil principles, was anathema to Conscience Whigs, including Dana. "I told 'em . . . I would not do it," Dana wrote on September 1 after leading members of the Free Soil Party met to discuss the possible arrangement.[5]

Conscience Whigs believed Sumner was of the same mind, but he "knew the advantages of rowing toward his objective with muffled oars."[6] Sumner discretely aligned with political kingmaker Henry Wilson to divide the spoils of the 1850 election if Democrats and Free Soilers won a majority of seats in the legislature. In exchange for support of the Democrats' choice for governor (who would control patronage), lieutenant governor, and speaker of the House, Democrats offered Free Soilers the choice for the U.S. Senate.[7]

Although Whigs retained a legislative plurality after the 1850 election, Democrats and Free Soilers held a slim majority if they voted as a bloc. The coalition proved sufficiently stable to elect Democrat George S. Boutwell as governor. But when it came time for Democrats to complete the bargain, the election of the Free Soil candidate to the Senate proved elusive. The Free Soilers had nominated Sumner though their most prominent figure, Charles Francis Adams Sr., confessed to "a lurking jealousy of Sumner's purity of purpose."[8]

The Massachusetts legislature began balloting in January 1851. Democrat defections left Sumner five votes short of election on the first ballot. On the fourteenth ballot a month later, Sumner found himself nine votes short of a majority. Sumner's refusal to assist Dana when Shadrach was seized as a fugitive slave was directly related to the "delicacy" of the arithmetic. But nothing could be less delicate than the political infighting that accompanied Sumner's studied protestations of disinterest. Like Dana, Sumner asserted that political office "must seek me," but unlike Dana he had no qualms about shifting positions when necessary to make himself electable.

When it became clear that the arbitrariness of the Webster-initiated prosecutions dismayed many legislators—if not Boston's establishment—Sumner "apparently decided that high principle was good politics."[9] Less than a month after Sumner refused to join in the defense of Charles Davis in the first rescue case, Dana noted, "Sumner and I have been drawing up laws to meet the dangers and outrages of the Fugitive Slave Bill at the request of [a] Committee of the Legislature."[10] Dana and Sumner drafted legislation to extend the prohibition of the use of state authority and resources to implement the new Fugitive Slave Act. The state's "Latimer law," adopted in 1843 after the fugitive slave George Latimer was seized and held in a Boston jail for rendition to his Southern master, made it unlawful to use state facilities to confine fugitive slaves.

Dana proposed a provision that would prohibit Massachusetts volunteer militia from serving as a posse under the direction the U.S. marshal to enforce the fugitive slave law. Sumner characteristically drafted a more extreme provision that would prohibit a slave owner from having legal counsel when attempting to claim a fugitive. Dana advised against the provision "as . . . it has an odious look & will answer little purpose."[11] Sumner, once committed to a course of action, was never one for moderation. The Dana-Sumner draft did not become law, but the two men were soon to be in common cause. Daniel Webster was about to strike again.

Webster and his Boston allies had three related objectives, each of which the secretary of state was determined to achieve in April 1851. In the Massachusetts legislature, "Webster Whigs" continued to oppose

Sumner's election to the U.S. Senate. The longer the deadlock went on, the better, since Webster believed the next election would restore a Whig majority. To ensure Whig allegiance, Amos Lawrence and William Appleton began a fund to "assist" Whig legislators who could not attend to their businesses because of the protracted balloting. Lawrence made the requisite public disclaimer (the subscription was "not intended to be used for influencing any member in an improper manner") but privately wrote to Samuel A. Eliot that "everything is being done to prevent Sumner's election that . . . can be."[12]

Webster also sought to ensure that the next rescue case prosecutions resulted in convictions. It was essential, Webster told President Fillmore, to convict at least "some" of those who had been charged with aiding in escape of Shadrach. Dana's successful defense of the first rescue case caused consternation at the White House. "Lunt is not a good lawyer," Webster wrote to the president in the aftermath of the dismissal of the Davis prosecution.[13] Dana had run circles around the U.S. district attorney and Webster knew it.

The secretary of state emphasized the point in a stinging letter to Lunt: "These causes are of the utmost importance. We wish them conducted by the best talent & experience of the bar." Webster authorized the U.S. attorney to retain Boston's leading lawyers, Rufus Choate and Benjamin R. Curtis, as special prosecutors in the rescue cases. When neither was available, Webster told Lunt that he "must be fully aware of the consequences if just decisions should fail to be obtained through any want of skill on the part of those who manage the trials."[14]

Of even greater importance to Webster than blocking Sumner's election and securing rescue case convictions was the absolute necessity of capturing a fugitive slave in Boston and returning him to slavery. Webster-for-president petitions were already in circulation. Webster's political viability—at least as he saw it—depended upon a successful rendition to blot out the stain of the Shadrach rescue.

In March, Boston's U.S. marshal's office sought to seize alleged fugitive slaves thought to be in New Bedford, but high seas thwarted the plan. Then on the evening of April 3, 1851, federal marshals (assisted by Boston police) cornered Thomas Sims, a diminutive twenty-three-year-old, in a dark alley. Surrounded, Sims drew a knife and in his struggle to escape stabbed a deputy U.S. marshal in the thigh. Sims was quickly subdued and dragged to a waiting carriage. As the carriage sped through the Boston streets, Sims shouted to passersby, "I am in the hands of kidnappers!"[15]

It was worse than that. Sims had been seized as a fugitive from slavery pursuant to a federal warrant issued only hours before by Commissioner George Ticknor Curtis. Like Shadrach before him, Sims was brought to the federal courtroom in the Boston courthouse. This time Curtis was ready. A round-the-clock detail of armed men guarded the room while another force of more than a hundred secured the entrances to the building. A regiment of militia and specially deputized constables reinforced police presence.

The next morning, Friday April 4, 1851, illustrated the extent to which Webster and those he represented were willing to go to maintain power. The Boston courthouse was literally in chains. A heavy iron chain encircled the building. Additional chains barricaded all walkways. The chains were neither low enough to step over nor high enough to walk under. Judges had to stoop to enter. Dana could not believe it: "If our people bear these indignities & assumptions of power over their rights & privileges, instead of being slave catchers they ought to be slaves themselves."[16]

There could be little doubt that the unlucky Sims was the example Webster sought. The young man was the property of Georgia slave master James Potter. Sims, a skilled bricklayer, was occasionally hired out by his master to do work in the port of Savannah. In February 1851, Sims stowed away in the forecastle of a Boston-bound merchant ship. He was discovered when the ship entered Boston Harbor. The ship's master and mate locked him in a cabin, where they beat him (Dana unsuccessfully sought the arrest of both master and mate). The resourceful Sims pried open a lock and rowed a dinghy to shore. Sims attempted to send a message to his wife in Georgia, but it was intercepted and his master immediately sent to Boston an agent who retained the services of attorney "Colonel" Seth Thomas, the lawyer of choice for slave owners. Commissioner George Ticknor Curtis quickly granted Thomas's request for a warrant to seize Sims.[17]

There was simply no chance that Curtis would refuse to return Sims to slavery—nor was there any real possibility that a federal judge would intercede to block the rendition. The only forum that could reasonably be expected to hear from lawyers for Sims was the Massachusetts Supreme Court. But once again Chief Justice Lemuel Shaw refused to even consider a petition for habeas corpus. This time, though, Shaw was persuaded that it would be more politic, in light of the public reaction to the capture of Sims, to hear formal argument.

Dana—perhaps because he had experienced Shaw's refusal in the Shadrach case—was surprised by Shaw's decision to schedule oral argument before the full court. On Monday morning, April 7, "I was called in suddenly and was not prepared for more than an opening."[18] Robert Rantoul, an antislavery Democrat who had also volunteered to assist Sims, made the bulk of the argument. The arguments of Dana and Rantoul were strands of antislavery legal arguments that had been woven in the 1840s by noted lawyers active in antislavery litigation, including Salmon Chase, William Seward, and James Birney.[19]

Dana thought Rantoul's presentation "a very striking and forcible argument considered as a speech to the people" but did not believe it was "calculated to meet the difficulties in the minds of the Court."[20] The idea that slavery could be ended by legal argument was folly to abolitionists like Garrison and Wendell Phillips. They maintained that scrupulous adherence to the formalism of the legal system—and a Constitution that recognized slavery—compelled judges who followed the law to reject antislavery arguments. To Garrison abolitionists, the decision of Chief Justice Shaw was bound to be more proof of the futility of relying on the judicial process to eliminate slavery.[21]

Dana and Rantoul completed their argument on behalf of Sims at 1:00 P.M. At 3:00 P.M. the unanimous decision of the Massachusetts Supreme Court was read by Chief Justice Shaw. Shaw's lengthy opinion was unlikely to have been written in two hours. The courtroom was filled with Boston's "first merchants," who were specially permitted entry.[22] They did not gather in anticipation of a ruling that the Fugitive Slave Act was unconstitutional.

They heard what they came to hear. The Massachusetts chief justice declared the Fugitive Slave Act of 1850 constitutional in all respects. In rejecting the arguments of Rantoul and Dana that Congress was without authority to adopt legislation to enforce the Fugitive Slave Clause of the Constitution, Shaw relied on the opinion of Justice Joseph Story in the 1842 decision of *Prigg v. Pennsylvania* upholding the Fugitive Slave Act of 1793. Story declared the Fugitive Slave Clause essential to the creation and maintenance of the Union. Shaw reasoned, as had Story, that therefore Congress had the authority to exercise all powers necessary and proper to give effect to the clause.

Nor did Shaw accept the contention of Dana and Rantoul that commissioners in fugitive slave hearings were exercising judicial powers that required their appointment pursuant to Article III of the Constitution. Shaw considered the fugitive slave hearings administrative, negating a constitutional claim to either judge or jury. "The law of 1850," wrote Shaw, "stands precisely on the same ground with that of 1793," and to claims of unconstitutionality "the same answer must be made."[23] "What a moment was lost," wrote Emerson, "when Judge Shaw declined to affirm the unconstitutionality of the fugitive slave law."[24]

A unanimous opinion of the Massachusetts Supreme Court written by its chief justice, citing precedent from the great Joseph Story, cloaked Webster's arbitrary application of the Fugitive Slave Act with legitimacy. Dana was not surprised by the decision: "The National Power, sustained by the interests of politicians, traders, & manufacturers overpowers the authority of the State Courts." He was disgusted when Chief Justice Shaw "actually went under the chain to get to his Court." Dana refused to submit to the indignity: "I either jump over it, or go round to the end."[25]

Dana and other Vigilance Committee lawyers defending Sims found themselves in a legal struggle almost as desperate as Sims's fight to escape the dark alley. Samuel Sewall, who had been briefly imprisoned by the marshal's office when he went to the courthouse on the night Sims was seized, sought a habeas petition on behalf of Sims in the U.S. district court. It was denied. Sumner joined Dana in a petition to U.S. Supreme Court Justice Levi Woodbury sitting as circuit judge in Boston.

"We found Judge Woodbury at his room at the Tremont House."[26] Dana believed he had also found a fatal defect in the government's basis for holding Sims prisoner. When Shaw upheld the fugitive slave law, advocates for Sims persuaded the Boston sheriff to issue a state criminal warrant for the arrest of Sims for the stabbing in the alley. Because Sims was being held under the authority of a fugitive slave warrant, which was only civil process (a slave was only property), Dana reasoned that the U.S. marshal must release Sims to the custody of the Boston sheriff because a civil warrant must yield to criminal process.

Even if Sims was convicted in state court on a charge of assault—an unlikely outcome if Dana represented Sims before a Massachusetts jury—a jail term in Boston was preferable to slavery in Georgia. Dana was dismayed at the sheriff's reluctance to serve the state criminal warrant on the U.S. marshal: "I do not believe there is moral power [enough] on the side of the State, in opposition to the National government, in Boston to enable the Sheriff to serve a criminal process."[27] The sheriff did warn the marshal that a state criminal warrant for the arrest of Sims had been prepared and could be served at any time. The marshal asked for twenty-four hours to consider the issue, at the end of which he informed the sheriff that Sims was being held under a federal criminal warrant that charged Sims with stabbing a federal officer.

Dana urgently pressed Judge Woodbury to convene a hearing to determine whether Sims had been informed that he was being held under a federal criminal warrant: "After a long consultation during which I made three journeys to my office & the Law Library to satisfy the judge . . . and which lasted until 7 o'clock, he agreed to open his court. Accordingly at 8 pm the U.S. Circuit Court was opened & we presented our petition." The best evidence of the strength of Dana's argument that Sims was being held illegally was the reaction of the U.S. marshal, who sent for Webster's handpicked lawyers: "Messrs. [Rufus] Choate & [Benjamin R.] Curtis . . . soon arrived in carriages."[28] Judge Woodbury granted a motion to delay further proceedings until the next day, Friday at 3:00 P.M.

But for Dana, "it happened, most unfortunately & provokingly for me, that the Charlestown flats case . . . had been especially assigned for Friday, before a committee of the Legislature." Dana had been retained by investors who sought to fill in seventy-five acres of Boston harbor mudflats for development. The matter promised the most lucrative fee he had yet received. Dana had already made several appearances before the Whig-dominated committee. It never occurred to Dana—as it surely did to others—that the timing of legislative hearings can serve many purposes. It was a remarkable stroke of good fortune for Choate and Curtis that Dana was compelled to attend a hearing that "was to take all day & there was no escape from it." Dana had to "give up my connection with the Habeas Corpus, in which my heart & pride & best feelings were engaged & take to the flats case which was a matter of mere pecuniary speculation."[29]

Dana's clients showed no interest in enabling Dana to finish in time for the 3:00 P.M. hearing. "It was mortifying to see how absorbed the petitioners were in their mud scheme, coming to my office, & talking over the square feet & the lines, without so much as looking out of the window or asking a question about the case of the poor slave, so touching to humanity, so great as a question of constitutional & political law." The result was as Dana feared: "All day I was employed in this case & at night learned that Judge Woodbury remanded the prisoner."[30]

The vise of legal logic now began to close on Sims. Colonel Thomas, lawyer for the slave owner, reminded Judge Woodbury that because Sims had been remanded to the legal custody of his master, the master-and-slave relationship was reestablished. The lawyer for the master was lawyer for the slave. That, wrote Dana "of course put an end to all further proceedings," except for the judge's "political clap-trap speech, intended for the Southern markets." Dana had little regard for Woodbury, whom he described as a man "who could not distinguish fraud except through intellectual process."[31]

On Friday April 11, 1851, Commissioner George Ticknor Curtis, as expected, issued a judgment ordering the rendition of Sims to Georgia and slavery. Even Benjamin R. Curtis must have cringed at his brother's attempt to portray the ruling as humanitarian. George Ticknor Curtis cited testimony of the master's agent that Sims's mother had begged for his return. Commissioner Curtis expressed his confidence that slave states would provide "a full and final trial" to returned fugitives. "Give me a knife!" cried Sims, "and when the Commissioner declares me a slave, I will stab myself in the heart, and die before his eyes! I will not be a slave!"[32]

A handful of Vigilance Committee members plotted to rescue Sims from the courthouse by having him jump from his third-floor window onto mattresses that were to be placed below. Before they could act, iron bars were installed over the small window. Dana, whose office abutted the courthouse, could see "poor Sims . . . looking through the grates of his prison." It outraged Dana: "Our Temple of Justice is a slave pen! Our officers are slave hunters & the voice of the old law of the State is hushed & awed into silence before this fearful Slave power which has got such entire control of the Union."[33]

Sims's transfer was not expected until the next day, but federal and Boston authorities did not care to run the risks of either a rescue attempt or Webster's ire. At four in the morning, police and volunteers marched Sims to Long Wharf under cover of darkness. A few abolitionists jeered at the procession, but the brigade of several hundred armed men formed a square around the chained Sims. He was placed aboard the brig *Acorn* and taken back to Savannah and slavery.

Webster triumphantly reported the news to President Fillmore, who responded in kind: "I congratulate you and the country upon the triumph of law in Boston. She has done nobly. She has wiped out the stain of the former rescue." Slave owner James Potter expressed his gratitude to Boston's establishment for return of his slave by a notice in Boston newspapers commending those who had been "conspicuous in their effort to serve us."[34]

Frederick Douglass had a different view: "Daniel Webster has at last obtained from Boston . . . a living sacrifice to appease the slave god of the American Union."[35]

The efforts of Benjamin R. Curtis on behalf of Webster were less successful in the legislature. Although Curtis informed Webster that Sumner's election could be prevented indefinitely, a Whig legislator apparently defected when the vote was by sealed ballot. On April 24, 1851, Sumner was elected to the U.S. Senate on the twenty-sixth ballot by a margin of one vote." It was a matter of great rejoicing," wrote Dana. A procession formed and marched to Dana's father's house, "thinking I lived there." Dana's father told them his son was in Cambridge and the crowd gave "three cheers for R. H. Dana, Senior" who—true to form—told the gathering he was too ill to speak. Webster *was* ill—"grieved and mortified." Black armbands of "mourning" were worn on State Street. Benjamin R. Curtis drew up a public indictment signed by every Whig legislator denouncing Sumner's election as immoral and illegal.[36]

Neither Dana, who would be attacked on a Boston street after defending the last fugitive slave ever seized in Massachusetts, nor Sumner, who would be beaten on the floor of the U.S. Senate for excoriating slavery, foresaw the chain of violence that was to follow. But it is doubtful Thomas Sims was surprised. Upon his return to Savannah he was whipped nearly to death in the public square. The next time the U.S. government exercised its authority in the matter of Thomas Sims was when the Union Army took Vicksburg and Sims was liberated.[37]

12

BOYCOTT

Dana was thirty-five years old in the spring of 1851, when proper Boston's distaste for him began to coalesce. They were the "best people," toward whom Dana felt an instinctive affinity. Yet "in the mind of wealthy and respectable Boston almost anyone was to be preferred to Dana." Dana's outspoken opposition to Webster came at a time when Beacon Hill resented such criticism as "outrages on decency."[1]

Prosecution of political opponents could be a useful tool against citizens without social standing, as Daniel Webster and George Lunt soon hoped to prove by the trials of three African Americans charged with aiding the rescue of Shadrach Minkins. It was too blunt an instrument to be used against a Brahmin. District Attorney Lunt's crude threat to Dana had not worked. But Lunt, despite his authority as federal prosecutor, could never be mistaken for a Bostonian of influence. (When asked why he no longer stayed in Boston's Tremont House, Webster said it was because he "was tired of seeing the District Attorney walking up & down the passage-ways.")[2] To apply social and economic pressure sufficient to compel Dana to choose between comfort and conscience required sophistication. Brahmin Boston was up to the task.

On Monday April 14, two days after Sims was put on board the ship to slavery, a Boston newspaper contained, wrote Dana, "the first attack on my character which has yet appeared. My Free Soil friends have always congratulated me upon having escaped personal attacks." Indeed, he noted, "it was only a few days ago that Sumner was alluding to this fact." Dana recognized that the article was likely to be the first of several, though he could not have prepared for the volume or duration: "As the ice is broken, I suppose I must share the fortune of war of all political actors."[3]

In May the Boston newspapers subjected Dana to a barrage of criticism, orchestrated by George Ticknor. Several articles were signed "X". They were written by George S. Hillard, whom Ticknor preferred for such work. It was Hillard who refused Dana's "Cruelty to Seamen" essay unless Dana cleared it with Justice Story, and it had been Hillard whom Webster praised in his Seventh of March speech as "a young man . . . of whom the best hopes may be entertained." Sumner responded to the fusillade with a letter to the *Commonwealth*. Dana was grateful for the support, though Sumner "attacked the merchants and praised me which he need not have done."[4]

Ticknor's effort to isolate Dana went far beyond prompting newspaper attacks. There were very few Free Soilers who had social standing in the drawing rooms of Beacon Hill, but those who did "were made to feel in many ways the contempt felt for the cause they espoused." Ticknor had often hosted Dana (and Sumner) at the exclusive gatherings in the library of his Park Street mansion. In May 1851 Ticknor sent Dana a note they were never to speak again. It was intended as more than a social rebuff. It was aimed at fatally wounding the social standing of the young Brahmin. But Dana—unlike Sumner—was impervious to social slights "for the reason that no doubt as to his social position ever entered his mind."[5]

George Ticknor's effort to marshal the ranks of proper Boston against antislavery agitation was predicated on his view that in New

England, "[Negroes have] never thriven . . . and always will remain an inferior caste;—a shiftless, inefficient race of men."[6] Franklin Haven, a Boston banker from the superior caste, had demonstrated the efficiency of his race by gathering a group of forty financiers and businessmen to ensure that Secretary of State Webster looked after their interests. Dana knew the arrangement was efficient. He wanted to know if it was honest.

In early April, Dana gave a speech in Worcester on behalf of Free Soil congressman Charles Allen, in which he asserted that a corrupt bargain existed between Daniel Webster and Boston's most influential men. Dana claimed that Haven—at Webster's request—solicited funds from prominent Bostonians (and New Yorkers) to induce Webster to become Fillmore's secretary of state. On May 19 the banker emerged from the shadows with a letter to the *Boston Evening Transcript* to reply to "this calumny."

Haven responded that the "bargain which Mr. Dana calls 'corruption in high places' would be so if it had been made." It was a response on behalf of men sure of their absolute power. In fact, Dana's allegation was true. Even Haven could do no better than deny the request had come from Webster (although it had) and excuse the money that changed hands as a gift "from the honorable men . . . in Boston . . . [to] a great statesman, who had made a great sacrifice of his pecuniary interests."[7]

Webster needed no incentive to pursue the rescue case prosecutions, which he believed advanced his presidential prospects, but President Fillmore reminded him of the need to make "satisfactory arrangements for the trials of the rescuers." "It is very important that these criminals should be punished," asserted the president. "Their crime is contagious and they must not escape with impunity."[8] The contagious crime was treason. "The act of taking away Shadrach was an act of clear treason," declared Webster. "I speak this in the hearing of men who are lawyers. I speak it out to the country; I say it everywhere on my professional reputation. It was treason and nothing less."[9]

District Attorney Lunt—spurred by Webster—now began the first of the prosecutions intended to convict three leaders of Boston's African American community: merchant James Scott, community leader Lewis Hayden, and attorney Robert Morris. Each was charged with violating the Fugitive Slave Act by aiding the escape of Shadrach Minkins. The May newspaper attacks on Dana coincided—as was intended—with the start of the trials.

It is difficult to conceive of anything more disruptive to the concentration one needs to try a case before a jury than learning that the community in which one lives intends to ruin you. "Mr. Dana ought to think that he has enough of it . . . I am sorry he appears to have so little of the blood of his worthy ancestors in his veins," Webster wrote to Franklin Haven on May 29.[10] The next day George Ticknor formally broke off social relations with Dana, and three days later the Boston establishment called for a boycott of Dana's law practice.

Amid his defense of African American merchant James Scott, an article in the June 2 *Boston Daily Advertiser* called "on all the merchants to withdraw their business from me, & to proclaim non-intercourse."[11] The article asserted that Dana and his ilk were attacking members of the community "as far above them as the pulpit is above the kennel,—a patriot above a pirate." The anonymous writer conveyed the establishment's message: "a decent self respect in those who are thus assailed demands that confidential relations . . . should cease."[12] The article was signed "Son of a Merchant" and was again the work of Hillard at Ticknor's instigation. ("Lawyer of a merchant" would have been more accurate than "son of"—though other sobriquets undoubtedly occurred to Dana.)

The threat to squeeze Dana financially was real. He was the only Free Soil lawyer in Boston who depended on his court practice for a living. Dana knew that "there was a combination of the monied and social power of Massachusetts to crush us." Nor did it prove to be an empty threat. Charles Francis Adams Jr. began his legal career in Dana's office and believed Dana's income was seriously impaired: "It kept the rich clients from his office. . . . It is impossible to say how many clients were prevented from going to Dana during his years of active practice by considerations of this sort; but the number was unquestionably large and the interests they represented larger still."[13]

Two decades later, Dana acknowledged that his defense of the rescue cases "cost me my professional success in Boston for the next six or eight years—the critical period of a lawyer's life." He added, "I doubt I have ever recovered from it entirely."[14] But lives—lawyers' lives included—are lived one day at a time. The choice Dana had to make in June 1851 when Boston's establishment sought to intimidate him was whether to continue to defend those charged with violating the Fugitive Slave Act.

On the day the "Son of the Merchant" called for the boycott, the *Boston Courier* editorialized about Dana's allegation of Webster's corrupt bargain: "Of Mr. Richard H. Dana . . . it will not be forgotten . . . that he has cast aspersions equally infamous and false upon the man who has rendered more service to New England than the gratitude of her people can ever repay . . . upon the man who has more influence at this moment on her condition than any other man alive."[15]

The same day, Dana received a species of threat familiar to anyone who has had the experience of disturbing the status quo. An anonymous letter, signed "A Whig Merchant," purported to give Dana a friendly warning: "Although a stranger to you personally, . . . I hope you will take no notice of the miserable attacks upon you in some of the papers here. I allude especially to the article in the *Courier* this morning. . . . I really hope you will not condescend to notice the attacks in question." There was the chance that Dana would actually ignore the paper, so the "Whig Merchant" made the threat explicit: "Venom like *death* loves a *shining* work. The friends of Mr. Webster and the fugitive slave law are preparing a sword for their purpose, and will bring everything to bear, of course."[16] "I shall not reply now happen what will," wrote Dana in his journal, "they do not desire either to elicit truth or to do justice."[17]

Dana expected to defend each rescue case without co-counsel but was joined by antislavery lawyer Senator John Hale of New Hampshire. Dana was impressed with Hale—"an excellent companion . . . a queer mixture of natural gentleman & rough country trader."[18] His participation was welcomed by Dana after Webster's attempt to get Rufus Choate and Benjamin R. Curtis to join the prosecution; Webster's third choice, Salem lawyer Nathaniel Lord, agreed to appear with Lunt.

The government's case against African American merchant James Scott again relied in part on the testimony of Deputy Marshall Frederick Brynes, so thoroughly discredited by Dana during Lunt's bungled attempt to prosecute Charles Davis. U.S. District Court Judge Peleg Sprague, of whom Dana usually thought highly, "repeated with emphasis, all the reasons given by the U.S. Attorney for believing the government testimony & disbelieving ours."[19] The case was given to the jury at noon on June 5. At 5:30 P.M. the jurors reported a deadlock, but Judge Sprague ordered them to resume deliberations. The next morning, after twenty-one hours of deliberations with no verdict in sight, the court discharged the jury. They had split six to six. It was a triumph for the defense.

District Attorney Lunt immediately moved to impanel a new jury for the trial of Lewis Hayden. The government's case was strong—Hayden would later admit he played a pivotal role in the rescue—but Lunt was again faced with Dana and Hale for the defense. Hayden had much at risk (his wife was a fugitive from slavery) but was as difficult to intimidate as Dana. While the jury deliberated, Hayden attended a dinner for English abolitionist George Thompson. When it was announced that the jury was locked up for the night, the guests burst into applause. At 9:00 A.M. the following morning the jury reported it could not reach a verdict.[20]

Webster immediately wrote to Franklin Haven: "The great point is, to let it be known . . . that the friends of the Union in Massachusetts are determined & will not take any backward step, under any circumstances."[21] The Union's "friends" were doing their utmost. Though Dana had been subjected to prosecutorial threat, social ostracism, and economic boycott, he had not been openly shunned by his fellow lawyers. That changed when the leader of the Boston bar, Rufus Choate, made clear what its members should think of an attorney who objected to returning a man to slavery. Choate was unable to fulfill Webster's request that he join Lunt in prosecuting the rescue cases, but he wrote the U.S. attorney that he would "feel great pride and pleasure in assisting in these important trials . . . [to] vindicate the law of the land and the honor of the Bar."[22]

In July 1851, Choate was the principal speaker at the bar's anniversary celebration in memory of Justice Story, who had died in 1845. Emerson noted "the disgusting obsequiousness" with which Choate and Webster were received by "New England societies."[23] The day before the gathering, Dana learned from Sumner that Choate was preparing remarks that would assert that a lawyer's duty was to uphold the Fugitive Slave Act. Dana "begged [Sumner] to go to the dinner & told him that if anything was said against us, we would make a fight. But he declined."[24]

Dana went alone. Upon seeing Dana, Choate said, "I am sorry you are coming. I shall have to offend you. You had better reconsider." Choate claimed that preservation of the Union "in the scale of enlightened morality, was a greater & higher virtue than refusing to surrender a fugitive slave."[25] The bar's most celebrated attorney declared "loyalty to Law is the new duty which times demand of the legal profession." There was little doubt among the audience of lawyers whom Choate had in mind when he said: "Let the babblers against the Law contemplate Socrates in his cell about to quaff the poison which Athens presented him."[26] Dana thought the remarks "ill mannered & improper." He responded "in a pleasant way, but so that that they should feel it."[27]

Dana's self-esteem was critical but incomplete protection against the pressure, which was taking a greater toll than he realized. In early July he felt sick to his stomach and "ran for a bowl, expecting to vomit at an instant, when I fainted entirely away & fell to the floor, striking my eye against the bedpost." Dana passed it off as his tendency "to feel faint in sickness." He could at least look forward to a change. The same month, Dana decided "to buy land . . . to build a house & have a *home*."[28] But the best cure was the usual one. A day after he closed on a Cambridge lot adjacent to Longfellow's house, Dana left for Halifax and points east. It was August again.

If Dana made any return to the brothels of Halifax Hill, he did not record them. He listened with interest to a wagon driver's account of "female virtue in the country towns of Maine." It accorded with Dana's knowledge that "it is notorious that Maine furnishes the chief supply of the Boston market in girls of the town." A drunken steward on the steamer to New Brunswick awoke Dana at 5:00 A.M. "I struck him a blow which laid him flat on the cabin floor." When Dana lodged with a garrulous host, he wrote, "I had rather live on cheese & garlic, in a windmill than to endure him one day more." Dana added "yet he means well"—a sign he was beginning to unwind.[29]

Soon Dana was deep in the Maine woods. He welcomed the company of hunters, trappers, and lumberjacks, the latter "a class by themselves, like sailors." His appetite returned: "I never relished fish so much in my life, as seated in the open air, in the early morning, on the banks of the lake, by the side of this cool spring, under the shadow of these noble mountains, the clouds & fog rolling off before the risen sun." Dana's canoe "floated . . . in profound silence . . . in harmony with the falling of the night shadows . . . the northern lights shooting up their spears into the dark sky & the long-drawn, plaintive, musical cry of the loon."[30]

Asleep by the campfire, Dana was "dreaming of reading a controversy in the *Daily Advertiser* . . . Mr. Ticknor [spoke of] . . . his family connections [and] political influence." Dana awoke to sunrise and birdsong.

He needed renewal as much as integrity to confront the Ticknors of the world. Dana found it in *"the vicissitudes of a day, in a boat! . . .* It takes me completely from all cares of life. I forget I am anything but a sailor." His thoughts wandered back to his days before the mast, "and I dream over the events of that parentheses in my life." If he could not sail or hike, "I will rather lie down & bask in the sun, or throw stones in the air and catch them . . . than . . . allow one thought of business, or law or literature to enter."[31]

It seemed to Dana that "once a year, for three weeks or a month, is not too much for such relaxation, for an abandonment to nature & nature's unsophisticated men, in a city living lawyer."[32] Especially, one could add, when the lawyer was Dana, the year was 1851, and the city was Boston.

13

THE LITTLE DARKY LAWYER

The legal community to which Dana returned in the
fall of 1851 was keeping score. In the four rescue cases initiated by U.S.
Attorney Lunt to date, there had not been a conviction. The prosecution
of Charles G. Davis was dismissed before trial for lack of evidence, and
the trials of James Scott and Lewis Hayden resulted in hung juries. A
fourth prosecution begun the previous June against black attorney
Robert Morris had been continued—over Dana's objection—when Lunt
realized the case was going badly for the government.

But when it came to picking winners and losers, the Boston bar had
no difficulty choosing sides in the confrontation over the Fugitive Slave
Act. Rufus Choate—who had instructed attorneys on their duty to uphold the law—was offered a position on the U.S. Supreme Court by Web-

ster. When he declined, Webster turned to forty-two-year-old Benjamin R. Curtis, who had worked with Choate to ensure that Thomas Sims was sent back to slavery.

Secretary of State Webster's recommendation of Curtis was welcomed by President Fillmore. Curtis had prepared an opinion as a private lawyer defending the constitutionality of the Fugitive Slave Act. Widely circulated among the Boston bar, it was intended, Webster wrote to Fillmore, to "silence the small lawyers."[1] The appointment of Curtis to the vacancy created by the death of Justice Levi Woodbury had a more specific purpose: it was meant to intimidate the brave lawyers.

Webster orchestrated the nomination not because he needed Justice Curtis on the Supreme Court but because he needed Judge Curtis in Boston. In one of the most remarkable letters of acceptance of a judicial appointment in the history of American law, Curtis wrote to President Fillmore on October 7, 1851: "On my return home, after an absence of ten days in a distant city, where I went to discharge a professional engagement, I received from the Secretary of State a commission as an Associate Justice of the Supreme Court of the United States." After a perfunctory expression of thanks, Curtis advised the president to immediately renew judicial circuit assignments, "as there is to be a term of the Circuit Court in Boston on the 15th instant, at which my presence is very desirable."[2]

Three days later, Curtis took office as the presiding judge in Boston. He "wasted no time before issuing a grand jury charge that laid down a chilling interpretation of treason."[3] Webster had already expressed his view that the rescue of Shadrach Minkins satisfied the "levying War" element of the treason clause of the U.S. Constitution. To this, Judge Curtis added that criminal liability for treason extended to persons performing "any part, however minute, or however remote, from the scene of the action, and who are actually leagued in the general conspiracy."[4] This was the first time—but not the last—Dana was to confront the use of "constructive treason" to further political interests.

The judge's treason charge to the grand jury was a warning to opponents of the Fugitive Slave Act and it was published as such in Boston newspapers. Dana conceded that the Curtis charge was "a remarkably clear lawyer-like performance." But he profoundly disagreed with the Webster-Curtis attempt to weave a wide net of treason. "Under our Constitution treason is—treason!" wrote Dana. "It is an attempt to overthrow the State & nothing less."[5] Definitions mattered. Treason was punishable by death.

But Dana faced a more imminent challenge. U.S. Attorney Lunt could now place on the scales of justice the weight of Webster's handpicked judge. Lunt immediately renewed the prosecution of Robert Morris for aiding and abetting the escape of Shadrach Minkins. Dana detested the federal prosecutor's willingness to do Webster's bidding by targeting Boston's black community, upon whom the fugitive slave law "falls with the terrors and blackness of night."[6]

And he despised Lunt for playing to the public by deliberately demeaning Morris. In the preliminary hearing in the first rescue case, a witness for the prosecution made an insulting reference to Morris, who was attending the hearing. Dana was incensed at Lunt's reaction and immediately called him on it:

> DANA: When one . . . by his industry and abilities has raised himself to the dignity of a place in this bar, it was with mortification I heard him insulted, yesterday on the stand . . . as "the little darky lawyer" . . . it was with deep regret that I saw the representative of the government lead off the laugh of the audience against him.
>
> LUNT: This is false.
>
> DANA: Do you deny you did so? It was seen and noticed by us all. I spoke to you at the time.
>
> LUNT: I only smiled. I cannot always control my muscles.
>
> DANA: I am sorry you could not control them on this occasion. It led off and encouraged others who take their cue from persons in high stations.[7]

"There is a method of exclusion more terrible than a merely formal one," Henry Bowditch had said when Macon Allen, the first black attorney known to have been admitted to the practice of law, left Boston within two years.[8] Lunt's laughter when his witness called Robert Morris "the little darky lawyer" was evidence enough of informal barriers. For proof of formal exclusion, one need not look far. In 1850 there were 24,000 lawyers in the United States. Robert Morris was the only other black attorney.[9]

Admitted to the Massachusetts bar in 1847, by 1851 Morris was already a well-known figure among Boston's black community and white bar. Undaunted by attempts to ostracize him, Morris became the first

African American lawyer to successfully try his case to a jury. When the white jury returned a verdict for his client, a black laborer suing for unpaid wages, a courtroom crowded with residents of the black community erupted in applause. In 1850 Morris joined with Charles Summer to challenge segregation in Boston public schools. Chief Justice Shaw rejected their argument in a "separate but equal" analysis that was still being cited sixty years later when the U.S. Supreme Court applied the analysis to a challenge to segregated railroad cars, but the case brought Morris notoriety and made him a leader of Boston's African American community.[10]

Yet whatever his outward manifestations of confidence, the anxiety of the twenty-eight-year-old Morris may be imagined as the full weight of the prosecutorial authority of the U.S. government began to press upon him. A conviction could bring six months in jail, but worse for one who had overcome so much, it almost certainly would lead to disbarment. Dana was a fearless advocate, but he was only eight years older than his client. It would not have cheered Morris to read Dana's journal entry on the eve of trial: "I must be a lawyer, it would seem. Sometimes I think I am. Sometimes I feel astonishingly ignorant of the law."[11]

Dana sought to have the June proceedings made a part of the record, but in an indication that Webster did not believe Lunt's prosecution of Morris had begun well, Judge Curtis ruled that the prosecutor could start over. Dana's first line of defense to the prosecution of Morris was that Commissioner George Ticknor Curtis, known derisively as the "Little Expounder," erred in issuing a warrant for Shadrach Minkins without proof that he was a slave.

Dana asserted that the law of Virginia where Shadrach had been enslaved provided that no persons shall be slaves except descendants of females who were slaves in 1785. No finding had been made by Commissioner Curtis that Shadrach was such a descendant. It was, of course, exceedingly convenient for the government that Commissioner George T. Curtis was the brother of Judge Benjamin R. Curtis. Judge Curtis rejected Dana's contention that the Fugitive Slave Act required a showing of descent.[12]

Prosecutor Lunt secured the presence of both a slave master and a slave catcher to prove Shadrach's slavery. John Debree traveled from Virginia to testify that Shadrach was his slave. His "slave catcher," John Caphart, testified that he had seen Minkins sold by a sheriff at the door of a Virginia courthouse. Caphart was chilling figure. Dana wrote that in eleven years of practice, "I never met with anything so cold blooded as the testimony of that man."[13] Caphart thought nothing of beating a sailor nearly to death when at sea, nor did he think twice about flogging slaves, adding that he had reduced his charge from 62 cents to 50 cents a head.[14]

The prosecution's case against Morris was credible for the same reason it been strong against Lewis Hayden—both men were involved in planning the rescue. District Attorney Lunt called witnesses who had seen Morris whispering to Shadrach moments before the rescue. That could be explained by Morris's role as counsel, but testimony that the young attorney had been seen at points along the route of escape was more difficult to counter. Witnesses for Morris placed him away from Shadrach's route, but the "alibi" testimony was not strong. Dana wisely called character witnesses who vouched for the defendant's faithfulness to the rule of law.

Dana's co-counsel, John Hale, sought to argue that the jury was the ultimate arbiter of law and fact, and therefore could acquit Morris if they believed the Fugitive Slave Act to be unconstitutional. Judge Curtis did not intend to allow Hale—who was to be the Free Soil candidate for president in 1852—to argue the constitutionality of the law to the jury under any circumstance, but Curtis correctly declared that issues of law are the exclusive province of the judge.[15]

On November 11, 1851, after a week of trial, Judge Curtis charged the jury. Dana considered the charge impartial. It was eminently fair in the court's instruction as to witnesses, but the new judge's view of the net of criminality cast by the fugitive slave law must have alarmed Dana to say nothing of Morris. The jury was instructed that the defendant could be found guilty "even if it [does] not appear that he aided in the rescue, yet if he was present, and did nothing to prevent it, this would render him guilty under the statute."[16]

The jury received the case at 2:30 P.M. At 9:30 the next morning it announced it had reached a verdict. A verdict was not welcome news. The trials of James Scott and Lewis Hayden were victories because the juries had not reached verdicts. Jurors had split evenly on Scott's guilt and nine of twelve had voted to convict Hayden. Unanimity was not a good sign for Morris.

"Have you reached a verdict?" intoned the clerk. "We have," answered the foreman. "What say you?" asked the clerk. "Not guilty," responded the foreman.

Dana's journal made only passing reference to the verdict in the immediate aftermath of the trial: "The chief secular events of the week are the elections. The coalition (Free Soil & Democrat) has probably carried both branches of the Legislature.... The other event is the acquittal of Morris. I hope this will end the rescue cases." It did not, but he noted that, despite the fact that his defense of fugitive slaves and their rescuers had put his law practice in economic peril, "[my interest] in my profession has increased in the last year."[17]

Construction of the new Cambridge house was progressing, "which gives me much pleasure in the hope of having a home for myself & family after living so long in tents." And at a ball at the close of 1851, he and Sarah "danced every dance except the waltzes." Dana overheard a guest asking "who that beautiful young lady was." He was delighted with the reply: "She is the mother of five children."[18]

But perhaps the best explanation for Dana's contentment came at the year's end, when he received "as gratifying a testimonial as I ever received & perhaps ever shall receive." Robert Morris sent Dana a present of eight volumes of the works of the English jurist Hallam, "a superb London edition beautifully bound."[19] Morris included a note:

> Dear Sir:
>
> A number of our colored citizens, deeply grateful for your most able and manly defence of the parties indicted for the rescue of Shadrach, and anxious to show, even by a slight token, their heartfelt respect for your character, and their cordial appreciation of your invaluable service in the rescue trials, ask you to honor them by acceptance of the accompanying volumes of the historical works of Hallam. In his writings we seem to discern a kindred spirit to your own, since they are everywhere animated by that strong sentiment of *Liberty protected by Law*, which lives in your own breast, and which has in all later times so honorably distinguished the truly great constitutional lawyers, the Erskines and Broughams of England.
>
> I am, sir, with the highest respect,
>
> Your friend and servant,
>
> *Robert Morris*[20]

As Dana waited for the verdict in the Robert Morris prosecution, Herman Melville awaited publication of a new novel. The two friends had corresponded while Melville worked on the book. "About the 'whaling voyage,'" wrote Melville to Dana, "I am half way in the work, I am very glad your suggestion so jumps with mine. It will be a strange sort of book, tho I fear."[21] *Moby-Dick; or, The Whale* was published by Harper on November 14, 1851, two days after the Morris acquittal.

Dana first met Melville in 1847. "Mr. Herman Melville is expected to take tea with us tomorrow. He would like to meet you," a Dana cousin wrote on July 8.[22] The twenty-eight-year-old author of *Typee* and *Omoo* was the fiancé of Elizabeth Shaw, the daughter of Chief Justice Lemuel Shaw. There was much for the two young men to discuss, given their shared experiences as common seamen, but that had to wait. Sarah was aghast at Melville's account of sailors in the South Seas. "Imagine Miss Shaw's feeling at the having of such a lover known to the world. How could one survive the beastliness of it!"[23]

Chief Justice Shaw gave a dinner party for his daughter and new son-in-law in July 1848, which Dana attended. A few nights later Melville was Dana's dinner guest at Boston's Parker House. Dana had just made his political debut as chair of the Boston Free Soil meeting. It is certain that he found Melville more sympathetic to his views than the chief justice, who was a Webster Whig then and always.[24] Dana and Melville were of the same mind when it came to the treatment of sailors. When Dana recommended Melville for a consulship, he emphasized Melville's "unusual degree" of knowledge of a sailor's life because it would enable his friend to "stand clear" of the "inducement of trade & consignments which lead so many consuls to neglect seamen & lend their influence indiscriminately in favor of owners & masters."[25]

In the winter of 1849 Melville joined his wife in Boston for the birth of their first child. Melville borrowed books from the Boston Athenaeum (on Judge Shaw's card) and dined with Dana. "Melville has made a visit here," wrote Dana to his brother Ned, "and I have passed two nights with him at Parker's. . . . He is incomparable in dramatic story telling."[26] The evening's stories may well have included some of Melville's experiences on a U.S. man-of-war, for Melville was then at work on his *White-Jacket or The World in a Man-of-War.* In October he wrote to Dana that the forthcoming book would be "rather man-of-*warish* in style," adding "but you, who like myself, have experienced in person the usages to which a sailor is subjected, will not wonder, perhaps, at anything in the book." Melville signed the letter "fraternally yours—a sea-brother."[27]

Dana read more than an echo of his own experience in Melville's flogging scenes, which replicate the horror Dana depicted in *Two Years Before the Mast*. Dana must have found particularly striking the passage in which Melville's flogged sailor called out "My God! Oh my God!" as Dana's shipmate, John the Swede, had screamed "Oh Jesus Christ! Oh Jesus Christ!" The sailors' cries elicited similar responses: "I would not forgive God Almighty!" from Melville's fictional captain; "Jesus Christ can't help you now," from the very real Captain Frank Thompson.[28]

But Dana knew Melville was writing from life, not literature. A letter (now lost) from Dana to Melville in the spring of 1850 praised *White Jacket*. Melville was flattered: "I am specially delighted at the thought, that these strange, congenial feelings, with which after my first voyage, I for the first time read *Two Years Before the Mast,* and while so engaged was, as it were, tied & wedded to you by a sort of siamese link of affectionate sympathy—that these feelings should be reciprocated by you, in your letter, and be called out by any *White Jacket* & *Redburn* of mine—this is indeed delightful to me."

Melville answered one of Dana's questions about the book (yes, there was such a jacket, which Melville supposed "is now somewhere at the bottom of [the] Charles River") but deferred another. Dana was curious about the "real names" of the officers in the book, but Melville demurred from putting their names in "pen & ink": "I will tell you all when I next have the pleasure of seeing you face to face."

Melville's letter regaled Dana with an account of Melville's London meeting with Moxon, the English publisher, to whom Dana had provided a letter of introduction. Moxon published *Two Years Before the Mast* but declined Melville's *White Jacket* (because of copyright issues). Melville wrote to Dana that Moxon's reception reminded him "of that Greenland whaler discovered near the Pole, adrift & silent in a calm with the frozen form of a man seated at a desk in the cabin before an stand of icy ink."[29]

By the fall of 1851, four years after their first meeting, Dana and Melville were again leaving the safe harbors to which they had returned. Melville wrote his father-in-law that his desire for the success of the books he had written "springs from my pocket & not from my heart. It is my earnest desire to write those sorts of books which are said to 'fail.'"[30] Chief Justice Shaw was as enthusiastic about his son-in-law's definition of a successful author as he was about Dana's equally deviant idea of a successful lawyer.

Measured by earnings, the sea brothers were failed writers. Harper did not pay an advance for *Moby Dick,* and Melville's royalties from the book (after deductions due Harper) were slightly more than $500, twice what the publisher had paid for *Two Years Before the Mast.*[31] But Dana considered Melville a man "of note in the Republic of letters." When Melville asked for Dana's help in seeking a consulship in Florence, Dana wrote Charles Sumner, "I like the notion of such consulships going to men of letters . . . & Melville is a capital good fellow, good manners & feelings."[32]

In a letter of introduction to the English publisher Moxon, Dana depicted Melville as a "most agreeable gentleman of one of our best families."[33] But he knew his friend could never be mistaken for those whom Dana described in *Two Year Before the Mast,* as people who "never walked but in one line from their cradle to their graves."[34] In *White Jacket* Melville honored Dana's deviation from the slavish shore: "But if you want the best idea of Cape Horn, get my friend Dana's unmatchable *Two Years Before the Mast.* But you can read, and so you must have read it. His chapters describing Cape Horn must have been written with an icicle."[35]

Dana may have paid his own tribute to a man who was a sea brother before he was the son-in-law of Chief Justice Shaw. In July 1853 a schooner under the command of Captain Austin Bearse compelled a brig entering Boston Harbor to surrender a slave. The exploit aroused the ire of defenders of the Fugitive Slave Act, including Lemuel Shaw. Bearse later wrote that when his part became known, "many people would not patronize my boat after what I had done."[36] The boat was, in fact, surreptitiously in the service of the Committee of Vigilance. Dana took part in the committee's decisions, including "those that touched on nautical matters, such as the acquisition of vessels for the rescue of fugitive slaves."[37] The schooner was christened *Moby Dick.*

Dana about 1840. The twenty-five-year-old lawyer "still wore his hair long, sailor-fashion, and contemporaries recorded that he rolled a little in his gait, by no means unconscious of exuding the same air of outdoor hardiness which he brought back from Cape Horn." Courtesy of the Longfellow House, Washington's Headquarters National Historic Site, Cambridge, Mass.

The Brig *Pilgrim.* Courtesy of the Santa Barbara Historical Museum, gift of Georgiana
Lacy Spaulding and Mildred Lacy Williamson.

Hauling Hides. Courtesy of the San Diego History Center.

The *Alert*. Dana drew this sketch for Sarah. Courtesy of the Longfellow House,
Washington's Headquarters National Historic Site.

A page from Dana's journal. The entry of February 15, 1851, recorded his confrontation with Chief Justice Lemuel Shaw. Courtesy of the Massachusetts Historical Society, from the Collection of the Massachusetts Historical Society.

Joseph Story. Justice Story was beloved by Harvard Law students, to whom, wrote Dana, he was "an elder brother, the patriarch of a common family." Courtesy of the Library of Congress.

George Ticknor. Ticknor's elite position among Brahmins was so well
recognized that it was said Boston society was more aptly named "Ticknorville."
Courtesy of the Longfellow House, Washington's Headquarters National Historic Site.

Charles Sumner in 1846. Of the many abolitionist meetings held in Boston in the early days of the antislavery movement, William Lloyd Garrison said, "Mr. Sumner's presence was never recognized at any one of them. Why he never came—at least among the curious to hear—I know not." Courtesy of the Longfellow House, Washington's Headquarters National Historic Site.

Rufus Choate. Choate's skill as a trial lawyer mesmerized lawyers and juries
alike. It was, wrote Dana, as if "by the side of our time-enduring granite,
there had risen, like an exhalation, some Oriental structure, with the domes
and glittering minarets of the Eastern world." Courtesy of the Longfellow House,
Washington's Headquarters National Historic Site.

Lemuel Shaw. "The Chief Justice! We contemplate him as the East Indian does
his wooden-headed idol—he knows that his is ugly, but he feels that he is great."
Choate's notorious toast was not made in Shaw's presence. Courtesy of the Library
of Congress.

The Club. A representative picture of those who "thought Boston was a club—their club." Benjamin R. Curtis (standing, left), a Webster loyalist, was rewarded with a seat on the U.S. Supreme Court. Other members of the influential Curtis clan are seated far left and far right. Massachusetts Supreme Court Chief Justice Shaw is seated in the middle. Courtesy of the Longfellow House, Washington's Headquarters National Historic Site.

Dana the advocate in 1849. The thirty-four-year-old lawyer would spend
the next five years immersed in the defense of fugitive slaves and their rescuers.
Dana's role in the cases "kept the rich clients from his office." Courtesy of the
Longfellow House, Washington's Headquarters National Historic Site.

Robert Morris, the only African American lawyer in Massachusetts (and perhaps the United States) at the time. Dana was incensed when the federal prosecutor led courtroom laughter mocking "the little darky lawyer." Courtesy of the Social Law Library, Boston.

Daniel Webster, 1851. Dana, disillusioned by "the great man of the age,"
wrote: "With all his gigantic powers there is one thing he lacketh. . . . He will run
no personal risk for a principle." Courtesy of the Library of Congress.

An urgent warning to Boston's African American community after the seizure of fugitive slave Thomas Sims in April 1851. Courtesy of the Library of Congress.

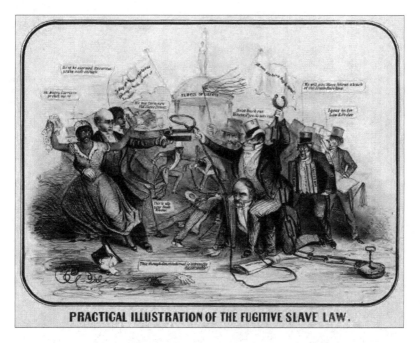

PRACTICAL ILLUSTRATION OF THE FUGITIVE SLAVE LAW.

Practical Illustration of the Fugitive Slave Law, 1851. Secretary of State Daniel Webster holds a copy of the Constitution while a slave master rides his back. Courtesy of the Library of Congress.

Anthony Burns is marched back to slavery by the "marshal's guard" on June 2, 1854. Charles Emery Stevens, *Anthony Burns: A History* (Boston: John P. Jewett, 1856).

Cover of the contemporaneous account of the seizure, trial, and rendition
of Anthony Burns, published in 1854. Courtesy of the Longfellow House,
Washington's Headquarters National Historic Site.

Sarah Dana about 1868. Courtesy of the Longfellow House, Washington's
Headquarters National Historic Site.

Dana's first house still stands in Cambridge. Dana wrote to Sarah when the house was sold: "I sat in the dining-room with many thoughts and meditations on our seventeen years there, when our children were infants and little girls and we were almost young." Courtesy of the Longfellow House, Washington's Headquarters National Historic Site.

Richard Henry Dana Sr., Richard Henry Dana III, and Richard Henry Dana Jr.
Courtesy of the Longfellow House, Washington's Headquarters National Historic Site.

The bail hearing for Jefferson Davis, held at U.S. District Court,
Richmond, Virginia, in May 1867. Courtesy of the Library of Congress.

Herman Melville, 1870. As respectable looking as "sea brother" Dana.

Courtesy of the Library of Congress.

Dana in 1872. "My life has been a failure." Courtesy of the Longfellow House, Washington's Headquarters National Historic Site.

The Dana statue at Dana Point, California. Photo courtesy of Brian E. J. Martin.

14

THE CLUB

The government's failure to convict Robert Morris was the fourth time in ten months that Dana stymied the Webster-initiated rescue case prosecutions. The secretary of state was not deterred. At the close of 1851 Webster wrote to Boston banker Franklin Haven, "It is a time for doing whatever is to be done. The question narrows to a single point. All will come right, if Massachusetts stands firm and inflexible."[1] But the "single point"—adherence to the Fugitive Slave Act—could not be narrowed.

In April 1852 Dana traveled by railcar to New Haven to argue a case. On the way, he read *Uncle Tom's Cabin,* published a month earlier: "It was a singular fact that four persons were reading this book, each unconnected with the other, in one car." Dana had a fond memory of its author,

Harriet Beecher Stowe, whom he had met when he was twelve and she, eighteen. Stowe "seemed like a person that might fall in love, as well as take a pun."[2]

Uncle Tom's Cabin introduced Americans to a man Dana had already met. The slave trader Haley of Stowe's novel was based upon John Caphart, the witness used by U.S. Attorney Lunt in the rescue trials to prove that Shadrach Minkins was a slave. When some critics suggested that Stowe's portrayal of Haley's cruelty was exaggerated, the author wrote to Dana that it was testimony in the rescue trials that "helped me essentially in an insight into the character of a negro catcher." Stowe asked Dana to forward his cross-examination of the man "who professed to have been a whipper of the South & who told of his regular terms of a head."[3]

Dana replied with an account "the accuracy of which you may reply upon." He informed Stowe that Caphart was portrayed by the prosecution to be "merely a policeman of Norfolk, Virginia." But prior to Caphart taking the stand in the Robert Morris trial, "someone in the room gave me a hint of the occupations of many of these so-called policemen . . . which led to my cross-examination."[4] Stowe cited an excerpt of Dana's cross-examination to refute claims that her fictional slave catcher was a creature of her imagination:

> Q. I suppose you flog women and girls, as well as men.
>
> A. Women and men.
>
> Q. Mr. Caphart, how long have you been engaged in this business?
>
> A. Ever since 1836.
>
> Q. How many Negroes do you suppose you have flogged, in all, women and children included?
>
> A. [Looking calmly around the room] I don't know how many niggers you have got here in Massachusetts, but I think I should have flogged as many as you've got in this state.[5]

The impact of Dana's cross-examination of John Caphart on Harriet Beecher Stowe is well-documented. Its effect on Justice Benjamin R. Curtis must be guessed, but the new judge overruled prosecutor Lunt's objections to Dana's questions. Six years later, Justice Curtis—who as a Webster Whig had once asserted that fugitive slaves "have no right to be *here*"—dissented in the *Dred Scott* case and resigned from the Supreme Court.[6]

Given the influence of *Uncle Tom's Cabin* in arousing the nation to the horror of the Fugitive Slave Act, few prosecutors in the history of American law have ever made a worse choice of witnesses than did U.S. Attorney Lunt when he called John Caphart to the stand in pursuit of Webster's single point. But nothing diminished Webster's interest in securing rescue cases convictions.

In June 1852, Lunt commenced the prosecution of Eizur Wright, the fifth defendant tried for aiding the rescue of Shadrach. Wright, the publisher of the anti-Webster paper *Commonwealth*, had less involvement—if any at all—than the three defendants (Scott, Hayden, and Morris) whose cases had gone to a jury. Wright declined Dana's offer of representation, confident that he could handle his own defense. It was almost a disaster. The jury deadlocked, eleven jurors voting to find the defendant guilty. Dana believed Wright would have been acquitted if he had been represented. The result, however, did give rise to the belief among abolitionists that God always provided "a faithful juror."

Dana remarked upon the phenomenon: "It seems as if Providence always raised up at least one faithful man on each jury to prevent a conviction in these cases." A year after the rescue cases, Dana was approached by a man whom he recognized as a former juror. Dana learned that the man had also driven the wagon in which Shadrach had hidden when spirited out of Boston. Dana found it incredible that "Lunt and the U.S. Marshal raked the district of Massachusetts to find a jury that would convict . . . subjected the whole jury to special investigation—actually packing the jury—and yet succeeded in getting into the jury-box the one man who had been instrumental in [getting] Shadrach . . . out of the jurisdiction."[7]

At the end of the summer of 1852 Dana faced an excruciating decision. His commitment to the principles of the Free Soil Party and his brilliant advocacy in opposition to the Fugitive Slave Act made him the first choice to preside over a Faneuil Hall meeting to ratify the Free Soil presidential candidacy of John Hale. Only four years away, the demise of the Whig Party and the birth of a Republican Party would owe much to its Free Soil antecedents. If Dana could not foresee the precise shape of national politics to come, he recognized that his political future was at a crossroad.

Charles Francis Adams Jr. knew Dana well and believed that, given his temperament, Dana could have political success only if he, "like John

Adams—who . . . he most resembled—pursu[ed] the course which John Adams pursued,—that is, by throwing himself body and soul into a rising popular cause and absolutely identifying with it."[8] Adams gave up his law practice to join the American Revolution.

Dana noted that he was "never more distressed in my life to make a decision." He set forth the principal reason for not accepting the invitation to preside over the meeting—"Cannot engage in politics. My profession requires all my time & mind"—as well as the best reason for accepting it—"the threats made against me in the papers."[9] Henry Wilson, the political kingmaker so critical to Charles Sumner's success, urged Dana to accept, as did Charles Francis Adams Sr., leader of the Massachusetts Free Soilers.

Dana's journal records his decision: "Very reluctant & quite unsatisfied determined to decline. Did so. I do not know that I ever so much regretted [the] want of property, to enable [me] to do a great public duty."[10] Dana's journal entry was dated August 26, 1852, the very day of Charles Sumner's "Freedom National" speech to the U.S. Senate. It was the speech that made the lawyer who refused to join Dana in the first rescue case the most famous opponent of the Fugitive Slave Act in the country.[11]

Dana's decision was understandable but consequential. To have reached the Senate by Sumner's path, or to have married for property, required calculation. Dana was not a calculating man—he was a romantic one. His fateful decision to depart the political playing field in 1852 was a mistake not because of miscalculation. It was a mistake because he did not follow his heart.

There was no doubt, however, that Dana made the most rational decision. The Dana family, immediate and extended, depended for their support solely on Dana's income from his law practice. In 1848 Dana had taken on Frank E. Parker as a law partner. It was a fortuitous choice. Parker, a quiet bachelor, excelled where Dana did not. His expertise in trusts and estates and competence in office management provided stability to the partnership.

Dissolution of his partnership would not have been the only cost of a decision to fully engage in politics. The Danas moved into the first home of their own in March 1852. "It is a beautiful house," wrote Dana. "Sarah has selected the wall-papers & carpets & furniture with . . . such exquisite taste that it looks like a fairyland." Dana devoted two nights to arranging his study—"for the first time in my life . . . [I have] a private room with my own furniture & papers & books about me." Husband and wife "congratulated each other like children at a play."[12]

With the birth of Richard Henry Dana III in 1851, the Danas now had five children: Sally (10), Ruth Charlotte (8), Elizabeth (6), and Mary (4). Dana enjoyed his family. Leaving by train one Saturday morning, he was too rushed to take Ruth Charlotte with him as he had promised. Once aboard, he found himself "so much affected by the thought of the dear little girl's disappointment" that he got off at the next stop and returned home.[13] His daughter was delighted.

"The first caller we had at our new house was Prof. Longfellow! May it be a good omen!" Dana exclaimed in his journal.[14] It was. The Danas raised their family there, and son Richard married the girl next door, Longfellow's daughter Edith. When Dana and Sarah moved to Boston, Dana returned to the house on a Christmas Eve before it was sold. He wrote to Sarah: "I sat in the dining-room with many thoughts and meditations on our seventeen years there, when our children were infants and little girls and we were almost young."[15]

Sarah and Dana were compatible again. Dana—who had a sailor's faith in omens—recounted the remarkable recovery of the gold pencil case Sarah gave him ten years earlier—"I have lost it several times but always found it again." This time it seemed gone for good. Sarah insisted on returning to the spot where Dana thought he lost it: "We looked over one ledge & then a second & were just giving up when S. saw it in the sand, where it had lain 8 weeks. I received it as more than a new gift."[16]

In mid-September 1852, Dana hosted a supper for Sumner "just from his first session in Congress & his great speech on the Fugitive Slave Law." There had been a concerted effort to prevent Sumner from speaking, but the freshman Senator spoke for three hours. Sumner told Dana that during the speech "Webster came in & stayed about an hour . . . the gallery was full. Several were in tears."[17]

Sumner's assertion that that the Fugitive Slave Act was unconstitutional echoed legal arguments that Dana had made. But Sumner's address to the Senate was a sensation not for what he said about the law—but for what he said about those whom the law enslaved. "Beware of the groans of wounded souls," declared Sumner in closing, "oppress not to the utmost a single heart, for a solitary sigh has the power to overset a whole world." Alabama Senator Jeremiah Clemens rose to assert that no reply to Sumner was necessary because "the barking of a puppy never did any harm." Only three senators supported Sumner's motion to repeal the Fugitive Slave Act.[18]

It was business as usual in Boston as well. Lunt's obstinacy, incompetence, and disregard for the truth astounded Dana. The district attorney misrepresented to the court his reason for rescheduling a case in which Dana was involved. Dana asked Rufus Choate if he believed Lunt was a man who would fabricate stories to conceal his mistakes. Choate, who saw Lunt almost daily, replied, "When I last knew him, he was."[19]

The prosecutor was determined to secure a rescue case conviction. James Scott, Lewis Hayden, and Elizur Wright could all be retried because of hung juries. Lunt chose to first retry Wright because the government had come within one vote of convicting the unrepresented defendant in the previous trial. Nor was there any doubt of Webster's interest in the case. When the rescue prosecutions began, the secretary of state wrote to President Fillmore: "It is of great importance to convict Wright."[20] This time Wright accepted Dana's offer of representation.

On October 25, 1852, two days into the trial, came news that Daniel Webster had died. "No death since that of Washington has excited so general a grief," wrote Dana that evening. There was sentiment "that the country has sustained an irreparable loss." For Dana, Webster with "all his greatness and smallness" was a "great sun . . . gone down in a cloud."[21] Forty-eight hours later, Wright stood with Dana to hear the jury's verdict: not guilty.

The Boston bar proposed a resolution eulogizing Webster as a great voice that "*never failed* to support the cause of the oppressed."[22] Dana objected.

On the first day of January 1853, Dana was at his office reconciling bills and accounts. It was "the worst day of the whole year . . . I wish it were kept as either a holy day or a holiday."[23] Dana had reason to resist embarking on the New Year. The boycott of his practice was beginning to tell. State Street merchants openly snubbed Dana when seeing him on the street. Dana's response was characteristic—he ignored the slights and worked harder.

Dana never allocated his advocacy on the basis of a client's ability to pay or social standing. His caseload now took him to rural courts that did not often see a Boston lawyer. He obtained a verdict of $3,200 for a country client, noting with some pride, "This is considered a large verdict for a Norfolk jury of farmers." Trying a case in Dedham, Dana remarked on a remnant "of the old pomp & parade of court week." The judge and lawyers boarded at the same tavern with "a stray guest from Boston." When court was to begin, the sheriff "with a long white rod comes to the tavern & stands by the door and precedes the judge on his way to court—two plain citizens walking through the mud together."[24]

In Plymouth, an ill Dana could find no lawyer to take his place at trial. The judge "offered to adjourn telling me I was too ill to go on, but I determined . . . to have it over . . . my duties seem too pressing to be avoided." To further supplement his income, Dana began lecturing again. He delivered seven lectures in January (his new topic was Edmund Burke). In early March, Dana recorded a day that followed an evening lecture in North Bridgewater. He returned to Boston in the morning to make an argument before the Massachusetts Supreme Court, took a train to Dedham to begin a jury trial, traveled to Charleston in the evening to give another lecture, and then went back to Boston to prepare a witness for another trial, "all this time eating nothing but a few figs & sandwich in the coach."[25]

The Boston establishment's shunning of Dana affected his health and wealth, but it had no effect on his conscience. In February Dana called upon Lunt to urge him to dismiss the remaining rescue cases. He reminded the federal prosecutor that James Scott, the African American merchant whose case had been the first to go to a jury, had been living under the threat of retrial for over twenty months. Dana told Lunt that "such a course was unprecedented in criminal & especially political trials." Lunt replied that "he supposed I knew that the Secretary of State had taken these cases into his own hands & that he had been obliged to do as Mr. Webster said & not as he wished." Lunt observed that "*perhaps the fellows had been punished enough.*" (Dana's journal contains the pointed aside: "What right had he to punish?") The district attorney, however, refused to dismiss the remaining cases, saying "perhaps he would try one of them in May."[26] Lunt never failed to meet one's expectations.

Dana attended a dinner for New Hampshire senator John Hale, which provided Dana the opportunity to express his admiration for Hale's work to pass legislation that outlawed flogging in the merchant service and U.S. Navy. Dana's *Two Years Before the Mast* and Melville's *White Jacket* gave the public glimpses of flogging brutality. Dana thought all would benefit "by protecting American seamen from this disgrace." He was delighted to record "a compliment which . . . pleased [Hale] much." The crew of the U.S.S. *Germantown* just arrived from the coast of Africa, "manned the rigging & gave three cheers" for the senator who ended flogging.[27]

Hale told Dana that corruption was rampant in Congress, and Sumner told Dana the same when he visited him in Cambridge. Rhode Island senator Charles James was "notoriously purchasable." Sumner also corroborated Hale's observation that members were often too drunk in the evening to hold sessions. There was worse. Sumner told Dana of his conversation with Senator John Davis, who was about to retire. It had been Davis who "overslept" rather than introduce Free Soiler Sumner to his colleagues. The senior senator from Massachusetts said to his junior colleague: "Sumner, do you wish to know the result of thirty years of observation of Congress?" Sumner replied that he should value it very much. "Well," said Davis, "the result of my observation of a long congressional life is that Slavery controls everything here."[28]

Boston's Cotton Whigs exercised similar control in the Massachusetts legislature. Despite the enhanced strength of the Free Soil–Democrat coalition, constitutional reforms were stymied by the Whig Party's plurality. Proposals to abolish imprisonment for debt, remove property qualifications for voting, and implement a secret ballot could not secure the two-thirds vote needed (in two successive legislatures) to amend the Massachusetts Constitution.

In 1852 voters narrowly approved a ballot measure, proposed by the Free Soil–Democrat coalition, for a constitutional convention. The proposal provided that delegates to the 1853 convention need not live in the town that elected them. Henry Wilson, the political architect of the coalition, worked diligently to ensure that the coalition had a majority of delegates. Wilson's interest had much more to do with diluting the political base of Boston Whigs than with substantive constitutional reform.

Dana was elected by Free Soilers in Manchester, where he had a summer home. He was opposed by a Democrat as well as a Whig, so he had "the satisfaction to know that I was elected without a coalition & am therefore under [no] obligation."[29] Dana was delighted when Sumner was elected from Marshfield by defeating Daniel Webster's son on March 7, the anniversary of Webster's infamous speech.

Dana's decision to participate in a time-consuming constitutional convention, when less than a year before he chose not to fully engage in politics, was due to a combination of factors. First, without a political debt to any party, he could speak independently. "What do I care about . . . party? Nothing at all!" he exclaimed at one point during convention debate.[30] But the most significant reason was a change at home. At the end of October 1852, Dana noted, "a general debility seems to have seized [Sarah] and her nervous system is entirely out of order." Dana's father made a similar observation: "Richard's wife is not looking well . . . there is an appearance of exhaustion & the nervous system is a good deal affected."[31]

The strain of managing the household even with help, the frequency of pregnancies, the financial pressure, and Dana himself contributed to Sarah's continuing anxiety. Male physicians advised that the malady was often present in married women of Sarah's social status. Accordingly, in the spring of 1853 plans were made for Sarah to take the fashionable "water cure" at a retreat in Brattleboro, Vermont. The children were dispersed to various relatives, though eleven-year-old Sally and nine-year-old Ruth Charlotte were sent to Miss Porter's, a boarding school even more exclusive than Sarah's retreat. Dana was more distraught than the girls: "Poor dear things! I was the only one to shed tears, unless they shed them after I left!"[32] The Cambridge house, a little more than a year old, was rented to help pay for Sarah's treatment and the girls' school.

On his own again, Dana was soon deeply engaged in the work of the constitutional convention. It proved to be a forum ideally suited to his strengths. Quick in debate, fluent in speech, meticulously prepared, and willing to work eighteen-hour days, the thirty-eight-year-old Dana outshone older and more prominent men. The disdain for political parties that made him unsuitable for politics gave Dana the standing to speak to the merits of proposed constitutional amendments irrespective of party interest: "The people of Massachusetts were not put here to carry out their will upon the earth. We were put here to do justice, to protect the weak, to resist the might, and to secure to each his right."[33]

Dana found himself aligned with Conservative Whigs when he opposed an amendment to elect judges. Democrats and Free Soilers asserted with some justification that lifetime appointments enabled the Whigs to control the judiciary, but Dana—who had better reason than any lawyer to know the consequences of judicial appointments for political motives—resisted the amendment. Dana's defense of judicial independence prompted Rufus Choate to congratulate Dana for a "magnificent" speech. Choate, attending as a Whig delegate, spoke the next day to even greater effect. Dana justly remarked that Choate's plea for an independent judiciary was "such a speech as a man may be happy to have lived to hear."[34]

But if Boston Whigs were pleased with Dana's alignment with their judicial interest, they were indignant at his support of Free Soil–Democrat proposals that threatened the Whig political base. Dana's speech on behalf of amendments to give greater representation to smaller communities (already disproportionately represented at the expense of urban dwellers) angered Boston's establishment. George Ticknor Curtis expressed the displeasure of his caste that support for a "monstrous scheme . . . of radicalism" should come from "the lips of one her own sons."[35]

Dana was at no risk of being misunderstood. "My sympathies," he declared, "go with the Soil first, the Sea next, and the Loom last." Dana did have an affinity for "the ancient town system to which the people are ardently attached." His counter to the fact that Boston's population was underrepresented included his disparagement of the city's "floating alien population."[36] But Boston's Conservative Whigs could never be mistaken as advocates for that population. They opposed the amendments because they sought to retain political control in a city where they held economic power and there was no secret ballot.[37]

In fact, the result of the debates over constitutional amendments to alter legislative apportionment had little to recommend it to those interested in true reform. All parties jockeyed for advantage and the final product was so unappetizing that even voters could see what went into the sausage. The proposed "reforms" were narrowly rejected in November. Dana could not decide "whether I am most pleased or disappointed with the result." He was most thankful for the "preservation of the judiciary."[38]

But Dana's opposition to the establishment's interests compelled Brahmin Boston to call Dana to account during the constitutional convention. Once again the messenger was lawyer George Hillard, "the special representative in the Convention of that social element [that] disapprov[ed] [of] . . . Dana."[39] Dana had noted Hillard "riding out like a lap-dog in the coach of Mr. & Mrs. Ticknor."[40] Hillard delivered a blunt message. Gesturing toward Dana and turning to the assembly of the most prominent members of the Boston establishment, Hillard declared: "I regret that my friend from Manchester [Mr. Dana] should have felt himself called upon to add . . . to a sentiment towards Boston which has increased, is increasing, and ought to be diminished. . . . As the bread that he and I both eat comes from the business community of Boston—from men, some of whom are rich, all of whom hope to be rich, it does not become us . . . to strike at the hand that feeds us."[41]

Dana was immediately on his feet: "My friend reminded me and it is not the first time in the course of my life that I have been reminded of it, that the bread that he and I both eat comes from the business community of Boston, and we should not strike at the hand that feed us. The hand that feeds us? The hand that feeds us! *Sir, no hand feeds me that has any right to control my opinions!*"[42]

Dana's fiery reply somewhat chastened Hillard, who approached Dana shortly after the exchange expressing his hope that it would not interfere with their social relationship: "I said, 'No, certainly not,'" Dana recorded in his journal. "He seemed a good deal affected and said that he did not mean . . . what he said. . . . I asked him what he did mean. Said he, 'I mean this. I mean that if a man lives in Boston and feels about her position and action as you do, if a man disapproves of her characteristics and interest and conduct, he ought either to keep silent or leave the city.'"

"Said I, 'is that your opinion Hillard?' He said it was. I told him that principle would do in a club or in a society but not in a community of equal rights. I told him that that sentiment came from persons who thought Boston was a club—their club."[43]

15

THE PRESUMPTION OF FREEDOM

On the morning of May 25, 1854, Dana was passing the Boston courthouse on the way to his office when "a gentleman told me there was a fugitive slave in custody in the United States Courtroom." Dana immediately made his way to the federal courtroom on the third floor. Upon entering he saw "a Negro sitting in the usual place for prisoners, guarded by a large corps of officers." The young man appeared "completely cowed and dispirited." Dana observed "a large scar on his cheek which looks much like a brand," a scar on his left hand, and most noticeably—a broken right hand "from which a large piece of bone projects."[1]

Dana quickly offered to act as his lawyer. "It is no use," replied the prisoner, "They will . . . get me back, and if they do, I shall fare worse if I resist." Dana responded that "there might be some flaw in the papers, or some mistake & that he might get off." To this the man "seemed entirely helpless [to reply] . . . the great thing on his mind seemed to be the fear that any delay & expense . . . would be visited upon him when he got back & that his best policy was to conciliate his master the best he could."[2]

Twenty-one-year-old Anthony Burns had reason to be afraid. Less than twelve hours before, he had been a free man on a Boston street walking home from work. Suddenly conscious of being followed by a half-dozen thugs, Burns froze. The white men who surrounded him were hoodlums—but they were also specially deputized agents of the U.S. government.[3]

Burns did not know it, but two Virginians had arrived in Boston and secured a warrant for his arrest as a fugitive slave. Now, as darkness fell, Burns was informed by Deputy U.S. Marshall Asa Butman that he was under arrest. It had been Butman who arrested Thomas Sims three years earlier. Despite deputizing six of Boston's more notorious enforcers, the deputy marshal thought it best to avoid the chance that Burns might resist. He told the young man he was being arrested for a jewelry store robbery.

The temporarily relieved Burns, who knew of his innocence of any robbery allegation, agreed to go quietly. But whatever apprehension Burns had about being wrongfully accused of robbery must have turned from dread to terror as he was picked up bodily by the "specials" and carried to the courthouse. On the steps stood U.S. Marshal Watson Freeman with drawn sword. Burns was hustled up the stairs to the federal courtroom. Surrounded by armed guards, a bewildered Burns was locked in the jury room. The door opened and a man entered tipping his hat in greeting: "How do you do Mr. Burns?" It was his master.

Anthony Burns had been enslaved to Charles Suttle since the age of six. When "Tony" turned seven, Suttle hired him out to others. At sixteen, Burns's right hand was crippled in a sawmill accident. The injury diminished his value as a slave, but the resourceful Burns had taught himself to read and was useful enough to be leased to a Richmond pharmacist. The young man's familiarity with the Richmond wharves enabled him to plan an escape with the help of a Boston-bound sailor.

In February 1854 Burns stowed away on a ship that reached Boston before the month's end. Burns found work at odd jobs before being hired as a clerk in a Brattle Street clothing store owned by a deacon in Boston's most prominent African American church. The deputy marshal and his "specials" had staked out the store on the night they tracked and seized Burns.

The marshal's office and lawyers for the slave owner expected the hearing returning Burns to slavery to be as abrupt and surreptitious as his seizure. At precisely 9:00 A.M., Fugitive Slave Commissioner Edward G. Loring took the bench to begin the truncated rendition proceedings. Loring, a probate judge and lecturer at Harvard Law School, had issued the warrant for the arrest of Burns.

Dana's unwelcome presence was compounded by the arrival of Reverend Leonard Grimes, who hastened to the courthouse when rumors of the seizure reached the black community. Other members of the Vigilance Committee, including lawyers Robert Morris and Charles Ellis, and abolitionists Wendell Phillips and Theodore Parker, arrived as well. Grimes was permitted to speak briefly to the shackled Burns, who was still surrounded by the band of city hoodlums. The marshal's reliance "on the most depraved class of men in the community" could not have given Burns faith in the process. Even more intimidating was the appearance of slave owner Charles Suttle. "He sat in full sight of the poor negro all the time," noted Dana. "I could not get over a feeling that [Burns] had seen cruel usage."[4]

The intimidation provided attorney Seth Thomas—the lawyer for slave owners in the Shadrach and Sims proceedings—the chance to move quickly. Dana could not represent Burns unless Burns consented to representation. Anxious to complete the hearing before more sympathizers came, Suttle's lawyers began to introduce testimony from William Brent, who had accompanied the slave owner from Virginia.

When Brent was asked to relate what the prisoner had said on the night he was seized, Dana could no longer sit still: "May it please your Honor. I rise to address the court as amicus curiae (friend of the court). I cannot say that I am . . . counsel for the person at the bar. Indeed, from the few words I have been able to hold with him . . . I am satisfied he is not in a condition to determine whether he will have counsel or not. . . . Under these circumstances I submit to your Honor's judgment that time should be allowed to the prisoner to recover himself from the stupefaction of his sudden arrest . . . to . . . determine what course he will pursue."[5]

Suttle's attorney immediately protested Dana's intervention, asserting its only purpose "is to try to induce [Burns] to resist the just claim which he is now ready to acknowledge." Moreover, added counsel for the slave owner, the delay "will cause great inconvenience to my client and his witness both of whom have come all the way from Virginia."

Dana countered that a claim of "inconvenience" was an affront to Commissioner Loring: "I know enough of this tribunal to know that it will not lend itself to the hurrying of a man into slavery to accommodate any man's personal convenience." He artfully analogized the acceptance of Burns's "acknowledgment" to a court's acceptance of a guilty plea in a criminal case: "It is but yesterday that the Court refused to receive a plea of guilty from a prisoner without the fullest proof that the prisoner . . . understands its meaning. . . . In a case involving freedom or slavery for life, this Court will not do less."

Dana knew that Loring was a staunch supporter of the Fugitive Slave Act. Related by marriage to the Curtises (Commissioner George T. and Justice Benjamin R.), Edward Loring was a stalwart Conservative Whig. But Dana believed Loring could be persuaded to speak to Burns: "I say to your Honor, as a member of the bar, on my personal responsibility . . . that he is not in a fit state to decide for himself what to do . . . Even without a suggestion from [me] the Court would of its own motion see to it that no . . . advantage was taken."

Here was the tipping point. All that followed in what was to become the most notorious fugitive slave case in American history depended upon Loring's ruling on a motion that was made by a lawyer who was not before the court. But Dana's "standing" to request the delay was predicated on a stronger foundation than court procedure. It emanated from his character.

Commissioner Loring called Burns to the Bench. Dana described the exchange in his journal entry that evening: "The Commissioner . . . told him what his rights were and asked him if he wished time to consider what he would do. The man made no reply & looked around bewildered, like a child. Judge Loring again put the question to him, in a kind manner, & asked him if he would like to have a day or two & then see him again. To this he replied, faintly, 'I would.' The judge then ordered a delay until Saturday." Dana observed Marshal Freeman whispering to Loring, who replied, "No. He must have a necessary time." Freeman again said something to the commissioner, who "replied rather sharply, 'No Sir.

I shall give him all reasonable delays.'" Dana thought it likely that Loring would execute the fugitive slave law, but observed the judge's conduct was "considerate and humane."[6]

Marshal Freeman's palpable anxiety was well founded. The "rescue" of Shadrach Minkins three years before had overpowered court security. Opposition to the Fugitive Slave Act was now far greater. It was clear that the longer the rendition of Burns was delayed, the greater the risk of an attack on the Boston courthouse.

Particularly troubling was the possibility that Burns would decide to accept legal representation, thus ensuring an extended hearing. The U.S. marshal prevented Reverend Grimes, Deacon Pitts (Burns's employer), and Wendell Phillips from meeting with Burns. They went to Dana, who sent a note to Loring lecturing at Harvard Law School, asking him to urge the marshal to allow access to Burns. Loring did so and Freeman grudgingly allowed the three men to talk to Burns, who told them he wished to have a lawyer.

The young man provided a power of attorney to Phillips, who asked Dana to represent Burns. Dana engaged Charles Ellis to assist him. In the early evening of Friday, May 26, Dana was finally able to confer with Burns: "He was confined in a small room, in the 3rd floor . . . of the Court House with some 6 or 8 men in the room with him. The men were of the rough thief catching order & were smoking & playing cards." Dana and Burns "withdrew to a window & talked quietly." Dana found Burns to be "a very different man from what he was the day before." He was "self-possessed, intelligent & with considerable force both of mind & body." Burns told Dana he "was in fear of his master, who, he said was a malicious man if crossed."[7]

The same evening Dana noted that "a great meeting is to be held at Faneuil Hall." Abolitionists were talking openly of "rescuing" Burns by force. But to Dana, "the most remarkable exhibition is from the Whigs, the Hunker Whigs, the Compromise men of 1850 . . . Men who would not speak to me in 1850 & 1851, & who were enrolling as special policemen in the Sims affair, stop me in the street & talk treason. This is all owing to the Nebraska bill. I cannot respect their feeling at all, except as a return to sanity. The Webster delusion is passing off."[8]

Even more astonishing was an offer from Amos A. Lawrence. Lawrence told Dana "it was not the Free Soilers only who were in favor of the liberation of slaves." Lawrence said "conservative, compromise men" had authorized him to ask Dana "to offer any amount of retainer . . . to employ some eminent Whig counsel" to work with Dana. Dana who was representing Burns without fee, made inquiries of those who "would answer Mr. Lawrence's description," including Rufus Choate and future Supreme Court justice Nathan Clifford. There were no takers.[9]

On Saturday morning May 27, 1854, Dana awoke to stunning news. An attempt to free Burns from the Boston courthouse had been made after Friday evening's meeting at Faneuil Hall. Led by Thomas Wentworth Higginson of the Vigilance Committee and Lewis Hayden, whom Dana had successfully defended in the Shadrach rescue attempt, the attack was repulsed by deputies stationed inside the courthouse.

The door of the courthouse was breached when the attackers used a beam taken from a construction site as a battering ram. Shots rang out and the card-playing "specials" guarding Burns on the third floor doused the lights and cowered in a corner, though the door was barricaded by seven massive iron bars. In the melee on the first floor, twenty-four-year-old James Batchelder, a special deputy (whom Dana described as having "volunteered three times to assist in catching & keeping slaves"), was killed.[10]

Dana was told "in secrecy" of Higginson's role in leading the courthouse attack. "I knew his ardor & courage," wrote Dana, "but I hardly expected a married man, a clergyman, & man of education to lead the mob."[11] Dana learned that Theodore Parker and Dr. Samuel Howe had also volunteered to lead a "rescue." Dana did not think the time for bloodshed had come, but if "gentlemen" invoked the forcible right to resist, Dana believed—as he asserted in the first rescue case—that their place was at the head of the resistance.

If there was to be further resistance, the U.S. government was prepared. When Dana arrived at the courthouse on Saturday morning, the building "was filled with hireling soldiers of the standing army of the U.S. . . . . ready to shoot down good men, at a word of command." Detachments of U.S. marines from the Charlestown Navy Yard and Fort Independence had arrived during the night at the urgent request of Marshal Freeman. Boston's mayor, Jerome Smith, had called out the state militia. Freeman's telegram informing the president that the marshal had "availed [him] self of the resources of the United States" was answered by telegraph: "YOUR CONDUCT IS APPROVED. THE LAW MUST BE EXECUTED. FRANKLIN PIERCE."[12]

Burns was already in the courtroom by the time Dana was able to make his way through the legions of troops. Armed "specials" surrounded the handcuffed young man. The court was "packed with creatures of Freeman."[13] Dana and his junior counsel Charles Ellis had a single objective at the Saturday hearing—to delay the proceedings to gain time to prepare a defense. Suttle's lawyers objected that "the only duty of your Honor is to grant a certificate of removal." Loring was urged to fulfill his duty quickly, given "the excited condition of the public mind." Suttle's lawyer, Seth Thomas, asserted that the request for delay was an "attempt to render the fugitive slave law invalid. It is no less treason . . . than it would be to go the other end of the courthouse and rescue a man convicted for murder."

Dana thought "the petty, mean voice & manner of Thomas" his best foil.[14] The "simple question," Dana reminded Loring, was whether the defense should have reasonable time to prepare. The contention of Suttle's attorneys that the hearing should be concluded because of the risk of "disturbance" was "an argument that can be addressed to no court, for it is a confession of weakness that the law is not strong, and therefore the man must suffer." Commissioner Loring agreed that "excitement in the community" was not a sufficient reason to hasten the hearing, but he granted a continuance only to Monday, an indication that he did not believe that Dana would have a defense to make.

That concern was shared by Reverend Leonard Grimes, who thought the only real chance Burns had for freedom was if he could be purchased from Suttle. Attorney Edward Parker, junior counsel to Seth Thomas, "seemed ashamed of what he was doing."[15] Parker hinted at Saturday's hearing that Suttle might accept payment for Burns. Grimes got confirmation that Suttle was interested if $1,200 could be raised by that evening. Grimes began a frantic effort to raise the money (Parker said he would contribute $400 himself) and Commissioner Loring actively encouraged the effort.[16]

The effort of Reverend Grimes was strenuously opposed by the U.S. attorney for Massachusetts, B. F. Hallett. Dana had as little respect for Hallett as he had for his predecessor Lunt. Prosecutor Hallett once asked Dana to withdraw a client's guilty plea because his fees depended upon the case "going to the jury."[17]

Hallett's objection to Reverend Grimes's plan to purchase Burns's freedom stemmed in part from concern that he would not be reimbursed for expenses in securing the courthouse if the Burns case did not go to trial. Grimes made a last futile attempt on Monday morning to arrange the sale. But Edward Parker did not appear for an 8:00 A.M. meeting in Commissioner Loring's chambers. He was with Seth Thomas, Charles Suttle, U.S. Attorney Hallett and Marshal Freeman. The trial of Anthony Burns was to begin in three hours.

Dana was preparing as well. The view from his Court Square office "presented on that morning a strange and alarming scene in free Massachusetts." Below, "a vast throng of citizens . . . constantly increasing from early dawn, surged . . . through the Square in unappeasable excitement." The courthouse itself resembled "a beleaguered fortress" where "the mingled soldiery of Massachusetts and the United States presented themselves, with firearms, as at . . . a rampart."[18]

Shortly before 11:00 A.M., Suttle's lawyers (both with weapons), Suttle, and U.S. Attorney Hallett ("whose business there did not clearly appear") entered the courtroom. Anthony Burns was brought from the third-floor "jury room" where he had been imprisoned. Dana more accurately called it a "slave pen." On either side of Burns, as well as in back of him, sat "brutal-looking men . . . with pistols and bludgeons lurking in their pockets." Dana again had to pass the bayonets. At one point in the proceedings "he was kept waiting on the stairs until it was the pleasure of the Marshal to permit him to pass on."[19]

Dana and his junior counsel Charles Ellis faced a greater challenge than access. They were still without a plausible strategy to defend Burns. The Fugitive Slave Act provided that in a rendition proceeding, a slave owner need only provide a transcript obtained from the local court where the slaveholder resided as "full and conclusive evidence of the fact of escape and that the service or labor of the person escaping is due to the [master]." Suttle had obtained the requisite transcript from a Virginia court in accordance with the law's provisions.[20] Dana examined the record and could find no flaw.

Under the circumstances the best Dana and Ellis could do was to try to extend the hearing an additional day while hoping that Suttle's lawyers would somehow bungle their case. Ellis began by objecting to the forum: "This room is packed with armed men . . . even counsel [bear] arms. We protest, also against conducting this case, when all its avenues and apartments are filled with military." Hallett rose immediately to object to the remarks. Though the U.S. attorney was neither representing

Suttle nor prosecuting Burns, he wanted it known that "the President of the United States has approved . . . the efficient aid [by] which the Marshal has, both armed and unarmed [prevented] further violence and murder."

Suttle's lawyers sought to move the hearing quickly by relying on the record they made when Burns first appeared in court. But Dana immediately objected, arguing that Burns had not been represented when the evidence was presented. Loring accepted Dana's assertion that the hearing should begin "as though the arrest had just been made."

William Brent was the primary witness for the slaveholder. Brent had acted as Suttle's agent in Virginia, "leasing" Burns to assorted employers. Brent asserted that the prisoner was Anthony Burns. But in the course of his testimony Brent swore that he had last seen Anthony Burns in Richmond on March 20, 1854. Burns told Dana that he had been in Boston since the first of March. It was the opening Dana was looking for: "If the claimant's counsel had merely put in his record & introduced evidence that the prisoner was the person named in the record, we should have had no defense except the constitutional objections, which, of course, Judge Loring would overrule."[21]

Dana knew Burns was telling the truth, but Commissioner Loring would not be able to evaluate the young man's veracity. The Fugitive Slave Act expressly provided that "in no trial or hearing under this act shall the testimony of such alleged fugitive be admitted in evidence."[22]

The presence of Burns in Boston on the date Suttle's agent swore he saw him in Richmond might be proved by other witnesses, but Dana had no idea who those witnesses might be. Once again Dana asked Loring for a delay. The commissioner recessed the hearing for forty minutes, which enabled Dana to alert others of the need to locate witnesses who could testify that Burns had been in Boston since early March. Charles Ellis spoke for the rest of the afternoon in a transparent but successful effort to gain more time. Loring finally adjourned the hearing at six P.M., instructing Dana to present his evidence, if any, the next day.

Suttle's lawyers had no reason to think that Dana and Ellis could do more than filibuster to the inevitable end of the hearing. Indeed, when Charles Ellis made the opening statement for the defense, he added little to what had already been said. He reiterated that the defense had not been given enough time to prepare: "a day in a case . . . when if it involved only his coat, the wheels of justice could not be turned in months." Ellis again objected to having "to meet a case with our opposing counsel armed, hemmed in with armed men, entering court with muskets at our breasts, trying a case under the muzzle of their guns."

Then, reminding Commissioner Loring that Suttle's witness had sworn that Anthony Burns was in Richmond on March 20, Ellis said: "We shall call . . . witnesses to show . . . beyond question that the prisoner was in Boston on the first of March . . . and has been here ever since." It was upon the "identity" of Burns that Dana sought to pivot the case: "They have but one witness, and one piece of paper. The paper cannot identify, and the proof of identity hangs on the testimony of one man. It all hangs by one thread. That man is Mr. Brent."

The defense called its first witness, Boston laborer William Jones, to establish that Burns was living in Boston when Suttle's agent claimed to have seen him in Virginia. Suttle's lawyers were unconcerned because the witness was not a white man. U.S. Attorney Hallett's deliberately audible reference to "perjury" was heard in the courtroom as Jones took the stand. But William Jones was a credible witness. A cross-examination of several hours by an incredulous Seth Thomas could not shake the essence of Jones's testimony: that Jones and Burns had worked together as window washers in early March at the Mattapan Works, a factory in south Boston. A series of witnesses followed, corroborating Jones. To the dismay of Suttle's lawyers, many of the defense witnesses were white.

The bookkeeper at Mattapan Works testified that he remembered Burns asking how much Jones had been paid. The witness was able to fix the date in early March by reference to a notation in the cash ledger, a copy of which was introduced as evidence. Other employees also testified they had seen Burns at the factory well before March 20, the date when Brent claimed to have seen Burns in Richmond.

Dana made a particular point of emphasizing the testimony of James Whittemore, a director of Mattapan Works, who swore he saw Burns working there on March 8 or 9. Whittemore was a member of the Boston City Council and an officer in the "Pulaski Guard," a quasi-militia organization committed to enforcement of the law. Over the objection of Suttle's lawyers, Dana elicited Whittemore's political affiliation ("Hunker Whig") to bolster his credibility as a disinterested witness. The defense closed with its ninth witness, a Boston police officer, who testified that while employed at the Mattapan Works he had seen Burns working there in early March.

Rebuttal witnesses called by Suttle's attorneys could not refute the evidence that the prisoner had been in Boston continuously since the first of March. Brent had sworn he saw Anthony Burns in Richmond on March 20. It was, said Dana, "the one fact of which Mr. Brent is sure." If that were so, "the prisoner is not the man." Dana found it "extraordinary" that neither the Virginia record nor Brent mentioned "the most noticeable thing possible in identifying a slave," the condition of his right hand. A slave's right hand "is the chief property his master has in him." Suttle's escaped slave was described as having a "scar" on his right hand. "A scar!" exclaimed Dana. "The prisoner's right hand is broken, and a bone stands out from the back of it, a hump an inch high, and it hangs almost useless from the wrist." It was what Dana had first noticed about the young man, aside from his frightened state.

There was little doubt that if proof of "identity" was confined to the evidence of Brent's description, it was too contradictory to establish that Suttle's agent had identified the right man. Moreover, Dana provided the commissioner with a legal rationale that gave Loring the opportunity to free the prisoner while adhering to the fugitive slave law.

Dana noted that the law provided two methods of proving the elements necessary to return a fugitive to slavery. One approach (Section 10) was based upon the record obtained from a Virginia court, and the commissioner "has only jurisdiction to inquire whether the person arrested is the person in [the record]." The other method (Section 6) "authorizes the court to try the questions of slavery and escape as well as identity and requires them to be tried by evidence taken here." Dana argued the provisions were exclusive and by choosing to introduce evidence of identity under Section 6, Suttle's lawyers must also prove slavery and escape without resort to the record introduced under Section 10. "We say the two proceedings cannot be combined."

Dana's legal analysis might have been compelling to a commissioner disinclined to enforce the Fugitive Slave Act. But federal appointment as a commissioner came to those whose political, social, and legal views were consistent with strict enforcement. Dana knew that Loring might allow evidence under both sections. Worse for Dana's "identity defense" was the possibility that Loring would consider the "testimony" of a witness who could not testify.

On the night of May 24, when Burns was abducted from a Boston street and carried bodily to the third floor of the Boston courthouse, Virginians Charles Suttle and William Brent carefully orchestrated their parts. Suttle was advised by his lawyer that any admissions elicited from the seized man would be useful in court. The dramatic appearance of the slave owner accompanied by the "leasing agent" had the intended effect upon the terrified Burns. When Charles Suttle tipped his hat and said, "How do you do Mr. Burns?" the prisoner—according to Brent's account—replied, "How do you do Master Charles?" Brent testified that Suttle then asked: "Why did you run away?" to which Burns replied, "I fell asleep on board the vessel where I worked." According to Suttle's agent, Suttle said, "I make you no promises and I make you no threats," and the young man indicated he was willing to return to slavery.[23]

Dana vehemently objected to this testimony, arguing that the admissions of an alleged slave while in custody, made to the master who claims him, should not be received as evidence. Commissioner Loring provisionally allowed Brent's testimony but indicated that Burns's statements would not be considered if they were coerced. The evidence was closed.

Dana's extraordinary trial advocacy on behalf the alleged fugitive altered expectations. "Wonder and hope" rose among those who sympathized with the prisoner, while there was "a marked change" in the slave owner's lawyers, "whose countenances . . . gave place to unfeigned anxiety and alarm." On Wednesday May 31, 1854, "amidst the deepest silence," Dana rose to begin his summation. The federal courtroom was not spacious. The "few good citizens present . . . took their seats quietly." Some seats were kept empty "as silent witness to excessive fears." The most conspicuous spectators, "now appearing as officers of justice, were convicted criminals."[24]

Dana was about to make one of the finest summations in the history of American law. He spoke from scribbled notes no bigger than his hand. Dana needed nothing more—the argument was written in his heart. He despised the use of authority to demean human dignity. Here was a far, far greater outrage than a schoolmaster's beating of a schoolboy or a shipmaster's flogging of a seaman. The unprecedented collusion among the U.S. attorney, U.S. marshal, U.S. military, and Boston thugs appalled Dana.

Dana first called out U.S. Attorney B. F. Halleck: "I congratulate . . . the government of the United States, that its legal representative can return to his appropriate duties, and that his . . . presence will no longer be needed here in a private civil suit for the purpose of intimidation." Dana "congratulated" U.S. Marshal Freeman "that the ordinary respectability of his character is no longer to be in danger from the character of the associates he is obliged to call about him."

Dana had run the gauntlet of U.S. troops lining the stairs and corridors of the Boston courthouse each day. On one occasion the officer in charge had been so drunk that Dana protested to military authorities. Now Dana "congratulated" "the officers of the army and navy, that they can be relieved from this service . . . and can draw off their noncommissioned officers and privates both drunk and sober, from this fortified slave-pen to the custody of the forts and fleets of our country, which have been left in peril, that this great republic might add to its glories the trophies of one more captured slave."

Dana's sharpest barbs were aimed at "the marshal's guard," specially selected from Boston's criminal class. Dana "congratulated the city of Boston . . . the city has never been so safe as while the marshal has had his posse of specials in this court house. Why, sir, people have not felt it necessary to lock their doors at night, the brothels are tenanted only by women, fighting dogs and racing horses have been unemployed." The "specials," 120 strong, listened stone-faced. Their leader, Louis Varell, known by various aliases, took note of Dana's taunt. Varell was a dangerous man, feared by those he recruited. One of the "specials" was an ex-prize fighter and enforcer for Varell. They would see Dana again.

Turning to Commissioner Loring, Dana expressed his hope—if not belief—"that the decision of your Honor will restore to freedom this man . . . whom fraud and violence found a week ago a free man on the soil of Massachusetts." If the hearing's result consigned a man "to perpetual bondage," Dana declaimed, "I would say—let this session never break up! Let us sit here to the end of that man's life, or to the end of ours."

But a less perfect justice required Dana to do the work of an advocate. He began by addressing the standard of proof. Dana sought to persuade Loring that the stakes in the case were greater than when a man is on trial for his life. There, he reminded the court, "all jurists" approved of the maxim that it was better that nine guilty men should escape than one innocent man should suffer.

"How much more should be applied to a case like this, where on the one side there is something dearer than life . . . and on the other only the value of a few hundred pieces of silver." "Liberty," Dana asserted, "is dearer than life." Men risked their lives "for pleasure, for glory, for gain, for curiosity . . . men have sought for death, and digged for it as for hid treasure. But when do men seek for slavery, for captivity."

"We have before us a free man," declared Dana. "We have a right then, to expect from your Honor a strict adherence to the rule that this man is free until he is proved a slave beyond every reasonable doubt." Dana reminded the court that the slave owner must prove ownership, service and labor owed, escape, and identity. "Colonel Suttle . . . says all this. Let him prove it *all*. Let him fail in one point, let him fall short the width of a spider's thread, in the proof of all his horrid category, and the man goes free."

Suttle's lawyers had fallen well short of that width, if the commissioner confined his evidence to court testimony. Dana contended that the elements of slavery and escape could only be proved by introduction of the record from the Virginia court. He urged Loring to reject it for these purposes: "I pray your Honor, earnestly, to confine [the Virginia court] record—the venomous beast that carries the poison to life and liberty and hope in its fang—to confine it in the strictest limits. It deserves a blow at the hand of every man who meets it."

But Dana's most compelling argument turned upon the issue of identity. Suttle's lawyers had chosen to rely on Brent's testimony to prove that Suttle's slave and the man seized by the "specials" were one and the same man. Their proof, however, was undermined by Brent's statement that he saw Anthony Burns in Richmond on March 20. Dana reminded Loring that there were "discovered mistakes" when free men had been wrongly identified as escaped slaves, but "who can tell . . . you the undiscovered mistakes? The numbers who have been hurried off, by some accidental resemblance of scars, or cuts, or height, and fall as drops, undistinguishable into the black ocean of slavery."

Dana's mistaken-identity defense depended upon persuading Loring that the "admissions" made by the young man on the night he was seized could not be introduced into evidence as a matter of law—and ought not to be considered as a matter of justice: "I regret, extremely, that you did not, sir, adopt the rule that in the trial of an issue of freedom, the admission of an alleged slave, made to the man who claims him, while in custody . . . should not be received." Such a ruling "would have been sustained by reason and humanity and precedent."

Loring's failure to apply the rule compelled Dana to argue that "the facts of this case show enough of intimidation to throw out the evidence." Dana first sought to show that Brent's testimony was unreliable. "Brent testified that he understood the young man to say he was willing to return to slavery. This we know is not true," declared Dana. If the alleged fugitive was willing to go back, then why, asked Dana, did they not send word to his place of employment and ask him to meet Suttle? "No sir, they . . . seized him by fraud and violence . . . and hurried him into bonds and imprisonment. Some one hundred hired men, armed keep him in this room, where once Story sat in judgment—now a slave-pen. One hundred and fifty bayonets of the regulars and fifteen hundred of the militia keep him without. If all that we see about is necessary to keep a man who is willing to go back, pray, sir, what shall we see when they shall get hold of a man who is not willing to go back?"

Dana recognized that Loring could resolve the conflict in the identity testimony only by resort to "the admission of the prisoner, made to Col. Suttle on the night of the arrest." Now—as Dana approached the end of his four-hour summation—every particle of his being reached for the combination of reason and eloquence that might unlock the injustice of using a man's own words to send him into slavery. Dana emphasized the circumstances of the arrest: "He was arrested suddenly, on a false pretense . . . and hurried into custody, among strange men, in a strange place, and suddenly, whether claimed rightfully or claimed wrongfully, he saw he was claimed as a slave and his condition burst upon him in a flood of terror. This was at night."

Dana made an impassioned plea to Loring: "You saw him, sir, the next day, and you remember the state he was then in. You remember his stupefied and terrified condition. . . . Sir, the day after the arrest you felt obliged to put off his trial two days because he was not in a condition to know or decide what to do. . . . What must it have been [that night]?"

Suttle's attorneys argued that the slave owner's statement ("I make you no promises and no threats") was evidence that there was no intimidation. Dana knew how masters conveyed messages. He asserted that Suttle was warning the young man: "It is according to the course you take now that you will be treated when I get you back. . . . Was ever man more distinctly told it would be better for him if he acquiesced in everything, yielded everything, assented to everything?" Dana urged

Loring to "give little or no weight to testimony so liable, at all times, to misconception, misrecollection, perversion and, in this case, so cruel to use against such a person under such circumstances."

One final "presumption" remained. It was neither a rule of evidence nor a rule of law. It would decide the case. But the final judgment would not be made by a court. Dana's plea for the young man he represented was a plea to their country: "You recognized, sir, in the beginning, the presumption of freedom. Hold to it now, sir, as to the sheet anchor of your peace of mind as well as of his safety. If you commit a mistake in favor of the man, a pecuniary value, not great is put at hazard. If against him a free man is made a slave forever. . . . The eyes of many millions are upon you, sir. You are to do an act which will hold its place in the history of America, in the history of the progress of the human race. May your judgment be for liberty and not for slavery, for happiness and not for wretchedness; for hope and not for despair."

The slave owner's lawyer of choice, Seth Thomas, made the closing argument for Suttle. Attorney Thomas said he too had congratulations to offer—though his were sincere: "He would congratulate also, the city of Boston that order was supreme; that Faneuil Hall that cradle of law as well as liberty was closed today against treasonable and insane speech." The Fugitive Slave Act of 1850, Thomas reminded Loring, "has been held [constitutional] by the Supreme Court of this State, all the judges concurring." Confident "in the majesty of the law," Attorney Thomas regretted only "the extraordinary bitterness of opposing counsel."

Dana did not conceal his disdain for Thomas, whom he considered "a small pattern of a man in every way, moral and intellectual." Dana was not alone in thinking the Thomas argument "poor," nor were those who told Dana that "it is the best speech I ever made" exaggerating. "Even the 'guard' were somewhat affected by it," Dana recorded that evening in his journal, "and many of them said they wished the man would get off." But Dana's confidence in the justness of his case and power of his argument was tempered by an observation: "Judge Loring paid a great attention to all that related to the identity, but took no notes of my points as to the record, the escape and the title. This puzzled me a good deal." The most likely interpretation, as Dana surely knew, was that Loring intended to rely on the Virginia record as proof of escape and service owed.[25]

That meant the fate of an alleged fugitive slave—and all that was to follow—turned on identity. And the proof of identity hinged on whether Commissioner Loring thought a young man was intimidated when seized at night from a Boston street by armed men, locked in a federal courtroom, and confronted by his master.

16

WHO CAN TELL WHAT A DAY
MAY BRING FORTH

At the close of arguments Wednesday afternoon, Commissioner Loring advised the parties that he would render his decision at 9:00 A.M. on Friday, June 2. The growing belief that the young man would regain his freedom was enhanced by Dana's brilliant summation. Thomas Wentworth Higginson, who had gone to Worcester to avoid arrest in the aftermath of the attack on the courthouse, received a report of the trial's progress: "R. H. Dana, Jr. feels . . . a good deal of hope, and others, cool and intelligent think so too."[1]

Dana's defense precipitated the confrontation most feared by the U.S. government. The fugitive slave rendition hearing was intended to facilitate the expeditious and obscure transfer of a seized slave. Instead, "millions await the decision of his fate in anxious suspense . . . the heart of a nation is aroused . . . in the great struggle between the moral sense of a people and the written law backed by armed power."[2]

The crisis in Boston had been building for days, a gathering storm that on the day of decision could only burst. No one in the city was indifferent. Reports of spontaneous acts of support or defiance filled special hourly editions of Boston newspapers. Harvard law students from the South formed a daily escort for "Colonel" Suttle. Soldiers were said to have gone hungry because "colored waiters refused to prepare food for the military."[3]

Marshal Freeman asserted that "if bloodshed is to be prevented in the public streets, there must be such a demonstration of a military force as will overawe attack." Secretary of War Jefferson Davis agreed. With President Pierce's approval, Davis dispatched the Army's adjutant general to Boston with orders to mobilize a sufficient force to quell disturbances and, if needed, to march the fugitive to Long Wharf for transfer back to Virginia by the U.S. Navy. U.S. Attorney Hallett, armed with express authority of President Pierce to "incur any expenses necessary" to enforce the Fugitive Slave Act, informed Boston mayor Jerome Smith that federal authorities could discharge their duties only if "the whole military and police force of the city" was mobilized.[4]

Public sympathy for the alleged fugitive slave, as well as the "Latimer Law," which prohibited Massachusetts officials from assisting in the rendition of fugitive slaves, made the mayor hesitant to grant the request. Now with Loring's decision imminent, the mayor "has done what a weak man almost always does, he has gone too far." Smith placed 1,500 troops of the Volunteer Militia under the discretionary command of their general—an act that Dana denounced as an illegal imposition of "martial law."[5]

Early Friday morning, Court House Square began to fill in anticipation of the decision. As crowds gathered, it was thought prudent to supplement the troops already present. At 7:30 A.M., a detachment of the Fourth Regiment, U.S. Artillery, brought a heavy brass cannon to the front of the courthouse, "ostentatiously loaded in sight of all the people." At 8:00 A.M. the assembled crowd was read the mayor's decree: "To the Citizens of Boston: To secure order throughout the city this day, Major General Edmands and the Chief of Police . . . are clothed with full discretionary powers to sustain the laws of the land. All well disposed citizens, and other persons are urgently requested to leave those streets which it may be found necessary to clear . . . and, under no circumstances, to obstruct or molest any officer, civil or military, in the lawful discharge of his duty."[6]

Dana arrived at the courthouse by 8:30 A.M. to find Burns already there, surrounded by "this horrible pack, 'the guard.'" The young man was dressed in a new suit. A Boston paper reported that forty dollars had been raised by the "specials" to outfit him. Dana approached Marshal Freeman and asked if he knew the commissioner's decision. Freeman said he did not. Dana asked whether there were any other arrest warrants for the prisoner and the marshal responded there were none. Dana was hopeful enough to tell the marshal that "if the decision was in favor of the prisoner, I proposed to give him my arm and conduct him through the guards and soldiers into the street. Freeman replied that he would prefer to clear the square first."[7]

The commissioner entered the courtroom punctually at 9:00 A.M. looking "haggard." Although Dana had argued that the Fugitive Slave Act was unconstitutional, he knew there was no chance of Loring agreeing. The commissioner resorted to the "wise words of our revered Chief Justice [which] may well be repeated now, and remembered always." Dana did not revere the chief justice. "Shaw is a man of no courage or pride," wrote Dana when Shaw failed to object to federal control of the Boston courthouse during the rendition hearing. Loring quoted Chief Justice Shaw's "national compact" reasoning that Dana found so abhorrent: "the regulation of slavery . . . to prohibit States by law from harboring slaves was an essential element in [the Union's] formation."[8]

But this was a trial that turned on the facts, not the law. As Dana feared, Loring's failure to take notes when Dana contended that the Virginia court record ought not to be admitted was a bad sign. The commissioner decided the record was admissible. It was therefore conclusive, said Loring, as to the facts of the escape and to the service and labor owed to the master: "The identity is the only question I have a right to consider."

As the commissioner read his methodically reasoned decision, Dana's hope—and the heart of the young man he defended—must have leapt when Loring declared "between the testimony of the claimant and respondent there is a conflict, complete, and irreconcilable." But when he added, "The question now, is whether there is other evidence in this case which will determine this conflict," Dana knew what was to come. "The evidence is of the conversation which took place between Burns and the claimant on the night of the arrest," declared the commissioner. Loring reiterated William Brent's account of what was said when Burns was confronted by Suttle: "He was asked if he was willing to go back, and he said 'Yes, he was.'" In the courtroom, the young man silently mouthed "No!"[9]

Loring declared the statements made by Burns to Suttle satisfied "my mind . . . beyond a reasonable doubt" of the identity of Anthony Burns. Of the fact there was never doubt but of the lawfulness of the evidence to prove the fact, the commissioner merely asserted, "Had [the statements] been procured by hope or fear they would have been inadmissible; but of that I considered there was no evidence." Therefore, explained the commissioner in the logic and language of the law: "I consider the claimant entitled to the certificate from me which he claims."

Loring gathered his papers and left the bench. But those in the courtroom "remained in their places and for some moments the dead silence continued unbroken." Dana was irate: "Convicted on an *ex parte* record, against the actual evidence, and on his own admission made at the moment of arrest to his alleged master! A tyrannical statute and a weak judge!"[10]

But his immediate concern was "the poor prisoner. He looked the image of despair." Dana and Reverend Grimes remained with Burns in the courtroom for an hour. Grimes told Burns that the government and slaveholders were taking him back to Virginia only as a "point of honor," and that he would soon return. That lifted his spirits some, but Burns "expressed fear he should be forgotten and if sold with his weakened right hand, he would be sold 'down the river.'"[11]

Military and civil authorities were preparing to move Burns the third of a mile from the courthouse to Long Wharf, where a vessel was awaiting the prisoner. "I told him I should accompany him to the Cutter and Mr. Grimes offered to go with us also. I told the Marshal of our intention to go down with Burns." Marshal Freeman objected. Dana was incensed. It was the first instance in the eight-day ordeal when the lawyer "of moderate temper" lost his. Marshal Freeman "winced under the pressure," but after consultation with "military officers" the marshal denied Dana permission to accompany Burns—or to speak to the prisoner in confidence.[12]

Dana told Burns of the marshal's order. "I . . . gave him my hand . . . and bade him goodbye . . . Mr. Grimes also followed suit . . . bidding him to trust and hope in God." Dana and Grimes left the courtroom and remained in front of the courthouse. The "entire Square [was] cleared of the people, and filled with troops. Every window was filled, and beyond the lines drawn by the police was an immense crowd. . . . Nearly all the shops in Court and State Street were closed and hung in black and a huge coffin was suspended across State St., & flags Union down."[13]

At 11:00 A.M. troops on Boston Common were ordered to begin clearing Court and State Streets. Each solider was supplied with eleven rounds of ammunition. The dispatch of Boston police was temporarily delayed when Boston police captain Joseph Hayes resigned rather than take part in facilitating the return of Burns to slavery. At 2:30 P.M. "the vile procession" was ready to move.[14]

Burns was placed in the middle of a square of 120 "specials" armed with cutlasses and revolvers. He was adorned in the suit chosen by his captors, replete with a blue silk handkerchief, but he resisted one offering. Burns refused to be shackled. The "specials" themselves were at little risk, since their "square" was flanked by detachments of U.S. marines, a company of U.S. army infantry, and the U.S. artillery with cannon. Dana "walked slowly down the streets at a considerable distance in the rear of the procession." Although he made no note of it, Dana was "cheered lustily." As the procession moved toward the wharf, it was met, said Dana, "with a perfect howl of Shame! Shame! & hisses."[15]

The U.S. Navy revenue cutter *Morris* was anchored in Boston Harbor. Suttle and Brent were already aboard. The steamer *John Taylor* was at Long Wharf to transfer Burns, Deputy Marshal Butman, six of the "marshal's guard," and the Fourth Artillery attachment with cannon to the *Morris*. "When I heard the news that [the procession] had safely reached the end of the wharf, and that the cutter was steaming out to sea," wrote Dana, "I returned to my office."[16]

Dana remained there until about 8:30 P.M. before going to nearby Parker House, where he and two friends talked "gloomily enough" about the day's events. Worse, Parker's was filled with "the marshal's guard, deputies, and others who had volunteered with them . . . making themselves conspicuous by loud, triumphant talking." Dana made plans to leave but realized he had missed the 9:00 P.M. omnibus to Cambridge. Dana and a friend, Anson Burlingame, decided to walk to Cambridge. Dana had often made the thirty-minute walk before, but in the tumult of the past week, "many were armed." Dana purposely carried no weapon:

"I had a special duty to perform . . . and felt I should do it all the better if I relied on nothing but . . . moral power."[17]

As Dana passed Stoddard Avenue, "a vile neighborhood," Burlingame was suddenly pushed from the crowded sidewalk. Dana remembered "observing a commotion on my left . . . and instantly I [received] a terrible blow over my right eye . . . I thought for the moment it was by an iron bar." Dana was knocked senseless to the pavement, "pretty well covered with blood."[18] Two men were seen running back toward Stoddard Avenue.

Dana was struck just above the right eye. His glasses were broken, and cheekbone badly bruised and bloodied: "If it had hit the eye it would have destroyed it. If it had hit the temple, I have little doubt it would have broken it in." When Dana regained consciousness, "people came about me and I recollect insisting . . . that I was not hit intentionally until several told me they had seen . . . the blow." Burlingame took Dana to a doctor, where "the swelling was reduced considerably." It was nearly midnight when Dana reached home by coach: "Sarah had gone to bed. I took no light into her room and told her of my injury, representing it as a light matter, and not telling her the truth until the next day."[19]

Remarkably, Dana was back at work within a few days. But the trial of Anthony Burns and the assault on Dana stirred the country. The *New York Daily Tribune* was headlined THE BOSTON SLAVE CASE ATTEMPT TO ASSASSINATE RICHARD H. DANA. Sumner wrote Dana that the attack would "tell on slavery more than on you."[20] Two years later, a ferocious assault on Sumner would be far more telling.

Dana received "letters of compliment and congratulation and condolence and sympathy from all quarters which have been very gratifying for me." Longfellow wrote Sumner, "Dana has done nobly acting throughout with the greatest nerve and intrepidity." Dana observed "for once, since 1848, my position seems to be in accordance with that of the powers that be in Boston." Dana's brother-in-law did not get the message, instead writing to Dana that the "thwack" was deserved for one "who indulges in such seditious sneers at . . . Law."[21]

Amos Lawrence succinctly expressed the suddenness of the change: "We went to bed one night old fashioned, conservative . . . Whigs, and waked up stark mad Abolitionists."[22] The transformation was prompted by passage of the Kansas-Nebraska Act, signed into law by President Franklin Pierce the very week Burns was sent back to slavery. Introduced by Illinois senator Stephen A. Douglas to advance construction of a transcontinental railroad (and increase his own net worth), the new law repealed the Missouri Compromise of 1820. The Act proposed to organize land in which slavery had been prohibited into the territories of Kansas and Nebraska—and to leave the issue of slavery to popular sovereignty.

"The change wrought by the Nebraska bill is astonishing," wrote Dana. "The 'Webster Whigs' . . . feel they have been deceived by the South . . . I do not [know] how many who hardly spoke to me from 1850 to 1853 and whom I heard of in all quarters as speaking [against] me bitterly, come up to me with the freedom and warmth of old friends and talk as though there had never been any difference between us. This is not always easy to bear." Hardest of all was Dana's knowledge that the Burns case "is precisely the same as that of Sims. But, then, we were all traitors & malignants, now we are heroes & patriots." Dana believed he knew the cause: "The truth is Daniel Webster was strong [enough] to subjugate, for a time, the moral sentiment of New England. . . . He deceived half the North, but they are undeceived."[23]

A consequence of the change of heart among the many who had been "hostile or unpleasant" to Dana was a concerted effort to find those who assaulted him. "It is all fair weather sailing now," Dana ruefully observed. Before the month ended, a suspect was arrested: "He is a very strong man, a bully going by the aliases of Oxford, Huxford and Sullivan." Dana could not identify his attackers, as he was struck from behind, but upon entering court the suspect asked loudly "which of those gentlemen is Mr. Dana?" Dana asked Huxford if he was one of "marshal's guards." The suspect said he was. Dana observed, "It is quite impossible that he did not know me, as I had been before the guard constantly for five days."[24]

Bail was set at $1,500 and was immediately posted by Louis Varrell, the leader of Boston's underworld. Huxford jumped bail. Dana thought "it was an arranged thing—that the bail would be paid by contribution, perhaps the United States paying part." In fact, "Varrell was in high wrath" because Huxford had been expected take the rap for the assault. Varrell's thugs tracked Huxford to New Orleans and brought him back to stand trial. Huxford was convicted on the testimony of two witnesses, who identified the defendant as the sole perpetrator of the assault, and was sentenced to two years imprisonment. One morning Huxford's lawyer called upon Dana with news that his client was out of prison "and asked me if I had any objection to seeing him . . . assuring me that Huxford had no ill will against me at all." Dana immediately agreed and learned the details of the attack.

Louis Varrell was entertaining his "specials" at a Stoddard Street saloon on the night Burns was sent back to slavery, when he saw Dana "passing by in the strong gaslight." Varrell said he'd give ten dollars to the first man who would join him in assaulting Dana. "Huxford was to strike me a . . . blow on the right side of the head, which was expected to knock me toward . . . Varrell . . . [who] was to catch me with a blow on the left side as I was falling . . . but . . . I did not fall according to the program . . . so Varrell . . . lost his share of the work." It was Varrell who procured the two witnesses, who swore truthfully that Huxford assaulted Dana but falsely that it was Huxford alone.[25]

Huxford knew enough not to implicate Varrell. Among his other qualifications, Varrell had thrown a woman off a bridge to her death. Varrell continued to prosper long after the Dana episode, as an official of the New York Customs House. He survived several bribery allegations, but at age seventy-three was convicted of attempted murder when he shot the surveyor of the Port of New York.[26]

Dana's narrative made colorful an assault that might have killed him, but he found only horror in slavery. Shortly after the Burns rendition, an African American resident of Boston came to Dana for advice. Robinson had been freed by his master but asked Dana if there was any danger of being reclaimed as a slave. Dana told him "that his former master had no more right to carry him off than he had to carry me, but that there was a legal certainty that he would be delivered up to him if [his master] made a claim." The reason was "the damnable character of the 10th section" of the Fugitive Slave Act. As in the Burns trial, a record obtained from a Southern court was conclusive of the facts of slavery and escape. A master could swear that Robinson "escaped" from slavery and owed service and labor. Once identity was established, "a free man would be sent into slavery."[27]

Dana was interested in Robinson's history. His visitor told him he had been "bred up by slave dealers." Dana asked about flogging but was told that slave traders rarely flogged because the lash left marks that diminished a slave's value: "The common punishment was to strip them, make them bend over a log, fasten their hands and feet and beat them over the seat with a board [with] holes bored through it. This raised blisters. They then broke the blisters with a cowhide and dressed them down with a little brine." One description must have struck Dana with particular force, given the "generosity" ascribed to the marshal's guard when they dressed Burns in a new suit: "Each slave in the jail had a new suit of clothes and when any purchasers came they were dressed in the new clothes, the boys had their faces washed and greased, to make them shine."[28]

The fate of newly clothed Anthony Burns was as uncertain as the destiny of a divided nation. Franklin Pierce's policy of fugitive slave law enforcement in 1854 was no different from Millard Fillmore's in 1851. But Fillmore had Daniel Webster. Pierce had Jefferson Davis. Even a president from New Hampshire could not defuse Boston's explosive response to the U.S. government's role in sending Burns back to Virginia slavery. "A few more such victories," declared the *Richmond Examiner*, "and the South is undone."[29]

Dana was soon back to the ordinary practice of law. He refused to accept a check from the Boston Vigilance Committee for his defense of Burns, though Wendell Phillips's letter described it "not as compensation but as grateful acknowledgment merely of your efforts . . . in securing justice to fugitive and freeman." Dana responded: "I hope the members of the bar in Massachusetts will never fail to be ready to render this service gratuitously to the cause of humanity and liberty. A portion of my time and the application of such influence and ability as I may possess, is the only contribution I have to make."

On January 1, 1855, the Vigilance Committee again sought to recognize Dana's defense of Burns, noting, "You have declined all pecuniary compensation for these laborious and painful services." The practice of presenting an inscribed piece of silver plate memorializing acts of valor was a tradition in the British Navy. The committee asked Dana to accept "the accompanying piece of plate [for] . . . our own gratification . . . to preserve and hand down to your children and your children's children this record of your noble act."

Dana accepted the plate "as a memorial of the event, [rather] than as a testimonial to myself." His letter to the committee said as much about Dana's character as it did about his view of a lawyer's life: "The labors of a lawyer are ordinarily devoted to questions of property between man and man. He is to be congratulated, if though but for once, in any signal cause, he can devote them to the vindication . . . of rights." The defense of Anthony Burns, wrote Dana, was "a privilege for which I ought rather to give than receive compensation."

The plate bore the inscription:

TO

RICHARD H. DANA, JR.

FOR HIS

MANLY AND GRATUITOUS DEFENCE

OF THE

UNALIENABLE RIGHTS

OF

ANTHONY BURNS,

WHO WAS

KIDNAPPED AT BOSTON MAY 24TH

AND DOOMED TO ETERNAL BONDAGE JUNE 2D, 1854

FROM A FEW OF HIS FELLOW CITIZENS[30]

The inscription on the plate reflected more than Dana's act. It was evidence that in 1854, even those most opposed to slavery could not foresee its end.

"Little Charlotte had a birthday party, her 10th birthday at which nearly 50 of her schoolmates & friends were present," Dana noted on the last day of June. By then Anthony Burns was back in Virginia. He was bound hand and foot in chains and thrown into a six-by-eight-foot cell in Richmond's most notorious slave pen. Incredibly, Burns managed to a write a letter to "Lawyer danner Boston/Massachusetts." Burns hid paper and pen on his person and was able to obtain ink from other incarcerated slaves. He fastened the letter to a piece of brick and tossed it through the window grates when he saw another slave outside the jail fence. First misdirected to a James Dana, the letter was dated August 23, 1854.[31]

Burns wrote "My Dr. Mr. Danner . . . I am yet Bound in Jail and are wearing chings Night and day." The manacled slave told Dana, "I am for Sale . . . And if you will get Sum of your friends to come . . . and not say that he come from Boston . . . And Ask [Suttle] . . . what he will take . . . you can get me Low he would take $800 dollars for me . . . Anthony Burns don't rite to me until I tel you." It is not clear when the letter reached Dana. He certainly would have known that Suttle did not respond to an offer from Reverend Grimes to purchase Burns for $1200. The return of Burns to slavery was as symbolically significant to the South as to the North. Suttle chose not to risk the ire of fellow Southerners who vehemently opposed any sale that would enable Northerners to free Burns. In November 1854 Burns was sold at auction to David McDaniel, a North Carolina slave trader.

In December Burns sent Dana a second letter: "I am Living with A man who is A trader. But he says he will Not sell me . . . write to me and call me James Black of Rock Mount North Callina for if you call my name I will Not get it . . . When I fine I can get letters from you then I will write to you all the News and what I wount you to Dow for me." It is not clear when Dana received it, but early in 1855 a letter from a woman who lived in Rocky Mount, North Carolina, to her sister in Amherst, Massachusetts, told of McDaniel's ownership of the famous Anthony Burns.[32]

McDaniel responded affirmatively when asked if he would sell Burns to Bostonians, "if it can be done without any public excitement." There was, in fact, plenty of drama before Reverend Grimes was able to meet the slave trader and slave in a Baltimore hotel. McDaniel faced down a crowd in Norfolk, Virginia, that learned Burns was to be sold to Northerners. On February 27, 1855, Grimes paid $1,300 to the master, and Burns headed North a free man.[33]

In March Burns gave speeches to large crowds in New York and Massachusetts, recounting his return from slavery. At month's end he paid a visit to Dana. "Anthony Burns called to see me, with his clergyman Rev. Mr. Grimes to thank me for my defense & to pay his respects. He appeared very well, in good health & spirits. He seems a modest, conscientious man & his story must be drawn from him."[34] The two men conversed for several hours.

Burns told Dana of his imprisonment. "He was put in a Slave jail & kept there . . . in irons, both on hands & on feet until November except during a few weeks when he had a violent fever & the irons were taken off by order of the physician. These irons were not for security, but for punishment." The young man told Dana that when Suttle put him up for auction, the crowd was so hostile that Suttle "got a gang of some 20 or 30 men to protect him . . . because . . . he was afraid [Burns] would be injured so as to reduce his value." His new owner, McDaniel, "was obliged to carry him away by night, for fear of the mob."

From his office, Dana pointed out to Burns "the window of the room of the Court House where he was confined." Only Burns could have been more incredulous than Dana at the turn of events since Loring's verdict nine months earlier: "What a change . . . now he visits the scene of his agony of trial, a hero, a martyr, with crowds of the learned & intelligent . . . listening to his words!"

Dana at thirty-eight must have considered June 2, 1854, when Anthony Burns was "doomed to eternal bondage" and Dana himself nearly killed, the single worst day of his life. But now as he stood with the twenty-two-year-old Burns gazing at the very spot where "the die turn[ed] for slavery," Dana was moved to write, "Who can tell what a day may bring forth! Who can tell what other things & which are the men that are to move the world."

17

DUTY

"I have just read *The Heir of Redclyffe*. Oh that my eyes were rivers & my head a fountain of tears!" Dana exclaimed in November 1854.[1] The two-volume romantic novel by English author Charlotte Mary Yonge was a book of rank sentimentality without literary merit. Dana loved it.

His identification with the book's hero ("Guy! Poor, dear, noble Guy!") was complete: "There is something in Guy that reminds me of myself . . . his love of adventure, his devotion to the sea . . . his love of boats, his turn for romance & heroic adventure, his sober seriousness as a lover, the melancholy devotedness of his courtship, his youthfulness & elasticity—in all these I am reminded of some of the best points in my own life & character."[2] But, as was entirely typical of Dana, his romantic vision of virtue was a reminder of his own fallibility.

Guy was "pure"—Dana "far, far behind him in purity. I am impure." Guy was "a constant striver for victory"—Dana "only an occasional struggler." His hero was sure of eternal life. Wrote Dana, "heaven & the spiritual world are unreal to me & I have no power to bear mental suffering because I have no sure hold on what is beyond."[3]

For a man whose reading could not be considered frivolous (Dana's children saw him with a red-bound copy of Bacon's *Novum Organum* so often, they thought it all their father read), *The Heir of Redclyffe* had a disproportionate impact. It was not a healthy one. If he could not be as virtuous as his hero, "my duty is clear. I must support myself & my family . . . by my profession. This requires indefatigable labor."[4]

In the aftermath of the Burns trial and the assault, Dana's annual August ramblings were limited. He accepted an invitation to accompany an army engineer on an inspection of Maine lighthouses. The best part of the trip was "in a boat, going off & on & landing . . . I fairly renewed my youth & fancied myself again & again on my old duties on the coast of California." September brought the thirty-nine-year-old lawyer back to the reality of work and family. Dana's "anxious and uncertain" father confessed to a sense that he ought to work, but Dana observed that his father's "morbid sensitiveness . . . makes every day & every hour an unfit time to work at."[5]

Sarah continued to be unwell, though the cause remained uncertain. At a performance of the opera *Norma,* she "was faint & obliged to leave." Sarah's "nervous condition" caused her "fears for her health & even her life." The family physician assured her that she had no "disease of either heart or brain" and prescribed rest and "freedom from care." Dana noted that freedom from care was not easy for a mother with five children at home. Nor, he could have added, for a father who believed his duty to his family compelled ceaseless labor. During Sarah's "worst state," Dana was "taken ill, getting up at night, feeling suddenly sick & fainting & falling on the floor." The parents were spared worse when three-year-old Richard narrowly missed the stone steps to the cellar when he fell from his second-story nursery window.[6]

Dana could at least take some satisfaction from his work. The frigid stares on State Street began to thaw: "The change in public sentiment on the Slave Question is very great. Men who were hostile or unpleasant in 1851 are now cordial and complimentary."[7] Evidence of a shift in sentiment could be glimpsed in his caseload as well. Although Dana was still largely avoided by a social and merchant class that preferred Rufus Choate and George Hillard, Dana was too good a lawyer to be ignored by clients with money at stake. In May 1855, Dana's appearances before the U.S. Circuit Court in Boston included patent cases in addition to suits for seamen's wages. Dana could joust with any lawyer in any courtroom, but he preferred the "dignity" of admiralty court, free from jury trials with their "inflammatory appeals, pert replies, angry retorts, and noisy declamations."[8] The admiralty court appealed to his love of tradition, and few lawyers in America could match his knowledge of the sea.

It was Dana's rare combination of legal acumen and maritime experience that enabled him to successfully challenge centuries of English precedent that governed the "law of collision" at sea. The rule that ships on a collision course must each keep to the right continued to govern when one of the two ships was a powered vessel. Dana believed that when a sailing vessel met a steamer, it was the sailing vessel that should keep its course, placing the duty on the power vessel to avoid collision.

Dana carefully examined "every case of collision in England or America & made up my mind that there was a rationale which lay at the bottom of the whole law of collision which had never been expounded or even hinted at by any judge or commentator." He made a four-hour argument to Judge Peleg Sprague "illustrating it & enforcing it in every way in my power." Though unhappy with Judge Sprague's charge in the James Scott rescue prosecution for its partiality to the government, he thought Sprague the most learned admiralty judge in the country. Dana was not above suggesting to the court that its opinion could secure a place in legal history. "I . . . told him that he could do for the law of collision what the great Lord Holt did for the law of bailment."[9] Judges, like other mortals, are occasionally susceptible to the thought they can do something memorable.

Peleg Sprague was too good a jurist to allow specious argument or flattery to sway him. It was the power of Dana's reasoning (and Sprague's willingness to overrule precedent when it was demonstrably ill founded) that persuaded the court to declare in the case of *The Osprey* that a vessel under sail must keep to its course, while placing the duty to avoid collision on the power vessel.[10] Judge Sprague thanked counsel, as well he might since the rationale for the decision was entirely Dana's work. "I have a right to take some pride in this," wrote Dana.[11] The rule laid down in that case is still followed today, as familiar to recreational sailors as it is to international law, where it was codified. Many superb lawyers (and judges) since would envy having a case of such lasting consequence.

Dana's commitment to his family and practice gave him no time for politics, but the Massachusetts elections of 1854 made them impossible to ignore. In one of the most stunning outcomes in the history of American elections, the Know Nothing Party obliterated the state's electoral landscape. The new legislature was comprised of a Whig, a Democrat, a Republican, and 377 Know Nothings. Every statewide office from governor on down was held by a Know Nothing.[12]

"It was an entire surprise on everybody," said Dana, describing the movement as "a secret political organization . . . made up of religious & national hostility to the Catholics & Irish & a distrust of . . . the old parties."[13] The party's name came from the password ("I know nothing") but the label fit for other reasons as well. Within two years the Know Nothing Party's extremism (most evident in a notorious "investigation" of nunneries) led it to collapse as quickly as it had risen. Yet its impending demise was far from apparent in 1855 when the Know Nothing movement appeared to be unstoppable. The Know Nothing Party was embraced by many voters who were opposed to the fugitive slave law. Anti-Irish prejudice played a part as well, as Boston's Irish were thought to favor the law (the Irish were particularly conspicuous participants in the quasi-military guard that "escorted" Anthony Burns to the ship that took him back to slavery). One of the first acts of the new Know Nothing governor, Henry Gardner, was to dissolve Irish militia companies.[14]

The Know Nothings did know something. They knew that the easiest target in American politics is a judge who makes an unpopular decision. When the new legislature convened in early 1855, no decision was more universally condemned in the state than Judge Edward Loring's rendition of Anthony Burns. In March the "Committee on Federal Relations" began proceedings to remove Loring from his position as state probate judge. The committee alleged that Loring's decision when sitting as a federal commissioner in the fugitive slave act hearing was contrary to the public interest and "a shock to the popular sentiment."

It is difficult to imagine a better platform for a politically ambitious lawyer than the one the hearing opened for Dana. Opposition to the Fugitive Slave Act—the cause for which Dana had sacrificed economic well-being, health, social standing, and nearly his life—was now the coin of the political realm. No figure in Massachusetts could speak to the removal of Judge Loring with greater assurance than the lawyer who so fiercely confronted the judge who refused to acknowledge "the presumption of freedom." Dana directly challenged Loring's legal analysis in a widely read article, "The Decision Which Judge Loring Might Have Given."[15]

Petitions calling for Loring's removal flooded the legislature. The judge was burned in effigy. "Let him be a marked man forever," proclaimed a *Boston Commonwealth* correspondent.[16] Dana sought advice on whether to testify. But the guidance he looked for had nothing to do with his political opportunity. Dana wanted to know who would speak for an independent judiciary.

Dana succinctly summarized the argument against the removal of Judge Loring: "If . . . founded upon the notion that in discharging the duty of Commissioner in the Burns case, he acted from corrupt or willful motive, or was wanting in kindness & fairness of his treatment of Burns or his counsel, it is a mistake. If founded on the opinion . . . he ought to be removed because [of] his acting as a magistrate in a slave case, my own opinion is that it is far better for Massachusetts first to put herself right upon the record, to pass a law prohibiting such an act & then to punish all who trespass it."[17]

Dana attempted to enlist help in slowing the rush to judgment. He spoke with Franklin Dexter, a respected lawyer who shared Dana's antislavery views, and with eighty-five-year-old Josiah Quincy, the esteemed former Harvard president who had dealt with rebellious students (including Dana). "The advice of neither of these gentlemen was quite satisfactory," noted Dana. Dexter deferred because of his dislike of the "Curtis faction" that supported Loring, though if that were a basis for excusing oneself, no one had more reason than Dana. Quincy believed that the removal would not serve as precedent because decisions of the Know Nothing legislature would not be given weight. Dana called on Charles Francis Adams Sr. but he was away. "I could consult no more & was obliged to commit myself to action without further opportunity for advice."[18]

There are an inexhaustible number of reasons available to those who wish to avoid the ordeal of defending an unpopular principle before a hostile legislature. Dana chose to examine the reasons he ought to appear: "It seemed to me that no man in the state was in a situation to act with as much effect as I, seeing that I was counsel for Burns, known to be an opponent of the Fugitive Slave Law & hostile to Judge Loring & his set. It seemed to me that therefore it was my duty to come forward, not in his defence, but in defence of the principle [of judicial independence]."[19]

Abolitionists Theodore Parker and Wendell Phillips led the move to oust Loring. Parker's basis for advocating Loring's removal had the virtue of simplicity: "We ask for Loring's removal because we have a kidnapper as judge." Phillips's more nuanced testimony—and Dana's rebuttal—made vivid two conflicting antislavery theories of a judge's responsibility when confronted with a slavery case. For Dana, the lawyer, the issue was "How should a judge of integrity decide the case?" (Judge Loring, said Dana, "did not bring to the cause the high instincts of liberty, the original power, the independence which the cause required.") For Phillips, the moralist, the issue was "How can a man of integrity judge these cases?"[20] One's unfitness to be a judge, Phillips testified, arose the moment one agreed to participate in a judicial process that recognized a constitutional protection of slavery. It was Loring's acceptance of the appointment as commissioner, thus consenting "to aid in hunting slaves," that demonstrated "a merciless spirit, a moral blindness . . . that totally unfit a man for judicial office."[21]

Phillips was articulating the jurisprudential premise for abolitionists, who believed that the Fugitive Slave Clause of the Constitution compelled judges to make morally reprehensible decisions. In 1844 Phillips had written *The Constitution: A Pro Slavery Compact,* a fuller exposition of the view he so forcefully expressed when Chief Justice Shaw refused to block the rendition of fugitive slave George Latimer from Massachusetts. "The fault is in allowing such a constitution to live an hour," proclaimed Phillips."[22]

Dana rejected Phillips's contention that taking an oath to uphold the Constitution made a judge or commissioner unfit, but he recognized the sacrifices his fellow Brahmin had made to advance the antislavery cause: "The bright dreams of his youth, of professional and political distinction of high station, and the reflection of new honor upon an honored name he has inherited. . . . All this sacrificed because he would not misconstrue the Constitution."[23] It was a tribute that was equally applicable to Dana. Indeed, "the sight of Dana and Phillips tilting at each other" has been described as "a wonderful example" of each man "acting consistently with principle."[24]

But principle is seldom the focus of an inquisitorial proceeding. The committee began its hearing on February 20, 1855. Even the great hall of the Massachusetts Statehouse was not large enough to contain the spectators. Hundreds who could not find seats stood in the streets. Though Conservative Whigs, including George Ticknor Curtis, castigated the committee in print, none were willing to appear. Rufus Choate did not reprise his eloquent defense of judicial independence made in the more welcoming forum of the Massachusetts constitutional convention. Wendell Phillips ostensibly recognized the principle of judicial independence ("[removal] is a grave power and one to be used only on important occasions"), but in common with those who seek to remove a judge for an unpopular decision, Phillips found the occasion sufficiently important.[25]

"I had hoped . . . that others . . . would have appeared here to address you," Dana began, "but they have devolved the sole duty upon me." Dana's appearance arose solely from his own conception of duty, but no legislator could dispute Dana's statement that "[Judge Loring's] friends have not been mine."

Dana's explication of judicial independence was as much a statement of his own creed as political theory: "Any man, however weak, however odious has certain rights secured to him by the Constitution. If the legislature by accident or design, if the dominant political party, flush from the contest have sought to touch the hair of his head, he can appeal from them to the judges; and there is nothing on earth nearer Heaven, than when judges of the land vindicate the right of such a man against the popular sentiment, or popular interests of the hour."

Dana's dilemma was the same as it always is for defenders of judicial independence. It is a principle easy to honor in the abstract but difficult to apply in the specific of an unpopular decision. Dana put the issue in terms no legislator could misunderstand: "Recollect, Mr. Chairman, that this game of removal is a game at which two may play and . . . it is not easy to see the end." If Judge Loring was removed because he enforced the Fugitive Slave Act, "other judges, here or elsewhere, may be removed because they do not." This was more than idle speculation. In Wisconsin some judges had refused to execute the law, a decision that put them at risk of removal at the hands of a Democratic or Whig legislature.[26]

Dana had little chance of persuading legislators that there was greater benefit in protecting judicial independence than sacrificing it, given the public outcry against Loring. But the committee and the public had to acknowledge that Dana had standing to dispute the claim that Loring should be removed because his conduct in the Burns hearing made him unfit to be a judge.

Wendell Phillips testified that Loring was inhumane and arbitrary in his treatment of Burns. Dana observed "how subject we are to have our recollection affected by subsequent events." But Dana had something more than memory: "I have a habit, whenever I happen to be engaged in a matter of much public or private importance of making a record of the events as they transpire." A description of the demeanor of Judge Loring as "considerate and humane," contemporaneously recorded by the attorney most adverse to the court in the Burns hearing, could not be ignored.

Facts are sticky things for inquisitions. Dana's account prompted Wendell Phillips to return as a witness. He contradicted Dana's assertion that Loring told Dana the court would give Burns time to decide to retain counsel. If Dana was grieved that Phillips shaded the truth, he understood the motivation. The zealousness with which Phillips and Theodore Parker (and lawyers Robert Morris and Charles Ellis) sought Loring's removal was consistent with their unwavering opposition to the fugitive slave law. That could not be said of the Massachusetts legislature. Dana did not say it.

Dana knew that the legislature would vote to remove Judge Loring irrespective of his testimony. It is seldom a politic idea to tell hostile legislators what one really thinks of them. It can, however, have a cathartic effect on the speaker. By that measure, Dana must have felt terrific. He reminded the committee that in 1851 the Massachusetts legislature defeated a resolution "very moderate in character" condemning the Fugitive Slave Act of 1850. He added: "That same year, during the session of the legislature, under its very eye, occurred the rendition of Sims. The Court House was in chains . . . Massachusetts law was suspended. Courts were closed to all, except such as the U.S. marshal chose to admit. Massachusetts lay at the foot of the slave power. What did the legislature do? Nothing! Absolutely nothing!"

There is little benefit to softening one's remarks at this point. Moreover, there is a risk one has left things unsaid. Dana preferred not to take the risk: "Now, Mr. Chairman and Gentlemen, I put it to you as men of candor, I put it to every petitioner in this hall—has the legislature of Massachusetts done anything to condemn the fugitive slave law since its passage? Has she not rather refused to do so? Do you forget the condition of the two great parties of this country from 1850 to 1854. . . . Do you forget the condition of the Whig Party of Massachusetts? Do you forget the overpowering influence of Mr. Webster?" If one is calling out hypocrites, one ought not to neglect an example of their hypocrisy. Dana had one at hand: "So, far from flying in the face of the legislative will of Massachusetts, I fear Judge Loring has acted too much in accordance with it."

Two weeks after Dana's testimony, the committee issued a report calling for Loring's removal. Surprisingly, three members of the seven-member committee dissented. Part of the reason may have been the majority's reliance on the allegation that Judge Loring treated Burns inhumanely, despite Dana's evidence to the contrary. Dana did not secure other witnesses to corroborate his testimony because the committee assured him it did not intend to use the issue of Loring's demeanor as a basis for removal. When it did so, Dana objected and the majority was compelled to reopen the hearing for a day. Despite testimony from other witnesses who found Loring's conduct of the hearing to be fair, Dana's testimony was again rebutted by Wendell Phillips. Phillips asserted that he did not doubt Dana's veracity, "but only his memory."[27]

The committee reissued its report the next day without significant changes. Following debate in the house and senate, the legislature endorsed a measure calling on Governor Henry Gardner to remove Loring from the office of judge of probate. Astonishingly—at first glance—Know Nothing governor Henry Gardner refused to do so. Indeed, the governor's message to the legislature was a principled defense of judicial independence: "It may be pertinent to ask what the duty of judges is. Are they to expound the laws as made by the law-making power or are they to construe them in accordance with popular sentiment?"[28]

But in contemporary explanations of Governor Gardner's motives, "principle" is not often cited. The reason for Gardner's surprising refusal to remove Judge Loring was the governor's ambition to become national president of the Know Nothing Party. That objective could be achieved only with support from Southern members, who were increasingly unhappy with the antislavery sentiment of elements of the Massachusetts Know Nothing Party. Gardener's refusal to remove Loring was politically calculated to enhance his standing with Know Nothing Southerners at the party's upcoming national convention in June.

Dana recognized that Gardner's decision not to remove Loring was predicated on politics, not principle. The governor's message used every significant point Dana made before the committee, including his testament to the judge's conduct. Gardner's decision received a twenty-one-gun salute on Boston Common, and was praised in the newspapers most antagonistic to Dana. It was not to be the last time Dana's conception of duty served those least interested in his principles.[29]

The Know Nothings looked invincible when they assumed office in 1855. The voices of those who knew something were remarkably quiet. Charles Sumner refused to condemn the movement—either publicly or privately—despite its openly anti-Irish, anti-Catholic bias. Unlike Sumner, Dana had criticized the Know Nothing Party's racism: "I can understand the feeling of race, the rivalry and hostility of race, which has contributed to the growth of this . . . order. I have felt them myself. But I have known them to be unchristian, and have hoped not to be governed by them."[30]

The shifting political landscape worried Sumner, who owed his Senate seat to Henry Wilson's genius for coalition politics. The Know Nothing Party dismantled the legislative coalition of Free Soilers and Democrats that elected Sumner to the Senate. Wilson secretly cut a deal with the powerful Know Nothings in 1854 when he withdrew as the nascent Republican Party's gubernatorial candidate, ensuring Know Nothing Henry Gardner's election as governor. In exchange, the new Know Nothing legislature elected Wilson to the U.S. Senate to replace Whig Edward Everett, who had resigned.

By the summer of 1855 the influence of Southerners in the national Know Nothing Party made it more difficult for Massachusetts politicians to support the new party. At the Philadelphia convention of the national Know Nothing Party in June, Southern delegates adopted a platform declaring that existing federal law should be the "final and conclusive settlement" of the slavery question. Governor Gardner was compelled to give up his ambition to lead the national Know Nothing Party and follow Henry Wilson when the Massachusetts senator led a walkout of Northern delegates.[31]

The vacuum created by the Know Nothing's split over slavery offered the opportunity for a "fusion" of antislavery voters under the banner of a principled party. The uncertainty of the outcome prompted characteristic responses from politician Sumner and citizen Dana. Sumner left for points west, hoping to avoid any entanglement. Dana jumped in, seeking to establish an antislavery party free of Know Nothing prejudice. When Charles Francis Adams Sr. asked Dana to bring together antislavery citizens in a fusion party, he agreed to try. Dana forcefully objected to an alliance with the Know Nothing Party as an organization, though he welcomed antislavery individuals from the party.[32]

The new "Republican" Party of Massachusetts met in Worcester in September 1855. Governor Gardner, intent on any method that would secure him a coalition sufficient for reelection, sought the Republican nomination for governor by professing support for the strong antislavery plank of the Republican platform. Dana pointedly said Free Soilers would never accept a candidate who did not have "character to fall back on."[33]

Gardner led on the first ballot, but a speech by Dana on behalf antislavery Whig Julius Rockwell swayed delegates. "When Gardner had the plurality & all seemed to be gone, . . . I made the chief speech which everybody tells me decided the [nomination for Rockwell]," wrote Dana to Sarah. Dana considered the instrumental role he played in ensuring that the Republican Party was untainted by Know Nothingism "the greatest work" of his life.[34] He refused the party's nomination to be the Republican candidate for attorney general, believing he had greater influence as a private citizen. At last able to support a political party devoted to antislavery principles, Dana canceled his lectures in order to campaign.

But Know Nothingism had not yet run its course. Henry Gardner repudiated "Mr. Dana's convention" and accepted renomination as the Know Nothing candidate for governor. To do so, Gardner disavowed the antislavery position he had taken at the Republican meeting. The issue was drawn as Dana sought: "We think the triumph of the Republican cause to be of the greatest importance in the cause of freedom in the struggle with the slave oligarchy." But "nativism and whiggery" prevailed. Gardner was reelected governor. Republican candidate Rockwell was supported by less than 30 percent of voters.[35]

Although the new Republican Party Dana shaped in Massachusetts did not do well in the 1855 election, the campaign did produce benefits. The clear choice between the Dana-drafted antislavery principles of the Republican Party and the Know Nothing nativist platform prompted Sumner to take a stand. "Boldly if belatedly," Sumner joined Dana in concluding that a "party, which beginning in secrecy, interferes with religious belief, and [discriminates] on the accident of birth, is not the party for us." Dana presided at a Faneuil Hall preelection assembly where "Sumner made a noble speech."[36]

Despite Sumner's talent for rationalization, Dana admired him. Sumner regularly had Sunday dinner at Longfellow's home, followed by tea at Dana's. Sumner once told Dana "an anecdote of himself . . . which is another proof of the great extent . . . that [every] man makes his own fortunes." Sumner's father did not intend to provide his son with much education, but the little boy studied on his own. One morning as his father was shaving, Charles "astonished him by reciting & reading Latin." His father enrolled him in Boston Latin School. Dana noted that Sumner "was universally acknowledged as the best scholar" at Harvard Law School. It was Sumner's brilliance rather than family influence that persuaded Justice Story to provide Sumner with letters of introduction to English aristocracy, and from there Sumner "made his own way."[37]

The reelection of Know Nothing governor Gardner concerned Sumner, who feared (correctly) that Gardner had designs on Sumner's Senate seat. Senator Sumner became surprisingly quiet again ("our mute representative," mocked the *Boston Courier*). Theodore Parker advised Sumner to counter Gardner's ambition by taking a "more decided course . . . against slavery."[38] The opportunity came in the debate over "bloody Kansas." The Kansas-Nebraska Act of 1854 opened the Kansas territory to competing free-soil and pro-slavery settlers. The "New England Aid Company" sponsored Northern émigrés, while residents of slave state Missouri were encouraged by slave interests to immigrate to adjacent Kansas. Each faction organized governments.

In April 1856 Dana attended a Boston gathering of the Emigrant Aid Society, where he met New Englander Charles Robinson, "governor-elect" of free-soil Kansas. He was impressed with "this plain, self-made man." "Verily every true born Yankee is a maker of constitutions, a founder of empires, a builder of cities, a subduer of nature & regulator of men."[39] Yankees, however, were not the only inhabitants of Kansas or the U.S. Senate. The debate among senators over competing claims to Kansas was bound to be acerbic, given the volatility of sectional passions. But the Northern narrative of outrages against oppressed free-soil settlers by "murderous" Southerners—if wholly accepted as fact—was particularly suited to Senator Sumner's talent for rhetorical excess.

Sumner was always deaf to the extraordinary power of his invective. When in 1846 Sumner attacked Robert Winthrop for the congressman's vote in support of the Mexican War ("Blood! Blood! is on the hands of the representative from Boston. Not all great Neptune's ocean can wash them clean"), Winthrop wrote to Sumner, "You have not weighed the force of your own phrases."[40] At least as telling was Sumner's belief that he was the injured party when Winthrop broke off social relations. Martyrdom came easily to Sumner.

On May 19, 1856, Sumner began his "Crime against Kansas" speech in the Senate. It continued into a second day and was marked by language that was vitriolic even by Sumner's standards. Elderly South Carolina senator Andrew Butler was a particular target of scorn, Sumner going so far as to mock the senator's impaired speech. "He cannot ope[n] his mouth but out flies a blunder." Sumner declared that if the senator and South Carolina itself were "blotted out of existence" civilization would lose less "than already gained by the example of Kansas, in its valiant struggle against oppression." From the back of the Senate chamber, Senator Stephen Douglas muttered, "That damned fool will get himself killed by some other damn fool."[41]

Two days later, thirty-six-year-old South Carolina congressman Preston Brooks, a cousin of Senator Butler, approached Sumner as he sat as his desk in the Senate. "I have read your speech," began Brooks while raising a cane over the seated Sumner. A blow stunned Sumner, who tried to rise as the enraged Brooks repeatedly struck Sumner. The bloodied senator, frantic to avoid the assault, stood with such force that he ripped the desk from the bolts that secured it to the floor. Eyes filled with blood, the blinded Sumner staggered forward while Brooks beat him until the cane splintered. Sumner collapsed unconscious on the Senate floor.[42]

Dana presided at a Cambridge meeting expressing his outrage at "the brutal, murderous and cowardly" attack. "I think of you every hour of the day," Dana wrote to Sumner. "You haunt me. Mrs. Dana cannot sleep because of you and my children cry tears of anger and pity." Brahmin Boston had a different lament. "Sumner is not merely [the Republicans'] champion but their martyr, and his election for the next six years is now certain," said George Hillard.[43]

Though Sumner, Kansas, and politics filled newspapers as well as Dana's thoughts, Dana was soon away from all when he took a long-anticipated trip to England in the summer of 1856. Dana's fame as author of *Two Years Before the Mast,* his defense of Anthony Burns, and his close association with Sumner opened every door of the English aristocracy. Dana thought he was treated well because his hosts "necessarily take a foreigner somewhat at his own valuation of himself." Even as he paid homage to the titled elders of English aristocracy, Dana identified with youth. A young British officer who had distinguished himself in the Crimean War reminded Dana of "Frank Parkman" (if Parkman "had fine health"): "clever, dashing, lucky, brave youth of rank and fortune."[44]

At a lavish dinner Dana vied with "several bachelors" for the attention of an attractive young woman. Dana "plunged into a competition of gallantry, and notwithstanding the disadvantages of years, and marriage, [my competitors] said it was a fair heat, and complimented me by saying it was rather brilliant." At forty-one, Dana was aptly described as "in the young maturity of his powers—eager, observant, loyal, enthusiastic and humorous."[45]

On a September morning in 1856 Dana entered New York Harbor on his return from England: "Here is a bright piercing sun, and clear sky, and all nerves set to concert pitch. . . . Here is youth, hope, progress and earnest action."[46] The qualities Dana valued in both individual and country were to be exhibited in Parkman's *The Oregon Trail.* But stress sets nerves to a different pitch than adventure. Dana was about to enter the modern world.

18

BREAKDOWN

In October 1856, Charles Francis Adams Jr., grandson and great-grandson of presidents John Quincy Adams and John Adams, respectively, began the study of law in Dana's office. Young Adams was, of course, fully cognizant of the long association of the Dana and Adams families: "Indeed, my very name bore testimony to the fact, for my grandfather had given his third son the middle name Francis, after Francis Dana, the former Chief Justice of Massachusetts. Nor was this an ordinary case of compliment through name-giving; on the contrary, it recalled historic memories, and was associated with . . . great events."[1]

Adams was not to witness great events in the three years he spent in Dana's law office from 1856 to 1859. Yet he could readily see Dana's qualities, which he described in superlatives seldom used by any Adams.

Dana was "a man of the finest mental qualities . . . with faculties of observation and a power of description rarely equaled."[2]

It was Henry Adams, Charles's younger brother, who famously asked what could become of a child raised in the traditions of seventeenth- and eighteenth-century Boston "when he should wake up to find himself required to play in the game of the twentieth?"[3] The middle of the nineteenth century was not yet the twentieth, but the game Dana was required to play is familiar enough. Dana, said Charles Francis Adams Jr., whose family wealth made the game easier, "was doomed to waste his life in the work of earning a living."[4]

"Waste" was not a fair verdict on Dana's life as a whole, but it was an accurate description of what young Adams saw from his ringside seat. Nothing in Adams's portrayal of Dana's life during this period is unfamiliar to the twenty-first century, much less the twentieth: "In common with most of his profession who lived in suburban towns, Dana through all the more depressing season of the year can scarcely be said, except on Sundays, to have ever seen his home by daylight. He left it when the sun was just risen, to get back to it long after dark."[5]

At times Dana would be in court every day for weeks. The cases were more often "fighting petty causes in inferior courts" than "battling over great principles in supreme tribunals." When Dana was in trial, his "hurried midday meal would be eaten or more properly speaking would be swallowed."[6] Following an afternoon in court, Dana would return to the office to meet clients, prepare witnesses, and get ready for the next day's arguments.

Dana was never without his ubiquitous green bag filled with briefs and memoranda necessary for work at home. He tried, not always successfully, to be with his family in Cambridge by seven P.M. Evening "dinners" were not yet in vogue (the midday meal was intended to be substantial), dinner then being tea and toast. Dana often devoured everything within his reach. In answer to Sarah's question about his appetite, "it would presently appear that, intent upon his case and its preparation, during recess he had wholly forgotten to get any dinner at all, and since breakfast nearly twelve hours before, had been living on air alone; and that, too, the vile air of the crowded courtroom." After some time with the children, Dana would "disappear into his library, the green bag would be emptied of its papers, and the lawyer would be immersed in the study of his case until bedtime."[7]

Dana's unsustainable pace—as well as his brilliance as a trial lawyer—were on full display in the "Dalton divorce case," a sensational trial that mesmerized Boston. Dana represented Mr. Dalton, who was suing his young pregnant wife for divorce. Dana's client was an unsympathetic figure because the public thought Dalton had gotten away with murder. The belief was understandable because Dana had successfully defended Dalton against the charge he murdered his wife's alleged lover.

Dana, trying the case alone, battled Rufus Choate and Henry Durant, widely considered "the strongest combination the [Boston] bar could supply."[8] While Choate and Durant spelled each other, Dana was on his feet for days in a hot, ill-ventilated courtroom. Closing arguments were expected to be lengthy in a culture that looked to trials for entertainment. The lawyers did not disappoint. Choate's closing was ten hours long. Not to be outdone, Dana took twelve hours over two days for his summation. It was more than 60,000 words—the length of a small book. Boston newspapers put out special editions reporting it.

The judge was as antagonistic as the public to Dana's client. Adams watched in "open mouthed astonishment" while the court gave a three-hour charge that "openly harangued the jury" on behalf of Choate's client, young Mrs. Dalton.[9] The jury could not reach a verdict. When it was learned that ten of the twelve jurors voted for the despised Mr. Dalton, the result was considered a great triumph for Dana.

But Adams believed that Dana's astonishing display of advocacy was sadder to look back on than it was to witness at the time: "The work was killing; . . . here was a man qualified by nature to do something which the world would not willing permit to die, letting himself out as an intellectual athlete and using up health and life in wordy wrangles over the domestic infelicities of a foolish boy who had married a wanton school-girl." To the outside world, Dana was a picture of "that unconscious composure which comes from self-confidence and courage." Yet even those qualities do not suffice if one needs—as Dana surely did—one's legal work to be for a greater purpose than a client's interest. The rescue and fugitive slave cases were behind him. Dana was not gaining energy from a great cause. He was drawing on the self-discipline he learned at sea by which "he went forth and came in, got up and lay down."[10]

Dana managed to spare time to campaign for the 1856 Republican presidential candidate, John C. Fremont. Though Democrat James Buchanan won, "the election has been as successful as a defeat can be." The "great result" was a united North and Sumner's reelection. Dana noted, "Sumner has been here several times. He is not yet recovered." In February 1857 the Danas' sixth and last child was born. Sarah was "doing well." Angela Henrietta Channing Dana was the couple's fifth daughter. "It is not a son," wrote Dana, "but I am too grateful for [Sarah's] relief & life, to admit to one feeling of disappointment."[11]

There was to be no August sojourn for Dana in the summer of 1857. Neither a wife with six children nor a law partner who covered Dana's cases the summer before were likely to be enthusiastic about another of Dana's August rambles. Dana did spend time with Sarah, the children, his father, and members of the extended family at the Manchester summer house he bought for his father. Though Dana loved the spot, time with the family did not rejuvenate him the way his usual August adventures did.

A July Fourth visit to New York City had to suffice, but Dana made the most of it. A trip to the Bowery placed him on the edge of a gang war between the "Bowery Boys" and the "Dead Rabbits." Dana watched from a turned-over handcart. "My companions on the handcart were a decent Irishman . . . & a girl about 12 years of age." It was more than a skirmish—eight were killed, including one shot through the head not far from Dana. "As it was getting towards twilight & the neighborhood was dangerous . . . I left the scene." The next morning the papers were filled with news of the fight. "There were such fears of a second outbreak, that I went down to the bad district after church & spent nearly two hours in . . . & about Five Points." Three days later, Dana was in Northampton with Sarah, "a beautiful town . . . with taste & style of refined life."[12]

Whatever else may be said of Dana's pattern of driving himself to the point of exhaustion eleven months of the year, and then renewing himself by escaping to adventure, it always seemed to prepare him to shoulder the duties of the next year. The 1856 summer trip to England and the shorter stay in Manchester in August 1857 were not the rugged physical excursions of previous Augusts. By 1858 Dana found his duties "so constant" that "instead of a journey this summer I spent three weeks at my father's at the seashore." A more significant indication of the press of work was Dana's neglect of his journal. He made only one entry for 1858, listing "chief causes of interest," which included the Dalton divorce case and the defense of "Reverend" I. S. Kalloch.[13]

The prosecution of "Reverend" Kalloch was an even more notorious case than the Dalton divorce. Dana's client, a preacher of uncertain denomination, was charged with having illicit relations with one of his married parishioners. Among the obstacles Dana confronted was evidence that Kalloch and his paramour had sex in a bar. Needless to add, it was a case in which the public took a profound interest.

Once again Dana astonished fellow lawyers, the public—and undoubtedly his client—when the jury announced it could not reach a verdict. Boston newspapers put out extra editions including a "Full Report of R. H. Dana's Argument for the Defense of Rev. I. S. Kalloch." When the prosecutor decided to dismiss the adultery charge rather than retry the case, an exuberant Kalloch gleefully admitted his guilt. Dana said his client "kicked up his heels" and went west. Kalloch eventually became mayor of San Francisco. Proper Boston was shocked. Dana pretended to be.[14]

There was no break from the demands of his law practice, but there was a monthly event that Dana eagerly anticipated. "I believe I have no where mentioned the [Saturday] Club," Dana noted in August 1857. The informal club—"an important and much valued thing"—was a gathering of fourteen for midday dinner at Boston's Parker House on the last Saturday of each month. The club "had an accidental origin" because it grew out of Ralph Waldo Emerson's habit of dining with a few friends when he came into Boston from Concord on the last Saturday of each month.[15]

Emerson solicited Dana's interest in "a sane & amiable club." Its only object was to dine together once a month, though in Dana's view "it is to be composed of persons of distinction." The club's first members included Longfellow, Louis Agassiz, James Russell Lowell, and Oliver Wendell Holmes Sr. Later additions included historians Prescott and Parkman, poet Whittier, and novelist Hawthorne. Sumner and Charles Francis Adams Sr. eventually became members as well.[16]

Although the club had no rules and kept no records, a unanimous vote was required to admit a new member. When the club started, Dana thought fourteen members were "as many as we think it best to have." The group grew to include more than twice that number. James Russell Lowell claimed that Dana's attachment to the tradition of fourteen members was so determined that it was necessary to wait until Dana was absent to propose new members. Lowell seldom missed an opportunity to portray himself more generously than his peers, despite "his school-masterish pleasure in snubbing others," but Dana did object to voting on new candidates without all members present. Irrespective of the tradition of fourteen, he certainly welcomed the inclusion of Sumner and Parkman.[17]

It is easy to lament, as others have, the absence of a Boswell to capture the conversations of the only club of Americans that could be said to approach the eminence of the celebrated London club of Johnson, Burke, Reynolds, et al. By custom, Longfellow sat at one end of the long dinner table, Agassiz at the other. Emerson was usually seated to Longfellow's left, and Dana was often seated across from Emerson. Dana was delighted with his dinner companion, whom he found to be more a man of the world than he expected of a transcendentalist: "Emerson is an excellent dinner-table man, always a gentleman, never bores, or preaches, or dictates, but drops and takes up topics very agreeably, and has even skill and tact in managing his conversation."[18]

Emerson was pleased as well. Although Dana did not take a lead in conversation unless politics or history was the topic, "he told a story, very well, when he chose." One of the members of the club recalled: "The club would settle itself to listen when Dana had a story to tell. Not a word was missed, and those who were absent were told at the next club what they had lost. Emerson smoked his cigar and was supremely happy, and laughed under protest when the point of the story was reached."[19]

As enjoyable as the Saturday Club dinners were for Dana, they were small relief from the pressures of practice. Few of his lengthy cases involved large sums, and Adams believed Dana "scarcely made a living" from the law. Though Adams found Dana's "habits . . . [and] household simple," family demands made it appear otherwise to Dana.[20] Brother Ned returned from eight years abroad, most of them at Dana's expense. At home Ned was an even greater burden. Sarah's treatments for her nervous condition were expensive, as were the costs of private schooling for the Dana daughters. Dana's father was perfectly comfortable in his permanent state of pecuniary embarrassment.

When in 1858 Dana was offered the Republican nomination for a seat in Congress, his "want of property" must have distressed him as greatly as it did in 1854 when he agonized over the invitation to lead the Free Soil meeting at Faneuil Hall. This time Dana was too pressed to record either the offer or his refusal. The financially secure Charles

Francis Adams Sr., father of Dana's associate, accepted the nomination and was elected to Congress. Young Adams continued to witness Dana "working under a pressure and with a disregard of the laws of health which could lead to but one result."[21]

In February 1859 Dana, "being a little fatigued," welcomed "the notion . . . suddenly suggested to me that I can go to Cuba." It was "as great a change of scene as is possible to get in so short a time & is too tempting to be relinquished." The suddenness of Dana's decision was evident in his remark that none outside of his family and law partner knew of his plan "for it is not well, on professional grounds to [be] off on a tour."[22]

There was intense American interest in Cuba's future (as there always seems to be). Dana kept a journal of his political, social, and scenic observations. When he returned in early March, he transformed his journal into a manuscript, *To Cuba and Back: A Vacation Voyage.* Published by Ticknor and Fields in May 1859 (he did not approach Harper Brothers), Dana dedicated it "to the gentlemen of the Saturday Club." The book sold surprisingly well, going through more than a dozen editions.

Political and social changes have long since outdated much of the book, but Dana's descriptions still entice. Of his approach to the Morro Lighthouse, where his ship arrived too late at night to enter the port, Dana wrote: "We rise and fall on the moonlit sea: the stars are near to us, or we are raised to them; the Southern Cross is just above the horizon; and all night long, two streams of light lie upon the water, one of gold from the Morro, and one of silver from the moon. It is enchantment. Who can regret our delay, or wish to exchange this scene for the common, close anchorage of a harbor?"[23]

The trip to Cuba was interesting but hardly restorative. Dana worked feverishly to get his manuscript ready for publication because he needed the royalties to defray his lost income and the cost of the voyage. On his return, a full docket of cases awaited. The duties of advocate, Dana noted, "do not admit of being partly performed. The advocate can no more half try a case, than a general can half fight a battle, and every large trial is a crisis of hard work at its close, which taxes & tests the power of endurance."[24]

Several weeks after his return from Cuba, Dana was in the midst of yet another trial. During a break he wolfed down "a quantity of cold corned beef & returned to Court." "No man," wrote Adams, "can through many years stand a life like this. He is, though he rarely knows it, living on his capital." Dana had exhausted his. He collapsed during a court recess.[25]

Dana was advised by his doctor that only "long rest and recreation" could restore his health. Several plans were proposed. Of those suggested, Dana concluded "none suits me so well as a voyage around the world."[26] Twenty-five years after his first voyage, Dana was again leaving the slavish shore.

19

AROUND THE WORLD

A voyage around the world "has been the dream of my
youth and maturer years," Dana wrote on July 20, 1859—the last entry
in a journal he had kept for eighteen years. The dispatch with which
Dana was able to arrange a trip that left behind his wife, six children,
and a law practice for over a year, suggests that the dream was a greater
spur than the diagnosis. But Dana was right when he observed, "I have
over-worked for the last two years. . . . My system is out of order."[1]

Rufus Choate had also left on a voyage. Choate's reputation for hard
work exceeded even Dana's. Five years earlier Choate was touched by Dana's empathy when Choate was exhausted by work. Dana told the older
lawyer, "You have worked harder than any man," to which Choate replied,
"I do it to drown sorrow." Choate's daughter suffered from mental illness.

On the day Dana was to depart, "the last thing I did of a public nature was to speak at the Bar Meeting on the death of Choate."[2]

Choate's sudden death abroad made Dana's eulogy nearly extemporaneous. "That, he of all men, should have died under a foreign flag!" Dana exclaimed. But Choate—who valued literary talent as much as legal talent—would have been pleased with the words of one who possessed both. "I can truly say . . . taking for a moment a simile from that element which he loved as much as I love it," said Dana, "that in his presence I felt like the master of a small coasting vessel that hugs the shore, that has run up under the lee to speak a great Spanish galleon freighted with silks and precious stones, spices and costly fabrics, with sky-sails and studding-sails spread to the breeze . . . her decks peopled with men in strange costumes, speaking of strange climes and distant lands."[3]

Dana's striking simile was appropriate to Choate, whom he found almost exotic in mind and manner, but Dana was already thinking of strange climes and distant lands. As soon as he finished his remarks, Dana was off to New York to board the steamer *Star of the West*. A quarter-century earlier, Dana's first voyage to California had taken five months. The railway across the Isthmus of Panama made passage around Cape Horn unnecessary, shortening the journey to two weeks. On August 1, 1859, Dana wrote home: "In the morning I was sailing on the Atlantic, and in the evening I was sailing on the Pacific. So on my birthday I crossed a continent!"[4] He boarded the steamer *Golden Gate* and on the evening of August 13, forty-four-year-old Dana entered San Francisco Bay, which last he saw as a twenty-year-old sailor aboard the *Alert*.

In the winter of 1835–1836 the search for hides "on the remote and almost unknown coast of California" had brought Dana's ship "into the vast solitude of the Bay of San Francisco." Beyond a gravel beach lay "dreary sand-hills . . . and beyond them higher hills steep and barren, their sides gullied by rain." The Spanish Mission Dolores "as ruinous as the Presidio [was] almost deserted with but a few Indians attached to it." There "were no other human habitations . . . except above the landing a shanty of rough boards" where an "enterprising Yankee" traded with the hide ship and the Indians.[5]

Now, as the *Golden Gate*, "gay with crowds of passengers . . . and brilliant with lighted saloons and state-rooms," entered San Francisco Bay, "stretching from the water's edge to the base of the great hills, and from the old Presidio to the Mission, flickering all over with lamps of its streets and houses lay a city of one hundred thousand inhabitants." Though it was midnight, "the city was alive from the salute of our guns, spreading the news that the fortnightly steamer had come." Dana made his way through densely crowded streets "as alive as by day, where boys in high-keyed voices were already crying the latest New York Papers." By 2:00 A.M., Dana was "comfortably abed in a commodious room in the Oriental Hotel which stood . . . on the filled up cove . . . where we used to beach our boats from the *Alert*."[6]

When Dana awoke to the city by the bay, "I could scarcely keep my hold on reality at all." Before him lay "the sole emporium of a new world" with "its store-houses, towers, and steeples; its court-houses, theaters, and hospitals, . . . its fortresses and light-houses; its wharves and harbor with their thousand-ton clipper ships, more in number than London or Liverpool sheltered that day."[7] Dana would take a clipper ship to China, but it was a month before it sailed—time for Dana to see the new California.

"State pride of Californians very strong," he noted, though the state had been admitted to the Union only nine years before—and nearly everyone was from somewhere else. It seemed to Dana that almost all had read *Two Years Before the Mast*. "The customs of California are free and any person who knows my book speaks to me." Those few who were on the coast in 1835–1836, professed to remember Dana; he thought this unlikely but conceded that "the novelty of a collegian coming out before the mast" attracted more attention than he was aware of at the time.[8]

Part of San Francisco was built "over the water on piles, streets, shops and all, the sea flowing under them." Much of the rest was built on sand, wooden planking covering the streets. The climate was "cold all summer. People wear woolen clothes . . . thin clothes—never." The city was "a great fruit and flower market." Dana noted approvingly that the city kept "European hours."[9]

He delighted in the change in individuals as well. A church deacon Dana knew in Boston was now a deacon in San Francisco: "What a change! Gone was . . . the solemn non-natural voice, the watchful gait, stepping as if he felt responsible for the balance of the moral universe!" Instead Dana saw a man who "walked with a stride, an . . . open countenance . . . his voice strong and natural—in short, he had put off the New England deacon and become a human being."[10] Dana was always intrigued by "human beings," and the characters he met in California were as rich as the country that attracted them.

On a steamer from San Francisco to the new Navy Yard at nearby Mare Island were General Vallejo, who "remembers me as a boy in the *Alert*'s boat in 1836," and "old Mr. Yount, the famous pioneer and woodsman, the first white settler in Napa Valley." Both insisted that Dana come to Napa, and Dana was "glad to do it—as Napa Valley is the pride of California." Vallejo's "princely estates" once encompassed nearly all of Napa and Sonoma, but the general's investment in making Vallejo the state capitol was lost after the California legislature abandoned the buildings put up at Vallejo's expense. Napa land became valuable ("$50 to $100 an acre," reported Dana), so "Old Yount's" 12,000-acre ranch was "a principality." Dana reached the ranch at night to a "hearty welcome" at an "old log house . . . huge chimney and large logs and . . . timbers burning on the fire."[11]

Dana was fascinated by Yount's stories of early California days, when Napa Valley was full of "Grisslies." More intriguing to Dana than Yount's account of California's notorious bears was "*Yount's famous dream,* as told by him to me." Yount said that for three successive nights he dreamt of coming upon a mountain pass where "men, women and children were 'snowed up' starving to death." Yount said he had been so disturbed by the dream that he told it to others, describing the mountain pass (where he had never been) and the physical features that appeared in his dream. Fellow trappers said they knew of such a place, and a group was assembled to hike to the pass. There they discovered the "Donner Party" of pioneers trapped in the mountain pass by a treacherous storm, the survivors of whom had eaten their dead.

"All I can say is that Yount believes what he tells of the dream . . . Yount is a man of unimpeachable integrity . . . and does not exaggerate." General Vallejo vouched for the story, as did others. Dana's predisposition to believe Yount was undoubtedly strengthened when he asked the wife of his guide how she came to California. He could get nothing more than "over the mountains," but learned that she was one of only five of eleven in her family who survived the ordeal. Dana, to whom the woman had served a meal, was quick to note, "Her family did not eat their dead."[12]

Dana's journey to Northern California came after he fulfilled his own dream: a return to Southern California, where first he landed in the brig *Pilgrim*. No August ramble could have had more meaning than August 20, 1859, when he took a steamer that made stops between San Francisco and San Diego. Dana noted that the steamer was free of San Francisco Bay in two hours, "which, in the *Alert*, under canvas ... took us full two days." But now "we are [in] an unromantic, sail-less, spar-less, engine-driven hulk!"[13]

Dana could supply the romance. Rounding Point Conception and approaching Santa Barbara he wrote: "There is the old white Mission with its belfries ... the same repose in the golden sunlight and glorious climate ... there roars and tumbles upon the beach the same grand surf of the great Pacific as on the beautiful day when the *Pilgrim*, after five months' voyage dropped her weary anchors here." Dana paid his compliments to another of Santa Barbara's attractions—the beauty of its women. He visited Doña Augustia, whom he had described so vividly in *Two Years Before the Mast*. "Her daughter told me that all the travelers who come to Santa Barbara called to see her mother." Dana still found Doña Augustia "enchanting." She was another example, noticed Dana, "of the preserving quality of the California climate."[14]

At "Pueblo de los Angeles" Dana found "a large and flourishing town of about twenty thousand inhabitants." One of Dana's former shipmates on the *Pilgrim*, Henry Mellus, had settled there. Mellus drove Dana around Los Angeles. There was much interest in "the distinguished advocate and author ... who contributed in no small degree to render the vicinity of Los Angeles famous." An observer reported: "Dana bore all his honors modestly, apparently quite oblivious of the curiosity displayed toward him and quite as unconscious that he was making one of the memorable visits in the early annals of the town."[15]

Dana continued his cruise down the coast. In the clear moonlight he caught a glimpse of San Juan Capistrano and its cliff where twenty-four years before he had hung by a rope to retrieve a few hides—"a boy who could not be prudential, and who caught at every chance for adventure." When Dana approached "the little harbor of San Diego ... the quiet little beach," he looked in vain for remnants of the hide houses. It was early morning and Dana "wished to be alone, so I ... was quietly pulled ashore in a boat and left to myself." In his mind's eye, Dana saw the past: "the *Alert* . . . the poor dear old *Pilgrim,* the home of hardship and hopelessness, the boats passing to and fro; the cries of the sailors at the capstan or falls; the peopled beach; the large hide-houses, with their gangs of men; and the Kanakas interspersed everywhere."[16]

All were gone. "I alone was left of all, and how strangely was I here!" Dana's emotions "were sad and only sad." He pondered why: "Why should I care for them,—poor Kanakas and sailors, the refuse of civilization, the outlaws and beach-combers of the Pacific!" He wondered at their fates— "doubtless nearly all were dead . . . in fever-climes, in dens of vice, or falling from the mast or dropping exhausted from the wreck." But one reason for Dana's melancholia was not the thought that most were dead. It was an emotion the forty-four-year-old lawyer felt more keenly: "If . . . the deadlier enemies that beset a sailor's life on shore have spared them . . . the light-hearted boys are now hardened middle-aged men."[17]

Dana took one last opportunity to replicate the lightness of youth. He rode horseback from the mission to the town at "full run, as Ben S[timson] and I did in 1835." Then it was by hulking steamer back to San Francisco, where the "noble clipper ship" *Mastiff* awaited—bound for Hong Kong and, Dana, hoped, the adventure of travel. The ship departed San Francisco on September 10, 1859. Dana was delighted by the 1,200-ton *Mastiff,* one of the latest (and last) examples of the glorious clippers "built in Donald McKay's best manner." The twenty-man crew worked the "newest fashions of rigging." Dana greatly preferred a sailing vessel to a steamer: "no noise, no smell of oil, no tremor, as still as the country after city."[18]

He liked, too, the *Mastiff*'s captain, William Johnson, "a seaman by birth, well-educated." Captain Johnson held a quarter-ownership interest in the ship, which served as his home. His wife was aboard, and in addition to the ship's expensive library, the Johnsons kept a menagerie—many cats and dogs (including a 125-pound English mastiff, which followed the captain everywhere) and four kangaroos. In addition to the six "cabin passengers," there were 175 Chinese "steerage passengers" below decks. Dana noted that the "Chinese burn lamps and smoke [though] Captain Johnson forbids it."[19]

Four days out of San Francisco "on a quiet afternoon . . . at about 5 P.M." Dana heard the cry "Fire in the ship!" Smoke began to pour up the hatches. All hands were called to rig a hose for the pump. "Officers . . . report that between decks all on fire . . . and fire in the lower hold." There was no hope of saving the ship. Captain Johnson issued the order to lower lifeboats. There were not enough boats and there was gunpowder on board. The captain went below to retrieve the powder magazine and threw it overboard. Johnson was armed with a revolver and used it to threaten the Chinese passengers who were rushing for the lifeboats. It was a desperate situation, one in which Dana "on deliberate reflection believe it very doubtful if [we] could have saved one life."[20]

But "a British ship has been in sight the last two days sailing with us. She is several miles astern. Set our ensign union down, and half mast." Dana immediately volunteered to take charge of one of the lifeboats. For the next ninety minutes, as smoke poured out of the *Mastiff,* Dana captained one of five boats taking passengers off the burning ship and transferring them to the *Achilles,* the English ship two miles distant. "Captain Johnson asks me to see his wife safely in boat." Dana admired Mrs. Johnson's calmness as she was lowered by rope.

Dana came alongside the *Mastiff* for the last time at 6:30 P.M. "All the Chinese had been taken off. . . . Now attempt to save the animals." The English mastiff and two kangaroos were saved. "Captain Johnson asks me to come aboard . . . to see if anything else can be done. I do so. Very much fatigued by exertions in my boat, especially the steering oar, and head and lungs full of smoke." Johnson and Dana decided nothing more could be done, though the captain and chief mate would not leave the ship until the last.

Dana recorded the scene: "Flames burst out through deck at mainmast. Now nearly dark, and flames glow over the ocean. Mrs. Johnson anxious lest her husband stay too long. Two figures on the quarter deck. Now disappear and last two boats come. Captain Johnson comes on board, and the poor, noble *Mastiff* is abandoned. Flames mount the rigging; catch the sails and all a mass of fire. Foremast stands long, then drops, and only a burning hull. . . . The magnitude of the loss comes over [Captain Johnson] 'My ship Mastiff! My ship Mastiff! Is it possible she is gone!' "[21]

The *Achilles* landed its rescued passengers in Honolulu on September 27. Dana was now without passage to China. Ships bound for Hong Kong did not always stop in the islands. Dana spent the next six weeks in Hawaii in hopes he could secure a berth on a China-bound clipper. He immediately put himself to good use by defending Captain Johnson in a claim for salvage made by the captain of the *Achilles.* The

Mastiff carried nearly $80,000 in gold that was saved. The British captain sought the entire amount, plus expenses of the rescue. Appearing for Johnson in the local admiralty court, Dana succeeded in reducing the award to 10 percent of the demand.

It was Hawaii, not the courtroom, that Dana wished to see. With characteristic curiosity, Dana secured a private audience with King Kamehameha IV, the twenty-five-year-old leader of Hawaii's constitutional democracy. Dana was impressed: "A king is a king." The king's "easy manners . . . intellect and character" inspired Dana, not least because in Hawaii "seamen are better regulated and protected against landsharks than in any port in the States."[22]

Dana hired an outrigger canoe ("3 Kanaka men, one woman, and myself") to sail to a lava flow. "Exquisite moonlight night, steady land breeze, bright stars, still water floating along the coral reef, just clear of the surf." He made extensive notes on Hawaiian vocabulary and, as always, took note of the women, "riding astride, with long folds of yellow and striped cloth and a garland on the head and necklace of flower or berries." The native women "do not wear bonnets . . . in church and look better for it." Dana spent "a whole day in the hut with women . . . and managed to have considerable conversation with them." He was less successful when "by moonlight, [at] Waikiki, the sea bathing place," he tried to persuade a native "chiefess" to "throw off her clothes and jump in and swim off to the reefs." She pretended she could not swim. "Her mother . . . would have done it," Dana ruefully observed.[23] But Dana was younger then.

Adventure followed Dana even when unlooked for. Leading a more proper outing of "8 ladies, 9 gentlemen," all on horseback, over a new chain bridge, the structure suddenly gave way. Suspended ten feet above a rushing river, "the party [was] in great peril, thrown into the river, or in the wreck of the bridge, among kicking and struggling horses in deep water." Two of the younger men in the party and natives succeeded in saving those in the water. Dana's horse was carried away by the current, but Dana managed to get to the river bank with nothing worse than a broken toe. "No one lost and no one hurt (beyond bruises) but me. Wonderful escape."[24]

Dana was less lucky in his search for a berth to China. By mid-November it was clear that he would have to return to San Francisco and rebook passage. Dana's voyage back to San Francisco in the *Archi-*

tect, an old whaling ship, was decidedly unadventurous. There were only whalers aboard. "One man kept on, in a dull monotone, long stories, to me alone, the effect of which on my mind may be represented thus. '—whale—the whale—whales—the whale—the whale—.' "[25]

Dana arrived back in San Francisco on December 11, 1859. It would be another month before he secured new booking to China, so he again used his time to learn how the state of California was inventing itself. "Law and order" was more than a trite phrase. A traveler who left the city carried the "usual California rig"—a "belt with a revolver in holster & a knife in a sheath." California Supreme Court Justice Stephen Field told Dana that "from 1849-1856 [no judge] went into Court without a pair of Derringers in his pocket & a Bowie knife under his coat."[26]

The "San Francisco Committee on Vigilance," formed to summarily try, punish, and banish suspected criminals, was more effective than the rudimentary judicial system. (Dana did not know it, but Louis Varrell, who nearly killed Dana after the Anthony Burns trial, had been "exiled" from San Francisco by vigilantes in 1851.) The reluctance of San Franciscans to leave matters solely to judges was understandable. Three weeks after Dana arrived in San Francisco, the chief justice of the California Supreme Court shot and killed a former U.S. senator in a duel.[27]

Dana traveled to Sacramento, California's new capital, to see the legislature in action. He was astonished that the 120-member legislature had only three men of Spanish descent "in a country which was Mexican 13 years ago!" Dana added, "My friend Dela Guerra is . . . able & intelligent & has the most . . . patrician look of any man here." It was a new world. A man named Ryan approached Dana saying that they had met before. Dana did not remember until he was told, "I repaired your father's house in 1846." Dana recorded: "I began to inquire patronizingly after his success here, when he told me he was here as senator from Humboldt County! I had to come down several pegs."[28]

Dana observed "the universal habit of 'drinks' here, tells especially on the politicians." At a legislative caucus, a member drew a knife "& instantly as many as 20 pistols were cocked." The question of whether the legislator *"did right* in drawing his knife . . . is gravely discussed." Dana was relieved to retreat to a dinner where he met a woman who "knows how to blush—a lost art in California."[29]

On January 11, 1860, Dana was finally able to re-embark on his voyage to China. The 500-ton *Early Bird* was not a clipper ship but Dana thought it "a good sailer." The vessel sailed at midnight, but Dana did not go on deck as "this was my 8th time of passing the Golden Gate." He was quick to note that the ship carried 230 Chinese passengers in steerage, "fifty more than we had in the *Mastiff,* a ship double the size of this one." There were only three lifeboats. "In fact, in case of disaster we have *no resource* . . . This is very wrong. Still, we are in good spirits & hope for the best."[30]

Despite his knowledge that the *Early Bird* could not survive a mis-adventure like the *Mastiff*'s, Dana had "a sense of happiness—that makes me ready to sing!" Though "away from all I love . . . the air is pure & I am free from care,—eating, worrying care." The stomach pain that precipi-tated his collapse was gone: "Digestion makes good spirits." Two weeks out to sea, Dana climbed the mast "as well as when I was a sailor boy. . . . Regard it as proof of improved health."[31]

Dana's journey around the world took, by his calculation, "433 days, of which [I] spent about 233 days on water and 200 on land." He was on every continent "unless Australia be one which I will not admit."[32] A truly indefatigable traveler of insatiable curiosity, Dana seemed to visit every scene of natural beauty, historical significance, and local interest. He wrote letters home—sometimes thousands of words in length—describing people and palaces, schoolchildren and shipmasters, manners and meals.

Upon being given a highly ornamented Chinese envelope, Dana wrote: "What did not this wonderful people have before us? Gunpowder, printing, mariner's compass—& now *envelopes*!" The "industry & the pop-ulousness of China . . . has not been overrated," said Dana after seeing "large cities of 20, 50, and 100,000 inhabitants." He was even more im-pressed by the "self-possessed, gentle, dignified" bearing of those he met. "I never saw, in any country, or society better manners." It was "the ur-banity of 30 centuries." That contrasted sharply with Dana's opinion of American missionaries in China, whom he described as "second rate young men."[33]

A chance encounter on the streets of Hong Kong with a former pas-senger on the ill-fated *Mastiff* delighted him. A Chinese man approached Dana; "Ah! How you do? My glad to see you!" Dana shook hands with him but did not recognize him. "My in ship, burn-up. You savee." Dana noted "the good fellow seemed truly glad to see me."[34]

Dana described his visit to the "famous Flower Boats," floating brothels. No account written home was likely to be fully revealing, though Dana did describe "four young girls, with hair most extravagantly extended behind & dressed with flowers with faces conspicuously rouged." To "prevent all misconstruction as to purposes," Dana was accompanied by two gentlemen. Whether they were sufficient to their task may be doubted, as one "told our host . . . that I had never smoked an opium pipe, & was desirous to do so." In Dana's account the pipe had little effect—"I was not willing to risk it"—and "our whole stay was only about 15 minutes."[35]

Dana wrote of an exchange with a Buddhist priest that said much about East and West. Noting the "fat, jolly" image of Buddha, Dana asked the reason for the "laughing eyes." The priest declared that unlike Dana's God who "concerns himself with everything—Buddha does not." The priest added, "But, you see he is happy to see you." Dana replied: "Yes & equally so to see us go away." "Yes, yes, he cares for nothing," responded the Buddhist.[36]

Dana's "digestion" remained untroubled. A meal of rice, tea, and vegetables prompted him to contrast diets. "The Americans & English are not cooks . . . Think . . . of the great hunks & slices of heavy meat we all eat at home! Think of the head of the family, up to his elbows in blood, distributing half raw meat among his children . . . a few waxy potatoes, clammy bread & hard thick pie crust!"[37]

By April Dana was in Japan. His first view was of Nagasaki, "famous in the history of the long attempted contact of East with West. . . . How beautifully the town lies, at the foot of many topped gently sloping hills!" The Japanese children impressed Dana. "I am told the parental rule is gentle. I think in two days I have not seen or heard a crying child." At a school, eight-year-old boys looked "very lively & happy . . . in contrast with the stupor of . . . school, when I was of that age." Dana was shown drawings done by a Japanese artist. "They are as good as Audubon, possibly better."[38]

Dana's good fortune as a traveler was made vivid when he visited the island of Penang, off the west coast of the Malay Peninsula. "In that fairy-like scene of sea and sky and shore" Dana found the grave of George Edward Channing, a boyhood friend. They were at Harvard together, and Channing had come down to the dock to greet Dana when the *Alert* returned from California in 1836. Channing, too, had gone to sea, "not having consulted me as to the captain." The master was none other than the despised Frank Thompson. Both the master and Dana's friend died of a deadly fever. According to Dana, Channing caught the fever when he cared for the sickened Thompson. "I tried not to think that [Channing's] life had been sacrificed to the faults of another . . . who at least had suffered in death."[39]

In July Dana reached India. During the voyage a violent storm pitched Dana against a stanchion, breaking a rib. Laid up in Bombay, Dana read American newspapers and learned to his dismay that William Seward would not be the Republican presidential candidate in 1860. "My heart sinks at the nomination of 'Abe' Lincoln & Hannibal Hamlin." Dana recovered sufficiently to record the charms of Indian women: "What strikes me most is the free, graceful, queenly carriage of the women—even the poor women who carry water on their heads . . . no duchess that I ever saw walked so well."[40]

By August 25 Dana's direction and thoughts were turning toward home. In Venice ("where all my resolutions broke down") he noted that the date was his "wedding day." Dana stayed an extra two days in Venice and decided that people could be divided into two classes: "those who have seen Venice . . . & . . . those who have not seen it." One month later Dana neared the East Coast—"the Atlantic is heavy & dull after the Pacific & the Oriental seas." On September 27, 1860, "this day opens in America—home. . . . New York completes the circumnavigation of the globe!"[41]

Dana's breakdown was over. His country's was about to begin.

20

THE SUPREME COURT ARGUMENT
THAT SAVED THE UNION

"We had Richard Dana (the younger) just returned from a voyage round the world," wrote Longfellow of a Saturday Club dinner in September 1860. Dana had been gone for over a year. His Republican Party was on the verge of electing its first president. Dana was too late to campaign for Lincoln, but a speech on behalf of Republican candidates in Cambridge prompted a letter from former Harvard president Josiah Quincy, now eighty-nine and delighted with the student he once suspended: "I cannot refrain from expressing my gratification of finding you again in the political field, with armor bright, headpiece strong, sword sharp."[1]

The election of Abraham Lincoln provided the new Republican Party with its first opportunity to fill federal positions. Senator Sumner and

Congressman Adams pressed for Massachusetts Republicans. Sumner recommended Dana for U.S. attorney for Massachusetts, writing to him that "in conversing with the President on our Massachusetts cases I said as to Mr. Dana, he has already been nominated by general public opinion, and all that remains now is to register it."[2] Dana's nomination was sent to the Senate on April 12, 1861—the day Fort Sumter was fired upon.

Although the position of U.S. attorney was to some "an office which no leading barrister can afford to hold," Dana accepted the appointment and its $6,000 salary.[3] He was to hold it for the duration of the Civil War. Unlike his predecessors (Lunt, for one), Dana aggressively prosecuted abusive ship captains and slave traders. In a single year he convicted over thirty masters and officers for brutality to merchant sailors. Though prosecutions of abusive ship masters were far more frequent under Dana, his caseload was transformed by the need to condemn the "prizes of war."

President Lincoln's proclamation of April 1861 ordering the blockade of Southern ports was virtually simultaneous with Dana's first day as U.S. attorney. Vessels captured for running blockades were soon being brought to federal courts to be sold pursuant to "prize law." Proceedings varied in efficiency and honesty according to the competence and character of prosecutors and judges. Dana immediately implemented a prize law process in Boston that was more "honest, rapid, and inexpensive" than any other in the country.[4]

Maritime tradition and law gave ships' crews a share in the "prize money" from the sale of the seized ship and its cargo. U.S. District Court judge Peleg Sprague knew Dana well, and the combination of effective prosecutor and efficient judge prompted ship captains to often bring captured vessels to Boston, even though prize courts in New York and Philadelphia were nearer their blockade stations. But the challenge Dana met in implementing effective disposal of seized blockade runners was the least of the difficulties presented by the arcane jurisprudence of prize law.

In July 1861 the brig *Amy Warwick* was bringing a cargo of coffee from Rio de Janeiro to Richmond. The ship's captain later testified to an event that must have shaken the ship's small crew—and his wife and daughter, who were also aboard: "Saw a man-of-war . . . some two or three hours before she weighed anchor and bore down on us; did not alter course but hoisted American flag when she hoisted hers. . . . The ship brought us to by firing a gun, on which I hove to and waited for orders, and was much surprised to hear that there was a blockade on the port, and Virginia had seceded."[5]

The captured vessel was brought to Boston, where Dana initiated prize court proceedings before Judge Sprague. The *Amy Warwick*'s owners sought to prevent the government from selling the ship and its cargo (valued at $160,000), arguing that they did not know of the blockade, the vessel carried no contraband, and they, although residents of Virginia, were loyal to the Union. But of greatest significance was the legal question the case posed: "It is contended," said Judge Sprague, "that although this property might be liable to confiscation if the contest were a foreign war, yet that it is otherwise in a rebellion or civil war. This requires attention."[6]

Abraham Lincoln did not have to be told. The *Amy Warwick* and each vessel captured by the U.S. government in the early days of the insurrection were seized pursuant to Lincoln's blockade proclamation. The rights to interdict, seize, and dispose of vessels and cargo belonging to those residing in "enemy's territory" upon the implementation of a lawful blockade was a recognized principle of international law. But the right was predicated on a war between sovereign nations. President Lincoln's first blockade proclamation characterized the Southern secessionists as a "combination of persons" engaged in "an insurrection against the government of the United States."[7] The difficulty posed by this description was that a government engaged in the suppression of an insurrection could "close" its domestic ports but could not, according to accepted tenets of international law, "blockade" them. Why, then, did Lincoln not close Southern ports—a decision clearly within his executive authority and consistent with international law?

The question divided Lincoln's "team of rivals." Secretary of the Navy Gideon Welles, supported by Attorney General Edward Bates, argued strenuously against the blockade because its legal validity presupposed a conflict between two distinct nations. The issue of whether to close or blockade was revisited in the summer of 1861 when Congress, on July 13, specifically authorized the president to declare ports closed where the authority of federal customs collections was challenged. Lincoln requested his navy secretary to advise him whether the blockade should be continued. Welles responded in a lengthy memorandum asserting that a port closure would be "legally . . . impregnable" but a blockade was unlikely to be sustained by a federal court. Welles warned the president that the Union would face huge damage claims for selling vessels and cargoes as prizes if the blockade was declared illegal.[8]

Abraham Lincoln was a good enough lawyer to recognize the validity of the legal arguments espoused by his secretary of navy and attorney general, but he was president of the United States during a war. Secretary of State William Seward conveyed the view of the cabinet member who mattered most: the British foreign secretary, Lord Russell. Her majesty's government made clear it would not accept American "closure" of Southern ports that would expose British shippers to arrest as common smugglers. A "blockade," on the other hand, would enable England to exercise the rights of a neutral nation. The British message was coupled with the implicit threat that port closure could lead to direct recognition of the Confederacy and the intervention of the British fleet to preserve the shipping rights of British subjects. Secretary Welles acknowledged Lincoln's convincing rationale for choosing a legally problematic blockade over a legally sound closure: "The President said we could not afford to have two wars on our hands at once."[9]

In Boston, Judge Sprague—relying on a theory of prize law exhaustively briefed and vigorously argued by Dana—upheld the legality of the seizure and sale of the *Amy Warwick*. Justice Nathan Clifford sitting as circuit judge assented to Sprague's decision, but foreshadowed trouble ahead by declaring that if the issue came before the Supreme Court, "my mind is open on this great question."[10] Justice Clifford (a Maine native but Southern sympathizer) was not the only member of the Supreme Court believed to have "an open mind" on the question of whether Lincoln had acted legally in blockading Southern ports.

There had been one vacancy on the nine-member Supreme Court when Lincoln was elected president. In March 1861, shortly after Lincoln took office, Justice John McLean died. One month later Justice John Campbell followed his home state of Alabama out of the Union by tendering his resignation to the president. The six remaining members of the court included four justices (Wayne, Grier, Catron, and Nelson) who had joined Chief Justice Roger Taney in the *Dred Scott* decision of 1857. Justice Clifford had not been on the court at the time of the *Dred Scott* case, but as a Buchanan appointee he had made clear his agreement with the decision. Abraham Lincoln had already expressed his view that the judiciary did not comprehend the reality confronted by a president in a civil war. The judiciary, he stated, "seemed as if it had been designed not to sustain the government but to embarrass and betray it."[11]

By February 1863 the epic struggle between North and South had been raging for nearly two years. There were over a million soldiers under arms. At Antietam there had been more than 20,000 casualties in the bloodiest single day of battle in American history. But the U.S. Supreme Court in the *Prize Cases* was preparing to hear argument on an astounding question: Was it, in point of law, a war?[12]

Lawyers for owners of other ships seized under the purported authority of Lincoln's proclamation appealed from adverse prize court rulings in New York and Key West. In early 1862 attorneys for captured vessels, including the *Amy Warwick,* pressed Attorney General Bates to advance the cases on the Supreme Court calendar. Bates wavered despite the certainty that a hearing before the court as then composed would have led to an opinion adverse to the government. Asserting that he was being "urged in several quarters to ask for a special term," Bates asked William Evarts for advice.[13] Evarts, who had represented the United States in the prize court in New York, advised the attorney general that the government had little to gain by accelerating the case, especially when President Lincoln had yet to fill a vacancy on the court.

Confirmation of three Lincoln appointees to the court (Justices Swayne, Miller, and Davis) did not resolve the attorney general's greatest problem. Bates was no closer to a compelling legal theory with which to defend the blockade decision than he had been nearly two years earlier when he joined Secretary of Navy Welles in expressing doubts about its legality. The government's dilemma was well put by Chief Justice Taney's biographer: "The Supreme Court was in position to greatly embarrass the government in either of two ways. It might hold that the conflict was not a war . . . and that the prizes had been illegally taken. . . . Such a decision would make the government liable for huge sums in damages, and its psychological effect would be such as seriously to cripple the conduct of the war. On the other hand the court might hold that the Confederacy was an independent sovereign power and although holding the blockade to be legal, it might do it in such a way as to encourage the recognition of the Confederacy by foreign governments."[14]

The Supreme Court consolidated four prize cases for argument: the Mexican-owned *Brilliante,* seized on June 23, 1861, for attempting to run the blockade of New Orleans, and condemned as a lawful prize by the U.S. District Court in Key West; the British-owned *Hiawatha* and the Virginia-owned *Crenshaw*, each captured in Hampton Roads in May 1861, and condemned as lawful prizes by the U.S. District Court in New York City; and the *Amy Warwick*. Attorneys for claimant ship owners were among the country's most accomplished appellate lawyers—"a display of legal and forensic talent rarely equaled in the history of the Court."[15] They included prominent New York attorney Daniel Lord, who had sponsored Dana's admission to practice before the Supreme Court, and Washington lawyer James M. Carlisle, a brilliant advocate and a friend of Chief Justice Taney.

Edward Bates had been a rival of Abraham Lincoln's for the Republican presidential nomination in 1860, and his appointment as attorney general owed more to his political value than his legal acumen. But he at least had some knowledge of his shortcomings as an oral advocate. With the *Prize Cases* scheduled for argument in February 1863, Attorney General Bates began assembling the legal team to argue the most momentous case heard by the U.S. Supreme Court during the Civil War. His first choice almost cost the government its case. His last choice saved it.

As principal advocate for the government in the *Prize Cases,* the attorney general chose Charles Eames, a prominent Washington lawyer. Eames, a former newspaper editor and U.S. minister to Venezuela, was often used by Secretary Welles to represent the Navy Department. Given the secretary's long-standing reservations about the legality of the blockade, and his high regard for Eames, Welles undoubtedly influenced Bates's choice. Although the secretary's characterization of Eames as "the most correct admiralty lawyer in the country" is evidence of the reasonableness of the attorney general's selection, it is revealing to note a further description from Welles's diary. Eames, wrote the secretary, "did not love the practice of the law, but necessity impelled him. . . . Not endowed with a strong constitution, he broke down upon the pressure of certain great cases entrusted to him."[16] The Supreme Court was soon to make it clear that Charles Eames was a disastrous choice for the *Prize Cases*.

Attorney General Bates apparently intended to have Eames argue three of the four consolidated cases (*Brilliante, Crenshaw,* and *Amy Warwick*), though Eames—unlike opposing counsel—had argued the cases in neither the district nor the circuit courts. In the case of the *Hiawatha*, the attorney general assigned the argument to William M. Evarts and

Charles B. Sedgwick. Bates had already relied on Evarts's sensible advice not to expedite the *Prize Cases*. Sedgwick was a New York congressman and chair of the House Committee on Naval Affairs. Astonishingly, Attorney General Bates did not, in the first instance, consider Dana as counsel for the government, despite the evidence that Dana's work had persuaded one of the nation's most knowledgeable prize case judges of a novel legal theory that could preserve Lincoln's presidential authority.

Dana's had appeared only once before the Supreme Court as of 1862 and that may have been why Bates looked elsewhere. If so, the attorney general had very little familiarity with Dana's reputation for oral advocacy. Judge Sprague said that Dana "made the best arguments that I ever heard from anybody, except perhaps, some of Webster's." Frank Parker passed along the accolade to law partner Dana, noting, "This is, as Dr. Johnson would say, a compliment enhanced by an exception, if indeed, it be an exception, for Judge Sprague evidently doubted whether he could make it."[17]

The court scheduled twelve days of oral argument commencing on February 10, 1863, and ending on February 25. Even in a legal culture where lengthy argument was the norm, the grant of two weeks to oral advocacy emphasized the significance the court attached to the *Prize Cases*. Dana viewed the attorney general's preparation with increasing apprehension. As events were soon to prove, Dana had reason to question whether Charles Eames had the subtlety of argument the cause required. Charles Sedgwick's perfunctory brief was evidence that his selection owed more to the attorney general's view of Sedgwick's congressional significance than his legal standing. Dana had great respect for William Evarts, whom he had known since their days as Harvard Law School students. Though Evarts had successfully represented the government before the U.S. District Court and Second Circuit in the *Hiawatha* and *Crenshaw* cases, Dana correctly judged Evarts's argument to be an incomplete exposition on the law of prize.

Dana "by training at the bar and before the mast, no less than by the natural turn of his thought and habit of mind was better qualified to present the case on the side of the government as, in view of all the circumstances, it ought to be presented than any other lawyer in America."[18] On November 16, 1862, Dana wrote to Attorney General Bates offering to participate in the *Prize Cases* without fee. Dana's offer to assist in the argument before the Supreme Court was not initially welcomed by Bates and precipitated correspondence with an assistant attorney general that must have seemed demeaning to Dana: "I beg you to inform the Attorney General that I did not know, when I wrote him, that he retained counsel in such a manner as to include the *Amy Warwick*. I supposed that Mr. Evarts' retainer included only the cases he had argued . . . and I did not know that Mr. Eames had been retained at all."[19] One week later the assistant replied that Dana could participate if he wished.

Dana prepared for the *Prize Cases* in characteristic fashion. "Dana . . . was always absolutely absorbed in the one thing he was doing and this question of—was there a war? Could there be prize?—took absolute possession of him."[20] His advocacy owed much to the literary gift so apparent in *Two Years Before the Mast*. It was this "same faculty of seeing and describing" that enabled Dana to "[see] things clearly himself, and then [make] others see them as he saw them."[21] His method of preparing for argument was unorthodox. He looked to precedent last. Always a master of the facts, Dana first sought to identify fundamental principles and work out the reasoning that would apply the principles to the issue at hand. Only then would he examine precedent in light of the legal theory he had evolved.[22]

The legal quandary confronted by the government's attorneys was more easily stated than resolved. Could the U.S. government seize the ship and cargo of its citizens without any proof of treasonable acts, on the sole ground that their residence was in a part of the United States controlled by persons in rebellion against the government? Prize was permitted only in war. Congress had never declared war. The necessary predicate for the legality of blockade and the taking of prizes was a state of war between sovereign nations. But if the United States conceded that such a state of war existed between it and the Confederate States of America, foreign powers had a much greater incentive—some would argue an obligation—to recognize the Confederacy as a nation.

There was an added complication that only Dana grasped. Under prize law doctrine, the vessel and cargo seized pursuant to a lawful blockade must be "enemy's property," and the owners of the captured prize must reside in "enemy's territory." Both terms were fraught with potential extrajudicial consequences. The first would appear to condemn the property of U.S. citizens without proof of their disloyalty—or even, as the owners of the *Amy Warwick* insisted, in the face of loyalty to the Union. The second implicitly recognized the status of the Confederacy, for it was difficult to see how the United States could argue that the ship's owners were residents of "enemy's territory" without acknowledging that it was passage of secessionist ordinances that created the territory. As the first day of oral argument approached, there was very little evidence that a majority of the U.S. Supreme Court would see things as clearly as the government claimed to see them.

President Lincoln's three new appointees could be reasonably counted on to be receptive to the Lincoln administration's case. Chief Justice Taney could not. Of the five remaining justices, four of whom had sided with the Chief Justice in *Dred Scott*, only Justice Robert Grier provided a basis for hope. Justice Grier, sitting as a circuit judge, upheld the blockade in an appeal from the U.S. District Court in Philadelphia. Attorney General Bates, however, had little regard for Grier, whom he considered a "natural-born vulgarian." In a later case before the court in which Bates appeared for the government, the attorney general had been appalled when Justice Grier said to Bates from the bench: "If you speak, give that damned Yankee hell."[23]

Two other justices had also affirmed the blockade while sitting as circuit judges. Neither was likely to accept the government's argument. Justice Samuel Nelson affirmed the *Hiawatha* and *Crenshaw* condemnations with "a view to facilitate a hearing before the Supreme Court."[24] Justice Nathan Clifford's "openness" did not bode well for the government. That left as "swing votes" the two Southern justices who had refused to resign their seats during the war: Justice James Wayne of Georgia and Justice John Catron of Tennessee. Attorney General Bates could expect them to approach the *Prize Cases* with as much objectivity as their sympathies would allow, but it was clear that, absent a coherent and compelling legal theory to support the government's case, the cause would be lost.

"Contemplate, my dear Sir, the possibility of a Supreme Court deciding this blockade is illegal," Dana wrote to Charles Francis Adams Sr., the American minister to England. Dana thought "it would end the war."[25] At the very least, an adverse decision would subject the Union to immense damages when it least had the capacity to pay them. Depending on its scope, an opinion concluding the president had acted illegally in declaring a blockade could raise constitutional challenges to decisions already made by Lincoln pursuant to his interpretation of the war power. If there was no constitutional basis for Lincoln's blockade of Southern ports, where was the authority for the decision he had made to suspend habeas corpus nearly two years earlier? Or to emancipate slaves from states in rebellion against the government taken less than two months earlier?

The government's dilemma was not lost on the attorneys for the ship owners. James M. Carlisle opened argument on behalf of the Mexican owners of the captured schooner *Brilliante*. Carlisle argued, as did counsel for the captured vessels *Hiawatha* and *Crenshaw*, that there had been no intent to violate the blockade. But that was a question of fact and, as Carlisle well knew, was subsumed by the largest question of all: "To justify this condemnation, there must have been *war* at the time of this so-called capture; not war as the old essayists describe it, beginning with the war between Cain and Abel; not a fight between two, or between thousands . . . but war as known to international law—war carrying with it the mutual recognition of the opponents as *belligerents;* giving rise to the right of blockade of the *enemy's* ports, and affecting all other nations with the character of neutrals. . . . War, in this, the only sense important to this question, is matter of law, and not merely matter of fact."[26]

Carlisle made effective use of Lincoln and Seward's evasion of the war issue. The seizure of the *Brilliante,* Carlisle asserted, took place "when the President, casting about among doubtful expedients," used the navy under the Act of 1807 to suppress insurrection. Lincoln and Seward, Carlisle emphasized, denied to all the world that a war with its attendant rights and obligations existed between the United States and the Confederacy. Therefore, Carlisle maintained, blockade and prize jurisdiction could not have existed.[27]

The "most extraordinary part of the argument for the United States," claimed Carlisle, is that "the principle of self-defense is asserted; and all power is claimed for the President. This is to assert that the Constitution contemplated and tacitly provided that the President should be dictator. . . . It comes to the plea of necessity. The Constitution knows no such word."[28] The impact of Carlisle's argument is testified to by those to whom it was directed. Immediately after the hearing, Justice Catron wrote a congratulatory note to Carlisle expressing his hope that the argument would be reprinted in the court's reports. Justice Catron added that Justices Nelson and Clifford joined in the request.[29]

Charles Eames opened for the government. The record of his argument has not been preserved but the court's reaction to it is well documented. Justice Noah H. Swayne, whom the government counted as a certain vote for its position, told Attorney General Bates that Eames had made "no argument at all." Swayne complained that Eames had made a "speech" that had turned the hearing "into a farce."[30] The thrust of Eames's argument may be glimpsed in the remarks of Carlisle, who addressed himself to "counsel for the United States . . . [who] testifies, in well-considered rhetoric, his amazement that a judicial tribunal should be called upon to determine whether the political power was authorized to do what it has done."[31]

When a court has scheduled twelve days for oral argument, counsel does not open from a position of strength by questioning the court's decision to take the case. Justice Swayne provided further evidence of Eames's woeful performance by passing along to Bates a remark of the chief justice. Eames had unsuccessfully represented Union general Fitz-John Porter, court-martialed for misconduct at the Second Battle of Bull Run. After hearing Eames argue, Taney had said of the general that "he deserved to be convicted for trusting his case to such counsel."[32]

When Dana rose to argue the *Prize Cases,* "the supreme crisis, in jurisprudence as well as in war," was at hand.[33] Here in the midst of his country's most terrible storm was a peril equal to that Dana confronted when his ship nearly foundered in a fearsome gale off Cape Horn. Dana had the characteristic qualities of an accomplished appellate lawyer: quickness of mind, command of the law, and verbal dexterity. But that could be said of each of the eminent attorneys except the unfortunate Eames. Dana, however, possessed an extraordinary trait—first exhibited when he went to sea: "He displayed in a high degree . . . great quality of physical and mental nerve. . . . Never flustered even when taken unawares, Dana invariably rose to an equality with the occasion. As new difficulties presented themselves and danger increased he seemed to grow cooler and more formidable; what excited others only toned him up to the proper key, and thus it was in the moment of greatest peril that he appeared in most control of all his faculties."[34]

He first brilliantly framed the issue: "The case of the *Amy Warwick* presents a single question which may be stated thus: At the time of the capture, was it competent for the President to treat as prize of war property found on the high seas, for the sole reason that it belonged to persons residing and doing business in Richmond, Virginia?"[35] Upon this question, Dana proceeded to construct a logic that could compel only one answer.

Dana began with the law of prize applicable to cases of war with a recognized foreign power: property on the high seas owned and controlled by persons who themselves reside in "enemy's territory" is liable to capture as prize of war. His comprehensive knowledge of the law of prize and even greater capacity to educate the court provided a path through the political minefield of the terms "enemy's property" and "enemy's territory." Each phrase, Dana emphasized, was a technical term peculiar to prize courts. The owners of the *Amy Warwick* asserted that they were American citizens residing within an insurrectionary district but neither implicated in the rebellion nor disloyal to the United States.

Dana asserted that the right of the sovereign power to capture property on the high seas did not depend on any actual or presumed disloyalty of the property's owners. To the contrary, prize law made immaterial whether an owner was loyal, neutral, or disloyal. Nor was it material whether the seized cargo would directly benefit the enemy or whether the commerce was with neutral nations.[36]

The test, Dana maintained, was the "predicament" of the property. If found on the high seas and owned by persons residing in "enemy's territory," the property was subject to capture *jure belli*, a prize of war. Characteristically, Dana emphasized the reason for the right: "The reason why you may capture it is that it is a justifiable mode of coercing the power with which you are at war. The fact which makes it a justifiable mode of coercing that power, is that the owner is residing under his jurisdiction and control."[37]

The rule was clear enough when the war was between established sovereign powers, but why was it applicable to an "internal war" where the sovereign claiming the right of blockade denied the war was against another government? Here, again, Dana argued from first principles. In internal wars the sovereign can exercise belligerent powers. The object of the sovereign is to coerce the power that is organized against it and making war upon it. Insurrectionists can compel inhabitants of the territory controlled by the insurgency. Therefore, Dana maintained, the parent state has the same interest and right to capture property on the high seas for the purpose of coercing the rebel power, as it would if the insurrectionists were a sovereign nation.[38]

Dana brought an equal clarity of argument to the issue of "enemy's territory." The test, he argued, was whether the residence of the property's owner is within the jurisdiction and control of the enemy. Again

Dana coupled reason to rule and rule to example. The reason for the rule, he explained, was because captured property "must be condemned or restored to the claimant." If the *Amy Warwick* had been permitted to go to Richmond, Dana argued, duties would have been paid to the rebel government. Vessel and cargo could have been taken by the insurrectionists for military purposes with or without compensation. Indeed, he observed, if the owners of the *Amy Warwick* were as loyal to the Union as they claimed, it increased the likelihood that the Confederacy would confiscate the vessel.[39]

It was unnecessary, Dana asserted, to "draw a fine line" as to what constituted "enemy's territory." The occupation of Richmond by rebel forces was more than sufficient for the purposes of deciding the *Prize Cases*. Thus Dana neatly avoided drawing the court into the political thicket of whether articles of secession established a territorial sovereignty that might provide a basis for foreign recognition of the Confederate states as a sovereign country.[40]

Dana's careful explication of the law of prize resurrected a government case that had almost certainly been sunk by Charles Eames's argument. There remained, in Dana's words, "another branch of the question": whether the president could exercise the war power without a preceding act of Congress declaring war. Dana conceded that the right to initiate a war as a voluntary act of sovereignty was vested solely in Congress. Dana asserted, "The question is not what would be the result of a conflict between the Executive and Legislature, during an actual invasion by foreign enemy, the Legislature refusing to declare war . . . it is as to the power of the President before Congress shall have acted, in case of war actually existing."[41]

Dana argued that actions of Congress subsequent to Lincoln's April 1861 blockade proclamation had ratified the president's decision. The essence of his argument, however, was "the overwhelming reasons of necessity" derided by James Carlisle in his opening argument for the ship owners. "War is *a state of things,* and not an act of legislative will," Dana asserted. The president's authority to use the army and navy "within the rules of civilized warfare and subject to established laws of Congress, must be subject to his discretion as a necessary incident to the use, in the absence of any act of Congress controlling him."[42]

Oral argument concluded in the *Prize Cases* on February 25, 1863. Justice Swayne's confidential visit to Attorney General Bates occurred the very next day. The attorney general confided to his diary: "Mr. Eames who was entrusted by me, with the chief management of the *Prize Cases* . . . seems . . . in the conduct of the cases, [to have] made himself very obnoxious to the Court. . . . I am afraid that the feeling may endanger the *Prize Cases*."[43]

Bates now had some inkling of his grievous error in selecting Eames, but had yet to realize the significance of the fortuitous appearance of a sailor turned lawyer. The attorney general was apparently not privy to the "impulsive compliments" Dana's argument had prompted from the justice who was to write the majority opinion in the *Prize Cases*. In the words of one who was present: "After Mr. Dana had closed his argument, I happened to encounter Judge Grier who had retired for a moment to the corridor in the rear of the bench . . . and, in a burst of unjudicial enthusiasm he said to me, 'Well, your little 'Two Years Before the Mast' has settled that question; there is nothing more to say about it!"[44]

On March 10, 1863, the courtroom was full in recognition that the decision could have momentous consequences.[45] Justice Grier delivered the opinion of the court. His very first sentence revealed the profound effect Dana's reasoning had upon the majority. Justice Grier began by observing: "There are certain propositions of law which must necessarily affect the ultimate decision of these cases, and many others, which it will be proper to discuss and decide before we notice the special facts peculiar to each."[46]

Joined by the three Lincoln appointees (Justices Swayne, Miller, and Davis) and by Justice James Wayne of Georgia, Grier's decision adopted every significant argument Dana had advanced in support of the blockade. The "right of prize and capture has its origin *jus belli* and is governed and adjudged under the law of nations"; "it is not necessary to constitute war that both parties should be acknowledged as independent nations"; "the President was bound to meet [war] in the shape it presented itself, without waiting for Congress to baptize it with a name"; enemies' territory "has a boundary marked by lines of bayonets"; "whether property be liable as enemies' property does not in any manner depend on the personal allegiance of the owner."[47]

Dana's argument was unquestionably the key to the government's victory. Justice Catron of Tennessee, Justice Clifford of Maine, and Chief Justice Taney joined the dissent authored by Justice Samuel Nelson. Nelson's language provided a stark reminder of what was at stake in the

Prize Cases: "So the war carried on by the President against the insurrectionary districts in the Southern states, as in the case of the King of Great Britain in the American Revolution, was a personal war against those in rebellion . . . with this difference, as the war-making power belonged to the King, he might have recognized or declared the war at the beginning to be a civil war . . . but in the case of the President no such power existed. . . . I am compelled to the conclusion that no civil war existed between this government and the states in insurrection til recognized by the Act of Congress, 13th of July 1861; that the President does not possess the power of the Constitution to declare war or recognize its existence . . . and, consequently that the President had no power to set on foot a blockade under the law of nations . . . and in all cases before us in which the capture occurred before the 13th of July 1861 for breach of blockade or as enemies' property are illegal and void."[48]

The single-vote majority in the *Prize Cases* preserved Lincoln's capacity to carry on the war. One cannot know if "a defeat at the hands of the Court at this time would have shattered the morale of the union."[49] But the *Prize Cases* were "far more momentous" than any other cases arising out of the war.[50] And Dana expressed the view of the Lincoln administration when he wrote that the consequences of an adverse decision were "fearful to contemplate."[51] By securing a majority in the *Prize Cases,* Dana may well have deterred constitutional challenges to other actions essential to the Union's success, including the Legal Tender Act of 1862, the Emancipation Proclamation, and the Conscription Act of 1863.[52]

The significance of the *Prize Cases* decision was amply illustrated by attempts to "spin" the result. Those sympathizing with the South, including many in the North and in Europe, seized upon the phrase "enemy's territory" to argue that the Supreme Court had acknowledged the right of secession and the independence of the Confederate States. To counter misleading use of the court's decision, Dana published a pamphlet entitled "Enemy's Territory and Alien Enemies: What the Supreme Court Decided in the Prize Causes."[53] The pamphlet was widely circulated, and Dana's clarity impressed another fair stylist: Abraham Lincoln.

Dana visited Lincoln at the White House in May 1864. Superficially, there could scarcely be a greater contrast between two men. By the time of Lincoln's birth in a Kentucky log cabin, four generations of Danas had graduated from Harvard. Yet for all their dissimilarities each had the root of the matter in him. Dana had written of Lincoln that "his life seems a series of wise, sound conclusions, slowly reached, oddly worked out, on great questions."[54] That is an equally apt description of Dana's argument in the *Prize Cases*.

Dana wrote to Sarah of his visit with the president: "When I return, I will tell you of a high compliment he paid me, in a sincere, awkward manner." Lincoln had told Dana that he had read his *Prize Cases* pamphlet and that "it reasoned out . . . what he had all along felt in his bones must be the truth of the matter and was not able to find anywhere in the books, or to reason out satisfactorily to himself."[55]

It was, indeed, the highest of compliments. Dana confronted in the *Prize Cases* the critical challenge to a constitutional democracy in the time of war: "to keep the discrepancy between what had to be done and what could be done constitutionally, as narrow as possible."[56] The sailor-lawyer's extraordinary argument enabled the great work of the prairie-lawyer to continue because each felt in their bones that the Constitution mattered.

21

THE DUKE OF CAMBRIDGE

"Boston is draped in black," Dana wrote to his son in April 1865. "The poor have little pieces of black tied to the door and windows . . . Mr. Lincoln had a great hold on the affection of the people." It was a hold Dana felt as well: "I had come to know Mr. Lincoln well. I believe he had come to like & respect me. . . . The last time I saw him, he put his arms around me, as if he had been my father, and seemed to want to keep me."[1]

Dana believed Lincoln's death a great loss, though neither he nor the country could conceive its eventual magnitude. The month also brought the surrender of Richmond and of Lee's army. Reconstruction would mean "a generation of labor and vast problems to solve but that should depress no man." "You will be glad hereafter to have lived [in these times]," Dana told his son.[2]

Dana was less than six months from his fiftieth birthday, a half-dozen years younger than Lincoln at his death. Dana's service as U.S. attorney during the war years was exemplary—and in the *Prize Cases* of extraordinary importance—but "not what my temperament leads me to, or my qualities are best fitted for." Dana yearned to "serve in any post for which I am fit." What Dana sought most of all was a platform that would enable him to shape the country's future. "I perhaps made a mistake in declining the chance for Congress in 1861 but I acted against my inclinations in what I thought to be my duty."[3] It was the second time Dana had refused an offer of nomination, and each time the nominee had been elected. Dana was determined not to refuse a third time, if the chance came again.

Dana did not wait for a political platform to express his views on the most urgent issue of post–Civil War reconstruction. The question the country confronted was, "Upon what conditions should the Confederate states be re-admitted to the Union?" One view contended that the Confederate states had never seceded, but had been under the control of insurrectionists. Under that theory, war powers could no longer be exercised because the insurgency had been put down. A corollary argument asserted that the Southern states must be readmitted to the Union with their rights, privileges, and state constitutions intact.[4]

Dana was compelled to respond. He could speak to an interpretation of the war power with greater authority and expertise than any other lawyer in the country. Of far more importance to him, Dana believed that "if the dogma of State Supremacy is not destroyed, for practice as well as in theory, the war will have been in vain." Dana's opportunity to address the urgent question came on June 21, 1865, at a Faneuil Hall meeting called to consider the "Re-organization of the Rebel States." Dana worked as hard on what became known as the "Grasp of War" speech as on any argument he ever prepared. His son described him: "I can see him now . . . erect, with square broad shoulders, a graceful figure . . . curling hair and elastic step, walking up and down the room, his head a little to one side, his eyes slightly raised . . . developing the arguments in its support."[5]

Dana lost little time in disposing of the "insurrection" argument: "You cannot justify the great acts of our government for the last three years upon any other principle than the existence of war," Dana asserted to the Faneuil Hall assembly. He reminded his audience that belligerent powers exercised by the Union, including the right to seize vessels as prizes, were predicated on the Supreme Court's decision that the conflict between North and South was a war. Now, although hostilities had ended, the Confederate states were still "in the grasp of war."

Dana's construct differed from the more extreme views of Sumner, who argued that the seceding states had reverted to territorial status, and Thaddeus Stevens, who thought they were conquered provinces. Dana acknowledged that the Constitution provided no rules for the exercise of authority over the occupied states: "You might as well look there to find rules for lighting General Grant's cigar." Dana asserted that the source of authority lay in the war power—a power that did not cease merely because the fighting had stopped. "The conquering power may hold the other in the grasp of war until it has secured whatever it has a right to require." The "requirement" extended beyond the abolition of slavery. In Dana's view, it included extending the right to vote to newly freed slaves.

A "self-governing, voting, intelligent population" of freed slaves would, Dana told his audience, come "quicker than you think. They do not need half the care nor half the patronage we used to think." Dana recognized that "to introduce the free negroes to the voting franchise is a revolution." He had a profound appreciation of the failure to secure that franchise while rebel states were "in the grasp of war." Dana italicized his warning in printed copies of his speech: *"If we do not secure that now, in the time of revolution, it can never be secured except by a new revolution."*

Dana foresaw only two outcomes if rights for freed slaves were not secured—and "if either of those things happens, it is our fault": "either negroes submit forever, and not rise for their rights . . . [or] the poor, oppressed, degraded, black man, bearing patiently his oppression, until he can endure it no longer, ris[es] with arms for his rights." Dana knew there was as little chance of the first as there was of forever oppressing sailors before the mast. "It has got to be decided pretty quickly which you will have . . . [it] will not be slavery in name, but [the South's] institutions will be built upon the mud-sills of a debased negro population." Dana declared, "Our system is a system of states, with central power and in that system is our safety. States rights I maintain. State sovereignty we have destroyed." But he was mistaken; sovereign states were to rise again.

Dana was encouraged by the response to his speech. "My 'address' has attracted great attention in all parts of the land," he wrote Sarah. It was "read aloud in the chief Negro church after services." A visitor from France told Dana that the speech "was printed entire in the French papers, translated from the *London Times* which printed it." The American minister to France, John Bigelow, wrote to Dana expressing the view of the Johnson administration that "the [voting] franchise [for negroes] is not worth so much . . . as the equality of rights of the States." In September 1866 Dana submitted his resignation as U.S. district attorney. "I understand the President expects of those who hold . . . office sympathy with the. . . . [reconstruction] . . . measures he has suggested . . . I find myself unable to accord that sympathy and cooperation."[6]

Dana's resignation coincided with his hope there would be a vacancy in the congressional district of which Cambridge was a part. Incumbent congressman Samuel Hooper, who accepted the Republican nomination in 1861 after Dana refused it, was expected to retire. Though the Danas had recently moved to Boston, Dana held on to the Cambridge house, explaining to Sarah, "If Mr. Hooper declined re-election I wish to succeed him and think I can do it better from Cambridge than from Boston."[7]

Congressman Hooper did not retire, serving until he died a decade later. Dana professed in his "Grasp of War" speech "no particular right to be heard . . . but the critical questions your representatives . . . will soon be required to meet leads us to hope for your attention and consideration." Dana's innate capacity to influence the great issues of his time was immense. But he was not a political animal. The jungle of politics is a dangerous place to be without instincts—as he was about to find out.

In 1866 Dana was elected to the Massachusetts legislature as a representative from Cambridge. The decision to run for the one-year term made sense to Dana. The congressional vacancy had not arisen. Charles Sumner thought Dana's legislative promise (exhibited so brilliantly at the 1853 constitutional convention) far exceeded that of the most able men of Massachusetts. Dana had long thought a great legislative body would be the forum most suited to his talents.

The Massachusetts legislature has seldom been compared to the House of Commons. The legislature Dana entered in 1867 did not bring the comparison to mind. Characteristically, Dana's conception of duty compelled him to devote himself completely to legislative tasks. "Poor father is dreadfully busy," his daughter Elizabeth wrote in her diary. "He always has to be at the Legislature for they are likely to do something foolish when he is away."[8] Dana's presence undoubtedly prevented foolishness and worse on occasion, but his concept of legislative obligation did not endear him to his colleagues.

Dana's unwillingness to barter in the favors that are the currency of legislative politics hampered him. His failure to acknowledge members was often due to his poor eyesight, which never fully recovered from the measles (Dana had been mortified when, years earlier, he failed to recognize the English actor Macready "owing to my nearness of sight"). But Dana felt no obligation to hide his disdain for those he felt lacked integrity. "I admit . . . that I have the fault of showing contempt when I feel it."[9] Behind his back, legislators began calling Dana "the Duke of Cambridge."

Dana's only means of influencing legislators was through the power of his reason and rhetoric. During the two years he served, only once did he have the scope to exhibit that power. The result stands as a demonstration of what he might have accomplished had the issue—and the forum—been equal to his capacity.

The occasion was a pro forma debate on an act to repeal Massachusetts "usury law" that prohibited lenders from charging (and borrowers from paying) more than 6 percent interest on loans. Usury statutes had been part of Massachusetts law since the founding of the state—and had been ignored for nearly as long. Even if one conceded—as most did—that the usury laws were unenforceable, there was no political will for repeal because legislators had more borrowers (whom the law was thought to protect) than lenders among their constituents.

Neither the issue nor the speaker had the sympathy of the House when Dana rose to argue for the law's repeal.[10] Dana acknowledged he must "make converts of opponents." The only weapon at his disposal was the strength of his speech. Dana's argument marshaled all the weapons—logic, clarity, vivid illustration—that made him a great advocate.

Dana asserted the usury law's arbitrary rate of 6 percent interest divided capitalists into three categories: those who would obey the law ("this class is not large, and is diminishing yearly"); those who would invest their capital elsewhere at higher rates of return; and the largest class of all, "those who will disobey the statute and take all they can get."

The law's effect, said Dana, was to put "an honest but poor man" in the hands of the extortionist, "the middleman who holds the secret (of an illegal loan above six percent) in his hand." Without recourse to loans from reputable lenders at prevailing market rates, only "the pawn-broker . . . is open to him." "I shall vote for repeal of the usury laws," asserted Dana. "I do not think they aid the borrower but rather bring him to a worse condition than he would be in, in an open market. They have balked the humane purposes that gave them life."

To the astonishment of those in and out of the legislature, the usury statute was repealed by a margin of more than forty votes. But Dana had no instinct for the "politics" of an issue—nor would he have followed it had he possessed one. When bankers sought to hold a banquet in his honor, Dana refused to attend. Running for reelection in 1867, he ignored the storm of protest that arose when a local constable enforced a long-ignored temperance law. Although Dana thought prohibition foolish, his failure to seek repeal of the statute nearly cost Dana his seat.

Dana was always tone deaf to political repercussions. It was that trait—coupled with his extraordinary legal talent—that made him the ideal choice for those who sought to avoid responsibility for a decision posed by the end of the Civil War: Should Jefferson Davis be tried for treason?

22

TREASON

In October 1867 New York lawyer William Evarts, Dana's co-counsel in the *Prize Cases,* wrote Dana *"confidentially* to know whether you might accept a retainer from the Gov't to take part in the Jeff Davis treason trial if it should take place." The "greatest criminal trial of the age" was scheduled to begin in one month.[1]

The fate of Jefferson Davis had preoccupied the country for more than two years. Captured in Georgia on May 10, 1865, by Union troops, the Confederate president was imprisoned in Fort Monroe, Virginia. In May 1867, U.S. District Court judge John C. Underwood, sitting in Richmond, released Davis on $100,000 bail to the "deafening applause" of those in the courtroom.[2] The bail money was raised by Northerners led by *New York Tribune* editor Horace Greeley, who personally guaranteed $25,000 of surety, as did Cornelius Vanderbilt. It was the latest and most vivid illustration of the extraordinary shift in Northern sentiment since the Civil War's end. Although "Hang Jeff Davis!" was still a rallying cry of Radical Republicans, there was no longer agreement in the North that Davis should stand trial.

By late 1867 when Evarts asked for Dana's help, the potential consequences of a Jefferson Davis treason trial—or the dismissal of the treason indictment—were fraught with political and legal risks. Indeed, the sole unifying "principle" among those responsible for determining if the Davis trial should proceed—from President Andrew Johnson to Chief Justice Salmon Chase to Attorney General Henry Stanbery to the U.S. district attorney for Virginia, Lucius Chandler—was that someone else should make the decision.

There had been no shortage of lawyers eager to act as special prosecutor when the conviction of Jefferson Davis seemed assured. But as the challenge of securing a guilty verdict from twelve Virginian jurors became more apparent, the political benefit of being the prosecutor became less obvious. Evarts had been retained in 1865 as special counsel by then attorney general John Speed. In turn Evarts had chosen former Massachusetts attorney general (and governor) John H. Clifford to assist him. Clifford resigned in August 1866, writing to the new attorney general, Henry Stanbery, "If it is the purpose of the government to proceed with the trial of Jefferson Davis upon the indictment pending against him in Virginia, I do not feel that any public or professional duty would require me to take part in the proceedings."[3]

One month before the scheduled start of the trial, Attorney General Stanbery wrote Evarts, "I need not suggest to you that no time should be lost in making full preparation for trial." Stanbery himself refused to appear in the Davis prosecution, informing Evarts that he intended to limit his court appearances to arguments before the U.S. Supreme Court. At Evarts's urging, Stanbery wrote to Dana on October 25, 1867: "I desire to employ you as assistant special counsel for the United States in the prosecution for treason now pending in the Circuit Court of the United States at Richmond, Virginia against Jefferson Davis."[4]

Evarts knew that Dana would consider the request a professional and public duty. He received notice of Dana's acceptance of the appointment three days later, and wrote to his new co-counsel, "The whole responsibility of the thing legal and political will be upon *us*."[5] Stated more accurately, Evarts would handle politics but Dana would bear the responsibility for prosecuting Jefferson Davis for treason.

On November 9 Dana received a telegram from Attorney General Stanbery: "MR. CHANDLER WISHES TO HAVE A CONSULTATION AS TO DAVIS CASE NEXT WEDS. MORNING. WILL EXPECT YOU."[6] The Davis trial was to begin in just over two weeks. Dana reasonably assumed that the U.S. attorney for Virginia had spent the six months since Davis was released on bail, preparing for trial. In fact, given the significance of the case, Lucius Chandler was the one of least prepared prosecutors in American history. He had failed to assemble even the most rudimentary list of exhibits and witnesses. Chandler's ineptness appalled Dana. He took some comfort in Evarts's belief that the start of the case might be postponed, but Dana was preparing for a historic trial. "Keep these letters carefully as I shall write no journal," he wrote to Sarah upon arriving in Richmond in late November 1867.[7]

The legal team assembled to defend Davis was composed of prominent lawyers, from North and South. The former Confederate president's primary counsel was Charles O'Conor of New York City, whom many considered to be the leader of the New York bar. As notorious for his defense of slavery as for his legal expertise, O'Conor owed much of his professional success to his skill in calculating Washington political interests. In the Jefferson Davis trial it was a talent of greater value than courtroom advocacy.

O'Conor capitalized on Northern concern that a treason trial might be transformed into a test of the constitutionality of secession. If sovereign states had the right to secede, a secessionist leader could not be guilty of treason. Jefferson Davis initially opposed his lawyer's strategy of delay because he hoped to defend the right of secession in court. Davis contended that the secession of his home state of Mississippi ended his citizenship and duty of loyalty to the United States.

O'Conor persuaded Davis that confidence in a Virginia jury might be misplaced. Judge Underwood, who was to preside with Chief Justice Chase, had countered the assertion that Jefferson Davis could not be convicted in Virginia: "I think it would be difficult but it could be done; I could pack a jury to convict him." O'Conor feared that Underwood would impanel "a mongrel jury" of emancipated African Americans and whites loyal to the Union.[8]

O'Conor shrewdly complained publicly about trial delay, while conveying to the Johnson administration his purported interest in seeing the constitutionality of secession addressed by the U.S. Supreme Court. The wild card in the high-stakes trial poker played by O'Conor was Chief Justice Salmon P. Chase. The chief justice, like each of his colleagues, was assigned a judicial "circuit" where he was required to preside (with the sitting U.S. district court judge) when the circuit court was in session. Chase was assigned to the judicial circuit that included Virginia.

Chief Justice Chase had gone to extraordinary lengths to avoid sitting in his circuit. He first objected on the grounds that Virginia was still under military law. When President Johnson issued a proclamation intended to alleviate Chase's objection, the chief justice countered that the newly enacted Judicial Circuits Act had not properly allotted the federal circuits. When Congress cured the supposed defect, Chase asserted he had scheduling conflicts. Each excuse he gave was legally plausible on its own, but taken together they revealed a political truth that was a secret to no one. Chase still harbored presidential ambitions and he was uncertain which result in a Davis treason trial would benefit him most. O'Conor calculated that the chief justice would not come to Richmond until he was sure it was politically advantageous.[9]

Jefferson Davis was already there. Dana described to Sarah his first look at the defendant: "Jeff Davis was at church, it being the same he always went to as President & from which he was summoned by Lee's telegram that his lines were broken & Richmond must be evacuated." Dana watched as Davis "walked off alone, bowing occasionally but not stopping to speak to anyone. Something of the old proud step remains, but it is a terrible fall."[10]

Dana reported to Sarah, "Evarts and I spent our day in our room making preparation on the law & evidence. . . . We have been reading over a mass of Jefferson Davis [material], letters, orders etc. some quite interesting just before & after great events—to extract the proper matter for proofs." Evarts wrote to Dana shortly before they arrived in Richmond, "We should not expect to try the case in the absence of the Chief Justice [but] . . . for the meantime I have arrived at the fact that J. D. used to wear a confederate uniform on great occasions and have a witness who can prove it, in the person of a colored waiter who came to me last evening."[11]

On Monday November 25, 1867, defendant Jefferson Davis and his lawyers—U.S. District Attorney Chandler and special prosecutors Evarts and Dana—and U.S. District Court Judge Underwood assembled at the Richmond courthouse to await the arrival of the chief justice. "This day when the great drama was expected nothing happened," Dana wrote to Sarah. "It was understood & reported that Chief Justice Chase was to be here and to charge the Grand Jury and the Court was postponed until 2:30 to await his arrival. The time came without him."[12]

Word came by telegraph that the chief justice was detained by his duties at the Supreme Court. Dana wrote to Sarah, "Tomorrow . . . the ceremony of Davis' appearance & the postponement . . . the Washington press speaks of the trial as certain to take place—perhaps the gov't encourages this line of report for reasons of its own." Prosecutors and defense lawyers agreed to a continuance until the following March 1868 when Chief Justice Chase would presumably be free of his term duties at the Supreme Court. O'Conor asked that his client not be "subjected to a renewal of the inconvenience" of returning to Richmond unless the trial was to commence. O'Conor's grasp of the political complications persuaded him that the case would not be tried. When Davis was released on bail, O'Conor had written to his wife: "The business is finished. Mr. Davis will never be called upon to appear for trial."[13]

Whatever confidence O'Conor had in avoiding the commencement of trial did not extend to ending the prosecution. Radical Republicans never tired of waving the bloody shirt of the Davis treason trial in the increasingly hostile political war over Andrew Johnson's reconstruction policies. Indeed, the search for grounds upon which to impeach the president began with the allegation that Johnson had orchestrated the trial delay. An investigation led by Massachusetts representative George Boutwell, chair of the House Judiciary Committee, sought evidence of Johnson's alleged role. Though Boutwell's committee could not substantiate the baseless allegation that Johnson was deliberately delaying the trial to protect Davis, U.S. Attorney Chandler testified before the Committee that the treason indictment he had obtained from the grand jury in May 1866 was deficient and that a new one was necessary.[14]

The renewed congressional focus on the status of trial preparation prompted Evarts to request Chandler to come to New York in January 1868. Chandler was expected to bring a draft of a new indictment, including a summary of the oral and documentary evidence submitted to the grand jury in Virginia. Chandler avoided a face-to-face meeting with Evarts, instead dropping off "his illegible minutes of evidence before the Grand Jury." An exasperated Evarts wrote to Dana that the prosecutor left "the same bundle of papers we looked over two months ago in Richmond and nothing else." Evarts added, "What do you say to a demonstration to the Atty. Gen. against trying it at all?" Dana immediately agreed. "I think it necessary to present [the matter] to the Attorney General in the most serious manner and at once—first, to urge the prosecution to be abandoned and second, to say that if it must go on, we cannot do it with Mr. Chandler as [U.S.] Attorney."[15]

But two weeks later Evarts wrote to Dana from New York: "Can you come here and draft a new indictment with me?" Dana obviously questioned the changed approach, because Evarts replied, "I do not wonder over your annoyance at the position of the Davis matter but there is no help for it . . . we must have a sufficient indictment." Evarts had second thoughts about joining Dana to persuade Attorney General Stanbery to end the prosecution. Instead Evarts suggested to Dana, "If you will draw a letter to the Attorney General giving it as the result of our deliberations . . . that the Gov't [would] do better to pursue no further in the cause and send it to me with your signature, I will add mine to it."[16]

Evarts, for the moment, had more need of Dana's extraordinary legal talent and devotion to duty than his letter. The woeful Chandler had still done nothing. Evarts sent Chandler a blistering note complaining of his "hurried visit to New York, upon which you merely left with me the unarranged maze of paper [for] Mr. Dana & myself." Evarts continued, "We are now within four weeks of the day assigned for the attendance of Mr. Davis for trial, and as far as I am aware, we are in precisely the same position as to preparation that we were November last."[17]

There was no choice under the circumstances, asserted Evarts, but to postpone the trial again. But there was a more urgent problem, as Evarts pointedly reminded Chandler: "The three years within which an indictment can be found is rapidly running out and will expire in April." Even Chandler had conceded (before Congress, no less) that the current indictment was legally deficient. The Civil War had ended in April 1865, which meant that unless a new treason indictment was secured before April 1868 the case of *United States v. Jefferson Davis* was likely to be dismissed. "Yet," Evarts admonished Chandler, "four weeks have now passed since your visit and I have not yet received any report of the evidence before the grand jury."[18]

"We must be prepared to take the matter upon us as soon as the materials are placed before us," Evarts wrote to Dana on February 24, 1868. "In the meantime I am expecting your letter in favor of stopping the prosecution."[19] The "matter" was a new treason indictment of the former president of the Confederate States of America; the "materials" were the evidence Chandler had not provided; and "we" meant Dana alone. Evarts would be busy. His new client, Andrew Johnson, had just been impeached.

Dana's draft letter setting forth the reasons the U.S. government ought to end the Jefferson Davis prosecution ("it will settle nothing in law . . . not now settled & nothing in fact which is not now history") reached Evarts shortly after the House of Representatives voted to impeach Andrew Johnson.[20] Although the impeachment charges did not include the unsubstantiated allegation that the president was deliberately stalling the prosecution of Jefferson Davis, Evarts realized that Johnson could not entertain recommendations that the Davis prosecution be dropped, no matter how compelling Dana's reasons. Nor could Johnson risk having the Davis case dismissed for the insufficiency of the treason indictment on the eve of the impeachment trial.

Evarts now had greater need of Dana than ever. He knew that signing—much less sending—Dana's letter to Attorney General Stanbery was out of the question. "I cannot make up my mind to send it, in the new situation," Evarts disingenuously wrote Dana. What Evarts most needed was Dana's assurance that he would "be ready to be summoned by telegraph" to draft a new treason indictment. On March 15, 1868, Evarts twice wrote Dana in increasingly urgent tones. "You must plan to . . . go to Richmond if necessary for *now* the responsibility is on *us*. . . . I will expect you as soon as steam can bring you." Dana arrived in Washington despite a heavy snowstorm that blocked train tunnels. "All along the route we were detained by drifts or trains off the track," he wrote to Sarah.[21]

Washington was immersed in a political storm as well. All talk was of the impeachment, with trial in the Senate to begin shortly. "I think there is a growing feeling that the impeachment lacks *basis*," wrote Dana, undoubtedly reflecting his conversations with Evarts, who was preparing the president's defense. Dana told Sarah he knew "nothing of the Jeff Davis matter yet. I shall see the officials tomorrow."[22]

Evarts wrote Dana that if he came to Washington to work on the new treason indictment, "we will take up, then, as well, the question of whether the trial itself should take place at all."[23] But only Dana—who did not evaluate legal questions in a political context—could have thought the decision to end the prosecution was really open for discussion. Evarts brought Dana to Washington for one reason: to send him to Richmond to re-indict Davis for treason and to do it before the statute of limitations expired.

Davis had been indicted for treason at least three times before Dana was given the responsibility of preparing a new indictment. Two of the indictments—one in Tennessee (where the U.S. attorney brought treason indictments against Davis and 2014 others) and one in the District of Columbia (where Davis was charged with being "constructively present" during a rebel raid on Washington in July 1864)—were legally deficient because Davis had been in neither Tennessee nor Washington when the alleged acts of treason occurred.[24]

The only pending treason indictment was secured by U.S. Attorney Chandler from a Virginia grand jury in May 1866. Chandler conceded he had drawn the indictment "very hurriedly." Dana did not need to be told. Chandler's indictment of Davis was an astounding document. The prosecutor for the United States alleged that Davis was "seduced by the instigation of the devil" to join "a great multitude of persons ... armed and arrayed in a warlike manner ... with ... dirks, and other warlike weapons."[25]

The "medieval verbiage" was because Chandler had used a treason form dating back centuries.[26] Though it was another example of Chandler's sloth, the archaic language was often invoked by American prosecutors (the treason indictment against Aaron Burr dismissed by Chief Justice John Marshall contained the same language.) Evarts sent Dana to Richmond to secure a new treason indictment, and neither he nor any other prosecutorial agent of the United States cared how it was done. But Dana—unlike Evarts, who had supported the Fugitive Slave Act—knew what it was like to be threatened with a treason prosecution by the U.S. government.

Justice Benjamin Curtis had given a Massachusetts grand jury a chilling definition of treason in 1851, when he asserted that persons "in any combination or conspiracy" who resisted with force the enforcement of federal law could be criminally liable for treason for performing "any part, however minute, or however remote from the scene of action."[27] Similar interpretations had been so often used by English judges to eliminate political opposition to the Crown that the term "constructive treason" was used to describe the practice.

The framers of the U.S. Constitution were acutely aware of the pernicious use of constructive treason and sought to eliminate it. Treason is the only crime defined in the Constitution: "Treason against the United States, shall consist only in levying war against them, or adhering to their enemies, giving them aid and comfort. No person shall be convicted of treason unless on the testimony of two witnesses to the same overt act or confession in open court."[28] But Dana knew that the constitutional protection against a charge of "constructive treason" was only as good as prosecutors and judges cared to make it. Dana had risked an indictment for constructive treason for opposing the fugitive slave law.

Dana understood that his duty as special prosecutor was to secure a new indictment of Davis before the statute of limitations expired, but he was determined do so in a charging instrument that did not rely upon the notorious precedents that Chandler had mimicked. The "devil and dirks" indictment included the ancient formulation that the defendant had acted "in order to fulfill and bring to effect . . . traitorous compassing, imaginations, and intentions." Despite the indictment's repeated general allegations that Davis did so by "war, insurrection, and rebellion," Chandler's charge was remarkably devoid of what overt acts Davis had done to levy war and where he had done them.[29]

Working from the morass of Chandler's grand jury notes and accumulated Confederate documents, Dana quickly organized an indictment that laid out the case of treason against Davis. The indictment dispensed with antiquated language that prosecutors had used since the days of Edward III in the fourteenth century. Dana alleged that Jefferson Davis "being a person owing allegiance to the United States" did "traitorously levy war." In place of Chandler's generalized allegations, Dana ensured the grand jury relied upon specific "overt acts" that alleged the presence and participation of Davis in actions that were deemed treasonous.

Drawing upon the testimony of Robert E. Lee, who appeared before the grand jury in November 1867, the indictment alleged, for example, that Davis "did, order, direct and command Robert E. Lee to assault . . . and . . . kill officers and soldiers in the military service of the United

States [at] Fort Steadman . . . in the District of Virginia within the jurisdiction of the court . . . and the said Robert E. Lee . . . and other persons unknown, in obedience to the command of Jefferson Davis, did then and there, assault, fight, wound and capture and kill said officers and soldiers in the military service of the United States."[30]

The grand jury returned the new treason indictment on March 26, 1868. The impeachment trial of President Johnson had begun in early March and lasted into May. Evarts made a fourteen-hour closing argument on behalf of his client, and on May 16, Andrew Johnson was acquitted, the Senate falling one vote short of the two-thirds necessary to remove the president from office. Chief Justice Chase presided over the impeachment trial, providing him with a truly legitimate reason for his absence from the Davis case, which was rescheduled for the last week of November 1868.

When the Senate refused to reconfirm Attorney General Henry Stanbery, who had resigned the position to help defend Johnson, the president appointed Evarts as attorney general. Dana urged Evarts to join him in advising President Johnson to end the Davis treason prosecution. Attorney General Evarts demurred: "I think you had better write me a spontaneous letter in regard to the case of Davis and I will give the matter prompt attention." Dana immediately did so, pointedly noting, "You now hold a post of official responsibility for the proceeding." Dana reminded Evarts, "You know how much my mind was moved, from the first, by doubts of the expediency of trying [Davis] at all."[31] He could have added—but did not—that Evarts shared those doubts.

Dana's letter emphasized the folly of the government's prosecution. He noted that the only constitutional question "was whether the levying of war against the United States which would otherwise be treason is relieved of that character by the fact . . . of secession." That question of law would not be given to the jury to decide, so "the only question . . . submitted to the jury will be whether Jefferson Davis took any part in the war." Dana posed the salient query: "As it is one of the great facts of history . . . why should we desire to make a question of it and refer the decision . . . to a jury?" Even the most careful jury selection could not ensure that "a traitor in heart" would not falsely swear loyalty to the Union. An acquittal or a hung jury "would be most humiliating to the government & people of this country & none the less so because it would be absurd."[32]

Dana acknowledged that the question of whether to prosecute Davis would present itself differently "if it were important to secure a verdict as a means of punishing the defendant." But "as for a sentence of death I am sure that . . . the people of the United States would not desire to see it carried into effect." Dana added: "I think the public interest in the trial has ceased among the most earnest and loyal citizens."[33] He was right, but he neglected politics.

There were uncertain political consequences if Andrew Johnson were to end the prosecution of Jefferson Davis. Radical Republicans were poised to ride U.S. Grant's coattails in the presidential election that was only a month away. Johnson—whose lame-duck presidency was not due to end until March 1869—feared a renewed impeachment effort. A decision to dismiss the treason indictment might provide Radical Republicans (whose election slogan was "Vote as you shot") with popular grounds for an impeachment.

Attorney General Evarts did not reply to Dana's August letter until October 1868, when he wrote, "I have placed a copy of that communication before the President accompanying with it a letter from myself, a copy of which I enclose for you information."[34] The enclosure was an instructive example of the difference between a lawyer with political instincts and a lawyer without them.

Evarts informed the president that he was transmitting a letter "from the honorable Richard Henry Dana of Massachusetts, associate counsel for the United States in the prosecution of Jefferson Davis . . . giving his (Mr. Dana's) view, in a careful and deliberate form as to the propriety of the Government's remitting further prosecution of the indictment." Evarts noted that he and Dana "acted together in making preparation for the trial which we both expected to take place last Spring." He acknowledged that "the opinions which Mr. Dana expressed were a subject . . . of conference while we occupied this common relation of counsel for the government."[35]

But at precisely the point in Evarts's letter of transmittal where Dana looked to the attorney general to declare the Davis prosecution should end, Evarts wrote, "Had I remained in a private professional relation to the case and to the government, [Dana's] communication probably would have borne my signature." It was a masterful example of a political art Dana neither possessed nor admired. Dana, unlike others, was not looking to avoid responsibility. His letter to Evarts closed: "If your views or those of the President should be in favor of proceeding with the trial, I feel confident that I can do my duty as counsel to the utmost." The attorney general replied: "I think nothing else should be said in the Davis trial until after the election."[36]

The politics of the Jefferson Davis prosecution compelled Evarts to use Dana again. The best evidence that there was more to be gained politically by ending the Davis case than continuing it came from the chief justice. Evarts expected a November 1868 hearing on the status of the Davis trial to be a pro forma matter in which the parties would agree to another trial delay. To the attorney general's surprise, Davis lawyers filed a motion to quash the indictment. The move was unexpected given O'Conor's strategy of avoiding any hearing on the merits of the government's case. Even more mystifying was word that Chief Justice Chase would be at the hearing.

Evarts sent Dana an urgent telegram: "THE COURT IN RICHMOND HAS FIXED THURSDAY OF THIS WEEK FOR HEARING THE MOTION TO QUASH THE INDICTMENT AGAINST JEFFERSON DAVIS UNDER THE OPERATION OF THE FOURTEENTH AMENDMENT OF THE CONSTITUTION, IT WILL BE NECESSARY FOR YOU TO ATTEND."[37] The suggestion that the recently adopted Fourteenth Amendment compelled dismissal of the treason indictment was as astonishing to Dana as the news that Chase would finally attend a hearing. It was scarcely a serious argument, and Dana had no doubt it would fail.

O'Conor had better reason to believe it would succeed. The chief justice had provided Jefferson Davis's lawyer with the argument. O'Conor spent little time figuring out why ("What may be the real objects of this practiced politician I know not") and wasted no time filing a motion to quash the indictment, asserting the grounds provided by Chase.[38] On Thursday, December 3, 1868, began the first and last hearing on the sufficiency of the treason indictment of the United States against the former president of the Confederacy, Chief Justice Chase presiding with U.S. District Court Judge Underwood.

O'Conor argued that the amendment's third section (prohibiting any individual who participated in an insurrection from holding public office if that person had previously taken an oath of allegiance to the United States) operated as a criminal punishment against Davis, who had previously taken the oath as a member of Congress. Thus, asserted O'Conor, Davis could not be prosecuted for treason as it would constitute double jeopardy. Dana began his appearance on behalf of the United

States by observing "the motion ha[s] been on a point unexpected to [me], and probably to the court."[39]

The chief justice's reply must have stunned Dana: "The court ha[s] not been surprised, as intimated by Mr. Dana, at the ground taken by the defendant. The course of the argument was anticipated, as it was expected that the point to be urged was the common principle of constructive repeal." Dana responded, "Probably nothing would more surprise the people of the United States than to learn that, by adopting amendment 14, they had repealed all the penalties against treason, insurrection, or rebellion."[40]

Chase was as determined to rule on the motion as he had been to avoid the case. Arguments were completed on Friday, December 4, and Chase intimated a decision would be made that day. But on Saturday a displeased chief justice announced "that the court had failed to agree upon a decision on regard to the motion made to quash the indictment against Mr. Jefferson Davis." Judge Underwood had refused to assent to Chase's reasoning. O'Conor quickly moved to have the fact of the disagreement certified to the Supreme Court for review. The record of the hearing closed with a remarkable notation by the reporter of the decision: "THE CHIEF JUSTICE instructed [me] to record him as having been of the opinion on the disagreement, that the indictment should be quashed, and all further proceedings barred by the effect of the fourteenth amendment to the Constitution of the United States."[41]

Whatever the political motives for Chase's extraordinary instruction to the court reporter, it was clear that the chief justice would vote to dismiss the treason indictment if the Davis appeal was heard by the Supreme Court. Evarts wished to avoid the ignominy of a court dismissal of the most significant treason case ever filed by the U.S. government. With November elections over, he at last seconded Dana's recommendation that the president end the prosecution. Evarts read Dana's letter to the president and cabinet. There was consensus that a final amnesty proclamation be issued, although Secretary of State William Seward, who was grievously wounded (as were two of his sons) in the Lincoln assassination plot, opposed leniency for Davis. Andrew Johnson made no final decision but asked Evarts to draft the proclamation.[42]

Evarts informed O'Conor that the United States would end the Davis prosecution if O'Conor, in turn, would agree to withdraw the question before the Supreme Court on the motion to quash the indictment.

O'Conor agreed, and on Christmas Day 1868, President Andrew Johnson issued a proclamation of general amnesty to all who participated in the rebellion against the United States. In February 1869 a notice of no prosecution was entered in the circuit court in Richmond in the matter of *United States of America v. Jefferson Davis.*[43]

Three years after it was to have begun, "the greatest criminal trial of the age" ended. Legal scholars identified one significant contribution from the political spectacle: "Along the way the process had managed to remove the last antiquated vestiges of English treason law from American jurisprudence in favor of the sounder principles announced in the Constitution."[44] The sounder principles did not come from "process." They arose from Dana's devotion to duty without regard to politics or self-interest.

It was all the more reason for others to remain wary. In the presidential papers of Andrew Johnson, Dana's letter bears a notation: "Richard Dana's opinion in reference to Jeff Davis' release. This opinion must be filed with care. A. J."[45]

23

THE RATING

Timing is everything in politics. Dana's experience was ample proof of the tried but true maxim. At age thirty he waited to be asked to run for office when first approached by a Whig emissary; at age thirty-seven he reluctantly withdrew from the political field when the Free Soil Party looked to him as a leader; in his forties he twice refused the Republican Party's nomination for Congress when election was all but ensured.

Dana's conviction that he must now at fifty-three seize the opportunities for elective office was as misguided as his earlier belief that he ought to ignore them. His decision to enter elective politics as a Massachusetts legislator was unwise but not fatal. Dana's political aspirations could be ended only if he made another egregious mistake of political timing. In 1868 he did.

Dana decided to challenge incumbent Republican congressman Benjamin F. Butler in Massachusetts' fifth congressional district (Essex County)—a county in which neither man lived. General Benjamin Butler was one of the most controversial figures of the Civil War era. He began his political life as a pro-South Democrat. Butler supported Jefferson Davis for president at the 1860 Democratic National Convention, and he was the unsuccessful Democratic candidate for governor of Massachusetts that same year.

Given command of Massachusetts volunteers at the outbreak of the Civil War, General Butler initially distinguished himself by occupying Baltimore, preventing the secession of Maryland. Butler's subsequent exploits, including his notorious administration of New Orleans, eventually led to an inglorious end to his military career. Lincoln mistrusted him and General Grant, furious at Butler's incompetence, relieved him of his command. Butler returned to Massachusetts, reentering politics as a Radical Republican. Butler's election to Congress in 1866 dismayed prominent Essex County Republicans, not least because of the tenuousness of the flamboyant congressman's connection to the county. Butler's memoirs contain the boast, "I was elected to Congress while I lived in a tent on the beach."[1]

In 1868 Butler attempted to block the Republican nomination of U.S. Grant for president. (Butler was never one to forget an adversary, as Dana was later to learn at his peril.) Butler's antagonism to the revered Grant and to the Republican Party's pledge to redeem government bonds in gold (Butler favored redemption in "greenbacks") prompted Essex County Republicans to seek an alternative candidate for Congress. Butler was, however, firmly in control of the requisite Republican state and county committees, and easily won renomination.

Butler's candidacy was anathema to a coalition of bankers and merchants in and out of Essex County. The retired president of the New England Mutual Life Insurance Company led a delegation—some of whom had ostracized Dana for opposing Webster and the fugitive slave law—to plead with Dana to challenge Butler and his "reckless" views on monetary policy.[2]

Although Dana was no more a resident of Essex County than Butler, he was assured that his summer home in Manchester would be viewed by voters more favorably than Butler's "tent." His new friends pledged to raise $10,000 for the campaign. Dana was further persuaded that an "alternative" convention could bestow upon him a nomination for Congress that would be equal in weight to "the shell of a nomination" Butler had engineered for himself.[3]

Accordingly, in early October 1868 Dana became an independent candidate for the fifth congressional district, enthusiastically accepting the nomination at a Salem meeting of supporters. Dana remained loyal to his antiquated idea of political candidacy: "You have called me to this post yourselves without a stir of mine." Dana had an equally quaint idea of how a campaign could be conducted: "In New England, the people meet quietly and soberly . . . to get light, to learn the facts and reason together." Butler had a more modern idea of campaign strategy.[4]

Butler's array of dirty tricks would give pause to the most cynical campaign consultant. Butler bribed reporters to castigate Dana. Butler's campaign workers owed their livelihood to the congressman's patronage and provided a network of enforcers to keep voters in line. "I welcome recruits and shoot deserters," joked Butler, but "execution" was unnecessary in a voting system where ballots were distributed by party workers who knew whether a "Butler" or "Dana" ballot was requested. "In this species of warfare General Butler was not to be excelled," observed Charles Francis Adams Jr. Nor, he could have added, was there ever a candidate less likely than Dana to meet trick with trick. The extremes to which Butler was willing to go exceeded those necessary to win, but Butler was looking to annihilate Dana.[5]

Venerable Essex County towns like Newburyport and Marblehead, once the bastions of the old Federalist Party tradition in which Dana was raised, had been surpassed by new industrial centers like Lynn, home to large shoemaking factories. There was little enough in Dana's campaign issue of bond redemption that spoke to shoemakers even if they cared to listen–which, Dana quickly learned, they did not.

An account of Dana's exchange with the "Butlerites" who dogged him throughout the campaign is a fair sample of what the outgunned candidate confronted. Dana sought to remind his audience that Butler (who was from Lowell) was no more a resident of Essex County than Dana:

> DANA: Fellow-citizens—
>
> CROWD: We ain't yer feller-citizens.
>
> DANA: Fellow-citizens of Essex—
>
> CROWD: You ain't from Essex—three cheers for Butler.
>
> DANA: I come from—
>
> CROWD: Cambridge—Cambridge.
>
> DANA: Well, now, what county is Cambridge in?
>
> CROWD: Middlesex.
>
> DANA: And what county is Lowell in?
>
> CROWD: Middlesex.
>
> DANA: Very good—I come from the same county from which your representative comes.
>
> CROWD: Three cheers for him.[6]

Few candidates for political office begin with the thought of losing. Dana believed he could win if "my case is properly put before the people." Dana never undertook any task with less than complete commitment to the "day's work" it entailed. He dove into the campaign—suspending his law practice, canvassing the district, and appearing wherever "there is an audience of a dozen to listen to me."[7]

Butler made certain the campaign was about Dana, not his case to the people. A widely circulated broadside contained a typical attack: "An aristocrat of the snobbiest sort, what has [Dana] in common with the working man? What knows he of the trials, the toils, the dangers of the hardy fishermen of your coast—unless the lately exhumed fossil *Two Years Before the Mast* be taken as a textbook for the mackerel fleet." Butler accused Dana of failing to prosecute "chief murderer" Jefferson Davis, shamelessly ignoring the fact that Butler favored Davis over Lincoln in 1860.[8]

Although there was a Democrat in the race as well, Butler's ruthless organization and Butler himself used all their weapons on Dana. An exhaustive list of baseless charges was leveled against Dana, but a candidate as skilled in demagoguery as Butler needed little more than an opening. Dana provided it when he unwisely responded to "the great accusation that Mr. Dana wears gloves!" Meeting with shoemakers in Lynn, he replied: "When I go down to my farm there at Manchester, if I want to cut down a tree I cut it down myself; and if I want cut a path through the dog-briar [I put on my working gloves]. . . . [When I gathered hides in California] I had to get into the vats and swash all those hides; and of all nasty work I think that is the nastiest."[9]

Two days after Dana's speech, the mayor of Lynn, who was also Butler's campaign manager, invited Butler to respond. The city's fire department, police department, two brass bands, a torchlight parade, and an enormous crowd of shoemakers greeted their congressman. Butler took some liberties with Dana's actual response—easy enough to do because Butler made a point of never appearing with Dana—but his audience loved it: "My opponent . . . in defending himself from the accusation of being an aristocrat admitted to you among other things that he wore gloves for the purposes of society. . . . I wear them to keep my hands warm and I advise you to do the same. As to the averment that it is necessary to be dirty in order to get to be your equal, I assure you I will not have to get into a manure pit to associate with you, but simply be a respectable, well-clad, decent American citizen."[10]

Dana had tried to point out that Butler was a far wealthier man (in fact he was a millionaire) by drawing attention to the contrast between their modes of travel: "[I drive a] one-horse wagon . . . but as we are riding along . . . we will hear a noise behind us and turning around see a carriage with two or four horses driven at full speed with perhaps out-riders on horseback, and it will come dashing by us covering us with dust and in that carriage will be my opponent."[11]

Butler thought enough of his response to include it in his memoirs as an example of his "stump speech" ability: "As to horses, when I came into this district . . . I found that my constituents had better horses; and I proposed to get as good a pair as I could, and I have got a good pair, and if you will come down and ride with me, I assure you we won't take anybody's dust." It was a specimen of a talent that made Butler—to Dana as well as others—"a nationally dangerous man."[12]

A candidate on the defensive is a candidate on his way to defeat, but Dana was eloquent in responding to the charge he was an aristocrat: "On that charge, I have only this to say: I know no word of mine can make me else than I am, whatever that may be. But let me suggest to you . . . that aristocracy which lives in ships' forecastles . . . that devotes its earliest labors to the cause of seamen against the wealthy and influential owners and masters . . . that takes up the cause of Negro slaves, and gave its best years . . . to a contest against the only oligarchy this nation ever saw . . . that has not a dollar it did not earn . . . is not dangerous to American liberties."[13]

Despite the repeated hammering, Dana never flagged. The group of bankers and merchants who encouraged him to run failed to fulfill their promises of financial support. The Democratic candidate made no appearances at all. Dana campaigned to the end. On the campaign's final day he spoke in Salem (or tried to—hecklers shouted "Put on your gloves!") and then rode to Manchester in the rain to make one last speech.[14]

No election in this country is preordained. A candidate who puts his heart and soul into a campaign invariably retains visions of an upset, despite what reason and others tell him. Dana had some basis for believing that given three candidates, voters might divide their vote relatively equally. Indeed, one of the calculations made by Dana's backers—though he did not recognize it—was that even if Dana lost, he could draw enough votes from Butler to enable the Democrat to win. The moneyed interests who solicited Dana to run were much keener on defeating Butler than electing Dana.

On election day Dana returned to Cambridge to vote because he had not become a registered voter in Essex County. That meant he could not even assure himself of one vote for Congress, but he intended to vote for General Grant, the Republican candidate for president. Dana was informed that his name had been stricken from the Cambridge voting list on the assumption he would be voting in Essex. Worse news soon followed.

Dana had lost—by a margin rarely seen in American electoral politics. Butler carried every city and town in the congressional district. Butler outpolled Dana better than six to one, receiving over 13,000 votes to Dana's 1,811. The Democrat, who had not campaigned, beat Dana by a more than two-to-one margin. Of the total votes cast, Dana received less than 10 percent. It was more than a landslide—it was an avalanche.[15]

The election results buried Dana's ambition for elective office. His generous and optimistic spirit was too much a part of his character to be long submerged, but "don't take it personally" advice comes only from those who have not been candidates. Political cartoons in Butler-paid newspapers made such effective use of the "Duke of Cambridge" caricature that the label stuck to Dana long after the campaign (more than a century later, the "tank ad" was to similarly cling to another Cambridge "Duke," Michael Dukakis, long after the 1988 presidential election).

The margin of defeat was painful, but more disappointing to Dana was the conduct of his "friends." Those who asked him to run abandoned the campaign when the loss looked inevitable. Other Massachusetts politicians (including Sumner) privately opposed Butler but would not say so publicly. Butler circulated the slander that Dana defended fugitive slaves only if paid to do so. "My old Free Soil & Abolitionist associates . . . standing by in silence & so giving it countenance is a hard thing to bear." Dana was philosophic about the experience. "I knew Butler & his campaign followers would do their worst to injure me when I had the part of the candidate and I do not complain." But, added Dana "this was baser than I thought possible."[16]

The day after the election, he was back at work, trying a case in Essex County. It required more than his usual fortitude. When Dana left the courthouse, he literally faced the music. "Butlerites"—bands and all— were still in the street celebrating his loss.[17]

Dana could take some solace in the knowledge that not all were applauding his demise. He was supported by "every minister . . . and schoolteacher . . . [by] retired shipmasters who have seen something of the world and farmers who are not carried away by the boisterous applause of ward meetings."[18] The editor of the *Nation* put it more simply: "Dana was defeated because he retains some old-fashioned views as to the value of the human mind."[19]

Dana had lost the game of politics. His crushing defeat at Butler's hands ended his prospects for elective office. "I have given up all expectations of public employment," Dana wrote to Sarah. "I should like to be relieved from the time-wasting of ordinary lawsuits . . . and to be able, the next eight or ten years to use my powers and knowledge in a larger sphere. . . . The objection is the old, old, story—I cannot afford it."[20]

Dana resumed the practice of law, reestablishing himself on Boston's Court Square in the same building that had been his office during the fugitive slave trials. At fifty-three, Dana found his practice less demanding (and more lucrative) than the one that caused his breakdown a decade earlier. Those who boycotted Dana before the Civil War sought his services.

He had more time to see his children, though now—except for twelve-year-old Angela—they were grown. The four eldest daughters were in their twenties (none had yet married) and his son was a year away from entering Harvard. Twenty-year-old Elizabeth ("Lily") noted in her diary: "I have forgotten to write down how lovely and kind Father is & how two or three times he has come home early with tickets to something he had heard me say I should like to see." Dana was always an affectionate father ("a man of sweet disposition," said his son), and the realization of the lost time with his children came late. To one who witnessed the unremitting pressure of Dana's practice when the Dana family was young, the sacrifice of domestic life by a man "of his kindly, bright, and affectionate nature [was] sad to contemplate."[21]

Dana was to make another sacrifice—as sad to contemplate in retrospect. It stemmed from Dana's familial impulse and concept of duty, and it was to shadow the remaining years of his life. It began as a service to a friend. It ended fourteen years later with the declaration that "Mr. Dana had in the Wheaton litigation been a victim of the bitterest and most unrelenting persecution [the judicial master] had ever known."[22]

Henry Wheaton "combined the advantages of the discipline of a barrister, the culture of a scholar [and] the experiences of a diplomat." That combination led to the authorship of Wheaton's acclaimed treatise *Elements of International Law*. First published in Philadelphia and London in 1836, several editions followed before Wheaton's untimely death in 1848. Wheaton's surviving son, Robert, studied law in Dana's office. "I may well call him my friend! I have met no other man, except my own brother, for whom I have had [the same] feelings."[23]

In 1851 twenty-five-year-old Robert Wheaton suddenly died. "In the evening I called at the house & saw the bereaved mother & sisters. Their case is one of desolation. A father & only brother.... gone within three years & all their earthly hope... & support taken from them!" Dana received a daguerreotype of Robert from Mrs. Wheaton, "a beautiful likeness & most highly prized by me. It brings his face daily before me."[24] Mrs. Wheaton and her two daughters moved to Cambridge, where they remained close to the Dana family.

Without a legacy, Wheaton's widow depended upon the sale of her deceased husband's *Elements of International Law* for income. A wealthy lawyer from Newport, Rhode Island, offered to help. William Beach Lawrence had been a friend of her husband and proposed to annotate a new edition. The widow gratefully accepted the offer and a new edition of Wheaton's book, edited by Lawrence, was published in 1855 by Little and Brown Company of Boston.

The advent of the Civil War raised urgent and novel issues of international law that prompted Lawrence to propose another revised edition of Wheaton's *Elements*. It also fed Lawrence's inflated idea of his standing as an authority on international law. Wheaton's original text was 400 pages. Lawrence's proposed new edition was more than 1,200 pages in length.

The mass of undigested citations and lengthy quotations accumulated by Lawrence all but buried Wheaton's book. Moreover, Lawrence demanded that publisher Little and Brown title the new 1863 edition *Lawrence's Wheaton on International Law*. C. C. Little acceded to the demand when Lawrence threatened to abandon the project, but the negotiations were so acrimonious that Little—who had married one of Wheaton's daughters—refused to speak with Lawrence again.

Dana had little knowledge of the deepening rift between Lawrence and Mrs. Wheaton, but he was familiar with the 1863 edition of *Lawrence's Wheaton*. Dana respected neither the edition nor the author. Indeed, a part Dana's impetus for publishing the pamphlet "What the Supreme Court Decided in the Prize Causes," which had so caught Lincoln's eye, was to refute Lawrence's claim that the *Prize Cases* recognized the right of secession. Lawrence's sympathy for the South was evident in his 1863 edition and was another reason for the Wheatons' displeasure with Lawrence.

Little and Brown, prompted by C. C. Little's hope of freeing his mother-in-law from the stigma Lawrence's editions had attached to her late husband's work, sought a new editor for a new edition. Mrs. Wheaton first asked Charles Sumner, who declined. She then turned to Dana, who initially refused because of his responsibilities as U.S. attorney. Mrs. Wheaton persisted and Dana finally agreed, "drawn to it from my interest in the subject and . . . friendship for the family." Dana worked "at my study in Cambridge, which for two years was a workshop and depot of international law."[25]

The happier result was the publication in 1866 of the eighth edition of *Wheaton's Elements of International Law*. Dana wrote more than 250 essay notes, on issues ranging from prize law to the Monroe Doctrine. The edition was widely acclaimed. Harvard conferred an honorary Doctor of Laws on Dana for the work. Seventy years later, Dana's edition was still valuable enough to be republished by the Carnegie Endowment for International Peace.[26]

If Dana could have foreseen the travail ahead, he would surely have foregone the honorary degree and future recognition. The first inkling of trouble was witnessed by Charles Francis Adams Jr., who in August 1866 joined Dana as a fellow passenger returning from Europe. Aboard ship "Dana tossed across to me a few newspaper clips which he had just received from America." Lawrence had publicly accused Dana of plagiarism. "I well remember the complete indifference with which he treated the whole matter," wrote Adams.[27]

In a world where slights did not turn into lawsuits, or litigation into vendettas, Dana would have been perfectly secure. But Dana did not live in such a world—though he was often the last to realize it. William Beach Lawrence was a species of litigant familiar to judges. Blind to any view but his own, obsessed with vindication by judicial ruling, and possessing unlimited means to fund court battles, Lawrence sought to try Dana by ordeal.

The ordeal began in October 1866 when Lawrence filed suit in the U.S. Circuit Court in Boston alleging that Little and Brown, Mrs. Wheaton, and Dana infringed on Lawrence's copyright interest in *Wheaton's Elements of International Law*. As far as Dana knew, the copyright of the several editions, including those edited by Lawrence, belonged to Mrs. Wheaton. Dana's introduction to the 1866 edition asserted, "This edition contains nothing but the text of Mr. Wheaton . . . his notes, and the original matter [I have] contributed. . . . The notes of Mr. Lawrence do not form any part of this edition."[28]

Dana's last unfortunate sentence was an accurate description, if by "notes" one meant—as Dana certainly did—original material contributed by the editor. The only resemblance between the Dana and Wheaton editions, said the judicial master who spent (literally) years in examining the books, was "that they were both printed on paper and bound in calf."[29] Lawrence, however, alleged that "notes" also meant the citations to cases, authorities, and treatises contained in annotations.

Lawrence could not plausibly establish a legal basis for his sweeping allegation of "literary piracy" (although that did not stop him from circulating the charges), but he had a basis for a copyright claim of which

Dana was unaware. In 1863 Lawrence had attempted to get Mrs. Wheaton to transfer the entire copyright for *Wheaton* to him. She refused but under financial pressure from Lawrence signed a memorandum that she would "agree to formally make no use of Mr. Lawrence's notes in a new edition without his written consent."[30]

The memorandum was an attempt by a neighbor, Harvard law professor Theo Parsons, to induce Lawrence to stop hounding the widow and to release to her money from the sale of a previous edition. Professor Parsons received a lengthy diatribe from Lawrence, who had become aware of Dana's work on a new edition. Parsons forwarded it to Dana, who replied, "If you can show me any reason I should read a letter of forty pages addressed to yourself which you won't take the trouble to read . . . answer or keep the document."[31]

In early 1866 an agitated Lawrence had appeared at Dana's office demanding to know if Dana was working on a new edition of *Wheaton*. When told by Dana that a new edition was to be published in a few months, Lawrence's agitation increased (Lawrence "was not regarded as conspicuous for his amiability").[32] Dana coolly informed Lawrence that any objection should be raised with Mrs. Wheaton and that he would complete the work unless stopped by her.

Dana could not know it, but seeds were now planted for a lawsuit that would ensnarl him for more than a decade. The case could grow only if a judge accepted two arguments of Lawrence: first, that the memorandum signed by Mrs. Wheaton conveyed a copyright interest to Lawrence even though it was never reduced to a formal agreement; and second that Dana had knowledge of the memorandum. Each of the possibilities was remote—unless Dana was unlucky enough to appear before a particularly hostile judge.

The presiding judge in the matter of *Lawrence v. Dana* was U.S. Supreme Court Justice Nathan Clifford. "That there was little love lost between Mr. Dana and Judge Clifford admits of no doubt," observed a contemporary of both. Dana was more direct: "Clifford hated me because . . . [of] the Prize Cases and [because I] never flattered him as most of the bar did."[33]

Still, even a personally hostile judge must have a basis for his decision beyond his dislike for a litigant. Lawrence had the resources to provide the basis. He permanently employed a lawyer whose sole function was to compare every annotation made in Dana's edition of *Wheaton* with every annotation made in Lawrence's. Unsurprisingly, there was considerable overlap (because both Dana and Lawrence were bound to cite similar cases and authorities when annotating a legal treatise on the same subject). In fact, according to Lawrence's view, there were over 600 pages of examples of Dana's use of Lawrence's notes.

There was virtually no way to respond to the "appalling labor" the obsessive Lawrence funded, though Dana was required to answer as best he could in the time he had. When the case was set for a hearing, the filing exceeded 1,000 pages. Dana attested under oath, "I never did in one instance, take a paragraph, note, sentence or clause of Mr. Lawrence's composition," but it was not enough.[34] To an almost limitless allegation of infringement was added the best legal talent Lawrence could buy. None other than Benjamin R. Curtis, former justice of the U.S. Supreme Court, and Dana's adversary from the fugitive slave days, appeared for Lawrence.[35]

With a different judge, Dana may have been spared testifying at all. But Judge Clifford concluded that the court sitting in equity would benefit from hearing Dana defend himself. A witness compelled to testify at length about voluminous material seldom remains unscathed at the hands of a trial attorney skilled in cross-examination. Curtis was extremely skilled. On the stand Dana conceded, for example, that he relied on some documents that had been translated into English without realizing that Lawrence had done the translation. The mistakes were trivial, but the almost incalculable amount of material could not be answered point by point.

Dana's reliance on his integrity ("It is not from such a man we are to expect a violation of literary privilege," asserted his lawyer) was not well calculated to persuade Judge Clifford. The judge certainly remembered an episode years before when Dana castigated Clifford for appointing an unqualified crony to a clerkship. Clifford undoubtedly took some satisfaction in observing that Dana's character defense "[did] not . . . rebut the particular proofs of the complainant."[36]

Thus, in September 1869 the fifty-four-year-old Dana, less than a year removed from his devastating loss to Butler, found himself awaiting a decision by an adverse court. "I well remember meeting Mr. Dana in his office the very day . . . he first learned of the . . . opinion of the court," wrote Charles Francis Adams Jr. "Though I had known him long and well, and had been witness to his bearing under many trying conditions, never until then had I seen him really discouraged and disheartened."[37]

It was the worst of all results. The court found that there was merit to Lawrence's claim, but could not determine how much. Judge Clifford concluded that the memorandum provided Lawrence an equitable right to a claim of copyright infringement, and further, that Dana had constructive notice of the claim (because Dana did not make further inquiry after returning the letter from Professor Parsons). The court refused to grant Lawrence his request for an injunction to stop the sale of Dana's edition of *Wheaton,* but the question of whether Dana's annotations infringed any right of Lawrence was referred to a judicial master.

Dana's dilemma was well put by Adams: "He stood convicted . . . but with sentence deferred until the extent of his misdeeds should be definitely ascertained. It might amount to nothing at all, or it might amount to a great deal; but until . . . the report of the master . . . ascertained whether it was one or the other, he was exposed at any time to attacks almost impossible to meet."[38]

The extent and length of the damage that the exposure caused Dana could scarcely be imagined (Sumner wrote Dana, "I have always thought that your only offense was in undertaking the work"). More than a decade later, Dana knew himself well enough to realize one of the causes. Writing to a friend, Dana said of Judge Clifford, "I treated him too much as I felt towards him, as has been too much my way with people, and which is not Christian nor wise."[39]

That realization was to come later. In 1869 Dana confronted the reality that "the subject [which] had occupied his mind to the exclusion of almost everything else . . . must now be gone over again before a new tribunal."[40] Lawrence had unlimited leisure and unlimited funds. Dana had neither. There was little choice for Dana but to accept the burden—as he had accepted the burden of hauling hides as a common seaman. But Dana was now entering that time of life when one is most likely to question the purpose of the voyage. Within the space of a year Dana had been found wanting in an election and in a court of law—two forums in which he placed the hopes of his professional life.

Dana's world was altered in other ways as well. In 1869 his brother Ned—three years younger than Dana—died at age fifty. Ned had been a burden from the days of his failed law partnership with his older brother, to his eight years of wandering abroad at Dana's expense. After returning home at age thirty-eight, Ned lived as a semi-invalid, dependent on Dana's income. But Dana was always devoted to his little brother. Oliver Wendell Holmes Sr.'s first memory of Dana was of "a little, rosy-faced, sturdy boy, piloting an atom of a lesser brother, Edmund, to and from the school-house."[41] Now the lesser atom was gone.

The copyright for *Two Years Before the Mast* at last reverted to Dana and his own edition was published. He had received unsolicited advice over the years of how to "improve" the book, including a visit from Horace Mann, who insisted that narrative had no value unless it conveyed useful facts and moral lessons. To "the schoolmaster gone crazy," Dana replied that the book "had *life* & the course he suggested would stop the circulation of the blood." Dana replaced the original concluding chapter of recommendations to improve working conditions of seamen with the much livelier "Twenty-Four Years After" describing his return to California in 1859.[42]

By the summer of 1870, Dana was worn down. Again it was August when he made his escape. Traveling to Scotland, Dana left the "tiresome hotels" with their "waiters in black coats and white ties." Dana longed "for an inn where I can have my chop and all to myself, with a neat 'Mary' or 'Lassie' to wait on me." Apparently he found it, for Dana was soon writing lyrical descriptions of the countryside to Sarah: "You will say I am bewitched by Scotland. I admit it."[43]

Invigorated by long hikes, Dana was also pleased that in England, at least, he was still thought an important American. Prime Minister William Gladstone met him for dinner, though it was not the social season and the Franco-Prussian War at its height. Dana returned home in early September, revived by his travel: "I had my usual luck; for, though in nothing else, I am lucky as a traveler."[44]

"Nothing else" included ill luck with money. Part of the reason was Dana's disinterest. He wrote to one of Sarah's relatives (who were always interested in Dana's financial status): "Wealth never attracted me. I like honor. I like adventure. I like romance, but I believe I am indifferent to wealth." In the crisis of midlife, Dana's perspective altered: "In my youth I thought it a fine thing to despise money, but forgot that I needed and ought to have the opportunities which cannot honestly be had without money, and I learned too late (as most learning by experience comes) that pecuniary anxieties disable a man in middle life more than ill health, or sorrows, or overwork."[45]

The "disability" began to lessen in 1871. Dana had retained land in Cambridge that became increasingly valuable as Boston expanded. Sale of these holdings, coupled with bequests from his aunts (who all their lives mourned the deaths of the brothers they were to have married), provided Dana with more financial freedom than he had ever had. The sale of his Cambridge house and an unexpected $10,000 inheritance from Ned, who was thought to be penniless, enabled Dana to reassess his plans. "Money has a great effect on my spirits," he reported to Sarah.[46]

The building boom and bequests had come too late for Dana's hope of elective office, but there was an opportunity abroad that appeared ideally suited to Dana's desire to exercise his talents on behalf of the public good. Hamilton Fish, Grant's secretary of state, negotiated the 1871 "Treaty of Washington" with England. Designed to resolve fishing and border disputes with Canada (then a part of the British Empire), the treaty also contained provisions to arbitrate claims of the United States against Great Britain arising out of the Civil War.

The "Alabama Claims" stemmed from the failure of the British government to prevent the construction and transfer of warships to the Confederacy despite the objections of the Union. The C.S.S. *Alabama* captured, sank, or destroyed more than sixty vessels before finally being sunk by the U.S.S. *Kearsage* in 1864. Under the terms of the treaty, a tribunal was to be established to decide the extent of the damages to be allowed the United States for the destruction caused by the *Alabama* (and other warships) constructed in England and used by the Confederacy.

Secretary of State Fish was to appoint an American representative to the tribunal, as well as two lawyers to represent the United States. Dana had great hopes of being selected to participate in the proceedings, which were to take place in Geneva, Switzerland. The expectation was well founded because the issues before the tribunal involved prize, maritime, and international law, all subjects of which Dana was a master. There was an added interest. Dana's old ship the *Alert* was sunk by the *Alabama*. "I love to think that our noble ship," wrote Dana, ". . . should have passed at her death, into the lofty regions of international jurisprudence and debate, forming a body of the 'Alabama Claims.'"[47]

Dana believed he had an excellent chance of being appointed to the tribunal, but was sure that if not, he would be offered one of the two counsel appointments. Sumner appeared to think so as well, writing to Dana, "The claims question with England will probably be one of the greatest international litigation trials in history." Dana was confident enough of his prospects to send Sarah and a daughter to Europe in advance. "It would be joyous . . . to go to Geneva on the great cause of the century," Dana wrote to daughter Elizabeth.[48]

The choice for American representative to the tribunal narrowed to Dana and Charles Francis Adams Sr., the American minister to England during the Civil War who protested the British government's failure to halt the departure of the *Alabama*. President Grant preferred Dana but left the decision to his secretary of state. Fish selected Adams, and appointed William Evarts to one of the two lawyer positions. Evarts expected Dana—with whom he had worked on the *Prize Cases* and Jefferson Davis prosecution—to be named the other lawyer.

Dana was not chosen. There could be only one explanation for the seemingly inexplicable result. Dana suspected it. He believed the secretary of state feared "the row Lawrence & his rabid Democratic friends would make." Dana was right. Lawrence had written an eight-page letter to Fish alleging that Dana was attempting to "evade his sentence by getting beyond the jurisdiction of the Court [in the Wheaton litigation]."[49]

Lawrence had once been a law partner with Fish. That did not mean the secretary of state gave credence to Lawrence's allegations. It meant something more serious—that Fish knew Lawrence's capacity to cause trouble. The Grant administration did not intend to go to the mat for Dana over a position of little consequence to it. But the time was to come when the president and secretary of state would fight desperately for Dana—and William Beach Lawrence would demonstrate how much trouble he could really make.

"Each man rates himself when he ships," wrote Dana in *The Seaman's Friend*. To misrepresent one's seafaring experience was an act of deception "to which . . . little mercy is shown on board ship." By 1873 Dana was well past the midpoint of his voyage. He was never an easy judge of others—or himself. The rating the fifty-seven-year-old Dana assigned to his passage was harsh: "My life has been a failure, compared with what I might and ought to have done."[50]

Dana was candid in his analysis of the reasons: "I could have prob-ably gone to Congress, and I am sure I should have distinguished my-self. But I had no money, and was obliged to refuse the offers of my friends. That was the career for me. I have no right to lay the fault wholly on the people and our institutions. I had my chance, and my want of means which was my own fault—certainly not the fault of the public—precluded me." Dana dismissed his "great success—my book" as "a boy's work done before I came to the Bar." The crisis of midlife prompted a melancholy letter to Sarah: "I took a long ride on horseback . . . [and thought of] your disappointments and my unintended neglects . . . and[my] fear that if I did not *work all the time* I should come to distress. Oh, it made me very sad."[51]

Dana's rating was the expression of a disappointed man but not an embittered one. His spirit was too buoyant to sink in self-pity. There was much in his life to enjoy. At a gathering of the Saturday Club, Dana was touched by Emerson's graciousness in asking for unanimous consent to make Dana's father, whom Dana had brought as a guest, an honorary member of the Club. The spring of 1874 brought news of Sumner's death. Longfellow, on behalf of Sumner's literary trustees, asked Dana if he would write Sumner's biography. Dana declined but replied, "This mark of confidence [is] one of the highest honors of life."[52]

On August 1, 1875, Dana turned sixty. His midlife melancholia evap-orated. "I cannot say I feel the touch of time," he wrote Sarah. "On the contrary, I really feel younger and more as if I had life before me than I have at anytime in the last eight years."[53] Dana must have believed he was prescient when a few months later he received a telegram with the most extraordinary news: President Grant had nominated Dana to be the American minister to England and sent his name to the U.S. Senate for confirmation.

24

ONE OF THEM DAMN
LITERARY FELLERS

The telegram bringing word of Dana's nomination to the Court of St. James's was the most joyful surprise of his professional life. "It comes to me unsought by me or any friend, the spontaneous act of the Administration." At least as rewarding was the nearly unanimous enthusiasm for the nomination from both sides of the Atlantic. The *New York Tribune* declared Dana's nomination "an agreeable surprise to Washington . . . the selection has been spoken of as good one and the Senate will without doubt promptly confirm it." The *London Times* reported, "Mr. Dana will on many accounts be welcome here," a sentiment echoed by the *London Daily News,* which noted, "The appointment . . . is said to have been generally approved in America and will give no less satisfaction here."[1]

To Dana it was—at last—evidence that merit trumped mendacity, and principles mattered more than politics. Dana asked Charles Francis Adams Sr. for guidance on ministerial dress and protocol. The expenses of the London mission were considerable, and Dana began economies at home to prepare for the move. In common with those who receive a universally praised nomination requiring legislative confirmation, Dana's real concern was that the vote might not be unanimous.

The confirmation process started with review by the Senate Committee on Foreign Relations, chaired by Senator Simon Cameron (Republican, Pennsylvania). The seventy-seven-year-old Cameron was one of the most powerful figures in the Senate. It was Cameron who reputedly defined "an honest politician" as "one who once bought, stays bought." If that political wisdom did not originate with Cameron, none could doubt his familiarity with the principle. Some thought Abraham Lincoln owed his nomination to Cameron's delivery of the Pennsylvania delegation at the 1860 Republican Convention. Certainly President Lincoln did not appoint Cameron as secretary of war as a reward for Cameron's military expertise or integrity—Cameron displayed neither, and in 1862 Lincoln dismissed him amid rumors of corruption.

By the time of Dana's nomination in 1876, Senator Cameron's skills were highly valued. The greatest challenge for professional politicians was how to succeed in a world the amateurs were ruining. Eight years of the Grant administration promoted corruption on a scale that staggered even old pros like Simon Cameron. President Grant found himself in need of "an impeccable successor" to his minister to England, Robert Schenk, who had persuaded prominent Englishmen to invest in a worthless Utah silver mine. For his services, proponents of the swindle paid Schenk $50,000. English investors were out $5,000,000. Grant—always loyal to his former army associates (Schenk was a Union general)—gave his friend time to escape England before directing Secretary of State Fish to recommend a replacement.[2]

The secretary of state was the most competent and honest member of Grant's cabinet—"a jewel in the head of a toad" in one historian's vivid description.[3] Fish knew that Dana's old nemesis Lawrence would object to Dana's nomination, but it had been five years since Lawrence's venomous threats to derail Dana's appointment as legal counsel in the Alabama Claims case. Even Benjamin Butler—notorious for settling scores with past political rivals—said privately Dana was "a good selection."[4]

"Democracy, rightly understood," wrote Henry Adams, "is the government of the people, by the people, for the benefit of Senators."[5] From the outset, rumors circulated that Dana's nomination "interfered with other arrangements contemplated by certain Senators."[6] The Grant administration had not informed Cameron in advance of Dana's nomination. The senator had "other arrangements" in mind, but they could be advanced only if he was lucky enough to find accomplices.

One week after Dana received his wonderful news, William Beach Lawrence and Benjamin Butler asked to appear before a secret session of the Committee on Foreign Relations to provide "evidence" of Dana's unfitness to be minister to England. Senator Cameron delightedly obliged. Lawrence's animus boiled over at the prospect of Dana receiving the most prestigious foreign post the country could bestow. Incredibly, the Wheaton litigation was still pending. The judicial master was in his seventh year of examining the thousands of citations Lawrence claimed Dana had infringed. Butler now saw an opportunity to embarrass two political enemies—Dana and Grant.

Even a legislative committee predisposed to act adversely on a nominee could not be expected to wade through the obsessive Lawrence's countless allegations. Cameron's committee needed a sharper instrument. The weapon they were provided bore all the marks of Butler's instinct for the jugular. The hundreds of pages of Dana's testimony in the Wheaton hearing contained Dana's statement that, "from the beginning to the end, [my brother and I] did not have, before us, nor in the house, nor did we look at Mr. Lawrence's *Wheaton.*" Butler alleged this was perjury.[7]

In fact, as Lawrence well knew, Dana was responding to the question of whether he consulted Lawrence's edition when at his father's house discussing his notes with his brother. Dana had never denied looking at Lawrence's edition—in fact, one of Lawrence's allegations rested on Dana's statement that he had examined Lawrence's text. Neither Butler nor Lawrence cared to make this distinction.

Dana was still basking in the glow of congratulatory notes ("There are two places for which I have always thought you preeminently fit. One is the Massachusetts senatorship & the other has just been offered you," wrote James Russell Lowell) when he received his first warning of trouble. Dana knew that "my maligner and enemy Mr. Beach Lawrence is at Washington doing his utmost to defeat my nomination. . . . I cannot think the Senate will give much heed." Congressman Henry Pierce of Boston telegraphed Dana that opposition seemed to be building, adding ominously, "Clifford, Lawrence, and Butler are the moving spirits."[8]

What mischief Justice Clifford—the judge in the Wheaton litigation—was up to remained unclear, but Dana knew the trouble Lawrence and Butler could cause. Unaware that the committee had already held a clandestine hearing, Dana sent a telegram to Massachusetts Senator George Boutwell: "IF CHARGES ARE MADE AGAINST ME I DEMAND A HEARING BEFORE THE COMMITTEE."[9] But the committee had already "instructed" Senator Cameron to inform the president that it intended to report adversely on Dana, and to ask Grant to withdraw the nomination.

Secretary of State Fish was outraged: "During the seven years I have been here, no nomination has been made which has received a more emphatic . . . approval from the public. What inducement is there to the President to seek persons of the highest character and qualification to be thus slaughtered in the house of their friends."[10] Fish informed Dana that the Senate Committee on Foreign Relations had already taken testimony from Lawrence and Butler. On March 16 Dana wrote to Senator Boutwell: "When I first heard that charges were to be made against me before the committee, my impulse was to demand a hearing. . . . I did not then know what the committee had done. . . . This morning I learn the facts authentically for the first time. I learn that the committee did give a secret *ex parte* hearing to two men known to be my enemies on personal grounds and on that hearing alone came to an adverse decision and acted upon it. They had no intention of seeking information from me or my friends." Dana continued: "I trust my dear Mr. Boutwell, that you know me well enough to know that I shall not ask to be heard before the committee under such circumstances. . . . There is nothing in the gift of the government which would induce me to go to Washington and submit a question touching my honor to a committee which has taken the course which has been taken by the Senate Committee on Foreign Relations."[11] The *Boston Evening Transcript* described the letter as "highly characteristic of its author, Danaish throughout, bold verging on audacity."[12]

Secretary of State Fish persuaded Grant not to withdraw Dana's name. A brief flurry of activity by Dana's supporters prompted him to ask Senator Boutwell to hold the "honor" letter. At the urging of friends, Dana dispatched to Washington the lawyer who appeared for him in the Wheaton litigation. It was a fool's errand, because even those few senators willing to meet with Dana's attorney could not digest the mountains of material necessary to rebut Lawrence. Butler, who was no longer in Congress, had a more effective tactic.

On Saturday, March 18, the *New York Tribune* printed a letter from General Butler that was a full-scale attack on Dana. Butler's double fusillade alleged literary piracy and perjury. Butler—never at a loss for the piquant phrase—summed up the allegation: "The gravamen of Mr. Dana's offence was not so much that of pirating the book, but that he swore he didn't." Dana recognized that the confirmation process had been—in his own pungent expression—"butlerized." Butler left nothing to chance, writing to a former army colleague who was now a senator from Alabama: "See Senators Clayton and Dorsey (both from Arkansas) for me and say that I will take it as a personal favor if they will interpose between me and my opponent for many years, Mr. Dana."[13]

Dana's March 16 letter to Senator Boutwell asserted, "I do not wish my nomination withdrawn. . . . If the Senate reject it . . . I trust I shall not fail of grace to submit with equanimity." Dana authorized release of the letter, later explaining to his son, "My only course was to refuse to go, and to give the true reason for it to the whole world. This enabled me to go down with flags flying and guns firing." *Harper's Weekly,* at least, agreed: "For Mr. Dana . . . to have written the letter is under the circumstances, a greater honor than to be minister of England."[14]

Conventional wisdom, then and later, concluded that Dana's refusal to appear before the committee scuttled his chance to be confirmed. "It is possible that was so," Dana wrote to his son, "[but] the humiliation of going before such a committee to vindicate my character against charges by Butler—a great office being the prize! . . . I cannot do it; my father could not do it, my grandfather could not have done it; nor his father, and my son would not have done it."[15]

Dana's nomination was sunk on April 4, 1876, in a closed-door session of the full Senate by a vote of 31-17. A coalition of Republican senators led by Cameron was unanimously joined by Democrats who were delighted to add to the embarrassment of Grant. Senator Cameron made good use of Dana's letter, having it read twice by the clerk to remind the Senate of Dana's affront to the committee. The *New York Evening Post* declared "a more disgraceful act was never committed by any legislative body than has just been committed by the Senate of the United States in the rejection of Mr. Dana." Mark Twain observed: "Noble system truly where a man like Richard Henry Dana can't be confirmed."[16]

There was more at work in Simon Cameron's rejection of Dana than the easily ridiculed letter of honor. Henry Adams—who scrupulously avoided the contact sport of politics—was a student of the game. A Cameron, he observed, was "the strongest American in America . . . because he understood his own class, who were always a majority, and knew how to deal with them, as no New Englander could." The Cameron machine "worked by coarse means on coarse interests."[17]

Six weeks after Dana's nomination was rejected, a curious reshuffling occurred in Grant's cabinet. Attorney General Edwards Pierrepont was nominated and easily confirmed as minister to England. Secretary of War Alfonso Taft—who had held the office for less than three months—became attorney general. The newly created vacancy in the post of secretary of war was filled by a forty-three-year-old "industrialist" without military experience.

As easily confirmed as Pierrepont and Taft, President Grant's new secretary of war was James "Don" Cameron, the son of Senator Simon Cameron. "It is asserted by those who pretend to know," reported the *Boston Herald* when the cabinet appointments were announced, "that the appointment of Donald Cameron to the Cabinet was on the carpet two months ago and that the plan of getting Pierrepont sent to England was even then contemplated. This fact is said to be the real explanation of Simon Cameron's opposition to the confirmation of Mr. Dana."[18]

When Dana's nomination was first announced, the *London Daily News* had written: "It is enough for us to know that Mr. Dana is the author of *Two Years Before the Mast,* the most charming as well as the most faithful description ever penned of the life of the common sailor. . . . It revives the old tradition. . . . If a poet could array a chorus well and give them stirring words to speak, it was presumed likely he could . . . manage a squadron. . . . Talent was talent."[19] In condemning Dana's nomination (but not the phrase) to political oblivion, Senator Cameron had a more prosaic response—"he's one of them damn literary fellers ain't he?"[20]

"I have made mistakes in life, but this is not one of them," Dana wrote to his son in explaining his refusal to testify before the Senate Foreign Relations Committee. Dana rightly concluded, "They would have degraded me and defeated my nomination both." He added, "Don't let this make you feel any the less patriotic. It only shows how much more the country needs the services of good men—how much the rising generation has to do for their State."[21]

The excesses of the Grant administration and the Senate's shabby treatment prompted Massachusetts "reform Republicans" to select Dana as a delegate-at-large to the 1876 Republican Convention. It was Dana's first political convention since his participation in Free Soil's Buffalo convention of 1848. The *New York Evening Post* considered Dana more than a delegate: "The people of the United States may elect him [vice-president]. 'Bristow and Dana' is not a hard-sounding phrase: suppose that before the end of the year we should hear it from a million mouths!"[22]

Dana, in fact, seconded the nomination of Benjamin Bristow, who much to the dismay of the Grant administration had used his position as secretary of the treasury to uncover the notorious "Whiskey Ring," a corrupt network of revenue officers, distillers, and treasury officials. The convention became a contest between James G. Blaine, closely identified with the corruption of the past eight years, and those determined to deny Blaine the nomination. On the seventh ballot, delegates coalesced behind Ohio governor Rutherford B. Hayes. Dana was instrumental in shifting Bristow delegates to Hayes, and met with the nominee. Dana told Hayes, "All we care about is reform."[23]

Hayes and the Democratic nominee, Samuel Tilden, portrayed themselves as reformers—with sufficient success to split the electoral vote and prompt the most corrupt presidential selection process in the nation's history. When the dust cleared, Hayes and the Republicans had been more adept than Tilden and the Democrats in procuring the required 185 electoral votes. The selection of Hayes (who had lost the popular vote) delighted Dana, not least because the new secretary of state was his old friend William Evarts.

Dana began to believe that a chance to perform great service for his country might be at hand. Discreet inquiries to the president and Evarts drew little more than vague assurances that the administration recognized his interest. Hayes owed more to others. But when the president came to Cambridge in June 1877 to accept an honorary degree, it was awkward to have nothing to offer to Dana, who hosted the president as a member of the Harvard Board of Overseers. The secretary of state had news for Dana. "Evarts said no word about foreign missions," Dana wrote to his daughter Charlotte, "but wishes me to engage in some professional work for the government, which is dignified and lucrative . . . At present a secret and not fully settled."[24]

Ironically, the position the Hayes administration offered to Dana arose from the 1871 Treaty of Washington that had prompted his unrealized desire to represent the United States in the Alabama Claims. Like the offer Dana had hoped to receive a half-dozen years before, he was to be counsel for the United States in arbitration proceedings before an international tribunal charged with resolving a dispute between countries. But the issue at stake was not the historic question of the obligation of England to America for reparations arising from the dramatic sea raids of the C.S.S. *Alabama*. Nor were the proceedings to be held in one of the great cities of Europe. Dana was asked to go to Halifax, Nova Scotia, to represent the United States in a quarrel with Canada over the value of mackerel.

The question was part of a long-standing trade controversy over the right of American fishing fleets to fish within the three-mile limit off the eastern coast of Canada. The Treaty of Washington—much to the displeasure of Canadian fishermen—provided Americans the right to fish the inshore banks. In return the United States agreed to eliminate tariffs on fish imported from Canada. Canadians believed the exchange to be unfair. The arbitration hearings were to determine if any money was due Canada, an issue that ultimately turned on the value of taking mackerel in Canadian waters.[25]

Dana accepted the appointment as counsel. One measure of its lack of prestige was Lawrence's apparent silence. But Dana reasonably assumed that Evarts was making the best offer available. Success in the arbitration—which Dana and the secretary of state fully expected—would enable Evarts to offer Dana a post of far greater significance.

Dana had always enjoyed Halifax, though some of its attractions of his earlier days were off limits now that Sarah and his youngest daughter were with him. The proceedings lacked the significance of the Alabama Claims arbitration, but they were not without interest to Dana. Characteristically, he immersed himself in the deep waters of three-mile limits, feeding habits of North Atlantic fish, and the economies of New England and Canadian fisheries.

The three-member tribunal appeared less interested. The American representative, Ensign Kellogg, was—notwithstanding his name—neither naval nor young. Kellogg was an elderly Whig who disconcertingly dozed while witnesses testified. The "neutral' member was Baron Maurice Delfosse, Belgian ambassador to the United States, to whom the State Department unsuccessfully objected as too favorable to British interests. By far the most vigorous member was Canadian Alexander Galt, who impressed Dana with his intelligence, energy, and pedigree.

The 1877 hearings began in the summer and lasted five months—in large part due to Dana's diligence. Dana's eight-hour closing argument lasted two days and served as a masterful summation of the extraordinary case he presented. Dana decimated Canada's claim for compensation, proving that the United States had given Canadians greater value in eliminating the tariffs than Americans received in the right to take mackerel within the three-mile limit.

Dana never exercised less than the full extent of his powers, irrespective of the case or controversy, and he did nothing less for mackerel. To the Canadian assertion that the wealth of Gloucester, Massachusetts, depended on the ease with which their boats took mackerel in Canadian bays, Dana responded: "Gloucester is a town full of widows and orphans, whose husbands and parents have laid their bones upon this coast, and upon its rocks and reefs, trusting too much to the appearance of fine weather as we all did last night, waking up this morning in a tempest."[26]

Nor was Dana oblivious to the capacity of his tribunal. To the question "How is the three-mile line to be determined?" Dana sought to put the arbitrators at ease with their confusion: "My purpose in making these remarks is, in part, to show your Honors . . . [that] international law makes no attempt to define what is 'coast.' We know well enough what a straight coast is . . . but the moment that the jurists come to bays, harbors, gulfs, and seas they are utterly afloat—as much so as the seaweed that is swimming up and down the channels."[27]

With the case submitted to the tribunal, Dana expected to wait several weeks for the arbitrators to sift through the voluminous exhibits and testimony. But on November 23, 1877—after only a single day's deliberations—the tribunal announced it had reached a decision. The arbitrators concluded that Canada was entitled to damages of $4,500,000. Dana was stunned. The tribunal provided no basis for its calculation. Dana immediately protested to the American member, the ineffectual Ensign Kellogg, that such an award ought not to be signed. Kellogg withdrew his consent, whereupon Alexander Galt and

Baron Delfosse issued a new order adding $1,000,000 to the damages due Canada.

It was a bizarre and inexplicable result. Dana grasped for a rationale as he attempted to explain the verdict to an astonished secretary of state. Evarts knew Dana's legal talent well enough not to fault him for his advocacy, but the excuses of Ensign Kellogg's woefulness and unfavorable wording of some provisions of the Treaty must have seemed as hollow to Evarts as they did to Dana. Both understood that the result ended any real possibility of Dana being asked to serve his country again. Dana did what he had always done—he went back to his "day's work." But one who knew him well noted that "the glad confidence of morning was . . . gone."[28]

"So far as Mr. Dana was concerned," wrote Charles Francis Adams Jr., "the chief result . . . was the agreeable relation, then established between himself, and members of his family and the family of Sir Alexander Galt . . . for whom personally, Mr. Dana conceived a high regard."[29] A Galt daughter was hosted by Dana before her wedding to a member of the Brahmin aristocracy.

Dana's "high regard" for Galt would have been considerably diminished had he known the explanation for the Halifax result. The British government had stacked the tribunal. The "neutral" Baron Delfosse "was fully trusted by the [British] Foreign Office." Galt was more than trusted—he was working on behalf of the British. Galt looked to the British Foreign Office for instruction and advised Canadian lawyers on the witnesses and evidence to be presented during the hearings.[30]

Galt's biographer lamely rationalized that, as member of the three-judge panel, Galt "wished to give a fair and impartial verdict [but was] convinced that an impartial verdict involved the recognition of the justice of his country's case."[31] For his services Alexander Galt was decorated in one of the English ceremonies Dana so admired. The best people always seemed to have the touch.

25

LAST VOYAGE

"Yes! I have taken the great step of giving up my profession and home to spend time enough in Europe to write my own work on international law. I am sixty-two-years-old ... my physician ... predicts for me a long life," an exuberant Dana wrote to James Russell Lowell in August 1878. Dana told Lowell, "I shall live plainly with Mrs. D. and two daughters." Charles Francis Adams Jr. saw no signs of ill health, anxiety, or disappointment when Dana departed: "On the contrary, he impressed me as being a strong, hale man of sixty, happy in his family and satisfied with his lot, enjoying the present and looking forward with satisfaction to the future."[1]

The Danas moved first to Paris, where Dana settled into a comfortable routine of working a few hours each day gathering materials for his book on international law, and enjoying the city. A cable in February 1879 brought news of the death of ninety-two-year-old Richard Henry Dana Sr., and Dana returned to Boston to settle his father's estate. His last appearance in a courtroom was a joust with Lawrence's lawyer. Dana wrote to a daughter in Paris, "To my surprise, I really enjoyed it—the old war cry and the cuts and slashes of the heady fight excited and interested me."[2]

In January 1880 the master issued his report in the *Wheaton* litigation. None of Dana's original material was found to have been taken from Lawrence and 146 allegations of gross plagiarism were reduced to fourteen instances of technical copyright infringement. The "complete vindication" came thirteen years after the case was filed and eleven years after the dispute was referred to the master.[3] But Dana was no longer concerned with his own career.

Two years earlier Dana had given Richard his law practice as a wedding gift when his son married Longfellow's daughter Edith. "Dickie" shared his father's passion for travel but not his diligence for work. Dana's former law partner, Frank Parker, complained of Richard's request to extend an already lengthy vacation because of "fatigue." "I do not see any evidence that he suffers from overwork," an exasperated Parker wrote to Dana in Paris.[4]

But Dana was a doting father, more excited to learn of his son's proximity to California than absence from a law office. "I am greatly interested to see how he likes *my* California," Dana wrote to daughter-in-law Edith while thanking her for the picture of new grandson Richard Henry Dana IV. Dana added, "In eighteen years or so, the boy will have to go round Cape Horn, for that is now about as much a duty of every Richard H. Dana as it is to be born in Cambridge."[5]

Writing from Paris, Dana asked his son to extend his trip: "Now my dear boy *you must* visit my places before you come home. . . . I want you to see Santa Barbara, San Pedro (and Pueblo de Los Angeles) and San Diego. . . . Stand on my old ground where I pegged & cut & cleaned hides." Dana advised Richard to "read my 'Twenty-Four Years After' as your guide. . . . I cannot tell you how much I depend upon you doing these things."[6]

Richard inherited few of his father's gifts but he was a dutiful son. "I reread *Two Years Before the Mast* and some parts of it several times to get all relating to these places," he wrote his father, adding, "This is the third time I have read the book and I enjoyed it this time much more than before. You know my faculties & love for reading have developed slowly."[7] Richard retraced some of his father's path, but it was not merely time that prevented him from seeing things as Dana saw them.

The Danas spent a second year in Paris but just before Christmas 1880 moved to Rome for the winter. They decided to stay in Italy. "This is . . . the land of beauty and romance . . . of vines, olives, figs, oranges and lemons, of beauty in nature and art, in the human form and movement and voice, in the blue islands, the blue wave, and the violet hillsides. . . . It is a dream of life," wrote Dana. The beauty extended to Rome's Protestant cemetery, where the couple visited the graves of Shelley and Keats. "Is this not the spot where one would wish to lie forever?" said Sarah. "It is indeed," Dana answered.[8]

They leased an apartment in Rome, first at 104 Via Frattina, then at 86 Via Sistina, both near the Spanish Steps. Dana immersed himself in research, where his working knowledge of French, German, and Italian enabled him to annotate volumes on international law in preparation for his book. A year after coming to Rome, Dana began writing. "I will tell you a secret," Dana said to Sarah on December 22: "I had all the day the most excruciating pain in my left side. All gone now."[9]

On Christmas Day, Dana went to ceremonies at St. Peter's, which delighted his sister Ruth Charlotte. "R. C.," as she was known in the family, had converted to Roman Catholicism. Sarah was always aghast at the thought Dana might follow the lead of his sister. They were originally confirmed in the Protestant Episcopal faith at St. Paul's in Boston but left because of its perceived failure to adhere to "high" Episcopalianism. (Dana was a founder of Cambridge's Church of the Advent, which adhered to the Episcopal practices he favored.) After Mass, Dana told Ruth Charlotte how well he felt, adding "I don't dare to boast for I don't know what's in store for such!"[10]

Dana had Christmas dinner in the Rome apartment of his friend William Wetmore Story. Story gave up the practice of law after writing the biography of his father, Justice Joseph Story, and was now a sculptor. He was, in fact, working on a bust of Dana. Dana enjoyed the festive gathering—he was in the high spirits that follow the disappearance of mysterious pain. On New Year's Day 1882, it returned.

Dana's physician diagnosed the discomfort as a touch of pneumonia. A day later Sarah wrote in her journal: "R. had a bad night & the pain in his chest was so violent that Dr. had to inject atropine . . . which made him wild. He talked without cessation French & Italian & everything earthy, struggling to get out of bed." Four days later, with no sign of improvement, the doctor was concerned enough to ask for a consultation. Sarah noted the new physician said "it was a dangerous complication but not imminent danger."

On January 6 Sarah wrote, "Richard was dreadfully excited & full of spasmodic action . . . but then in a comatose state which alarmed the doctor." At 9:30 P.M. Story came to visit and spoke to the doctor, who was about to leave. Suddenly the nurse attending Dana called for help. Sarah closed her journal entry of January 6, 1882: "And my husband was dead!"[11]

Four days later, Charles Francis Adams Jr. eulogized Dana before a somber gathering of the Massachusetts Historical Society: "He was not adapted for quiet times . . . he was no man for wire-pulling or making small points. . . . For him to succeed, it would have been necessary that he should have grown into prominence as the exponent of great principles. . . . Had this been his fortune, his courage, his quickness and resource of intellect, his aptitude for debate, his wonderful felicity of argument, language, and illustration, his love of conflict and absolute fearlessness in personal collision . . . would have . . . sustained him in place among the foremost."

Adams was measuring Dana by the achievements of Adamses. But even by that standard, "even for him, can that which he did accomplish be called really failure? I do not think so. It was merely that in his case the unusual was looked for; anything less than that was not accounted for him."[12]

But "the unusual" was the last thing Brahmin Boston looked for. James Russell Lowell, who was a "success"—assured in his own mind and by contemporaries of lasting fame as a writer and diplomat—rendered the conventional verdict on Dana: "He never had the public career he should have had . . . and it was from a quality of character pushed to excess. . . . He was a lofty-minded man, and would not meet his fellows on such terms . . . as is needful for success in a democracy. He might have been Senator from Massachusetts, Minister to England—indeed, he might have been anything but for this weakness."[13]

Sarah, recalling her conversation with her husband when they visited Rome's Protestant cemetery, decided Dana should be buried there.

When the marble stone—much simpler than the ornate monuments that surrounded it—was placed above her husband's grave, Sarah wrote in her journal, "Did not know what to think of it." Apart from "died in Rome" and Dana's name, country, dates of birth and death, there are only two words on the marker: "of Boston."

The news of Dana's death had come to E. H. Faucon, former master of the *Pilgrim* and the *Alert,* "so suddenly that I am dazed."[14] The elderly retired sea captain wrote to Richard Henry Dana III: "My first acquaintance of your father was at San Diego in July 1835. . . . His place as a boy before the mast, how he was berthed and lived and the work he had to do, I know all about. From first to last he never shirked or hung back, he was always ready."

Faucon retired to Boston, where he saw the effect of the pressures upon Dana: "He had greatly changed in appearance, & not for the better." But the captain rejoiced when, after Dana's second visit to California, "his healthy look had returned." Dana was preparing a new edition of *Two Years Before the Mast,* and "we sat up together in Cambridge, nearly the whole of winter's evening going through the whole book."

"Never from my first seeing him, did I ever know or hear of anything respecting him that was not of the highest credit," wrote Faucon. "As a frank and fearless boy who deliberately took his side without fear of the cost, spoke his mind with all plainness yet dignity and courteousness, I speak of him with the knowledge of many years."

Faucon was still "doubting the truth" that Dana was dead. The young sailor was before him: "I can see him now as distinctly as though it was this morning . . . the picture of rude health, cheeks, rosy and full and hardy, the whole face with that color given by active life, exposure to a hot sun, and all weathers."

Dana was leaving the slavish shore. The readiness is all.

NOTES

LONG   Longfellow House, Washington Headquarters National Historic
        Site, Cambridge, Massachusetts
MHS   Massachusetts Historical Society

INTRODUCTION

1. Bliss Perry, "Richard Henry Dana as a Man of Letters," *Proceedings, Cambridge Historical Society* 10 (October 26, 1915): 130.
2. Robert F. Lucid, ed., *The Journal of Richard Henry Dana, Jr.,* 3 vols. (Cambridge, MA: Harvard University Press, 1968), 1:xxxvi.
3. M. A. DeWolfe Howe, *Boston: The Place and the People* (New York: Macmillan, 1903), 295–296.
4. Charles Francis Adams, *Richard Henry Dana: A Biography,* 2 vols. (Boston: Houghton Mifflin, 1891), 1:127.
5. Ibid.
6. Philippe-Paul de Ségur quoted in Mark Danner, introduction to *Defeat: Napoleon's Russian Campaign* by Philippe-Paul de Ségur (New York: New York Review of Books, 2008), ix.

1. TRUE SPIRIT

1. Robert F. Lucid, ed., *The Journal of Richard Henry Dana, Jr.,* 3 vols. (Cambridge, MA: Harvard University Press, 1968), 1:15–16. Dana began his journal with an autobiographical sketch of his first twenty-six years, 1815–1841.
2. Charles Francis Adams, *Richard Henry Dana: A Biography,* 2 vols. (Boston: Houghton Mifflin, 1891), 1:4.

3. W. P. Cresson, *Francis Dana: A Puritan Diplomat at the Court of Catherine the Great* (New York: Dial Press, 1930), 19, 18.

4. Ibid., 385.

5. Lucid, *Journal,* 1:7–8.

6. Ibid., 8–9.

7. Ibid., 19.

8. Henry Adams, *The Education of Henry Adams* (1907; repr., New York: Vintage Books/Library of America, 1990), 17.

9. James Russell Lowell, *A Fable for Critics* (Boston: Houghton Mifflin, 1890), 61–62.

10. Lucid, *Journal,* 1:6.

11. H. W. L. Dana, "The Dana-Palmer House," *Proceedings, Cambridge Historical Society* 33 (1949–50): 10.

12. Ibid., 16.

13. Richard Henry Dana Sr., "The Son," in *The Idle Man* (New York: Wiley and Halsted, 1821), 18.

14. H. W. L. Dana, "Dana-Palmer House," 11.

15. James Russell Lowell, *Fireside Travels* (Boston: Houghton Mifflin, 1894), 36.

16. James David Hart, "The Education of Richard Henry Dana, Jr.," *New England Quarterly* 9, no. 1 (March 1936): 4–5.

17. Henry Adams, *Education,* 13.

18. Lowell, *Fireside Travels,* 28.

19. Lucid, *Journal,* 1:5.

20. Ibid.

21. Quoted in Adams, *Dana,* 1:4.

22. H. W. L. Dana. "Dana-Palmer House," 11; Lucid, *Journal,* 1:10.

23. Henry Adams, *Education,* 11; Lucid, *Journal,* 1:4

24. Lowell, *Fireside Travels,* 42.

25. Ibid., 24.

26. Cresson, *Francis Dana,* 11.

27. Quoted in Samuel Eliot Morison, *Three Centuries of Harvard* (1936; repr., Cambridge, MA.: Harvard University Press, 2001), 251.

28. Lucid, *Journal,* 1:20.

29. Morison, *Three Centuries,* 260.

30. Ibid., 118, 211, 230–232.

31. Ibid., 252

32. Lucid, *Journal,* 1:20.

33. Ibid., 1:20–22.

34. Harvard University Faculty of Arts and Sciences. Faculty Minutes 1806–1994. Vol. 11. 5 March 1832, p. 70. Harvard University Archives.

35. Lucid, *Journal,* 1:22–24.

36. Ibid., 1:22–23.

37. Ibid., 1:25; Dana to Dana Sr., 19 August 1832, quoted in Robert L. Gale, *Richard Henry Dana* (New York: Twayne, 1969), 27.

38. Lucid, *Journal,* 1:25-26.

39. Ibid., 1:26.

40. Ibid., 1:27.

2. PILGRIM

1. Richard Henry Dana Jr., *Two Years Before the Mast and Other Voyages* (New York: Library of America, 2005), 5-6.

2. Ibid., 10.

3. Ibid., 8, 11.

4. Ibid., 12.

5. Ibid., 14, 16-17, 21.

6. Ibid., 22, 25, 27.

7. Ibid., 27,28.

8. Ibid., 28-29.

9. Ibid., 30-31.

10. Ibid., 35-37 (emphasis in original).

11. Ibid., 37, 36 (emphasis in original).

12. Ibid., 40-44.

13. Ibid., 46-47, 50-51.

14. Ibid., 51, 49 (emphasis in original).

15. Ibid., 50.

16. Ibid., 54.

17. Ibid., 55-56.

18. Samuel Eliot Morison, *The Maritime History of Massachusetts, 1783–1860* (Cambridge, MA: Houghton Mifflin/Sentry, 1961), 266-268. Morison said of the sailors whose hide hauling made Boston firms wealthy, "Dana's book is their only monument—who would wish a better?" Ibid., 268.

19. Dana, *Two Years Before the Mast,* 57 (emphasis in original).

20. Ibid., 64.

21. Ibid., 69.

22. Ibid., 74.

23. Prudencia Higuera, "Trading with the Americans," in *California Heritage: An Anthology of History and Literature,* John and Laree Caughey (Los Angeles: Ward Ritchie Press, 1962), 126-128.

24. Dana, *Two Years Before the Mast,* 77.

25. Ibid., 82.

26. Ibid., 68, 76, 73.

27. Ibid., 76-77.

28. Ibid., 78-79, 166.

29. Ibid., 226, 77.

30. Ibid., 85–86.

31. Ibid., 87–88.

32. Ibid., 88–89.

33. Ibid., 90, 96.

34. Ibid., 96–100 (emphasis in the original). Dana's account of the flogging is one of the most compelling scenes in *Two Years Before the Mast*. The book's popularity prompted several sailor narratives in the antebellum period that explicitly compared the flogging of seamen to the flogging of slaves. Myra C. Glenn, "Sailor Narratives as Exposés of Flogging," in *Jack Tar's Story: The Autobiographies and Memoirs of Sailors in Antebellum America* (Cambridge: Cambridge University Press, 2010). Glenn noted that "Dana offered the most famous discussion of this issue," 112.

35. Dana, *Two Years Before the Mast,* 100. When Dana's book was published, his shipmate Ben Stimson wrote: "As regards the flogging scene, I think you have given a fair and unvarnished history of it, and if anything have been too lenient to Capt. Thompson for his brutal, cowardly, and unjustifiable conduct toward those men." Stimson to Dana, 16 March 1841, Dana Family Papers, MHS.

36. Dana, *Two Years Before the Mast,* 101.

37. Ibid., 104.

38. Ibid., 107–108.

39. Ibid., 110.

40. Ibid., 111 (emphasis in original).

41. Ibid., 223.

42. William Robert Garner, *Letters from California, 1846–1847,* ed. Donald Munro Craig (Berkeley: University of California Press, 1970), 104. Garner was as impressed as Dana with the horsemanship: "Perhaps there is no country in the world . . . where there are better riders." Ibid., 107.

43. Dana, *Two Years Before the Mast,* 111.

44. Ibid., 114.

45. Ibid., 113, 115.

46. Ibid., 115, 117.

47. Robert F. Lucid, ed., *The Journal of Richard Henry Dana, Jr.,* 3 vols. (Cambridge, MA: Harvard University Press, 1968), 1:27.

48. Dana, *Two Years Before the Mast,* 93.

49. Ibid., 117, 122.

50. Ibid., 123. To Dana the most appalling aspect of flogging was the use of a master's authority to ritualistically demean human dignity: "The ignominious character of the punishment is its sting." Dana to Haynes G. Watson, 6 March 1849, Houghton Library, Harvard University. For a perceptive analysis of Captain Thompson's flogging of Sam, see Samuel Otter, *Melville's Anatomies* (Berkeley: University of California Press, 1968). Otter observed that "Sam feels the force of the analogy between sailor and slave, and that force breaks him." 77.

51. Dana, *Two Years Before the Mast*, 131–132.

52. Ibid., 133. The promontory located about half way between Los Angeles and San Diego was known as San Juan but was named for Dana in 1894. Dana's description of the topography has prompted discussion of exact locations. See J. N. Sokolich, "Dana and the Perennial Questions," *Historical Society of Southern California Quarterly* 41, no. 1 (March 1959): 17–25.

53. Dana, *Two Years Before the Mast*, 135–137.

3. ALERT

1. Richard Henry Dana Jr., *Two Years Before the Mast and Other Voyages* (New York: Library of America, 2005) 137, 147 (emphasis in original).

2. Ibid., 139–141.

3. Ibid., 149–150.

4. Ibid., 152–153.

5. Benjamin Stimson to Dana, 16 March 1841, Dana Family Papers, MHS (emphasis in the original). Stimson teased Dana for not providing details "which might implicate yourself in some *love affair* . . . sitting at twilight on those majestic rocks with a lovely Indian girl sitting on your knee. . . . That you experienced these pleasures no one can doubt situated as you were, and knowing your love of romance." Ibid. (emphasis in original).

6. Dana, *Two Years Before the Mast*, 165.

7. Ibid., 168–169.

8. Ibid., 171, 182, 181.

9. Ibid., 185–190.

10. Ibid., 192–193.

11. Ibid., 207–209, 213.

12. Ibid., 215, 218.

13. Ibid., 220.

14. Dana to Dana Sr., 31 December 1835; Richard Henry Dana Jr., *Two Years Before the Mast, Edited from the Original Manuscript and from the First Edition, with Journals and Letters of 1834–1836 and 1859–1860*, ed. John Haskell Kemble, 2 vols. (Los Angeles: Ward Ritchie Press, 1964), 2:390–395.

15. Dana, *Two Years Before the Mast*, 222.

16. Ibid., 228–229.

17. Ibid., 229–232.

18. Ibid., 93.

19. Ibid., 234.

20. Ibid., 234–235.

21. Ibid., 239–240.

22. Ibid., 242–243.

23. Ibid., 247, 250–251.

24. Ibid., 251–252, 181.

25. Ibid., 255.

26. Ibid.

27. Ibid., 256.

28. Ibid., 256–257.

29. Ibid., 257–259.

30. Ibid., 264, 266–267.

31. Ibid., 276, 282.

32. Ibid., 282–283, 285.

33. Ibid., 283, 285, 287.

34. Ibid., 288–290.

35. Ibid., 290–291.

36. Ibid., 294.

37. Ibid., 296–297.

38. Ibid., 301, 304.

39. Ibid., 304–306 (emphasis in original).

40. Ibid., 310–311.

41. Nuttall had left Harvard in 1834 to travel west with the Wyeth expedition. Willis Linn Jepson, "The Overland Journey of Thomas Nuttall," *Madrono* 2, no. 17 (October 1934): 143–147. Dana, *Two Years Before the Mast,* 311, 272, 271.

42. Dana, *Two Years Before the Mast,* 316–317.

43. Ibid., 318.

44. Ibid., 318–319.

45. Ibid., 322.

46. Ibid., 324, 331–332.

47. Ibid., 307–308, 337.

48. Ibid., 341–342.

49. Ibid., 342–343.

50. Ibid., 343–344.

51. Ibid., 345–346.

52. Ibid., 346.

4. THE VOW

1. Robert F. Lucid, ed., *The Journal of Richard Henry Dana, Jr.,* 3 vols. (Cambridge, MA: Harvard University Press, 1968), 1:28.

2. Ibid., 1:35.

3. Ibid., 1:37.

4. Quoted in Robert F. Metzdorf, ed., *Richard Henry Dana, Jr., An Autobiographical Sketch (1815–1842)* (Hamden, CT: Shoe String Press, 1953), 2.

5. Lucid, *Journal,* 1:37.

6. R. Kent Newmyer, *Supreme Court Justice Joseph Story: Statesman of the Old Republic* (Chapel Hill: University of North Carolina Press, 1985), 239. The description of Judge Parker is attributed to Justice Story.

7. Ibid., 245.

8. Ibid., 249–250.

9. Lucid, *Journal,* 1:38; Newmyer, *Justice Story,* 261.

10. Lucid, *Journal,* 1:37.

11. Newmyer, *Justice Story,* 266; David Donald, *Charles Sumner and the Coming of the Civil War* (New York: Alfred A. Knopf, 1960), 22, 24; Lucid, *Journal,* 1:39.

12. Newmyer, *Justice Story,* 262.

13. W. W. Story, *Life and Letters of Joseph Story,* 2 vols. (Boston: Little, Brown, 1851), 2:321.

14. Newmyer, *Justice Story,* 253, 258–259.

15. Lucid, *Journal,* 1:38.

16. Kathryn Mudgett, "'Cruelty to Seamen': Richard Henry Dana Jr., Justice Story, and the Case of Nichols and Couch," *American Neptune* 62, no. 1 (Winter 2002): 47–65. The facts of the case are drawn from Mudgett's account unless otherwise noted.

17. *Boston Morning Post,* 29 May 1839.

18. Story, *Life and Letters,* 2:317.

19. Ibid., 2:314.

20. Ibid., 2:315–316.

21. Ibid., 2:316.

22. Richard Henry Dana Jr., "Cruelty to Seamen: Case of Nichols and Couch," *American Jurist and Law Magazine* 22 (October 1839): 92–107. All quoted excerpts are from Dana's article.

23. Story, *Life and Letters,* 317.

5. THE BOOK

1. Charles Francis Adams, *Richard Henry Dana: A Biography,* 2 vols. (Boston: Houghton Mifflin. 1891), 1:24.

2. Quoted in Van Wyck Brooks, *The Flowering of New England: 1815–1865* (New York: E. P. Dutton, 1936), 43.

3. Ibid., 44.

4. Quoted in H. W. L. Dana, "Allston in Cambridgeport," *Proceedings, Cambridge Historical Society* 29 (1943): 48. Allston married Martha Remington Dana, sister of Dana Sr. The two men shared an artistic temperament at odds with their culture. "All effort at originality must end either in the quaint or the monstrous," wrote Allston whose unfinished painting "Belshazzar" was decidedly the latter. Gordon S. Wood, *Empire of Liberty: A History of the Early Republic, 1789–1815* (New York: Oxford University Press, 2009), 574; Doreen Hunter, "America's First Romantics: Richard Henry Dana, Sr. and Washington Allston," *New England Quarterly* 45, no. 1 (March 1972): 3–6.

5. Richard Henry Dana Sr. to William Cullen Bryant, 13 May 1839, quoted in Robert F. Metzdorf, "The Publishing History of Richard Henry Dana's *Two Years Before the Mast,*" *Harvard Library Bulletin* (1953): 315.

6. Bryant to Dana Sr., 24 June 1839, Houghton Library, Harvard University.

7. Dana Sr. to Bryant, 12 June 1839, quoted in Metzdorf, "Publishing History," 316.

8. Dana Sr. to Dana, 29 January 1840, ibid., 317.

9. Bryant to Dana Sr., 24 June 1839, ibid., 316.

10. Dana Sr. to Bryant, 9 July 1839, ibid., 316–317.

11. Dana Sr. to Dana, 4 February 1840, ibid., 317.

12. Eugene Exman, *The Brothers Harper* (New York: Harper and Row, 1965), 106–109.

13. Dana Sr. to Dana, 4 February 1840, quoted in Metzdorf, "Publishing History," 317 (emphasis in original).

14. Dana to Dana Sr., 20 February 1840, ibid., 318.

15. Ibid.

16. Dana Sr. to Dana, 14 March 1840, quoted in Metzdorf, "Publishing History," 319.

17. Harper to Dana, 20 May 1840, ibid.

18. Robert F. Lucid, ed., *The Journal of Richard Henry Dana, Jr.,* 3 vols. (Cambridge, MA: Harvard University Press, 1968), 1:45.

19. Exman, *The Brothers Harper,* 130.

20. Lucid, *Journal,* 1:45.

21. Ibid., 1:44.

22. Brooks, *Flowering,* 115.

23. Bryant to Dana Sr., 15 October 1840, Houghton Library, Harvard University.

24. Dana Sr. to Bryant, 14 October 1840, quoted in Metzdorf, "Publishing History," 320.

25. Quoted in Lucid, *Journal,* 1:13.

26. Richard Henry Dana Jr., *Two Years Before the Mast and Other Voyages* (New York: Library of America, 2005), 351.

27. Brooks, *Flowering,* 309.

28. Dana, *Two Years Before the Mast,* 363, 356.

29. Lucid, *Journal,* 1:46.

30. Adams, *Dana,* 1:27.

6. BOSTON, BRAHMINS, AND THE BUSINESS OF LAW

1. Robert F. Lucid, ed., *The Journal of Richard Henry Dana, Jr.,* 3 vols. (Cambridge, MA: Harvard University Press, 1968), 1:46. J. Henry Harper's *The House of Harper* made no mention of grandfather Fletcher Harper's acquisition of Dana's book. Eugene Exman noted that "the brothers had a trade reputation . . . for driving a hard bargain." Eugene Exman, *The Brothers Harper* (New York: Harper and Row, 1965), 126–127.

2. Lucid, *Journal,* 1:46.

3. Ibid., 1:40–41.

4. Sarah Watson Dana Journal, 20 July 1837, Dana Family Papers, LONG.

5. Lucid, *Journal,* 1:43.

6. Ibid., 1:42.

7. Charles Francis Adams, *Richard Henry Dana: A Biography,* 2 vols. (Boston: Houghton Mifflin, 1891), 1:28.

8. Lucid, *Journal,* 1:49.

9. Henry Adams, *The Education of Henry Adams* (New York: Vintage Books/ Library of America, 1990), 35.

10. Dana to Abbott Lawrence, 14 December 1841, Dana Family Papers, Houghton Library, Harvard University.

11. Lucid, *Journal,* 1:52.

12. Quoted in David Donald, *Charles Sumner and the Coming of the Civil War* (New York: Alfred A. Knopf, 1960), 79.

13. Lucid, *Journal,* 1:51.

14. Ibid., 1:53.

15. Quoted in David B. Tyack, *George Ticknor and the Boston Brahmins* (Cambridge, MA: Harvard University Press 1967), 175.

16. Ibid., 174.

17. Josiah Quincy, *Figures of the Past* (Boston: Little, Brown, 1910), 316.

18. Lucid, *Journal,* 1:53.

19. Quincy, *Figures of the Past,* 116.

20. Quoted in Tyack, *George Ticknor,* 90.

21. M. A. DeWolfe Howe, *Boston: The Place and the People* (New York: Macmillan, 1903), 234.

22. Quoted in Tyack, *George Ticknor,* 178.

23. Quincy, *Figures of the Past,* 318.

24. Quoted in Donald, *Charles Sumner,* 29.

25. Ibid., 56.

26. Ibid., 79.

27. Lucid, *Journal,* 1:52.

28. Ibid., 1:59.

29. Quoted in Tyack, *George Ticknor,* 174.

30. Ibid., 177. Holmes first used "Brahmin" in his novel *Elsie Venner* (Boston, 1861). Its meaning as a term to signify Boston's wealthy aristocratic class was well enough understood that an anonymous author used it without definition in *Fair Harvard* (1869). Ronald Story, *The Forging of an Aristocracy: Harvard and the Boston Upper Class, 1800–1870* (Middletown, CT.: Wesleyan University Press, 1980), 196. Although the usage of "Brahmin class" did not gain currency until the 1860s, it may be taken to represent social elites in the "Whig Aristocracy" and "Boston Associates" who held political and economic power in antebellum Boston. Ibid., 4.

31. Quoted in Tyack, *George Ticknor,* 177. Tyack observed that "the rapid social rise of the patricians—the Cabots, Eliots, Grays, Perkins, Storys, Appletons, Lawrences, Bowditches, Dexters, Wards, Forbes and the

rest—testified to the possibility of acquiring high social position without a distinguished family tree." Ibid., 178.

32. Lucid, *Journal,* 1:57, 56.

33. Ibid., 1:57.

34. Ibid.

35. Ibid., 1:57–58.

36. Ibid., 1:58.

37. Quoted in ibid., 1:57.

38. Ibid., 1:xxxiii.

39. Kent Newmyer, *Supreme Court Justice Joseph Story: Statesman of the Old Republic* (Chapel Hill: University of North Carolina Press, 1985), 320–321.

40. Robert V. Remini, *Daniel Webster: The Man and His Time* (New York: W. W. Norton, 1997), 144–146.

41. Richard Henry Dana Jr., "Rufus Choate," in *Richard Henry Dana, Jr.: Speeches in Stirring Times and Letters to a Son,* ed. Richard Henry Dana III (Boston: Houghton Mifflin, 1910), 290–291.

42. Lucid, *Journal,* 2:666 (emphasis in original). Dana was opposing counsel and witnessed the memorable exchange: "It was a good many minutes before the Court & audience recovered its gravity." Ibid.

43. Donald, *Charles Sumner,* 31–32.

44. Lucid, *Journal,* 1:54.

45. Samuel Eliot Morison, *The Maritime History of Massachusetts: 1783–1860* (Boston: Houghton Mifflin, 1921; Sentry edition, 1961), 227, 259–260. All subsequent citations are to the 1961 edition.

46. Ibid., 257, 259.

47. Charles Francis Adams, *Richard Henry Dana: A Biography,* 2 vols. (Boston: Houghton Mifflin, 1891), 2:133.

48. Lucid, *Journal,* 1:98.

49. *United States v. Givings,* District Court, MA. 1 Spr. 75, April 1844.

50. Lucid, *Journal,* 1:107.

7. THE MASQUERADE

1. Charles Francis Adams, *Richard Henry Dana: A Biography,* 2 vols. (Boston: Houghton Mifflin, 1891), 1:42. Even a half century later, Adams asserted that an income of $2,500 for a lawyer in his second year of practice "would today in Boston, or indeed in New York or London for that matter, be looked upon as an exceptional success." Ibid.

2. Dana to Oliver Ellsworth Daggett, 3 October 1842, quoted in Adams, *Dana,* 1:44.

3. Robert F. Lucid, ed., *The Journal of Richard Henry Dana, Jr.,* 3 vols. (Cambridge, MA: Harvard University Press, 1968), 1:97.

4. Dana to Sarah Dana, 6 August 1843, Dana Family Papers, LONG.

5. Richard Henry Dana Sr. to Dana, 18 January 1865, Dana Family Papers, MHS.

6. Sumner received aid from textile magnate Samuel Lawrence among others. David Donald, *Charles Sumner and the Coming of the Civil War* (New York: Alfred A. Knopf, 1960), 44. Wealthy Bostonians "regularly raised subscriptions for Webster to supplement his income." Robert V. Remini, *Daniel Webster: The Man and His Time* (New York: W. W. Norton, 1997), 200.

7. Dana to Sarah Dana, 12 June 1849, Dana Family Papers, LONG.

8. Lucid, *Journal*, 1:126–127.

9. Ibid., 1:127–128.

10. Ibid., 1:68–69.

11. Ibid., 1:69–70.

12. Ibid., 1:71, 83.

13. Samuel Shapiro, *Richard Henry Dana, Jr.: 1815–1882* (East Lansing: Michigan State University Press, 1961) 25.

14. Lucid, *Journal*, 1:3, 80.

15. Ibid., 1:76–77, 121.

16. Ibid., 1:121.

17. Ibid., 1:77, 80.

18. Ibid., 1:80.

19. Ibid., 1: 83, 88.

20. Ibid., 1: 89. The preceding quotations relating to the death of Sarah Woods are from Lucid, *Journal*, 1:33–34.

21. Ibid., 1:92.

22. Ibid., 1:102.

23. Ibid., 1:114.

24. Ibid., 1:119.

25. Ibid.

26. Charles Dickens, *Pictures from Italy and American Notes for General Circulation* (Philadelphia: J. B. Lippincott, 1885), 285. Dickens noted: "Seamen frequent these haunts." Ibid.

27. Lucid, *Journal*, 1:120–121.

28. Ibid., 1:121–122.

29. Ibid., 1:153–155.

30. Ibid., 1:194.

31. Ibid., 1:194–195.

32. Ibid., 1:197–198.

33. Ibid., 1:212–214.

34. Ibid., 1:214.

35. Ibid., 1:214, 217, 220.

36. Ibid., 1:196.

37. Sarah Dana's journal, 28 January 1842, Dana Family Papers, LONG.

38. Lucid, *Journal,* 1:229.

39. Ibid., 1:230.

40. Ibid., 1:231.

41. Ibid., 1:232.

42. Ibid., 1:232–233.

43. Ibid., 1:233.

44. Ibid., 1:4.

45. Ibid., 1:255.

8. THE GREAT MAN OF THE AGE

1. Richard Henry Dana Jr., *The Seaman's Friend: A Treatise on Practical Seaman-ship* (Boston: Thomas Groom, 1879; 14th ed., Mineola, NY: Dover, 1997). The publisher's note to the Dover edition asserted that Dana's book "was indispensable to anyone wishing to put to sea in the mid-to-late nineteenth century" (v).

2. Dana, *The Seaman's Friend,* 215.

3. Robert F. Lucid, ed., *The Journal of Richard Henry Dana, Jr.,* 3 vols. (Cambridge, MA: Harvard University Press, 1968), 1:112.

4. Ibid., 1:118.

5. Charles Francis Adams, *Richard Henry Dana: A Biography,* 2 vols. (Boston: Houghton Mifflin, 1891), 1:50–63. Dana's lengthy letter was published in several Boston and New York newspapers in January 1843. Adams observed, "It is the judgment of a man whose judgment carried weight on this painful episode in our naval history, in regard to which opinions then were, and will probably always remain divided." Ibid., 1:50.

6. Lucid, *Journal,* 1:166.

7. Robert V. Remini, *Daniel Webster: The Man and His Time* (New York: W. W. Norton, 1997), 251.

8. Ibid., 199–200.

9. Ibid., 516.

10. Daniel Walker Howe, *What Hath God Wrought: The Transformation of America, 1815–1848* (New York: Oxford University Press, 2007), 590–595.

11. Ibid., 425.

12. M. A. DeWolfe Howe, *Boston: The Place and the People* (New York: Macmillan, 1903), 260–264.

13. Henry Mayer, *All on Fire: William Lloyd Garrison and the Abolition of Slavery* (New York: W. W. Norton, 1998), 127–131.

14. Lucid, *Journal,* 1: 162.

15. Ibid., 1:161.

16. David Donald, *Charles Sumner and the Coming of the Civil War* (New York: Alfred A. Knopf, 1960), 132.

17. Lucid, *Journal,* 1:162.

18. Ibid., 1:165.

19. Quoted in Remini, *Webster,* 521.

20. Lucid, *Journal,* 1:167.

21. Van Wyck Brooks, *The Flowering of New England, 1815–1865* (New York: E. P. Dutton 1936), 96.

22. Quoted in Donald, *Sumner,* 132.

23. Charles C. Calhoun, *Longfellow: A Rediscovered Life* (Boston: Beacon Press, 2004), 175.

24. Quoted in Remini, *Webster,* 587.

25. Lucid, *Journal,* 1:235–237.

26. Ibid., 1:254.

27. Ibid., 1:241.

28. Ibid., 1:244, 238.

29. Ibid., 2:498.

30. This and the preceding quotations relating to Dana's Mount Vernon visit are from Lucid, *Journal,* 1:247–250.

31. Ibid., 1:252–253.

32. Dana to Sarah Dana, March 3, 1844, quoted Adams, *Dana,* 1:109.

33. Howe, *What Hath God Wrought,* 677–679.

34. Lucid, *Journal,* 1:242.

35. Ibid., 1:254.

36. Ibid., 1:244.

37. Howe, *What Hath God Wrought,* 679–682.

38. Robert W. Merry, *A Country of Vast Designs: James K. Polk, the Mexican War, and the Conquest of the American Continent* (New York: Simon and Schuster Paperbacks, 2009), 81, 92–94, 110–111.

39. Remini, *Webster,* 599.

40. Ibid., 600–601; Robert F. Dalzell Jr., *Enterprising Elite: The Boston Associates and the World They Made* (New York: W. W. Norton, 1987), 194.

41. Lucid, *Journal,* 1:289.

42. Ibid., 1:203.

43. Ibid.

44. Ibid., 1:220–221.

45. Ibid., 1:322.

46. Ibid., 1:254–255.

9. THE INHERITANCE

1. Robert F. Lucid, ed., *The Journal of Richard Henry Dana, Jr.,* 3 vols. (Cambridge, MA: Harvard University Press, 1968), 1:347.

2. Elizabeth Ellery Dana to Ruth Charlotte Dana, 4 August 1848, Dana Family Papers, MHS.

3. Charles Francis Adams, *Richard Henry Dana: A Biography,* 2 vols. (Boston: Houghton, Mifflin, 1891), 1:128–129.

4. Dana to Edmund Dana, 21 July 1848, Dana Family Papers, MHS.

5. Richard H. Dana Jr., "Free Soil Meeting, 1848," in *Richard Henry Dana, Jr.: Speeches in Stirring Times and Letters to a Son,* ed. Richard Henry Dana III (Boston: Houghton Mifflin, 1910), 145.

6. Dana to Daniel Lord, 26 January 1854, quoted in Adams, *Dana,* 1:124–126 (emphasis in original). Adams observed: "There was also something peculiarly repulsive to Dana in the radicalism and extravagance of the anti-slavery agitators. . . . He adhered to [Free Soilism] on principle, regardless of self-interest, of his own dislike of its exponents, of personal and professional odium, and social ostracism." Ibid.

7. Lucid, *Journal,* 1:287.

8. Ibid., 1:286.

9. Daniel Walker Howe, *What Hath God Wrought: The Transformation of America, 1815–1848* (New York: Oxford University Press, 2007), 719.

10. Robert W. Merry, *A Country of Vast Designs: James K. Polk, the Mexican War, and the Conquest of the American Continent* (New York: Simon and Schuster Paperbacks, 2010), 240–244. Merry describes Polk's request for a declaration of war as "brilliantly crafted to leverage the death of American troops for maximum political effect" (244).

11. Quoted in Howe, *What Hath God Wrought,* 821. Casualty figures at Merry, *Country of Vast Designs,* 450.

12. Howe, *What Hath God Wrought,* 767–768. Merry, *Country of Vast Designs,* 286–289.

13. Dana III, *Speeches in Stirring Times,* 147–148.

14. Lucid, *Journal,* 1:347.

15. Dana to Sarah Dana, 8 July 1848, quoted in Adams, *Dana,* 1:135.

16. Lucid, *Journal,* 1:303; Dana to Sarah Dana, 23 August 1847, Dana Family Papers, LONG.

17. Sarah Dana, April 1848, Dana Family Papers, LONG.

18. Lucid, *Journal,* 1:353.

19. Dana to Sarah Dana, 21 July 1848, quoted in Adams, *Dana,* 1:135–136.

20. Dana III, *Speeches in Stirring Times,* 157.

21. Lucid, *Journal,* 1:355–356 (emphasis in original).

22. Dana to Elizabeth Daggett, 17 September 1848, quoted in Samuel Shapiro, *Richard Henry Dana, Jr., 1815–1882* (East Lansing: Michigan State University Press, 1961), 41.

23. Lucid, *Journal,* 1:355.

24. Dana III, *Speeches in Stirring Times,* 162–163.

25. Dana to Dana Sr., 11 July 1848, quoted in Shapiro, *Richard Henry Dana, Jr.,* 40.

26. Adams, *Dana,* 1:126.

27. Shapiro, *Richard Henry Dana, Jr.,* 41; Reinhard H. Luthin, "Abraham Lincoln and the Massachusetts Whigs in 1848," *New England Quarterly* 14, no. 4 (Dec. 1941): 619–632.

28. Dana III, *Speeches in Stirring Times,* 148.

29. Shapiro, *Richard Henry Dana, Jr.,* 42.

30. Robert F. Lucid, ed., *The Journal of Richard Henry Dana, Jr.,* 3 vols. (Cambridge, MA: Harvard University Press, 1968), 1:394.

31. Robert F. Dalzell Jr., *Daniel Webster and the Trial of American Nationalism, 1843–1852* (New York: W. W. Norton, Norton Library, 1975), 172–177.

32. *Congressional Globe,* "Seventh of March" Speech of Daniel Webster, 31st Cong., 1st sess., March 7, 1850.

33. Robert V. Remini, *Daniel Webster: The Man and His Time* (New York: W. W. Norton, 1997), 670, 676.

34. Dana to Edmund Dana, 13 March 1850, quoted in Shapiro, *Richard Henry Dana, Jr.,* 55.

35. Remini, *Webster,* 678.

36. Ibid., 685–686. Webster accepted the appointment as secretary of state only after seeking and receiving assurances that Boston and New York businessmen would supplement the "paltry" annual salary of $6,000. Abbott Lawrence's refusal to contribute stemmed from his belief that Webster had played a part in derailing Lawrence's nomination as Zachary Taylor's running mate in 1848. Millard Fillmore was nominated instead. Webster denied any role. Dalzell, *Trial of American Nationalism,* 148–149.

37. Fugitive Slave Act of September 18, 1850. See also Steven Lubet, *Fugitive Justice: Runaways, Rescuers, and Slavery on Trial* (Cambridge, MA: Harvard University Press, 2010), 42–44.

38. Webster to Millard Fillmore, 15 November 1850, *The Papers of Daniel Webster, Series One: Correspondence,* ed. Charles M. Wiltse et al., 7 vols. (Hanover, NH: University Press of New England, 1974–1985), 7:180.

39. Quoted in Gary Collison, *Shadrach Minkins: From Fugitive Slave to Citizen* (Cambridge, MA: Harvard University Press, 1998), 99.

40. Quoted in Stuart Streichler, *Justice Curtis in the Civil War Era: At the Crossroads of American Constitutionalism* (Charlottesville: University of Virginia Press, 2005), 51.

41. Lucid, *Journal,* 2:410.

42. Ibid., 2:410, 412.

43. Ibid., 2:412.

44. Ibid., 410–411. It has long since been established that a state judge is without authority to issue a writ of habeas corpus to release a prisoner from federal custody, but the law was unsettled when Dana sought the writ from Chief Justice Shaw. The supremacy of federal jurisdiction was not firmly settled until *Tarble's Case,* 80 U.S. (13 Wall.) 397 (1871), although the Supreme Court had earlier reached the same result in *Ableman v. Booth,* 62 U.S. 506 (1859).

45. Lucid, *Journal,* 2:410–412.

46. Frederic Hathaway Chase, *Lemuel Shaw: Chief Justice of the Supreme Judicial Court of Massachusetts, 1830–1860* (Boston: Houghton Mifflin, 1918), 279, 277.

47. Lucid, *Journal,* 2:411.

48. Ibid. Dana emphasized "bluff me off."

49. Ibid.

50. Ibid.

51. Ibid., 2:411–412.

52. Ibid., 2:412.

53. Collison, *Shadrach Minkins,* 163–165.

54. Lucid, *Journal,* 2:412.

55. *New Orleans Daily Picayune,* 2 March 1851, quoted in Collison, *Shadrach Minkins,* 140.

56. Daniel Webster to Moses Taylor et. al., 20 February, 1851, quoted in Collison, *Shadrach Minkins,* 255.

57. Proclamation, 18 February 1851, http://www.presidency.ucsb.edu /proclamations.

58. Federal prosecutors were not responsible to the attorney general. The Department of Justice was not established until 1870. See Cornell W. Clayton, *The Politics of Justice: The Attorney General and the Making of Legal Policy* (Armonk, NY: M. E. Sharpe, 1992), 16, 25. The appointment papers of a U.S. district attorney were signed by the president and the secretary of state.

59. Gary Collison, "'This Flagitious Offense': Daniel Webster and the Shadrach Rescue Cases, 1851-52," *New England Quarterly* 68, no. 4 (December 1995): 610-611.

60. Charles Francis Adams Jr., *Proceedings, Massachusetts Historical Society,* 19 (1881–882): 203.

10. A MONSTROUS THING

1. *United States v. Charles Davis: Report of the Proceedings at the Examination of Charles G. Davis, Esq. on a Charge of Aiding and Abetting in the Rescue of a Fugitive Slave* (Boston: White and Potter, 1851) (emphasis in original). Unless otherwise noted, remarks of Dana, U.S. District Attorney Lunt, and Commissioner Hallett are excerpts from this report.

2. Quoted in Gary Collison, *Shadrach Minkins: From Fugitive Slave to Citizen* (Cambridge, MA. Harvard University Press, 1998), 138, 136.

3. Daniel Webster, "Speech to the Young Men of Albany," 28 May 1851, in *The Writings and Speeches of Daniel Webster,* 18 vols. (Boston: Little, Brown, 1903), 4:275.

4. Robert F. Lucid, ed., *The Journal of Richard Henry Dana, Jr.,* 3 vols. (Cambridge, MA: Harvard University Press, 1968), 2:414. Note on usage: The office of federal prosecutor held by George Lunt was "United States Dis-

trict Attorney for the District of Massachusetts." The position is today referred to as "U.S. attorney" but was often called "district attorney" in the nineteenth century. The terms "U.S. attorney," "U.S. district attorney," and "district attorney" were used interchangeably by Dana's contemporaries to refer to a federal prosecutor, and they are used that way in this book.

5. Amos A. Lawrence to Samuel A. Eliot, 18 February 1851, quoted in Collison, *Shadrach Minkins*, 140.

6. Dana Sr. to William C. Bryant, 6 March 1851, quoted in Collison, *Shadrach Minkins*, 143.

7. Dana to George William Curtis, 19 September 1872, Dana Family Papers, LONG.

8. Webster, *Writings and Speeches*, 4:275.

9. Lucid, *Journal*, 2:414.

10. Quoted in Moorfield Storey, "Dana as an Antislavery Leader," *Proceedings, Cambridge Historical Society* 10 (October 26, 1915): 134.

11. Dana's statement reflected a distinction made by opponents of slavery in the "right of revolution." The oppressed had such a right. White sympathizers did not. As Robert M. Cover noted, "Dana's logic led straight to justification of the right of revolution for *slaves*." Robert M. Cover, *Justice Accused: Antislavery and the Judicial Process* (New Haven: Yale University Press, 1975), 106 (emphasis in original).

12. Lucid, *Journal*, 2:415.

11. CHAINS

1. Leonard W. Levy, "Sims' Case: The Fugitive Sale Law in Boston in 1851," *Journal of Negro History* 35, no. 1 (January 1950): 39–40.

2. Ibid., 40.

3. Robert F. Lucid, ed., *The Journal of Richard Henry Dana, Jr.*, 3 vols. (Cambridge, MA: Harvard University Press, 1968), 2:415.

4. David Donald, *Charles Sumner and the Coming of the Civil War* (New York: Alfred A. Knopf, 1960), 186.

5. Lucid, *Journal*, 1:406.

6. Donald, *Sumner*, 186.

7. Ernest A. McKay, "Henry Wilson and the Coalition of 1851," *New England Quarterly* 36, no. 3 (September 1963): 348–349.

8. Donald, *Sumner*, 194.

9. Ibid., 197. Donald noted that Sumner "cautiously declined to assist Dana" in the defense of Shadrach Minkins but came to the defense of Thomas Sims "when it became clear that Massachusetts opinion was outraged by the arbitrariness and cruelty of the arrest." Ibid. Sumner never appeared with Dana in the rescue cases.

10. Lucid, *Journal*, 2:416.

11. Ibid.

12. Donald, *Sumner*, 196.

13. Quoted in Gary Collison, "'This Flagitious Offense': Daniel Webster and the Shadrach Rescue Cases, 1851-1852," *New England Quarterly* 68, no. 4 (December 1995): 613.

14. Webster to George Lunt, 4 April 1851, in *Letters of Daniel Webster from Documents Owned Principally by the New Hampshire Historical Society,* ed. C. H. Van Tyne (New York: McClure, Phillips, 1902), 466–470.

15. Leonard W. Levy, *The Law of the Commonwealth and Chief Justice Shaw* (Cambridge, MA: Harvard University Press, 1957), 92; Steven Lubet, *Fugitive Justice: Runaways, Rescuers, and Slavery on Trial* (Cambridge, MA: Harvard University Press, 2010), 148.

16. Lucid, *Journal,* 2:424.

17. Levy, *The Law of the Commonwealth,* 92; Lubet, *Fugitive Justice,* 147.

18. Lucid, *Journal,* 2:420. Shaw's sudden decision to hear argument was prompted by a weekend visit from "a number of gentlemen of high standing." Levy, *Law of the Commonwealth,* 97.

19. Robert M. Cover, *Justice Accused: Antislavery and the Judicial Process* (New Haven: Yale University Press, 1975), 149, 161.

20. Lucid, *Journal,* 2:420.

21. Cover, *Justice Accused,* 169–171, 176–177. Cover's exemplary work illuminated the "moral-formal" dilemma inherent in the slavery cases. Ibid., 197–259. He considered Dana "a most visible symbol of the attempted reconciliation of formal values and antislavery." Ibid., 242.

22. Levy, *Law of the Commonwealth,* 101.

23. *In Re Sims,* 7 Cush. 285, 310 (Mass. 1851).

24. Quoted in Levy, *Law of the Commonwealth,* 101.

25. Lucid, *Journal,* 2:424.

26. Ibid., 2:422.

27. Ibid., 2:421.

28. Ibid., 2:422.

29. Ibid., 2:423.

30. Ibid.

31. Ibid., 2:423, 622–623.

32. Quoted in Lubet, *Fugitive Justice,* 154–155.

33. Lucid, *Journal,* 2:424.

34. Quoted in Lubet, *Fugitive Justice,* 155.

35. Quoted in Henry Mayer, *All on Fire: William Lloyd Garrison and the Abolition of Slavery* (New York: W. W. Norton, 1998), 412.

36. Lucid, *Journal,* 2:426–427; Donald, *Sumner,* 201–203.

37. Samuel Shapiro, *Richard Henry Dana, Jr.: 1815–1882* (East Lansing: Michigan State University Press, 1961), 64.

1. Charles Francis Adams, *Richard Henry Dana: A Biography,* 2 vols. (Boston: Houghton Mifflin, 1891), 1:128-129.

2. Robert F. Lucid, ed., *The Journal of Richard Henry Dana, Jr.,* 3 vols. (Cambridge, MA: Harvard University Press, 1968), 2:533.

3. Ibid., 2:425-426. At least twenty-one newspaper attacks upon Dana appeared by the end of July. Ibid., 2:426

4. Ibid., 2:428.

5. Adams, *Dana,* 1:128.

6. Quoted in David B. Tyack, *George Ticknor and the Boston Brahmins* (Cambridge, MA: Harvard University Press, 1967), 229.

7. Franklin Haven, letter to the editor, *Boston Evening Transcript,* 19 May 1851. The "gifts" Webster received from the Boston Associates were never spontaneous. See Robert V. Remini, *Daniel Webster: The Man and His Time* (New York: W. W. Norton, 1997), 146, 199-200, 685-686.

8. Fillmore to Webster, 16 April 1851, in *The Papers of Daniel Webster, Correspondence,* ed. Charles M. Wise and Michael J. Birkner, vol. 7, 1850-1852 (Hanover: Dartmouth College Press, 1986), 237-238.

9. Daniel Webster, "Speech to the Young Men of Albany," 28 May 1851, in *The Writings and Speeches of Daniel Webster,* 18 vols. (Boston: Little, Brown, 1903), 4:275.

10. Webster to Haven, 29 May 1851, Daniel Webster Papers, Houghton Library, Harvard University.

11. Lucid, *Journal,* 2:431.

12. *Boston Daily Advertiser,* 2 June 1851.

13. Dana to George William Curtis, 19 September 1872, Dana Family Papers, LONG; Adams, *Dana,* 1:129. The handful of other Brahmin lawyers who opposed the Fugitive Slave Act, such as Samuel Sewall and Ellis Gray Loring, did not have to earn livings practicing law nor were they Dana's equal as trial attorneys.

14. Dana to Curtis, 19 September 1872, Dana Family Papers, LONG.

15. *Boston Courier,* 2 June 1851.

16. "A Whig Merchant" to Dana, 2 June 1851 (emphasis in original), Dana Family Papers, MHS.

17. Lucid, *Journal,* 2:431. Dana's papers include a draft of a letter—apparently not sent—in which Dana says of the "arrangement" between the Boston Associates and Webster: "It is a dangerous business to be engaged in,—this making private donation to public officers who have control over public measures and immense patronage. It perils him who gives and him who takes." Dana to Charles Loring (draft), 12 June 1851, Dana Family Papers, MHS.

18. Lucid, *Journal,* 2:429; Richard H. Sewell, *John P. Hale and the Politics of Abolition* (Cambridge, MA: Harvard University Press, 1965), 141-142.

19. Ibid., 2:430.

20. Gary Collison, "'This Flagitious Offense'": Daniel Webster and the Shadrach Rescue Cases, 1851-1852," *New England Quarterly* 68, no. 4 (December 1995): 613-618.

21. Ibid., 618.

22. Choate to George Lunt, 29 March 1851, in Wise and Birkner, *Papers of Daniel Webster,* 7:224-225.

23. William H. Gilman et al., eds., *The Journals and Miscellaneous Notebooks of Ralph Waldo Emerson,* 16 vols., vol. 11, 1851 (Cambridge, MA: Harvard University Press, 1960-1982), 346.

24. Lucid, *Journal,* 2:438.

25. Ibid.

26. Samuel Gilman Brown, *The Works of Rufus Choate,* 2 vols. (Boston: Little, Brown, 1862), 1:173.

27. Lucid, *Journal,* 2:438.

28. Ibid., 2:436-437 (emphasis in original).

29. Ibid., 2:445, 444, 442.

30. Ibid., 2:447, 454, 450.

31. Ibid., 2:451, 455, 457 (emphasis in original).

32. Ibid., 2:457.

13. THE LITTLE DARKY LAWYER

1. Stuart Streichler, *Justice Curtis in the Civil War Era: At the Crossroads of American Constitutionalism* (Charlottesville: University of Virginia Press, 2005), 42-43.

2. Benjamin R. Curtis, ed., *A Memoir of Benjamin Robbins Curtis,* 2 vols. (Boston: Little, Brown, 1879), 1:156.

3. Streichler, *Justice Curtis,* 54.

4. Ibid., 54-55.

5. Robert F. Lucid, ed., *The Journal of Richard Henry Dana, Jr.,* 3 vols. (Cambridge, MA: Harvard University Press, 1968), 2:465.

6. Richard Henry Dana Jr., "Argument for Charles G. Davis," in *Richard Henry Dana, Jr.: Speeches in Stirring Times and Letters to a Son,* ed. Richard Henry Dana III (Boston: Houghton Mifflin, 1910), 208.

7. Ibid.

8. Stephen Kendrick and Paul Kendrick, *Sarah's Long Walk: The Free Blacks of Boston and How Their Struggle for Equality Changed America* (Boston: Beacon Press, 2004), 6.

9. Ibid.

10. Steven Lubet, *Fugitive Justice: Runaways, Rescuers, and Slavery on Trial* (Cambridge, MA: Harvard University Press, 2010), 142-143. Robert Morris was the protégé of Ellis Gray Loring, for whom he had clerked. In May 1846 Morris was married in a ceremony at Loring's house. William

Lloyd Garrison was a guest at the wedding and his presence at a Brahmin home "measured Garrison's ascent as well as Morris's." Henry Mayer, *All on Fire: William Lloyd Garrison and the Abolition of Slavery* (New York: W. W. Norton, 1998), 352. Despite Loring's hospitality, there was a decided social demarcation between even staunch Brahmin abolitionists like Wendell Phillips and abolitionists of more "common" origin, including African Americans. Dana admired Morris but it is doubtful he ever invited him to his home.

11. Lucid, *Journal,* 2:466.

12. Ibid.; Gary Collison, "'This Flagitious Offense': Daniel Webster and the Shadrach Rescue Cases, 1851-1852," *New England Quarterly* 68, no. 4 (December 1995): 619.

13. Dana to Harriet Beecher Stowe, 25 November 1852, Dana Family Papers, MHS.

14. Gary Collison, *Shadrach Minkins: From Fugitive Slave to Citizen* (Cambridge, MA: Harvard University Press, 1998), 111.

15. The U.S. Supreme Court later adopted Curtis's rationale in denying a jury's authority to decide questions of law in a criminal case. *Sparf & Hansen v. United States,* 156 U.S. 51 (1895).

16. Curtis, *Memoir,* 2:174.

17. Lucid, *Journal,* 2:469, 466.

18. Ibid., 2:466, 477.

19. Ibid., 2:478.

20. Charles Francis Adams, *Richard Henry Dana: A Biography,* 2 vols. (Boston: Houghton Mifflin, 1891), 1:211.

21. Melville to Dana, 1 May 1850, Dana Family Papers, MHS.

22. Ida Russell to Dana, 8 July 1847, Dana Family Papers, MHS.

23. Sarah Dana to Dana, 27 July 1847, Dana Family Papers, LONG.

24. Andrew Delbanco, *Melville: His World and His Work* (New York: Vintage Books, 2006), 153-155. Delbanco noted that a scene in Melville's *Pierre* echoed Dana's confrontation with Chief Justice Shaw. Ibid., 192.

25. Dana to Allan Melville, May 10, 1853, Herman Melville Papers, Houghton Library, Harvard University. Dana could be punctilious when asked to use his influence on behalf of acquaintances seeking positions, but he was unreserved in support of his friend. The letter he prepared for Melville's use in seeking a consulship asserted: "I cannot conceive of a more appropriate appointment and I sincerely hope it will be given to him. If I knew the President or the Secretary of State personally, I would take the liberty to write them. As I do not, I beg you to use whatever influence I may have in any quarter for his favor." Ibid.

26. Dana to Edmund Dana, 18 March 1849, MHS.

27. Melville to Dana, 6 October 1849, *Correspondence, The Writings of Herman Melville,* ed. Lynn Horth (Evanston: Northwestern University Press and The Newberry Library, 1993), 140-141.

28. William H. Bond, "Melville and 'Two Years Before the Mast,'" *Harvard Library Bulletin* 8, no. 3 (Autumn 1953): 362–365. Bond noted that just as the flogging scene in Melville's *White Jacket* resembled Dana's account of Captain Thompson's floggings, "so does Billy Budd's stammer resemble Sam's in precipitating their several crises." Ibid., 365.

29. Melville to Dana, 1 May 1850, Dana Family Papers, MHS.

30. Melville to Lemuel Shaw, 6 October 1849, in Horth, *Correspondence*, 138–139.

31. Eugene Exman, *The Brothers Harper* (New York: Harper and Row, 1965), 295–296; Lorie Robertson-Lorant, *Melville: A Biography* (New York: Clarkson Potter, 1996), 296.

32. Dana to Sumner, 21 March 1861, quoted in James D. Hart, "Melville and Dana," *American Literature* 9, no. 1 (March 1937): 55.

33. Dana to Edward Moxon, 12 September 1849 (copied excerpt), Henry Wadsworth Longfellow Dana Papers, LONG.

34. Richard Henry Dana Jr., *Two Years Before the Mast and Other Voyages* (New York: Library of America, 2005), 244.

35. Herman Melville, *Melville: Redburn, White-Jacket, Moby-Dick* (New York: Library of America, 1983), 452.

36. Austin Bearse, *Reminiscences of Fugitive-Slave Law Days in Boston* (Boston: 1880), 34.

37. Sidney Kaplan, "The *Moby Dick* in the Service of the Underground Railroad," *Phylon* 12, no. 2 (1951): 174, 176. Melville's admiration for Dana's advocacy on behalf of fugitive slaves may be glimpsed in a dedication to William Clark Russell wherein Melville praised Russell: "In his broader humane quality he shares the spirit of Richard H. Dana, a true poet's son, our own admirable *Man before the Mast*." *Published Poems: The Writings of Herman Melville,* ed. Hershel Parker (Evanston: Northwestern University Press and Newberry Library, 2009), 192.

14. THE CLUB

1. Daniel Webster to Franklin Haven, 4 December 1851, Houghton Library, Harvard University.

2. Robert F. Lucid, ed., *The Journal of Richard Henry Dana, Jr.,* 3 vols. (Cambridge, MA: Harvard University Press, 1968), 2:487, 519.

3. Harriet Beecher Stowe to Dana, 9 November 1852, Dana Family Papers, MHS.

4. Dana to Harriet Beecher Stowe, 25 November 1852, Dana Family Papers, MHS.

5. Harriet Beecher Stowe, *A Key to Uncle Tom's Cabin* (London: Sampson, Low, 1853), 6–7.

6. Stuart Streichler, *Justice Curtis in the Civil War Era: At the Crossroads of American Constitutionalism* (Charlotte: University of Virginia Press,

2005), 51, 145. The resignation of Curtis after his *Dred Scott* dissent has been ascribed to financial reasons or "what the justices had done to the Court as an institution." Ibid., 148. My own view is that the bitter exchange of letters between Curtis and Chief Justice Taney—who accused Curtis of improperly releasing the dissent in order to influence public opinion—made it impossible for Curtis to remain on the Supreme Court.

7. Charles Francis Adams, *Richard Henry Dana: A Biography,* 2 vols. (Boston: Houghton Mifflin, 1891), 1:216–217.

8. Ibid., 1:131.

9. Lucid, *Journal,* 2:502

10. Ibid.

11. David Donald, *Charles Sumner and the Coming of the Civil War* (New York: Alfred A. Knopf, 1960), 227–238.

12. Lucid, *Journal,* 2:484.

13. Ibid., 2:507–508.

14. Ibid., 2:484.

15. Dana to Sarah Dana, 24 December 1871, quoted in Adams, *Dana,* 1:215.

16. Lucid, *Journal,* 2:502.

17. Ibid., 2:503–504.

18. Donald, *Sumner,* 236–237.

19. Lucid, *Journal,* 2:509.

20. Webster to Fillmore, 9 April 1851, quoted in Gary Collison, *Shadrach Minkins: From Fugitive Slave to Citizen* (Cambridge, MA: Harvard University Press, 1998), 193.

21. Lucid, *Journal,* 2:513, 516, 512.

22. Ibid., 2:514. Dana wrote of the proposed resolutions: "One said Webster's great voice *never failed* to support the cause of the oppressed, etc. I requested them to alter this." He assented to a revised version that asserted Webster's voice *"often penetrated"* where there was oppression (emphasis in original). Ibid.

23. Lucid, *Journal,* 2:528.

24. Ibid., 2:537.

25. Ibid., 2:549, 536.

26. Ibid., 2:531–532 (emphasis in original). Of the ten individuals arrested for alleged violation of the Fugitive Slave Act in the rescue Shadrach Minkins, Lunt initiated prosecutions against the five most prominent: Charles G. Davis, James Scott, Lewis Hayden, Robert Morris, and Elizur Wright. Dana represented each of the five, obtaining a dismissal of the case against Davis, acquittals of Morris and Wright, and hung juries in Scott and Hayden. Lunt did not retry Scott or Hayden and in May 1853 dropped charges in all remaining rescue cases. Gary Collison, "'This Flagitious Offense': Daniel Webster and the Shadrach Rescue Cases, 1851–1852," *New England Quarterly* 68, no. 4 (December 1995): 623.

27. Lucid, *Journal,* 2:541; Richard H. Sewell, *John P. Hale and the Politics of Abolition* (Cambridge, MA: Harvard University Press, 1965), 138–139. Melville's description of a flogging in *White Jacket*—"You see a human being stripped like a slave, scourged worse than a hound"—echoed Dana's depiction of Captain Thompson's flogging of Sam: "A man—a human being made in God's likeness—fastened up and flogged like a beast!" Although each book contributed to the impetus to ban flogging, the movement for reform came from many sources. Myra C. Glenn, *Campaigns against Corporal Punishment: Prisoners, Sailors, Women, and Children in Antebellum America* (Albany: State University of New York Press, 1984), 123–124.

28. Lucid, *Journal,* 2:544.

29. Ibid., 2:536.

30. Quoted in Samuel Shapiro, *Richard Henry Dana, Jr.: 1815–1882* (East Lansing: Michigan State University Press, 1961), 75.

31. Lucid, *Journal,* 2:516. Richard Henry Dana Sr. to Mrs. Arnold, 16 November 1852, Dana Family Papers, MHS.

32. Lucid, *Journal,* 2:546.

33. Quoted in Shapiro, *Richard Henry Dana, Jr.,* 74.

34. Lucid, *Journal,* 2:557. Choate's great speech on judicial independence is better known, but Dana's is at least its equal. For a like-minded appraisal, see Robert M. Cover, *Justice Accused: Antislavery and the Judicial Process* (New Haven: Yale University Press, 1975), 301.

35. Shapiro, *Richard Henry Dana, Jr.,* 80.

36. Ibid., 76.

37. The Whigs opposed a secret ballot because in its absence they could compel "their defenseless employees to vote the 'right ticket' and the 'right ticket' for them was the Whig one." Michael Brunet, "The Secret Ballot Issue in Massachusetts from 1851 to 1853," *New England Quarterly* 25, no. 3 (September 1952): 354.

38. Lucid, *Journal,* 2:602

39. Adams, *Dana,* 1:237.

40. Lucid, *Journal,* 2:554.

41. Quoted in Adams, *Dana,* 1:237.

42. Ibid. (emphasis in original).

43. Lucid, *Journal,* 2:553–554.

15. THE PRESUMPTION OF FREEDOM

1. Robert F. Lucid, ed., *The Journal of Richard Henry Dana, Jr.* (Cambridge, MA: Harvard University Press, 1968), 2:625.

2. Ibid.

3. The facts surrounding the arrest and trial of Anthony Burns are drawn from Charles Emery Stevens, *Anthony Burns: A History* (1856;

repr., New York: Negro Universities Press, 1969); Albert J. Von Frank, *The Trials of Anthony Burns: Freedom and Slavery in Emerson's Boston* (Cambridge, MA: Harvard University Press, 1999); Steven Lubet, *Fugitive Justice: Runaways, Rescuers, and Slavery on Trial* (Cambridge, MA: Harvard University, 2010); and Earl M. Maltz, *Fugitive Slave on Trial: The Anthony Burns Case and Abolitionist Outrage* (Lawrence: University of Kansas Press, 2010). Citations to Stevens, *Anthony Burns,* are to the Negro Universities Press reprint.

4. Stevens, *Anthony Burns,* 82; Lucid, *Journal,* 2:626.

5. *Boston Slave Riot, and Trial of Anthony Burns: Containing the Report of the Faneuil Hall Meeting, the Murder of Batchelder, Theodore Parker's Lesson for the Day, Speeches of Counsel on Both Sides, Corrected by Themselves, Verbatim Report of Judge Loring's Decision, and a Detailed Account of the Embarkation* (Boston: Fetridge, 1854) (emphasis in original). Unless otherwise noted, all trial excerpts are drawn from this record.

6. Lucid, *Journal,* 2:626.

7. Ibid., 2:627–628.

8. Ibid., 2:628. The Kansas-Nebraska Act, repealing the Missouri Compromise of 1820 and opening the new territories to slavery, had just passed Congress and was signed into law by President Franklin Pierce on May 30, 1854.

9. Ibid.

10. Stevens, *Anthony Burns,* 43–45; Lucid, *Journal,* 2:628.

11. Lucid, *Journal,* 2:629.

12. Ibid.; Stevens, *Anthony Burns,* 273.

13. Lucid, *Journal,* 2:629.

14. Ibid.

15. Ibid.

16. For an extended account of the effort to purchase the freedom of Burns, see Stevens, *Anthony Burns,* 61–79.

17. When Dana refused to go to trial, Hallett's son said, "Well, we shall know how to accommodate you, when you ask a favor from us." Lucid, *Journal,* 2:623.

18. Stevens, *Anthony Burns,* 80.

19. Ibid., 82–85.

20. Maltz, *Fugitive Slave on Trial,* 56.

21. Lucid, *Journal,* 2:631.

22. Lubet, *Fugitive Justice,* 183.

23. Lubet, *Fugitive Justice,* 162; Maltz, *Fugitive Slave on Trial,* 58.

24. Stevens, *Anthony Burns,* 95, 97, 81–82.

25. Lucid, *Journal,* 2:632.

1. Samuel May to Thomas Wentworth Higginson, 30 May 1854, quoted in Albert J. Von Frank, *The Trials of Anthony Burns: Freedom and Slavery in Emerson's Boston* (Cambridge, MA: Harvard University Press, 1999), 167.

2. Robert F. Lucid, ed., *The Journal of Richard Henry Dana, Jr.* (Cambridge, MA: Harvard University Press, 1968), 2:673.

3. Lucid, *Journal,* 2:631. *Boston Slave Riot, and Trial of Anthony Burns: Containing the Report of the Faneuil Hall Meeting, the Murder of Batchelder, Theodore Parker's Lesson for the Day, Speeches of Counsel on Both Sides, Corrected by Themselves, Verbatim Report of Judge Loring's Decision, and a Detailed Account of the Embarkation* (Boston: Fetridge, 1854), 40.

4. Charles Emery Stevens, *Anthony Burns: A History* (1856; repr., New York: Negro Universities Press, 1969), 269; Earl M. Maltz, *Fugitive Slave on Trial: The Anthony Burns Case and Abolitionist Outrage* (Lawrence: University of Kansas Press, 2010), 84; Steven Lubet, *Fugitive Justice: Runaways, Rescuers, and Slavery on Trial* (Cambridge, MA: Harvard University, 2010), 209. Citations to Stevens, *Anthony Burns,* are to the Negro Universities Press reprint.

5. Lucid, *Journal,* 2:632.

6. Ibid., 2:634; Stevens, *Anthony Burns,* 141.

7. Lucid, *Journal,* 2:632–633.

8. Stevens, *Anthony Burns,* 114; Lucid, *Journal,* 2:631. All quotations of Loring are from his decision reprinted in Stevens, *Anthony Burns,* 114–123.

9. Von Frank, *Trials of Anthony Burns,* 203.

10. Stevens, *Anthony Burns,* 123; Lucid, *Journal,* 2:633.

11. Lucid, *Journal,* 2:633.

12. Stevens, *Anthony Burns,* 145; Lucid, *Journal,* 2:633–634.

13. Lucid, *Journal,* 2:634.

14. Ibid., 2:635; Lubet, *Fugitive Justice,* 215–216; Stevens, *Anthony Burns,* 142.

15. Lucid, *Journal,* 2:636; Maltz, *Fugitive Slave,* 91.

16. Lucid, *Journal,* 2:636.

17. Ibid., 2:636–637; Charles Francis Adams, *Richard Henry Dana: A Biography,* 2 vols. (Boston: Houghton Mifflin, 1891), 1:308.

18. Ibid., 2:636. Dana recounted the assault and its aftermath in greater detail in his 1876 lecture reprinted in Adams, *Dana,* 1:298–330.

19. Lucid, *Journal,* 2:636–637.

20. *New York Daily Tribune,* 5 June 1854; Sumner to Dana, 4 June 1854, quoted in Samuel Shapiro, *Richard Henry Dana, Jr.: 1815–1882* (East Lansing: Michigan State University Press, 1961), 92.

21. Lucid, *Journal,* 2:637; Longfellow to Sumner, 2 June 1854, LONG; William Watson to Dana, 9 June 1854, quoted in Von Franck, *Trials of Anthony Burns,* 225.

22. Quoted in Lubet, *Fugitive Justice,* 216.

23. Lucid, *Journal,* 2:637–638.

24. Ibid., 2:638.

25. Adams, *Dana,* 1:325–326.

26. Ibid., 1:328–329. "Varrell" had several aliases. "Luigi Varelli" may have been his real name, though he was also known as Louis Bireal and Louis Clark. Adams said Varrell was connected with "a notorious [Boston] brothel." Ibid.

27. Lucid, *Journal,* 2:639–640. Dana did not record Robinson's first name.

28. Ibid., 2:640–641.

29. Maltz, *Fugitive Slave,* 94.

30. Inscription and the exchange of letters at Adams, *Dana,* 1:291–294.

31. Lucid, *Journal,* 2:641; Stevens, *Anthony Burns,* 188–189, 193–194.

32. The letters from Burns from which this account is drawn are reprinted in Von Frank, *The Trials of Anthony Burns,* 287–289.

33. Ibid., 290.

34. Lucid, *Journal,* 2:672–673.

17. DUTY

1. Robert F. Lucid, ed., *The Journal of Richard Henry Dana, Jr.,* 3 vols. (Cambridge, MA: Harvard University Press, 1968), 2:663. Charlotte Mary Yonge, *The Heir of Redclyffe,* 2 vols. (London, 1853). The book had gone through seventeen editions by 1868 and never lost its charm for Dana. He visited Yonge in England.

2. Lucid, *Journal,* 2:663–664.

3. Ibid., 2:664.

4. Charles Francis Adams, *Richard Henry Dana: A Biography,* 2 vols. (Boston: Houghton Mifflin, 1891), 2:150; Lucid, *Journal,* 2:664.

5. Lucid, *Journal,* 2:656, 661.

6. Ibid., 2:675–676.

7. Ibid., 2:638.

8. Quoted in Samuel Shapiro, *Richard Henry Dana, Jr.: 1815–1882* (East Lansing: Michigan State University Press, 1961), 50.

9. Lucid, *Journal,* 2:663.

10. 1 Spr. 245, 17 Law Rep. 384 (1854).

11. Lucid, *Journal,* 2:663.

12. David Donald, *Charles Sumner and the Coming of the Civil War* (New York: Alfred A. Knopf, 1960), 268.

13. Lucid, *Journal,* 2:665.

14. Earl M. Maltz, *Fugitive Slave on Trial: The Anthony Burns Case and Abolitionist Outrage* (Lawrence: University of Kansas Press, 2010), 111–113; Albert J. Von Frank, *The Trials of Anthony Burns: Freedom and Slavery in Emerson's Boston* (Cambridge, MA: Harvard University Press, 1999), 236–239.

15. Dana's "decision" is reprinted in Charles Emery Stevens, *Anthony Burns: A History* (1856; repr., New York: Negro Universities Press, 1969), 254–261.

16. Quoted in Maltz, *Fugitive Slave,* 108.

17. Lucid, *Journal,* 2:671.

18. Ibid., 2:671–672.

19. Ibid., 2:671.

20. Robert M. Cover, *Justice Accused: Antislavery and the Judicial Process* (New Haven: Yale University Press, 1975), 178.

21. Quoted in Maltz, *Fugitive Slave,* 116.

22. Quoted in Cover, *Justice Accused,* 170.

23. All excerpts of Dana's testimony are from *Remarks of Richard H. Dana, Jr., Esq. before the Committee on Federal Relations, on the Proposed Removal of Edward G. Loring, Esq. from the Office of Judge of Probate, March 5, 1855* (Boston: Alfred Mudge and Son, 1855).

24. I. H. Bartlett, *Wendell Phillips: Brahmin Radical* (Boston: Beacon Press, 1961), 186.

25. Maltz, *Fugitive Slave,* 117.

26. Wisconsin became the site of an epic jurisdictional battle between the state and federal judiciaries. Sherman Booth, a Wisconsin abolitionist, was convicted of aiding in the escape of a fugitive slave in violation of the Fugitive Slave Act. The Wisconsin Supreme Court attempted to prevent federal judicial review of its decision that Booth was entitled to a writ of habeas corpus under state law. The U.S. Supreme Court rejected the claim that state judicial authorities could issue such writs to remove a prisoner from federal custody. The unanimous opinion, authored by Chief Justice Roger Taney, also expressed the view that the Fugitive Slave Act was "in all its provisions, fully authorized by the Constitution of the United States." *Ableman v. Booth,* 62 U.S. 506, 521 (1859).

27. Quoted in Maltz, *Fugitive Justice,* 128. As Maltz noted, Wendell Phillips actually questioned Dana's veracity as well. "I cannot imagine that it can be true," said Phillips of Dana's testimony that Judge Loring agreed to give Burns more time to decide whether he wished to have counsel. Ibid.

28. Quoted in Steven Lubet, *Fugitive Justice: Runaways, Rescuers, and Slavery on Trial* (Cambridge, MA: Harvard University Press, 2010), 225.

29. Dana's principled defense of an independent judiciary "cost him a great opportunity to make himself popular." Shapiro, *Richard Henry Dana, Jr.,* 99. John Albion Andrew showed no such reluctance while leading the ouster of Judge Loring in 1858 when Gardner's successor, Governor Nathaniel Banks, accepted the legislature's petition for removal. Two years later Andrew rode his wave of popularity to the governor's office. Edward Loring fared nearly as well. Although he lost his lectureship at Harvard Law School, President James Buchanan rewarded Loring for his adherence to the fugitive slave law with an appointment to the U.S. Court of Claims, where Loring served until 1877, his house an "unsurpassed" center of social Washington. Maltz, *Fugitive Justice,* 156.

30. Quoted in Shapiro, *Richard Henry Dana, Jr.,* 96. Sumner "refrained even in private letters" from condemning the Know Nothings. Donald, *Charles Sumner,* 269. Donald noted that Sumner "was once again in the exposed position of a senator without a political machine behind him." Donald, *Sumner,* 270.

31. Maltz, *Fugitive Slave,* 136–137.

32. Martin B. Duberman, "Some Notes on the Beginnings of the Republican Party in Massachusetts," *New England Quarterly* 34, no. 3 (September 1961): 364–370; Lucid, *Journal,* 2:677–680; Donald, *Sumner,* 271–274.

33. Quoted in Shapiro, *Richard Henry Dana, Jr.,* 100.

34. Dana to Sarah Dana, 26 September 1855, ibid., 101.

35. Lucid, *Journal,* 2:680; Donald, *Sumner,* 275. Although the Know Nothing Party received only 38 percent of the total vote, it was a plurality. The Know Nothing legislature had made a recent convenient change to the law which required only a plurality to elect the governor. Duberman, "Some Notes," 369.

36. Donald, *Sumner,* 274–275; Lucid, *Journal,* 2:680.

37. Lucid, *Journal,* 2:661–662.

38. Quoted in Donald, *Sumner,* 275–276.

39. Lucid, *Journal,* 2:688

40. Donald, *Sumner,* 146.

41. Ibid., 286.

42. Ibid., 294–295.

43. Shapiro, *Richard Henry Dana, Jr.,* 103; Dana to Sumner, 27 May 1856, quoted in Steven Puleo, *The Caning: The Assault That Drove America to Civil War* (Yardley, PA: Westholme, 2013), 129; Donald, *Sumner,* 303.

44. Lucid, *Journal,* 2:750, 758.

45. Lucid, *Journal,* 2:761; Adams, *Dana,* 1:360.

46. Lucid, *Journal,* 2:820.

18. BREAKDOWN

1. Charles Francis Adams, *Richard Henry Dana: A Biography,* 2 vols. (Boston: Houghton Mifflin, 1891), 2:128.

2. Ibid., 2:144.

3. Henry Adams, *The Education of Henry Adams* (New York: Vintage Books/ Library of America, 1990), 9.

4. Adams, *Dana,* 2:144.

5. Ibid., 2:137.

6. Ibid., 2:135–136.

7. Ibid., 2:136–137.

8. Ibid., 2:140.

9. Ibid., 2:142.

10. Ibid., 2:144.

11. Robert Lucid, ed., *Journal of Richard Henry Dana, Jr.,* 3 vols. (Cambridge, MA: Harvard University Press, 1968), 2:821, 832.

12. Ibid., 2:824, 827.

13. Ibid., 2:832–833.

14. *Boston Daily Bee,* 7 April 1857; *Richard Henry Dana, Jr.: Speeches in Stirring Times and Letters to a Son,* ed. Richard Henry Dana III (Boston: Houghton Mifflin, 1910), 31; Robert L. Gale, *Richard Henry Dana* (New York: Twayne, 1969), 78.

15. Lucid, *Journal,* 2:830.

16. Emerson to Dana, 12 May 1849, Dana Family Papers, MHS; Lucid, *Journal,* 2:830; M. A. DeWolfe Howe, *Boston: The Place and the People* (New York: Macmillan, 1903), 243–246.

17. Lucid, *Journal,* 2:830; Van Wyck Brooks, *The Flowering of New England, 1815–1865* (New York: E. P. Dutton, 1936), 512.

18. Lucid, *Journal,* 2:666.

19. Adams, *Dana,* 2:170, 167.

20. Ibid., 2:137.

21. Ibid., 2:153.

22. Lucid, *Journal,* 2:834.

23. Richard Henry Dana, Jr., *To Cuba and Back: A Vacation Voyage* (Boston: Ticknor and Fields, 1859), 28.

24. Dana to Charles Eliot Norton, 29 June 1859, Charles Eliot Norton Papers, Houghton Library, Harvard University.

25. Lucid, *Journal,* 2:836; Adams, *Dana,* 2:137.

26. Lucid, *Journal,* 2:836.

19. AROUND THE WORLD

1. Robert F. Lucid, ed., *The Journal of Richard Henry Dana, Jr.,* 3 vols. (Cambridge, MA: Belknap Press of Harvard University Press, 1968), 2:836.

2. Ibid., 2:622, 836.

3. Richard Henry Dana Jr., "Rufus Choate," *Richard Henry Dana, Jr.: Speeches in Stirring Times and Letters to a Son,* ed. Richard Henry Dana III (Boston: Houghton Mifflin, 1910), 294, 289.

4. Quoted in Charles Francis Adams, *Richard Henry Dana: A Biography,* 2 vols. (Boston: Houghton Mifflin, 1891), 2:178.

5. Richard Henry Dana Jr., *Twenty-Four Years After,* in *Two Years Before the Mast and Other Voyages* (New York: Library of America, 2005), 365.

6. Ibid., 366–367.

7. Ibid., 367.

8. Lucid, *Journal,* 3:908; Dana, *Twenty-Four Years After,* 370, 369.

9. Lucid, *Journal,* 3:846, 855–856.

10. Dana, *Twenty-Four Years After,* 368–369.

11. Lucid, *Journal,* 3:902–904.

12. Ibid., 3:905–906 (emphasis in original).

13. Dana, *Twenty-Four Years After,* 372, 375.

14. Ibid., 374–375, 377.

15. Ibid., 377; Maurice and Marco Newmark, eds., *Sixty Years in Southern California, 1853–1913: Containing the Reminiscences of Harris Newmark* (Los Angeles: Zeitlin and Ver Brugge, 1970), 227.

16. Dana, *Twenty-Four Years After,* 378.

17. Ibid., 378–379.

18. Lucid, *Journal,* 3:849; Adams, *Dana,* 2:180–181.

19. Adams, *Dana,* 2:180–181.

20. Ibid., 2:182, 185. Dana's account of the fire was printed in the October 22, 1859, *San Francisco Times,* but Adams relied upon Dana's manuscript notes because they gave "a more graphic picture of an exciting sea adventure." Adams, *Dana,* 2:180.

21. Ibid., 2:182–185.

22. Lucid, *Journal,* 3:865–866.

23. Ibid., 3:869, 884, 886, 873, 889.

24. Ibid., 3:879–880.

25. Ibid., 3:897.

26. Ibid., 3:850, 917.

27. Ibid., 1:328; Lucid, *Journal,* 3:916. Chief Justice David Terry shot and killed David Broderick, former senator from California, in a duel on September 13, 1859. Thirty years later Terry himself was shot to death by a bodyguard for former justice Stephen Field, who had been on the California Supreme Court with Terry. It is unlikely that it was a collegial court.

28. Lucid, *Journal,* 3:919, 915.

29. Ibid., 3:921–922 (emphasis in original).

30. Ibid., 3:925–926 (emphasis in original).

31. Ibid., 3:927–928.

32. Ibid., 3:1138, 1101.

33. Ibid., 3:960, 1040, 1039, 1043, 1050 (emphasis in original).

34. Ibid., 3:988.

35. Ibid., 3:971–972.

36. Ibid., 3:976.

37. Ibid., 3:955.

38. Ibid. 3:1003, 1008, 1029, 1030.

39. Dana, *Twenty-Four Years After,* 388–389; Lucid, *Journal,* 3:1071.

40. Lucid, *Journal,* 3:1078–1079.

41. Ibid., 3:1114, 1138.

1. Longfellow diary entry, 29 September 1860, and Josiah Quincy to Dana, 5 November 1860, both quoted in Charles Francis Adams, *Richard Henry Dana: A Biography,* 2 vols. (Boston: Houghton Mifflin, 1891), 2:248, 249.
2. Sumner to Dana, 14 April 1861, quoted in Adams, *Dana,* 2:257.
3. Adams, *Dana,* 2:257.
4. Samuel Shapiro, *Richard Henry Dana, Jr.: 1815–1882* (East Lansing: Michigan State University Press, 1961), 117–118.
5. Testimony of Charles Brown, Interrogatory No. 29, *United States of America v. The Brig Amy Warwick & Cargo,* in Admiralty, Circuit Court of United States, Mass. Dist., printed case, p. 27, Dana Family Papers, MHS.
6. *The Amy Warwick,* 2 Spr. 123, 1 Fed. Cas. 799 (1862).
7. "Declaring a Blockade of Ports in Rebellious States," 19 April 1861, http://www.presidency.ucsb.edu/proclamations.
8. David M. Silver, *Lincoln's Supreme Court* (Urbana: University of Illinois Press, 1957, repr. 1998), 105.
9. Gideon Welles, *Lincoln and Seward: Remarks upon the Memorial Address of Chas. Francis Adams, on the Late Wm. H. Seward* (New York: Sheldon, 1874), 124.
10. Brian McGinty, *Lincoln and the Court* (Cambridge, MA: Harvard University Press, 2008), 133.
11. Quoted in William H. Rehnquist, *All the Laws but One* (New York: Vintage Books, 2000), 59.
12. The *Prize Cases,* 67 U.S. 635 (1863).
13. Howard K. Beale, ed., *The Diary of Edward Bates, 1859–1866* (Washington, D.C.: Government Printing Office, 1933), 231. The attorney general's entry of February 14, 1862, noted that he met with attorneys "anxious to bring on the prize cases." Ibid.
14. Carl B. Swisher, *Roger B. Taney* (New York: Macmillan, 1935), 563–564.
15. Clinton Rossiter, *The Supreme Court and the Commander-in-Chief* (Ithaca, NY: Cornell University Press, 1951), 69.
16. Gideon Welles, *Diary of Gideon Welles,* 3 vols. (Cambridge, MA: Riverside Press, 1911) 3:67–68.
17. Adams, *Dana,* 2:277.
18. Ibid., 2:268–269.
19. Dana to Assistant Attorney General T. J. Coffey, 24 November 1862, letters received from Massachusetts, 1813–1864, National Archives, Washington, D.C.
20. Thorton K. Lothrop to Charles Francis Adams Jr., 25 August 1890, quoted in Adams, *Dana,* 2:418.
21. Ibid., 2:138.
22. Adams thought Dana's mind "was too fine for precedent." Charles Francis Adams Jr., *Proceedings of the Massachusetts Historical Society* 19 (1881–1882): 203.

23. Beale, *Diary of Edward Bates,* 340.

24. *The Hiawatha, The Crenshaw,* 12 F. Cas. 94 (1861).

25. Adams, *Dana,* 2:267.

26. The *Prize Cases,* 67 U.S. at 648–649 (emphasis in original).

27. Ibid., 643.

28. Ibid., 648.

29. McGinty, *Lincoln and the Court,* 135.

30. Beale, *Diary of Edward Bates,* 281.

31. The *Prize Cases,* 67 U.S. at 645.

32. Silver, *Lincoln's Supreme Court,* 118.

33. Ibid.

34. Adams, *Dana,* 2:143.

35. The *Prize Cases,* 67 U.S. at 650.

36. Ibid., 651.

37. Ibid., 651, 653.

38. Ibid., 654–655.

39. Ibid., 658.

40. Ibid., 659.

41. Ibid., 660.

42. Ibid., 659–661.

43. Beale, *Diary of Edward Bates,* 281.

44. Quoted in Adams, *Dana,* 2:269.

45. *New York World,* March 11, 1863; Silver, *Lincoln's Supreme Court,* 113–114.

46. *The Prize Cases,* 67 U.S. at 665.

47. Ibid., 666–674.

48. Ibid., 694–695, 698–699 (Nelson, J. dissenting).

49. Silver, *Lincoln's Supreme Court,* 116.

50. Charles Warren, *The Supreme Court in United States History,* 3 vols. (Boston: Little, Brown 1922), 3:103.

51. Quoted in Adams, *Dana,* 2:267.

52. Rossiter, *The Supreme Court,* 75.

53. Richard Henry Dana Jr., *Enemy's Territory and Alien Enemies: What the Supreme Court Decided in the Prize Causes* (Boston: Little, Brown, 1864).

54. Quoted in Adams, *Dana,* 2:274.

55. Ibid., 2:273–274.

56. Harold Melvin Hyman, *A More Perfect Union: The Impact of the Civil War and Reconstruction on the Constitution* (New York: Knopf, 1973), 101.

21. THE DUKE OF CAMBRIDGE

1. Dana to Richard Henry Dana III, 23 April 1865, 16 April 1865, Dana Family Papers, MHS.

2. Dana to Charles Francis Adams Sr., 3 March 1865, quoted in Charles Francis Adams, *Richard Henry Dana: A Biography* (Boston: Houghton

Mifflin, 1891), 2:275; Dana to RHD III, 25 April 1865, Dana Family Papers, MHS.

3. Adams, *Dana,* 2:281.

4. Michael L. Benedict, "Preserving the Constitution: The Conservative Basis of Radical Reconstruction," *Journal of American History* 61, no. 1 (June, 1974): 69–70. Dana's "grasp of war" formulation was cited as authority for reconstruction legislation, including the Fourteenth Amendment. Ibid., 72–76, 83.

5. Richard Henry Dana Jr., "The 'Grasp of War' Speech," *Richard Henry Dana, Jr.: Speeches in Stirring Times and Letters to a Son,* ed. Richard Henry Dana III (Boston: Houghton Mifflin, 1910), 240. All quoted excerpts are from the speech. Ibid., 243–272.

6. Dana to Sarah Dana, 16 July 1865, in Adams, *Dana,* 2:333; Dana to Sarah Dana, 15 September 1865, Dana Family Papers, LONG; John Bigelow to Dana, 8 August 1865, in John Bigelow, *Retrospections of an Active Life,* vol. 3, *1865–1866* (New York: Baker and Taylor, 1909-1913), 144; Dana to William Seward, 29 September 1866, in Adams, *Dana,* 2:336.

7. Dana to Sarah Dana, 15 September 1865, Dana Family Papers, LONG.

8. Quoted in Samuel Shapiro, *Richard Henry Dana, Jr.: 1815–1882* (East Lansing: Michigan State University Press, 1961), 133.

9. Robert F. Lucid, ed., *The Journal of Richard Henry Dana, Jr.* (Cambridge, MA: Harvard University Press, 1968), 1:290; quoted in Shapiro, *Richard Henry Dana, Jr.,* 136.

10. Excerpts are from Dana's speech of February 14, 1867, "Usury Laws," in Dana III, *Speeches in Stirring Times,* 118-144.

22. TREASON

1. Evarts to Dana, 17 October 1867 (emphasis in original), Dana Family Papers, MHS. The phrase "greatest criminal trial of the age" was used by newspapers as well as by lawyers in the case. Cynthia Nicoletti, "Did Secession Really Die at Appomattox? The Strange Case of U.S. v. Jefferson Davis," *U. Toledo Law Review* 41 (Spring 2010): 591.

2. *Case of Jefferson Davis,* 7 Fed. Cas. 63,79 (C. C. D. Va. 1867-1871).

3. Clifford to Stanbery, 15 August 1866, quoted in Nicoletti, "Did Secession Really Die," 609.

4. Roy F. Nichols, "United States vs. Jefferson Davis, 1865–1869," *American Historical Review* 31, no. 2 (1926): 275; Stanbery to Dana, 25 October 1867, Dana Family Papers, MHS.

5. Evarts to Dana, 28 October 1867 (emphasis in original), Dana Family Papers, MHS.

6. Stanbery to Dana, telegram, 9 November 1867, Dana Family Papers, MHS.

7. Dana to Sarah Dana, 24 November 1867, Dana Family Papers, MHS.

8. Nicoletti, "Did Secession Really Die," 628 n. 137.

9. Ibid., 616–621. Nicoletti noted that modern scholars conclude that the chief justice was motivated by political considerations rather than jurisdictional problems. I agree.

10. Dana to Sarah Dana, 24 November 1867, quoted in Charles Francis Adams, *Richard Henry Dana: A Biography* (Boston: Houghton Mifflin, 1891), 2:340.

11. Adams, *Dana,* 2:341; Evarts to Dana, 15 November 1867, Dana Family Papers, MHS.

12. Dana to Sarah Dana, 25 November 1867, Dana Family Papers, MHS.

13. Ibid.; Nichols, "United States vs. Jefferson Davis," 274.

14. Jonathan W. White, "The Trial of Jefferson Davis and the Americanization of Treason Law," in *Constitutionalism in the Approach and Aftermath of the Civil War,* ed. Paul D. Moreno and Jonathan O'Neill (New York: Fordham University Press, 2013), 128.

15. Evarts to Dana, 22 January 1868, Dana Family Papers, MHS; Dana to Evarts, 25 January 1868, Dana Family Papers, MHS.

16. Evarts to Dana, 9 and 16 February 1868, Dana Family Papers, MHS.

17. Evarts to Lucius Chandler, 18 February 1868, Jefferson Davis Trial Papers, Special Collections Research Center, University of Chicago Library.

18. Ibid.

19. Evarts to Dana, 24 February 1868, Dana Family Papers, MHS.

20. Dana to Evarts, 26 February 1868, Dana Family Papers, MHS.

21. Evarts to Dana, 3 and 15 March 1868, Dana Family Papers, MHS (emphasis in original); Dana to Sarah Dana, 22 March 1868, Dana Family Papers, MHS.

22. Dana to Sarah Dana, 22 March 1868, Dana Family Papers, MHS (emphasis in original).

23. Evarts to Dana, 15 March 1868, Dana Family Papers, MHS.

24. White, "Americanization of Treason Law," 122.

25. *Case of Jefferson Davis,* 7 Fed. Cas. at 70.

26. White, "Americanization of Treason Law," 127.

27. Stuart Streichler, *Justice Curtis in the Civil War Era: At the Crossroads of American Constitutionalism* (Charlotte: University of Virginia Press, 2005), 54–55.

28. U.S. Constitution, art. III, § 3.

29. *Case of Jefferson Davis,* 7 Fed. Cas. 70

30. Ibid., 85.

31. Evarts to Dana, 10 August 1868, Dana Family Papers, MHS; Dana to Evarts, 24 August 1868, Dana Family Papers, MHS.

32. Dana to Evarts, 24 August 1868, Dana Family Papers, MHS.

33. Ibid.

34. Evarts to Dana, 9 October 1868, Dana Family Papers, MHS.

35. Evarts to Dana, 9 October 1868 (enclosure), Dana Family Papers, MHS.

36. Evarts to Dana, 9 October 1868 (enclosure) MHS; Dana to Evarts, 24 August 1868, MHS; Evarts to Dana, 17 October 1868, Dana Family Papers, MHS.

37. Evarts to Dana, 30 November 1868, telegram, Dana Family Papers, MHS.

38. Charles O'Conor to Davis, 7 December 1868, *The Papers of Jefferson Davis,* vol. 12: June 1865–December 1870, ed. Lynda Casswell Christ (Baton Rouge: Louisiana State University Press, 2008), 332. O'Conor wrote: "The Chief Justice is thoroughly enlisted. His judgment is with you." Ibid.

39. *Case of Jefferson Davis,* 7 Fed. Cas. at 91.

40. Ibid., 92, 95.

41. Ibid., 102.

42. Nichols, "United States vs. Jefferson Davis," 281, 283.

43. Ibid., 284.

44. White, "Americanization of Treason Law," 132.

45. Copy in Dana Family Papers, MHS.

23. THE RATING

1. Benjamin F. Butler, *Autobiography and Personal Reminiscences of Major General Benjamin F. Butler* (Boston: A. M. Thayer, 1892), 920.

2. Samuel Shapiro, "'Aristocracy, Mud, and Vituperation': The Butler-Dana Campaign in Essex County in 1868," *New England Quarterly* 31, no. 3 (September 1958): 343–345.

3. Ibid.

4. Ibid., 345–346.

5. Ibid., 355; Charles Francis Adams, *Richard Henry Dana: A Biography,* 2 vols. (Boston: Houghton Mifflin, 1891), 2:344.

6. Adams, *Dana,* 2:345.

7. Samuel Shapiro, *Richard Henry Dana, Jr.: 1815–1882* (East Lansing: Michigan State University Press, 1961), 144.

8. Shapiro, "'Aristocracy, Mud,'" 348–349.

9. Ibid., 349.

10. Butler, *Autobiography,* 922.

11. Ibid.

12. Ibid., 921; Shapiro, *Richard Henry Dana, Jr.,* 143.

13. Quoted in Bliss Perry, *Richard Henry Dana, 1851–1931* (Boston: Houghton Mifflin, 1933), 13.

14. Shapiro, "'Aristocracy, Mud,'" 352.

15. Adams, *Dana,* 2:348; Shapiro, *Richard Henry Dana, Jr.,* 231. Although Shapiro attributed Dana's abysmal vote to his lack of common touch, Adams noted that six years later Butler's opponent received only 150 votes more than Dana. Adams observed: "The result only demonstrated once more the force of party discipline in popular elections, and showed